The Preacher and Preaching

Reviving the Art
in the Twentieth Century

Edited by
Samuel T. Logan, Jr.

Presbyterian and Reformed Publishing Company
Phillipsburg, New Jersey

Dedicated to the memory of
Samuel T. Logan
September 24, 1910 – August 21, 1985
"He who promised is faithful" (Heb. 10:23).

Copyright © 1986
Presbyterian and Reformed Publishing Company

Manufactured in the United States of America

Library of Congress Cataloging-in-Publication Data
Main entry under title:

The preacher and preaching.

Includes bibliographical references.
1. Preaching—Addresses, essays, lectures.
2. Clergy—Office—Addresses, essays, lectures.
I. Logan, Samuel T., 1943—
BV4222.P645   1986   251   85-32558

ISBN 0-87552-294-7

Published in Great Britain as:
Preaching: The Preacher and Preaching in the Twentieth Century
by Evangelical Press, 16/18 High Street, Welwyn, Hertfordshire AL6 9EQ

ISBN 0-85234-230-6

British Library Cataloguing-in-Publication Data available

---

86   87   88   89   90   5   4   3   2   1

Contents

Foreword

In 1980, two Westminster Theological Seminary students, Mr. James Pratt and Mr. Richard Craven, came into my office at the seminary to share an idea they had for a book on preaching. They had become convinced that the Reformed pulpit in the twentieth century was neglecting its incredibly rich heritage and failing to provide the kind of homiletical leadership it both could and should. Because of my own interest in the preaching of the Puritans and especially in the preaching of Jonathan Edwards, I immediately concurred with their concern.

We very quickly recognized the need to involve in our discussions someone with more expertise in the field, and we therefore approached Dr. Robert Godfrey, Professor of Church History at Westminster, who was at that time teaching a course entitled "The History of Rhetoric." Dr. Godfrey graciously consented to join us, and together we mapped out the project that has become the present book.

Our first step was to identify and contact approximately thirty leading Reformed pastors and homiletical scholars around the world and to ask them what they thought were the primary deficiencies of the contemporary Reformed pulpit. Most of those whom we wrote responded with excellent analyses and suggestions.

The four of us then spent a great deal of time sifting through the responses we received and trying to identify patterns within those responses. We ultimately came up with the categories that are the topics covered in each of the chapters in this volume.

Our next step was to identify individuals who were, in our

opinion, best qualified to write on the topics we had identified. After a number of months of writing back and forth, we received commitments from the various individuals whom we had identified. Of course, along the way, some of those whom we initially asked to write chapters declined, and others who at first agreed to write chapters later decided they would be unable to do so. Nevertheless, the final lineup of authors is remarkably close to that with which we began.

The various manuscripts came in over a period of two years, and by June of 1984, almost all of them were in hand. I had been granted a study leave from Westminster from July 1, 1984, through January 31, 1985, and I had determined, for a wide variety of reasons, to spend that study leave at Tyndale House in Cambridge, England. I therefore took all of the manuscripts with me and spent approximately two months of the study leave going over the manuscripts line by line, doing the difficult work of editing. I had a unique opportunity, consequently, to be the first to read this book and also to be the only one to see all of the excellent material that, for reasons of space and coverage, had to be edited out of the original manuscripts. I learned a tremendous amount as I read and edited, and I continue to pray fervently that the Lord will use these chapters to achieve the goal that Mr. Craven, Mr. Pratt, Dr. Godfrey, and I had originally envisioned— the strengthening of Reformed preaching to the honor and glory of the name of Jesus.

I do want to express my professional appreciation to each of the authors whose work is contained in this volume for his labors on this project. I certainly want to thank James Pratt and Richard Craven for suggesting the project and Dr. Robert Godfrey for his wisdom as we put it together.

I owe a debt of gratitude to the faculty and the board of trustees of Westminster Theological Seminary for granting to me the study leave that made possible the editing of this book. Thanks also are due to Dr. George Fuller, Miss Dorothy Krieke, Mrs. Viola Braun, Mr. Al Groves, and many others here at Westminster for covering the wide variety of my administrative responsibilities while I was on leave. Mrs. Billie Goodenough and Mrs. Shawna Jones deserve everyone's gratitude for their meticulous work in typing and retyping all of this material.

The opportunity to work at Tyndale House in Cambridge was a marvelous blessing in so many ways. As a center of evangelical Christian scholarship, Tyndale House provides both superb facilities for research and writing and marvelous Christian fellowship and support. My family and I deeply appreciated all that we received there, and I would extend my special thanks to Dr. Murray Harris, Warden of Tyndale House, and to Rev. Iain Hodgins, Bursar of Tyndale House.

On a more personal level, I would like publicly to thank my mother and my father for their Christian nurture, for their unfailing support, and for their continuing prayers. From them I have learned, among many other things, what it means to subsume all of my endeavors under the final goal of advancing the kingdom of Jesus Christ—and that is, of course, also the proper goal of biblical preaching.

Finally, my deepest appreciation goes to Sue and to Taly and to Eric. You made the time in Cambridge as delightful as it was productive. It's the greatest of joys to be involved in the work of Christ's kingdom with the three of you! *Merci beaucoup!*

Samuel T. Logan, Jr.
Academic Dean
Westminster Theological Seminary

Contributors

Jay E. Adams graduated from Johns Hopkins University and earned the B.D. from Reformed Episcopal Seminary, the S.T.M. from the Temple University School of Practical Theology, and the Ph.D. from the University of Missouri. Dr. Adams has pastored churches in western Pennsylvania and in New Jersey. For three years he was on the faculty of the University of Missouri. At present he is the Director of Advanced Studies at Westminster Theological Seminary in California and Visiting Professor of Practical Theology at Westminster Theological Seminary in Philadelphia. He also serves as Dean of the Institute of Pastoral Studies at the Christian Counseling and Educational Foundation located in Philadelphia. Dr. Adams is a frequent lecturer at ministerial and Bible conferences and the author of many books and articles, among them *Competent to Counsel* and *The Christian Counselor's Manual.*

John F. Bettler is a graduate of Westminster Theological Seminary and Chicago Theological Seminary where he received his doctorate in Pastoral Counseling. As Director of the Christian Counseling and Educational Foundation he comes into contact daily with the real struggles people experience in living the Christian life. As Adjunct Professor of Practical Theology at Westminster Theological Seminary, he brings that "life" dimension to his classes in homiletics. He maintains a full conference schedule, and his preaching is marked by practical, "how to" application of the Scriptures.

James Montgomery Boice is pastor of Philadelphia's historic Tenth Presbyterian Church, which he has served since 1968, and he is speaker on the international radio broadcast "The Bible Study Hour." He holds degrees from Harvard University (A.B.), Princeton Theological Seminary (B.D.), the University of Basel, Switzerland (D.Theol.), and Reformed Episcopal Seminary (D.D.). He is the chairman of the International Council on Biblical Inerrancy and the chairman and founder of the Philadelphia Conference on Reformed Theology. He is the author of more than thirty books on biblical theology.

Edmund P. Clowney is a graduate of Wheaton College and received the B.D. from Westminster Theological Seminary and the S.T.M. from Yale Divinity School. The Doctor of Divinity degree was conferred upon him by Wheaton College. He has served the Orthodox Presbyterian Church in Illinois and New Jersey and as editor of the Christian Education Committee. From his appointment in 1952 as Lecturer in Practical Theology at Westminster Theological Seminary, he went on to serve as Professor of Practical Theology, Acting Dean of the Faculty, and Dean of Academic Affairs. Dr. Clowney was inaugurated as President of Westminster Seminary in 1966 and held that position until his retirement in 1982. He has authored numerous journal articles and several books, including *Called to the Ministry*. He and his wife Jean now reside in Charlottesville, Virginia, where he is Associate Pastor of Trinity Presbyterian Church.

Richard M. Craven is the pastor of the Gettysburg Orthodox Presbyterian Church in Gettysburg, Pennsylvania. He received his M.Div. from Westminster Theological Seminary and is presently a Ph.D. candidate in hermeneutics and biblical interpretation at the seminary.

Lester De Koster was Professor of Speech at Calvin College in Grand Rapids, Michigan, from 1947-69. He was Chairman of the Department of Speech for eleven of those years and Director of the Library for both Calvin College and Seminary from 1951-69.

For the following eleven years Mr. De Koster was Editor of *The Banner*. He is co-owner, author, and Editor of the Christian's Library Press. He has co-authored six titles, has edited *Speaking in Public*, and is the author of *Communism and Christian Faith, Vocabulary of Communism*, and *How to Read the Bible*.

David A. Dombek is a graduate of Westminster Theological Seminary (B.D., 1972), Philadelphia. He is an actor, director, speech teacher, and drama coach. He has served as a lector in a Presbyterian church. Now a member in the Christian Reformed Church, he occasionally reads with his pastor a dramatic Scripture passage as a dialogue. Living in the Mid-West, he and his wife, Ellen, teach their children at home. He also writes, preaches, and teaches in his church's Sunday school.

Sinclair B. Ferguson is a native of Scotland where he received both his M.A. and his Ph.D. at the University of Aberdeen. He was in the pastoral ministry from 1971–82, most recently at St. George's Tron in Glasgow. He is an Assistant Editor of the Banner of Truth and his numerous books include *Discovering God's Will, Grow in Grace*, and *Know Your Christian Life*. Since 1982, Dr. Ferguson has been Associate Professor of Systematic Theology at Westminster Theological Seminary. He and his wife Dorothy have four children.

W. Robert Godfrey is Professor of Church History at Westminster Theological Seminary in Escondido, California. He received the A.B., M.A., and Ph.D. degrees from Stanford University and the M.Div. degree from Gordon-Conwell Theological Seminary. He has taught at Westminster (in Pennsylvania and in California) for eleven years. He is a minister in the Christian Reformed Church. He has contributed to *John Calvin: His Influence on the Western World, Scripture and Truth*, and *Discord, Dialogue and Concord*. He co-edited and contributed to *Through Christ's Word*, and he edited the *Westminster Theological Journal* for several years. He is married and has three children.

Erroll Hulse graduated with a degree in architecture from Pretoria University, before studying at London Bible College. He worked for the Banner of Truth Trust during its formative years and was pastor of the Baptist Church in Sussex for twenty-three years, during which time it grew from one member into a large and active fellowship. He has written several books including *The Believer's Experience.* From 1970 he has served as Editor of the bimonthly magazine *Reformation Today.* Mr. Hulse has been involved in planting several churches and has been instrumental in establishing ministers' conferences in Britain and abroad. He is at present the minister of Belvidere Road Church, Liverpool. He is married and has four children.

Glen C. Knecht, born in Ogdensburg, New York, graduated from Maryville College in Tennessee, attended Fuller Theological Seminary, and received the B.D. and Th.M. degrees from Princeton Theological Seminary. He also did additional postgraduate study at Conwell School of Theology, Pennsylvania. From 1957 to 1962 he was a missionary evangelist in Tabriz, Iran. He has held pastorates in Maryland and Pennsylvania and since 1983 has been senior pastor of First Presbyterian Church, Columbia, South Carolina. He and his wife, Betty Jane, have six children and three grandchildren. In addition to his preaching and pastoral responsibilities, he is on the board of Multiple Sclerosis for his area and is a member of the Steering Committee for CADRE (Citizens Advocating Decency and Revival of Ethics) for Richland and Lexington Counties.

Samuel T. Logan, Jr., a native of Vicksburg, Mississippi, received his B.A. from Princeton University, his M.Div. from Westminster Theological Seminary, and his Ph.D. from Emory University. He taught for nine years at Barrington College (now merged with Gordon College) and is currently Academic Dean and Associate Professor of Church History at Westminster Theological Seminary. He is an ordained minister of the Orthodox Presbyterian Church and did pastoral work in Philadelphia, Pennsylvania, in Scottdale, Georgia, and in Lafayette, New Jersey. He is married and has two sons.

Donald Macleod was born on the Island of Lewis off the Northwest coast of Scotland in November of 1940. After studying at the University of Glasgow and the Free Church College of Edinburg, he was ordained to the ministry of the Free Church of Scotland in 1964. From 1964 until 1978, he served in two pastoral charges, including ten years in the city of Glasgow, where he preached five times each week. In 1978, he was appointed as Professor of Systematic Theology at the Free Church College. Since 1977, he has served as Editor of *The Monthly Record* of the Free Church of Scotland.

Joel Nederhood has been a radio pastor since December 1960 for the Christian Reformed Church and has recently also been the preacher and host for the Faith 20 telecast of the Christian Reformed Church. He also preaches regularly in churches and is a conference speaker. He has written *The Church's Mission and the Educated American, God Is Too Much, The Holy Triangle*, and *Promises, Promises, Promises*, in addition to chapters that have appeared in other books and in magazines. He serves as the Director of Ministries of The Back to God Hour of the Christian Reformed Church.

James I. Packer was born in Gloucestershire, England, and educated at Oxford University, receiving degrees in classics and theology (D.Phil., 1954). Ordained in 1952, he served as assistant minister at St. John's Church of England, Birmingham and then became Senior Tutor at Tyndale Hall, an Anglican seminary, from 1955 to 1961. After nine years as Warden of Latimer House, an Anglican evangelical study center in Oxford, he returned to Bristol to become Principal of Tyndale Hall. When Tyndale Hall merged with two other evangelical colleges to become Trinity College, Dr. Packer became Associate Principal. Since 1979 he has been Professor of Systematic and Historical Theology at Regent College, Vancouver. Married and with three children, Dr. Packer has preached and lectured widely in Great Britain and America, and is a frequent contributor to theological periodicals. He was an editor of the *New Bible Dictionary* and *The Bible Almanac*. Among his writings are *Evangelism and the Sovereignty of God*, *Knowing God*, *Beyond the Battle for the Bible*, and *Keep in Step with the Spirit*.

James M. Pratt received his Master of Divinity degree from Westminster Theological Seminary. He is ordained to the ministry and is presently serving the First Baptist Church of Torrance, California, as Minister of Youth and Discipleship.

R. C. Sproul received the B.A. from Westminster College, the B.D. from Pittsburgh Theological Seminary, the Drs. from the Free University of Amsterdam and the Litt.D. from Geneva College. He is an ordained minister in the Presbyterian Church in America. As President and Founder of Ligonier Ministries in Orlando, Florida, he has in view a modern Christian Reformation that penetrates individual lives and, ultimately, all of society. Dr. Sproul is Professor of Systematic Theology and Apologetics at Reformed Theological Seminary in Jackson, Mississippi, and recently served as President of the Executive Committee of the International Council on Biblical Inerrancy. He is known for his lectures and seminars and is the author of fourteen books, including *In Search of Dignity*, *Classical Apologetics*, and *The Holiness of God*.

Geoffrey Thomas completed his studies at University College of Wales, Cardiff, and at Westminster Theological Seminary, Philadelphia. A Welshman with a Welsh-speaking wife and three daughters, he has been minister since 1965 at Alfred Place Baptist Church (Independent), Aberystwyth, a university town on the mid-Wales coast. He has preached through more than twenty books of the Bible and generations of university students have attended his preaching. He is an Assistant Editor of the Banner of Truth and the present Chairman of the Grace Baptist Assembly Organizing Committee. During his ministry in Aberystwyth, a Christian Book Shop and a home for the mentally handicapped have been opened to the town. Geoff Thomas is a conference speaker much in demand in many parts of the world.

J. Peter Vosteen received the B.A. degree from The College of Wooster in Ohio and the M.Div. from Westminster Theological Seminary, before going on for further graduate study in New Testament at Luther Theological Seminary in St. Paul, Minnesota. Ordained to the gospel ministry by the United Presbyterian Church of North America, he entered the ministry of the Christian Reformed Church in 1959, serving seven congregations in both the United States and Canada. He is currently serving as home missionary and pastor in Boise, Idaho and is frequently called on to conduct seminars and retreats.

Gwyn Walters, Professor of Ministry at Gordon-Conwell Theological Seminary, South Hamilton, Massachusetts, graduated B.A., B.D. from the University of Wales, and Ph.D. from the University of Edinburgh. Prior to his pastoring experience in Scotland, Wales, and the United States, he was exposed to the rich heritage of Scottish and Welsh preaching. He has preached in Europe, the Middle and Far East, and North America, and has taught preaching in several countries but mainly, and for nearly thirty years, at Gordon-Conwell. He served as President of the Academy of Homiletics.

Introduction: Why Preach?
J. I. Packer

By their questions, it has been said, you shall know them. Honest questions reveal what ignorance, doubt, fears, uncertainties, prejudices, and preconceptions lie within the questioner's mind. By asking questions, even more than by answering them, we lay ourselves open to each other and thereby become (to use the cant word) vulnerable. (That is why some people never ask questions! But those who never ask anything never learn anything either, so the unquestioning attitude is not really one to commend.) I take the question "Why preach?" on which I have been asked to write, to be an honest question, expressing honest uncertainty as to whether there is a viable rationale for pulpit work in our time. I blame no one for raising the question—indeed, I see many reasons why thoughtful people might well raise it—and I shall try to treat it as seriously, and respond to it as honestly, as I take it to be put.

Whose question is it, though? Does it come from a discouraged preacher? or from a weary listener? or from a pastoral organizer who wants more time for other things, and grudges hours earmarked for sermon preparation? or from a student of communication theory, who doubts whether pulpit monologue can ever convey as much as dialogue or discussion, or an audio-visual film presentation or TV? Perhaps the question comes from all four, and perhaps it does not matter for my present purpose which it comes from; for whoever voices it is putting into words real disillusionment with the medium and real doubt about the worthwhileness of the activity. Such disillusionment is, as we all know, widespread nowadays, and I am happy to acknowledge and accept it as the starting place for a discussion that, if God helps, will have a pastoral as well as a theological thrust. Throughout this essay I shall have all four sorts of disillusioned folk particularly in mind.

Like my fellow-contributors to this book, I propose to defend preaching. But lest you imagine that I am doing this simply to order, I begin with a personal statement. In the following pages I shall magnify and glorify the preaching ministry, not because I have been asked to (though indeed I have), nor because, as a spokesman for the Reformed heritage, I think I ought to (though I certainly do), but because preaching is of the very essence of the corporate phenomenon called Christianity as I understand it. By that I mean that Christianity, on earth as in heaven, is (I echo I John 1:4) fellowship with the Father and with His Son Jesus Christ, and the preaching of God's Word in the power of God's Spirit is the activity that (I echo Isa. 64:1 and John 14:21-23) brings the Father and the Son down from heaven to dwell with men. I know this, for I have experienced it.

For several months during 1948 and 1949 I sat under the Sunday evening ministry of the late D. Martyn Lloyd-Jones. It seems to me in retrospect that all I have ever known about preaching was given me in those days, though I could not then have put it into words as I can now. What I received then still shows me what to look and hope and pray for in listening, and what to aim at and pray for in my own preaching. And though I have read and heard much since those days, I cannot think of anything I perceive about preaching now that did not at least begin to become clear to me at that time. When I say, as frequently I catch myself doing, that preaching is caught more than it is taught, it is partly of my own discoveries during that period that I am thinking. I do not, of course, mean that I regard Dr. Lloyd-Jones as the only preacher I ever heard do it right; over the past generation I have been privileged to hear many other real preachers really preaching. I am only saying that it was Dr. Lloyd-Jones's ministry that under God gave me my standards in this matter. And standards are needed, for not all preaching is good preaching by any means. I suppose that over the years I have heard as much bad preaching as the next man and probably done as much myself as any clergyman you would like to name. Nonetheless, having observed how preaching is conceived in Scripture, and having experienced preaching of a very high order, I continue to believe in preaching and to maintain that there is no substitute for it, and no power or stature or sustained vision or close fellowship with God in the church without it. Also, I constantly maintain that if today's quest for renewal is not, along with its other concerns, a quest for true preaching, it will prove shallow and barren. You see, then, where I am coming from as I take up the question "Why preach?"

How is it, I wonder, that so few seem to believe in preaching as I do? I can think of several reasons why that might be, and to list them will be a good way of opening my subject.

First, *there has been much nonpreaching in our pulpits.* Not every discourse that fills the appointed 20- or 30-minute slot in public worship is actual preaching, however much it is called by that name. Sermons (Latin, *sermones,* "speeches") are often composed and delivered on wrong principles. Thus, if they fail to open Scripture or they expound it without applying it, or if they are no more than lectures aimed at informing the mind or addresses seeking only to focus the present self-awareness of the listening group, or if they are delivered as statements of the preacher's opinion rather than as messages from God, or if their lines of thought do not require listeners to change in any way, they fall short of being preaching, just as they would if they were so random and confused that no one could tell what the speaker was saying. It is often said, and truly, that sermons must teach, and the current level of knowledge (ignorance, rather) in the Christian world is such that the need for sermons that teach cannot be questioned for one moment. But preaching is essentially teaching *plus* application (invitation, direction, summons); where the *plus* is lacking something less than preaching occurs. And many in the church have never experienced preaching in this full biblical sense of the word.

Second, *topical preaching has become a general rule, at least in North America.* Sermons explore announced themes rather than biblical passages. Why is this? Partly, I suppose, to make preaching appear interesting and important in an age that has largely lost interest in the pulpit; partly, no doubt, to make the sermon sound different from what goes on in the Bible class before public worship starts; partly, too, because many topical preachers (not all) do not trust their Bible enough to let it speak its own message through their lips. Whatever the reason, however, the results are unhealthy. In a topical sermon the text is reduced to a peg on which the speaker hangs his line of thought; the shape and thrust of the message reflect his own best notions of what is good for people rather than being determined by the text itself. But the only authority that his sermon can then have is the human authority of a knowledgeable person speaking with emphasis and perhaps raising his voice. In my view topical discourses of this kind, no matter how biblical their component parts, cannot but fall short of being preaching in the full sense of that word, just because their biblical content is made to appear as part of the speaker's own wisdom. The authority of God revealed is thus resolved into that of religious expertise. That destroys the very idea of Christian preaching, which excludes the thought of speaking for the Bible and insists that the Bible must be allowed to speak for itself in and through the speaker's words. Granted, topical discourses may become real preaching if the speaker settles down to letting this happen, but many topical preachers never discipline themselves to become mouthpieces for messages from biblical texts at all. And many in the churches have only ever been exposed to topical preaching of the sort that I have described.

Third, *low expectations are self-fulfilling.* Most modern hearers have never been taught to expect much from sermons, and their habit is to relax at sermon time and wait to see if anything that the speaker says will interest them—"grab them," as they might put it. Today's congregations and today's preachers seem to be mostly at one in neither asking nor expecting that God will come to meet His people in the preaching, and so it is no wonder that this does not often happen. Just as it takes two to tango, so ordinarily it takes both an expectant congregation and a preacher who knows what he is about to make an authentic preaching occasion. A century ago and earlier, in Reformed circles in Britain (I cannot vouch for America), the common question to a person returning from a service would be, how he or she "got on" under the momentous divine influence of the preaching of the Word; nowadays, however, on both sides of the Atlantic, the question more commonly asked is how the preacher "got on" in what is now viewed as his stated pulpit performance. This shift of interest and perspective is a clear witness to the way in which, from being venerated as an approach by God, searching and stirring our souls, preaching has come to be viewed as a human endeavor to please, so that critical detachment now takes the place of open-hearted expectation when preaching is attempted. The direct result of our having become thus cool and blasé about preaching is that we look for little to happen through sermons, and we should not wonder that God deals with us according to our unbelief.

Fourth, *the current cult of spontaneity militates against preaching.* It is characteristic of some of the liveliest Christian groups today to treat what one can only call crudeness as a sign of sincerity, whether in folk-style songs with folk-style lyrics or in rhapsodic extempore prayer marked by earnest incoherence or in a loose and seemingly under-prepared type of preaching in which raw and clumsy rhetoric matches intellectual imprecision. Charismatic "prophecy" (unpremeditated applicatory speech, uttered in God's name) is an extreme form of this. But where interest centers upon spontaneity rather than substance, and passion in speakers is valued above preparation, true preaching must of necessity languish. Here is a further reason why some earnest Christians have no experience, nor suspicion, of its power.

Fifth, *the current concentration on liturgy militates against preaching.* This is noticeable not only in theologically vague and pluralistic sectors of Protestantism, where it might have been expected (since nature abhors a vacuum), but among evangelicals too. One of the striking movements of our time is the flow of evangelicals, nurtured as they feel in a world of religious individualism and kitsch, into churches where the austere theocentrism of set liturgies, harking back to patristic models, still survives. Many of them become Episcopalians, and I, an Episcopalian by upbringing and judgment, have no complaint about that. But it saddens me to observe that this liturgical interest, which has led them to leave churches that highlighted the ministry of the Word, seems to have elbowed all concern about preaching out of their minds. It is as if they were saying, "We know quite enough about preaching; we have had a bellyful of it, enough to last us all our lives; now, thankfully, we turn from all that to the world of ceremony and sacrament." But that attitude involves a false antithesis, for the genuine Reformed and Episcopal, not to say biblical, way is the way of gospel-*and*-liturgy, word-*and*-sacrament—the way that informs you in effect that you are free to hold as high a doctrine of the sacrament, the visible Word, as you like, provided that your doctrine of and expectation from the preached Word remain higher. But, generally speaking, the mind set of these refugees from nonliturgical Christendom subordinates preaching to congregational enactment of worship (of which preaching is clearly not thought to be a major part), and thus reduces its importance and lowers expectations with regard to it. Here is yet another reason why some Christians today do not share the high view of preaching that I myself uphold.

Sixth, *the power of speech to communicate significance has become suspect.* In the modern West, cool, dead-pan statements of fact are as much as is acceptable; any form of oratory, rhetoric, or dramatic emphasis to show the weight and significance of stated facts tends to alienate rather than convince. That entire dimension of public speech is nowadays felt to be murky and discreditable. This is largely due to the influence of the media, on which strong feeling both looks and sounds hysterical and artificial, and a calm and chatty intimacy is the secret of success. Part of that influence, too, is the numbing of emotional responsiveness by the constant parade of trauma and horror in news bulletins and programs on current affairs. Our sensibilities get dulled by over-stimulus; also, in self-defense against attempts to harrow our feelings, we cultivate a sense of noninvolvement; and we end up unable to believe that anything told us or shown us matters very much at all. One, two, three, and four centuries ago, a preacher could use words for forty or sixty minutes together, or longer in special cases, to set forth the greatness of God the King, of Christ the Savior, of the soul, of eternity, and of the issues of personal destiny that were actually being settled at that moment by reactions to what was being said, and the hearers would listen empathetically and believe him. Today such a response would be thought naive, and most folk would at an early stage become inwardly aloof from, and perhaps hostile to, what the preacher was doing, out of caution lest they be "conned" by a clever man putting on an act.

In the same sense in which Jonathan Edwards was a seventeenth-century Puritan born out of due time, Dr. Lloyd-Jones was a nineteenth-century preacher born late, and I cannot be thankful enough that I was privileged to hear him doing the old thing, despite the fact that, as he knew, some of his hearers thought of his preaching as just an entertaining performance, and others found his pulpit passion distasteful, maintaining throughout his thirty-year ministry at London's Westminster Chapel a preference for the cooler communicator who had preceded him. (I knew the congregation well enough to verify this.) But few preachers in my experience have had either the resources or (more important) the resolve to swim against the stream of suspicion and to follow the old paths at this point, and hence many in the churches never hear preachers deliberately and systematically use words to create a sense of the greatness and weight of spiritual issues. This also is a reason why my estimate of preaching is a minority view in today's Christian world, and why it is so widely held that other modes of Christian instruction are as good, if not better.

But what is preaching? My general view will have emerged already, but a full formal analysis seems desirable at this stage, before we attempt to go further.

First, then, a negative point. Preaching, I urge, should be defined functionally and theologically rather than institutionally and sociologically: that is, it should be defined in terms of what essentially is being done, and why, rather than of where and when it happens, and what corporate expectations it fulfils. The New Testament leads us to think in these terms, using one of its two main words for preach (*euaggelizomai*: literally, "tell good news") not only of Paul addressing a synagogue congregation at Pisidian Antioch and groups gathered in the marketplace at Athens, but also of Philip sitting in a chariot speaking of Jesus to its one occupant (Acts 13:32; 17:18; 8:35). Much modern criticism of preaching arises from observations of sermonizing in churches: hence the frequent wisecracks about the pulpit as a coward's castle, and the preacher as standing six feet about contradiction, and resentful references to preaching *at* rather than *to* the hearers. Of course, most attempts at preaching do take place in church buildings, but that is not the point. What I am urging here is that preaching should be conceived as an achievement in communication. Regarding sermons, my point is that once preaching is defined in this functional and theological way, the performances that draw such comments as I cited will be seen not to be good preaching, and perhaps not to qualify as preaching at all.

Putting the matter positively, I define preaching as verbal communication of which the following things are true:

1. Its *content* is God's message to man, presented as such. For the evangelical, this means that the source of what is said will be the Bible, and furthermore that a text will be taken (a verse, a part of a verse, or a group of verses), and the truth or truths presented will be, as the Westminster Directory for Public Worship put it, "contained in or grounded on that text, that the hearers may discern how God teacheth it from thence." The preacher will take care to make clear that what he offers is not his own ideas, but God's message from God's book, and will see it as his task not to talk for his text, but to let the text talk through him.

Also, as one charged, like Paul, to declare "the whole counsel of God" (Acts 20:26-27)—that is, all that God does for mankind and all that He requires in response—the evangelical preacher will relate the specific content of all his messages to Christ, His mediation, His cross and resurrection, and His gift of new life to those who trust Him (as Edmund Clowney points out in his chapter). In that sense, the preacher will imitate Paul, who when he visited Corinth (and everywhere else, for that matter, *pace* some wayward theories to the contrary), "resolved to know nothing . . . except Jesus Christ and him crucified" (I Cor. 2:2). That does not mean, of course, that the evangelical preacher will harp all the time on the bare fact of the crucifixion. It means, rather, that he will use all lines of biblical thought to illuminate the meaning of that fact; and he will never let his exposition of anything in Scripture get detached from, and so appear as unrelated to, Calvary's cross and the redemption that was wrought there; and in this way he will sustain a Christ-centered, cross-oriented preaching ministry year in and year out, with an evangelistic as well as a pastoral thrust.

2. The *purpose* of preaching is to inform, persuade, and call forth an appropriate response to the God whose message and instruction are being delivered. The response will consist of repentance, faith, obedience, love, effort, hope, fear, zeal, joy, praise, prayer, or some blend of these (see Samuel Logan's discussion of "The Phenomenology of Preaching"). The purpose of preaching is not to stir people to action while bypassing their minds, so that they never see what reason God gives them for doing what the preacher requires of them (that is manipulation); nor is the purpose to stock people's minds with truth, no matter how vital and clear, which then lies fallow and does not become the seed-bed and source of changed lives (that is academicism). The purpose is, rather, to reproduce, under God, the state of affairs that Paul described when he wrote to the Romans, "You wholeheartedly obeyed the form of teaching to which you were entrusted" (Rom. 6:17). The teaching is the testimony, command, and promise of God. The preacher entrusts his hearers to it by begging them to

respond to it and assuring them that God will fulfil His promises to them as they do so. When they wholeheartedly obey, he gains his goal.

3. The *perspective* of preaching is always applicatory (as John Bettler argues later in this volume). This point is an extension of the last. As preaching is God-centered in its viewpoint and Christ-centered in its substance, so it is life-centered in its focus and life-changing in its thrust. Preaching is the practical communication of truth about God as it bears on our present existence. Neither statements of Bible doctrine nor talk about Christian experience alone is preaching, not even if the speakers get excited, emphatic, and dogmatic, and bang the table to make their points. Religious speech only becomes preaching when, first, its theme is Bible truth, or rather, the God of Scripture, in the hearers' lives—when, in other words, it is about the Father, Son, and Spirit invading, inverting, illuminating, integrating, and impelling us, and about ourselves as thereby addressed, accused, acquitted, accepted, assured, and allured—and when, second, the discourse debouches in practical biblical exhortation, summoning us to be different in some spiritually significant way and to remain different whatever pressure is put on us to give in to unspiritual ways once more (Rom. 12:1-2).

The idea of practical biblical exhortation requires some comment. The traditional view was that biblical instruction and narrative reveal and illustrate general truths about God and man, and about the kinds of attitude and conduct that God loves and rewards on the one hand, and hates and judges on the other. The interpreter's task was then to distil those general principles out of the historical and cultural specifics of each passage and to reapply them to the modern world, on the assumption that whatever else has changed, God and man, sin and godliness, have not. The method of moving from what the text meant as the writer's message to his envisaged readership to what it means for us today was by principled rational analysis—a discipline requiring historical and exegetical finesse of the kind displayed in critical commentaries, plus light from the Holy Spirit for discerning the spiritual roots of modern life and so making a contemporary application of truth that goes to the modern heart. Startlingly, it appears that the classic account of this discipline is John Owen's *Causes, Ways, and Means, of understanding the Mind of God, as revealed in his Word, with Assurance therein: and a Declaration of the Perspicuity of the Scriptures, with the external Means of the Interpretation of them*, a work published in 1678. Though later books have of course updated and expanded many of Owen's points, none seems to cover all his ground. But however that may be, it is a matter of demonstrable fact that this is how Reformed and evangelical preachers have reached their practical biblical exhortations for more than 400 years, and indeed how they still do.

But since Barth it has become common to deny that Scripture reveals or embodies general principles about God's will for and ways with His human creatures, and to affirm instead that God speaks a new word directly through the biblical text to each new situation. On this view, the interpreter's task is (putting it in our post-Barthian jargon) to "listen to" and "wrestle with" passages till he feels that some "insight" triggered by them has become clear to him; then he should relay that insight as "prophetically" as he can. But with the discipline of identifying and correlating general principles removed, as this view removes it, and the analogy of Scripture (that is, its internal consistency, as the teaching of God) disregarded or denied, as it usually is by this school of thought, imprecision, pluralism, and relativism flood in whenever the attempt is made to determine what God is saying at the present time, and there is no way to keep them out. Here is not the place to analyze or critique this phenomenon in detail; suffice it to say that it is not at all what I have in mind when I speak of applicatory biblical exhortation as an integral part of preaching.

4. *Authority* is also integral to the notion of what preaching is, namely, as is now clear, human lips uttering God's message (again, Samuel Logan's chapter explores this point more fully). Preaching that does not display divine authority, both in its content and in its manner, is not the substance, but only the shadow of the real thing. The authority of preaching flows from the trans-

parency of the preacher's relation to the Bible and to the three Persons who are the one God whose Word the Bible is. As Erroll Hulse demonstrates later in this volume, it is only as the preacher is truly under, and is seen to be under, the authority of God and the Bible that he has, and can be felt to have, authority as God's spokesman. To spell this out: he must be evidently under the authority of *Scripture,* as his source of truth and wisdom; he must be evidently under the authority of *God,* as whose emissary he comes, in whose name and under whose eye he speaks, and to whom he must one day give account for what he has said; he must be evidently under the authority of *Christ,* as a subordinate shepherd serving the chief Shepherd; and he must be evidently under the authority of *the Holy Spirit,* consciously depending on Him as the sole sustainer of vision, clarity, and freedom of mind, heart, and voice in the act of delivering his message, and as the sole agent of conviction and response in the lives of his hearers.

Let Paul be our teacher here. "Unlike so many," he wrote, "we do not peddle the word of God for profit. On the contrary, in Christ we speak before God with sincerity, like men sent from God" (II Cor. 2:16-17). Here we see the transparency of a consciously right relationship to the authoritative message, the authoritative God, and the authoritative Christ. (Paul, of course, knew the authoritative message from oral instruction and personal revelation, whereas preachers today must learn it from Scripture, but this does not affect the principle of fidelity to it once one knows it.) "My message and my preaching," wrote Paul again, "were not with wise and persuasive words, but with a demonstration of the Spirit's power, so that your faith might not rest on men's wisdom, but on God's power" (I Cor. 2:4). Here we see the transparency of a consciously right relationship to the Holy Spirit as the one who authenticates, convinces, and establishes in faith. In this Paul stands as a model. Where these relationships are out of joint, the authority of preaching—that is, its claim on the conscience, as utterance in God's name—weakens to vanishing point. Where these relationships are as they should be, however, proof will be given again and again of the truth of Robert Murray McCheyne's dictum, that "a holy minister is an awful weapon in the hands of a holy God." In less drastic language Paul testified to what McCheyne had in view when he wrote, "We also thank God continually because, when you received the word of God, which you heard from us, you accepted it not as the word of men, but as it actually is, the word of God which is at work in you who believe" (I Thess. 2:13).

5.   Preaching mediates not only God's authority, but also His *presence* and His *power* (see Geoffrey Thomas's remarks below). Preaching effects an encounter not simply with truth, but with God Himself. There is a staggering offhand remark that illustrates this in I Corinthians 14, where Paul is arguing for the superiority of prophecy (speaking God's message in intelligible language) over tongues. "If the whole church comes together and everyone speaks in tongues, and some who do not understand or some unbelievers come in, will they not say that you are out of your mind?" (Expected answer: yes.) "But if an unbeliever or someone who does not understand comes in while everybody is prophesying, he will be convinced by all that he is a sinner and will be judged by all, and the secrets of his heart will be laid bare. So he will fall down and worship God, exclaiming, 'God is really among you!' " (I Cor. 14:23-25). Whatever else in this passage is uncertain, three things are plain.

First, prophecy as Paul speaks of it here corresponded in content to what we would call preaching the gospel—detecting sin and proclaiming God's remedy.

Second, the expected effect of such prophecy was to create a sense of being in the presence of the God who was its subject matter, and of being searched and convicted by Him, and so being moved to humble oneself and worship Him.

Third, in the experience of both Paul and the Corinthians, what Paul described must have occurred on occasion already, otherwise he could not have expected to be believed when he affirmed so confidently that it would happen. That which has never happened before cannot be predicted with such certainty.

There have evidently been times since the apostolic age when such things have been known to take place once more: the Puritan David Clarkson, for instance, in a sermon entitled *Public Worship to be Preferred before Private*, was presumably talking from experience when he declared, "The most wonderful things that are now done on earth are wrought in the public ordinances. Here the dead hear the voice of the Son of God, and those that hear do live. . . . Here he cures diseased souls with a word. . . . Here he dispossesses Satan. . . . Wonders these are, and would be so accounted, were they not the common work of the public ministry. It is true indeed, the Lord has not confined himself to work these wonderful things only in public; yet the public ministry is the only ordinary means whereby he works them."[1] What Paul describes is rare in our time, no doubt, but that does not make it any less part of the biblical ideal of what preaching is, and what it effects. Perhaps the point should be put this way: preaching is an activity for which, and in which, the awareness of God's powerful presence must be sought, and with which neither speaker nor hearers may allow themselves to be content when this awareness is lacking.

The above analysis was needed because the ordinary concept of preaching as sermonizing (filling a stated slot of time with religious monologue) is too loose and imprecise, and the usual definitions of preaching, as was said before, are not sufficiently functional and theological, for our present purposes. If the definition I have given draws criticism as being too narrow, I must endure it; but I cannot see that the New Testament will sanction any lower concept of Christian preaching, and therefore it is in terms of the view I have stated, this and nothing less than this, that I continue my argument.

Now that we have seen what preaching is, we can move on to the heart of this essay. We are now in a position to address directly the question of my title: Why preach?

First, it should be noted that here we have really two questions in one. Objectively, the question is, What theological reasons are there for maintaining preaching as a necessary part of church life?

1. David Clarkson, *Works*, vol. 3 (Edinburgh: James Nichol, 1865), pp. 193-94.

Subjectively, the question is, What convictions should prompt a person to take up, sustain, and keep giving his best to the task of seeking to preach according to these awesome specifications? I take the two questions in order.

With regard to the first, I herewith offer some theological reasons for regarding preaching as a vital and essential part of Christian community life in this or any age. The suspicion is voiced nowadays, as we have seen, that pulpit monologue is an inefficient way of communicating and that books, films, TV, tapes, and group study and discussion can all be fully acceptable substitutes for it. With this I disagree, and in this section of my essay I am consciously arguing against any such views. Certainly, preaching is communication, and communication must be efficient; there are no two ways about that. But preaching is more than what is nowadays thought of as communication. God uses preaching to communicate more than current communication theory is concerned with, and more than alternative forms of Christian communication can be expected under ordinary circumstances to convey. I have nothing against books, films, tapes, and study groups in their place, but the place where God sets the preacher is not their place. The considerations that follow will, I hope, make this clear.

First, *preaching is God's revealed way of making Himself and His saving covenant known to us.* This is an argument drawn from the nature of God's revelatory action, as Scripture sets it forth.

The Bible shows God the Creator to be a communicator, and the theme and substance of His communication since Eden, to be a gracious, life-giving relationship with believing sinners. All the factual information and ethical direction that He currently communicates through His written Word feeds into this relationship, first to establish it through repentance and commitment to Jesus Christ, and then to deepen it through increasing knowledge of God and maturing worship. This is the covenant life of God's people, which is both initiated and sustained through God's personal communion with them. Now the Bible makes it appear that God's standard way of securing and maintaining His person-to-person communication with us His human creatures is through the agency of persons whom He sends to us as His messengers. By being made God's spokesmen and mouthpieces for His message, the messengers become emblems, models, and embodiments of God's personal address to each of their hearers, and by their own commitment to the message they bring, they become models also of personal response to that address. Such were the prophets and apostles, and such supremely was Jesus Christ, the incarnate Son, who has been well described as being both God for man and man for God. That is the succession in which preachers today are called to stand.

Why does the New Testament stress the need for preaching (as it does in many different ways: see Matt. 10:6-7; Mark 3:14; 13:10; Luke 24:45-49; Acts 5:42; 6:2-4; 10:42; Rom. 10:6-17; I Cor. 1:17-24; 9:16; Phil. 1:12-18; II Tim. 4:2-5; Titus 1:3; etc.)? Not just because the good news had to be spread and the only way to spread news in the ancient world was by oral announcement, though that was certainly true. But it is also, surely, because of the power of "incarnational" communication, in which the speaker illuminates that which he proclaims by being transparently committed to it in a wholehearted and thoroughgoing way. Phillips Brooks was profoundly right when he defined preaching as "truth through personality." The preacher's personality cannot be eliminated from the preaching situation, and what he appears to be is a part of what he communicates—necessarily, inescapably, willy-nilly, and for better or for worse. So the preacher must speak as one who himself stands under the authority of his message and knows the reality and power of which he speaks; otherwise the impact of his personality will reduce the credibility of his proclamation, just as a man's baldness would reduce the credibility of any sales pitch he might make as a purveyor of hair restorer. The committed personality is in this sense integral to God's message, for God uses it to communicate his own reality as his messenger speaks. But for fullest awareness of the messenger's committedness we need to have him confront us in a "live" preaching situation; "canned" preaching on a tape, and "stage" preaching on TV, and "embalmed" preaching in the form of printed sermons are all unable to communicate this awareness to the same degree. Thus the need for preaching "live" remains as great as it was nineteen centuries ago. It is still supremely through preaching, that is, through the impact on us of the message and the messenger together, that God meets us, and makes Himself and His saving grace known to us.

How to communicate the reality of the God of Scripture across the temporal and cultural gap that separates our world from the world of the Bible has exercised many contemporary minds. It is not always noticed that God provides much of the answer to this perplexity in the person of the preacher, who is called to be a living advertisement for the relevance and power of what he proclaims. The flip side of this truth is, of course, that should a preacher's words and life fail to exhibit this relevance and power, he would be actively hindering his hearers' knowledge of God. I suspect that the widespread perplexity today as to the relevance of the New Testament gospel should be seen as God's judgment on two generations of inadequate preaching by inadequate preachers, rather than anything else.

Second, *preaching communicates the force of the Bible as no other way of handling it does.* This is an argument drawn from the nature of Scripture itself.

Holy Scripture is, in and of itself, preaching. From one standpoint, it is servants of God preaching; from another, profounder, standpoint, it is God Himself preaching. Some of its sixty-six books are already, explicitly, sermons on paper (I think of the prophetic oracles of the Old Testament and the apostolic letters of the New); some are not. But all of them without exception were written to edify—that is, to teach people to know the living God, and to love and worship and serve Him—and to that extent they all have the nature of preaching. To preach them is thus no more, just as it is no less, than to acknowledge them for what they are, and to let their content be to us what it already is in itself. The Bible text is the real preacher, and the role of the man in the pulpit or the counseling conversation is simply to let the passages say their piece through him. *Simply*, did I say?—but it is far from simple in practice! For the preacher to reach the point where he no longer hinders and obstructs his text from speaking is harder work than is sometimes realized. However, there can be no disputing that this is the task. And by preaching the Bible one makes it possible for the thrust and force of "God's Word written" (Anglican Article 20) to be adequately appreciated, in a way that is never possible through any type of detached study, or any kind of instruction in which a person speaks for or about the Bible as distinct from letting the Bible speak for itself. Bible courses in seminaries, for instance, do not beget an awareness of the power of Scripture in the way that preaching does.

Preaching the Bible is the affirming and exploring of the relation between God's Word (written and transmitted as Scripture by the agency of the Spirit, and now written on and applied to our hearts from Scripture by the same agency) and human lives—in other words, it is the exploring of its relation to ourselves. The activity of preaching the Bible (of which I take the public reading of Scripture to be part) unlocks the Bible to both mind and heart, and the activity of hearing Scripture preached, receiving what is said, meditating on the text as preaching has opened it up, and letting it apply itself to one's own thoughts and ways actually leads us into the Bible in terms of enabling us to comprehend and lay hold of what it, or better, God in and through it, is saying to us at this moment. Where such a personal relation to the Bible has not become part of one's life, though one may know much about its language, background, origins, and the historical significance of its contents, it remains in the deepest sense a closed book. And those who in this sense do not yet know what to make of the Bible will not know what to make of their own lives either. One way to express this is to say that our lives are in the Bible, and we do not understand them until we find them there. But the quickest and most vivid way in which such understanding comes about is through being addressed by the Bible via someone for whom the Bible is alive and who knows and can articulate something of its life-changing power. This is a further reason why preaching is always needed in the church: whenever preaching fails, understanding of Scripture in its relation to life will inevitably fail too.

Third, *preaching focuses the identity and clarifies the calling of the church as no other activity does.* This is an argument drawn from the nature of the church, as we learn it from Scripture.

In every age the church has had an identity problem, and in some ages an identity crisis. Why? Because the world always wants to assimilate the church to itself and thereby swallow it up, and is always putting the church under pressure to that end; and to such pressure the church, at least in the West, has constantly proved very vulnerable. The results of it can be seen today in the extremely weak sense of identity that many churches have. Their adherents think of them more as social clubs, like Shriners, Elks, Freemasons, and Rotarians, or as interest groups, like political parties and hikers' associations, than as visible outcrops of one worldwide supernatural society, and they are quite unable to give substance to the biblical thought that God's people, as the salt and light for the world, are required to be different from those around them. The problem is perennial, and there is always need to proclaim the Bible, its gospel, its Christ, and its ethics, in order to renew the church's flagging awareness of its God-given identity and vocation. Preaching is the only activity that holds out any hope of achieving this; but preaching can do it by keeping before Christian minds God's threefold requirement that His people be Word-oriented, worship-oriented, and witness-oriented. A comment, now, about each of these.

The church must be *Word-oriented:* that is, God's people must always be attentive and obedient to Scripture. Scripture is God's Word of constant address to them, and woe betide them if they disregard it (see II Chron. 36:15-16; II Kings 22:8-20; Isa. 1:19-20; Jer. 7:23-26; Rev. 2:4-7, 15-17, etc.). God's people must learn to "tremble at his word" (Ezra 9:4; Isa. 66:5), listening, learning, and laying to heart; believing what He tells them, behaving as He directs them, and battling for His truth in a world that denies it. Preaching, as an activity of letting texts talk, alerts Christians to the fact that God is constantly addressing them and enforces the authority of Scripture over them. The church must live by God's Word as its necessary food and steer by that Word as its guiding star. Without preaching, however, it is not conceivable that this will be either seen or done.

The church must also be *worship-oriented*: that is, God's people must regularly celebrate what God is and has done and will do, and glorify His name for it all by their praises, prayers, and devotion. The preaching of the Bible is the mainspring of this worship, for it fuels the devotional fire, constantly confronting Christians with God's works and ways in saving them (redeeming, regenerating, forgiving, accepting, adopting, guarding, guiding, keeping, feeding), and thereby leading them into paths of obedient and adoring response. Indeed, from this standpoint biblical preaching is implicit doxology throughout; the biblical preacher will follow Scripture in giving God glory for His works, ways, and wisdom at every turn, and will urge His hearers to do the same. This is the first reason why preaching should be regarded as the climax of congregational worship. From this flows the second reason, namely that congregations never honor God more than by reverently listening to His Word with a full purpose of praising and obeying Him once they see what He has done and is doing, and what they are called to do. But it is precisely through preaching that these things are made clear and this purpose is maintained.

Should it be objected that the liturgical drama of the Lord's Supper rather than the preached Word of Holy Scripture ought to be central and climactic in our worship, the appropriate answer is that without the preached Word to interpret the Supper and establish on each occasion a community context for it, it will itself become dark in meaning to us, and eucharistic worship will then be spoiled by waywardness and somnolence in our hearts. This is why, historically, Word and sacrament have been linked together as partners in the worship of God, rather than set against each other as rivals for our attention.

Finally, the church must be *witness-oriented*: that is, God's people must always be seeking to move out into the world around them to make Christ known and disciple the lost, and to that end they must "always be prepared to give an answer to everyone who asks [them] to give the reason for the hope that [they] have" (I Pet. 3:15). Apart from the preaching of the Word, however, the church will never have the resources to do this; it will constantly tend to forget its identity as the people charged to go and tell, and may actually lose its grip on the contents of its own message, as it has done many times in the past. History tells of no significant church growth and expansion that has taken place without preaching (*significant*, implying virility and staying power, is the key word there). What history points to, rather, is that all movements of revival, reformation, and missionary outreach seem to have had preaching (vigorous, though on occasion very informal) at their center, instructing, energizing, sometimes purging and redirecting, and often spearheading the whole movement. It would seem, then, that preaching is always necessary for a proper sense of mission to be evoked and sustained anywhere in the church.

Thus preaching is able to maintain the church's sense of identity and calling as the people charged to attend to God's Word, to obey it as His children, and to spread it as His witnesses. But there seems no way in which without preaching the eroding of this awareness can be avoided.

Fourth, *preaching has some unique advantages as a mode of Christian instruction.* This is an argument drawn from the nature of the church's teaching task.

Preaching is teaching, first and foremost. It is more than teaching; it is teaching *plus* application, as was said earlier; but it is never less than teaching. It is a kind of speaking aimed at both mind and heart, and seeking unashamedly to change the way people think and live. So it is always an attempt at persuasion; yet if its basic ingredient is not honest teaching, it is fundamentally flawed and unworthy. I shall now suggest that its monologue form, which is so often criticized as a hindrance both to teaching and to learning, is actually a great advantage in regard to both. Let me explain.

I grant that, because preaching is monologue, artifice is needed (some have it naturally, others have to acquire it) to ensure that hearers stay awake and are kept interested, involved, and thinking along with the speaker as he proceeds. But that is no hindrance when the preacher has the artifice and the congregation knows that it is there to learn. And when this is the case, the monologue form helps greatly. The preacher can use words to do what he could not do in ordinary conversation, or in discussion. He can, for instance, spend time building up a sense of the greatness of what he is dealing with: the greatness of God, or of eternity, or of divine grace. Thus he can educate his hearers' sense of the relative importance of things. Or he can pile up reasons for believing a particular truth, or behaving in a particular way, or embracing a particular concern, and so hammer his points home by cumulative impact. Thus he can deepen his hearers' sense of obligation. He can hold a mirror up to his hearers, exploring their actual states of mind, with their various conflicting thoughts, faithful and faithless, in a way that would otherwise require a full-length novel or play. He can search consciences and challenge evasions of moral and spiritual issues with a forthrightness that would be unacceptable in ordinary conversation, or in a casual chat. Also, as one who prays for the unction of the Holy Spirit for the delivery of his message, he can allow himself a more intense, dramatic, and passionate way of speaking about the awesome realities of spiritual life and death than everyday speech would sanction; then he may look to God to honor the vision of things expressed by his honest disclosure of his feelings and reactions. In short, he will see it as his responsibility to make his message as clear, vivid, searching, "home-coming" (Alexander Whyte's word for applicatory), and thus memorable, as he can, and to use all the rhetorical resources and possibilities of monologue form to that end. My point is simply that these resources are considerable, and if they are wisely used, hearers who are there to learn (as all hearers of sermons should be) will gain more from the sermon than they would do from any informal conversation or discussion on the same subject.

These things are said to encourage not the Spirit-quenching artificiality of "putting on an act," but the spiritual alertness, realism, and sheer hard work out of which effective communication of what Whyte called "the eternities and the immensities" is born.

Another thing that monologue makes possible is the exhibiting of individuals' problems as problems of the community, by bringing them into the pulpit for biblical analysis. By this means a wise preacher may in effect do much of his counseling from the pulpit, and in so doing equip his hearers to become counselors themselves. This is a further great advantage of the monologue form to those who have the wit to use it.

Educationists have a tag that there is no impression without expression, and teachers are taught that a third of every lesson in the classroom should be expression work. How can this requirement be met, it is asked, in the case of pulpit monologue? And how can there be effective learning from the monologue if it is not met? Organized discussion of sermons preached, congregational deliberation on the issues raised, and pastoral enquiry as to what changes (if any!) the preaching has effected in particular hearers' lives provide together the answer to these questions. That this threefold follow-up of preaching is in practice a rare thing may be a valid criticism of pastors, but it does not in any way invalidate monologue preaching from Scripture as a primary form of communication from God.

It is thus abundantly clear that no congregation can be healthy without a diet of biblical preaching, and no pastor can justify himself in demoting preaching from the place of top priority among the tasks of his calling. From the objective point of view, therefore, the question "Why preach?" is now answered. All that remains is to say something about the convictions that, under God, work in a person's heart to make him a preacher and to keep him preaching despite all discouragements, thus constituting his personal answer to the question "Why preach?"

Jeremiah told God that "the word of the Lord has brought me insult and reproach all day long. But if I say, 'I will not mention him or speak any more in his name,' his word is in my heart like a burning fire, shut up in my bones. I am weary of holding it in; indeed, I cannot" (Jer. 20:8-9). Does anything correspond to this in the experience of Christian preachers? The answer is yes. There is a God-given vision that produces preachers, and any man who has that vision cannot sleep easy without making preaching his life's work. The vision (that is, the awareness of what God sees, and wills to do, and to have His servants do) embodies a series of related convictions, somewhat as follows.

First, *Scripture is revelation*. Heaven is not silent; God the Creator has spoken, and the Bible is His written Word. God has made Himself known on the stage of history by prophecy, providence, miracle, and supremely in His Son, Jesus Christ, and Scripture witnesses to that. God has disclosed His will for the living of our lives, and the Bible proclaims His law. God undertakes, through the interpreting work of the Spirit who inspired Scripture in the first place, to teach us how this revelation bears on us; thus it is promised that His Word shall function for us as a lamp for our feet and a light to illuminate our path, as on a dark night. God's Word is described as a hammer to break stony hearts, fire to burn up rubbish, seed causing birth, milk causing growth, honey that sweetens, and gold that enriches (Ps. 119:105; Jer. 23:29; I Pet. 1:23–2:2; Ps. 19:10). The Bible is in truth, as the Moderator of the Church of Scotland tells the monarch in the British coronation service, the most precious thing that this world affords.

There is, then, available in this world a sure message from God, tried and true, unfailing and unchanging, and it needs to be proclaimed so that all may know it. The messenger who delivers it will have the dignity of being God's spokesman and ambassador. No self-aggrandizement or self-advertisement is involved, for the messenger neither invents his message nor asks for attention in his own name. He is a minister—that is, a servant—of God, of Christ, and of the Word. He is a steward of God's revealed mysteries, called not to be brilliant and original but diligent and faithful (I Cor. 4:1–2). Yet to be God's messenger—to run His errands, act as His courier, and spend one's strength making Him known—is the highest honor that any human being ever enjoys. The servant's dignity derives from the dignity of his employer, and of the work he is set to do. "Ministers are ambassadors for

God and speak in Christ's stead," wrote Charles Simeon. "If they preach what is founded on the Scriptures, their word, as far as it is agreeable to the mind of God, is to be considered as God's. This is asserted by our Lord and his apostles. We ought therefore to receive the preacher's word as the word of God himself."[2] There is no nobler calling than to serve God as a preacher of the divine Word.

Second, *God is glorious.* God has shown His wisdom, love, and power in creation, providence, and redemption, and all of His self-revelation calls for constant praise, since it is infinitely praise-worthy. Man's vocation, in essence and at heart, is to give His Maker glory (praise) for all the glories (powers and performances) that God shows him. The chief end of man is to glorify God, and in so doing to enjoy Him, and that for ever, as the first answer of the Westminster Shorter Catechism puts it. God's doings should be known and celebrated everywhere, and when His rational human creatures fail to honor Him in this way, they rob Him of His due, as well as robbing themselves of their own highest happiness. For human life was meant to be an infinitely enriching love affair with the Creator, an unending exploration of the delights of dox-ology, and nothing makes up for the absence of those joys that come from praise.

It is the preacher's privilege to declare the works of God and lead his hearers to praise God for them. "I will bless the Lord at all times; his praise will always be on my lips. My soul will boast in the Lord; let the afflicted hear and rejoice. Glorify the Lord with me; let us exalt his name together" (Ps. 43:1–3). Some have thought that what makes men into preachers is the desire to dominate, but what really animates them is a longing to glorify God and to see others doing the same.

Third, *people are lost.* Mankind's state is tragic. Human beings, made for God, are spiritually blind and deaf, and have their backs

2. Charles Simeon, *Let Wisdom Judge,* ed. Arthur Pollard (London: Inter-Varsity Press, 1959), pp. 188–89.

turned to Him. Whether clear-headedly or not, they are bent on self-destruction through self-worship and self-indulgence. Their souls starve in a world of spiritual plenty, and they mar their angelic abilities by their brutish and beastly behavior. Made for God's love, they bring down on themselves His wrath by defying His will. Made for glory, they are consigning themselves to hell. The preacher sees this, and compassion drives him to speak. He wants to take the arm of everyone he meets, point to Christ, and say "Look!" He sees his ministry as a form of Samaritanship to ravaged souls—an expression of love to neighbor, therefore, as well as of love to God. He is a man driven by zeal to share Christ.

Fourth, *Christ is unchanging.* "Jesus Christ is the same yesterday and today and forever" (Heb. 13:8). The Christ who is to be preached today is the Christ of whom Bernard wrote in the twelfth century,

> *Jesus, thou joy of loving hearts,*
> *Thou fount of life, thou light of men,*
> *From the best bliss that earth imparts*
> *We turn unfilled to thee again;*

and of whom John Newton wrote in the eighteenth century,

> *How sweet the name of Jesus sounds*
> *In a believer's ear!*
> *It soothes his sorrows, heals his wounds,*
> *And drives away his fear.*
> *Jesus, my Shepherd, Brother, Friend,*
> *My Prophet, Priest, and King,*
> *My Lord, my life, my way, my end,*
> *Accept the praise I bring.*   ·

So the preacher knows that when he depicts the Christ of the New Testament as the living Lord and Savior of guilty, vile, and helpless sinners today, he presents not fancy but fact, not a dream but a reality. The need of this Christ is universal; the adequacy of this Christ is inexhaustible; the power of this Christ is immeasurable. Here is a wonderfully rich message on which to expatiate, a gospel worth preaching indeed!

Furthermore, the preacher knows that Christ's way is to step out of the pages of the New Testament into the lives of saints and sinners through the speech that is uttered about Him by His messengers. In Gustav Wingren's words, "Preaching is not just talk about a Christ of the past, but is a mouth through which the Christ of the present offers us life today." "Preaching has but one aim, that Christ may come to those who have assembled to listen."[3] To be the human channel of Christ's approach in this way is unquestionably a huge privilege, and no preacher can be blamed for feeling it so and making much of his role accordingly.

Fifth, *persuasion is needed.* God treats us as the rational beings that He made us. Accordingly, He does not move us to Christian responses by physical means that bypass the mind, but by persuading us to obey His truth and honor His Son. The preacher, as God's mouthpiece, has the task of persuading on God's behalf, and the role is a vital one since where there is no persuasion people will perish. Preaching is the art not of browbeating, but of persuading, in a way that shows both respect for the human mind and reverence for the God who made it. Christian persuasion requires wisdom, love, patience, and holy humanness. It is a fine art as well as a useful one, and it becomes for preachers a lifetime study, concern, and challenge.

Sixth, *Satan is active.* The devil is malicious and mean, more so than any of us can imagine, and he marauds constantly with destructive intent. Though he is, as Luther said, God's devil, and is on a chain (a strong one, though admittedly a long one), he is tireless in opposing God, and sets himself to spoil and thwart all the redemptive work that God ever does in human lives. As one means to this end, he labors to ensure that preachers' messages will be either misstated or misheard, so that they will not have the liberating, invigorating, upbuilding effect that is proper to the

3. Gustav Wingren, *The Living Word* (London: SCM, 1960), pp. 108, 208.

preached Word. Preaching is thus, as all real preachers soon discover, an endless battle for truth and power, a battle that has to
be fought afresh each time by watchfulness and prayer. Preachers
know themselves to be warriors in God's front line, drawing
enemy fire; the experience is gruelling, but it confirms to them the
importance of their task as ambassadors for Christ and heralds of
God, sowers of good seed, stewards of saving truth, shepherds of
God's flock, and fathers guiding their spiritual families (II Cor.
5:20; Luke 8:4–15; I Cor. 4:1; Acts 20:28–32; I Pet. 5:2–4; I Cor.
4:15; Gal. 4:19). In the manner of front-line troops they frequently get scared by the opposition unleashed against them, but
they do not panic, and their morale remains high. The challenge
of beating back Satan by God's strength, like that of communicating effectively for Christ, is one to which they rise.

Seventh, *God's Spirit is sovereign.* Through the Spirit's agency in
both preacher and hearers, the Word of God becomes invincible.
If fruitfulness depended finally on human wisdom and resource-
fulness, no preacher would dare to speak a word, for no preacher
ever feels that in his communication he has been wise and resourceful enough. And if God's power was exerted only in helping the preacher to speak and not in causing the listeners to hear,
preaching, however wise and resourceful, would always be a barren and unfruitful activity, for fallen human beings have no natural power of response to the divine Word. But in fact fruitfulness
depends on the almighty work of God the Holy Spirit in the
heart. So preachers, however conscious of their own limitations,
may nonetheless speak expectantly, knowing that they serve a
God who has said (Isa. 55:10–11) that His Word will not return
to Him void. With this knowledge supporting them, it is the way
of real preachers to show themselves undaunted and unsinkable.

Such, in sum, are the convictions that produce *reformed* preachers. As we review them, it becomes very obvious that a "reformed" preacher in the seventeenth-century sense of that word,
which corresponded roughly to our use of "renewed" and "revived," will need to be a Reformed preacher in the twentieth-
century sense of that word, that is, Augustinian and Calvinistic in

belief; for all the seven items I have mentioned are characteristically Reformed tenets. Nor should this discovery surprise us, for it is a matter of historical fact that the Reformed tradition has been more fertile in producing reformed preachers over the centuries than has any other viewpoint in Christendom. I affirm with total confidence as I conclude, that able men with these seven convictions burning in their hearts will never need to scratch their heads, in this or any age, over the question whether preaching is a worthwhile use of their time. They will know that preaching God's gospel and God's counsel from the Scriptures was, and is, and always will be, the most honorable and significant activity in the world, and accordingly they will tackle this task with joy. It cannot, surely, be doubted that it will be a most happy thing if God increases the number of such preachers in our time.

PART ONE
THE MAN

1

The Minister's Call

Joel Nederhood

There is something strange about the subject *the minister's call.* One reason is that so few people actually have it, it might almost fit under the subject of abnormal psychology. Another is that it is totally subjective, and those who possess it in its strongest form find it difficult, even awkward, to express exactly what it is for them. And, of course, the subject is part of "religious experience," and many of us feel somewhat embarrassed whenever we venture into this area.

Even so, it is important to talk about the *call;* there are many concerned people in churches who would like to get some things straight about it. Maybe if they could understand what the call is, they would be able to understand their minister better. There is no question that he has been touched by something different from the influences that normally touch people, and possibly his call is the explanation for his behavior. Church members are deeply concerned about their preachers, after all, for they realize that in a curious way they are dependent on these individuals who in turn often seem dreadfully dependent on their congregations. There is, unfortunately, an ambivalence between churches and their pastors, and it is caused by the congregation's frequent puzzlement regarding just what it is that their pastor has and refers to, often in times of special stress, as his call.

But if there are certain questions and misgivings regarding the call within congregations, they also exist among ministers themselves. Some have simply abandoned any pretense of having any special call, and they have dedicated themselves to their work just

33

as any other professional might dedicate himself to his. If it is necessary to discuss the matter of *call* so that the churches will be better equipped to look for "called" pastors and to relate to them once they have found them, it is even more necessary for ministers themselves to possess clarity with respect to their understanding of their own call. They should know what the call is, and they should be sure that they have it; else they should get out of the ministry. And possessing certainty that God has called them to the ministry of the Word, they should neither waver nor vacillate in their pursuit of their calling. A minister who is sure of his call is among the most poised, confident, joy-filled, and effective of human beings; a minister who is not is among the most faltering and pitiable.

False Forms of the Call

It is important first of all to clear away some of the false forms the call can so easily take, for the trouble that churches are having nowadays with their ministers and that many ministers are having with themselves suggests that a significant number of people in the ministry these days are not truly called. Unfortunately, it may well be that some of the very people who insist on their calling most strenuously may in fact be responding to something that is not the call at all.

Certain elements of the ministry as we know it tend to call into play a variety of motivations that may strongly impel a person to enter this work without his having been authentically called to it. Consider that the ministry is practically the only activity these days that allows a person to speak uninterruptedly for extended periods of time to an audience that feels obligated to give attention to what is being said. Whatever one wants to say about the effectiveness of preaching so far as the congregation is concerned, there can be no doubt that for people who love to speak, preaching provides satisfactions duplicated nowhere else. If a preacher has some native talent and few scruples, there is virtually no limit to what he can accomplish with the people who listen to him.

Audience manipulation is practiced not only by the television industry; preachers do it all the time. And no tradition is exempt: Pentecostal ministers do it, but Reformed pastors can develop their ways, too. The attraction of the pulpit, in this naturalistic sense of attraction, can create a compulsion to preach that is real, but is not necessarily authentic.

Another motivation that can be very strong though by no means authentic relates to the automatic stamp of goodness the ministry gives to those in it. Today, of course, there is a cynicism abroad regarding ministerial virtue, but usually at the time a person begins to prepare himself for the ministry, he is unaware of this cynicism. In many instances, there is no more effective way to receive the approval of one's parents, and possibly of aunts and uncles as well, than to announce that one is preparing for the gospel ministry. All of us prefer to be considered very, very good rather than only moderately so, and consequently a person's entrance into the ministry in order to achieve approval is not exceptional.

We should not fail to notice, in addition, that the ministry provides a number of advantages that can tend to draw people to it. It is perhaps somewhat tactless to remember that there have been times when preparation for the ministry has exempted young men from military service, and young men who preferred not to endure the rigors of combat have felt the call during times when the draft was in operation. And speaking of the military, the fact that in many countries clergymen are brought into the services as part of the officer corps illustrates the special treatment traditionally given members of the cloth.

There are a wide range of perks that ministers receive, ranging from favorable treatment by the Internal Revenue Service to discounts on furniture and jogging shoes. In some instances, ministers can run a number of items such as their automobile licenses through their church's books and avoid sales tax. And then there are gifts; if nothing else, some congregations tend to be generous when ministers leave them, and though the sentiment may be suspect, the gift is nonetheless real. And with all of this, ministers are often well taken care of. Now, it is true that this varies from denomination to denomination; even so, many ministers whose income may be relatively low discover over the decades that they do all right in the long run. One thing is sure: they are usually exempted from participating in the hectic tension that is often part of earning a living these days.

What this all comes down to is this: the ministry is not a bad job, and there is no doubt that for some it is the best job they can get. And since a minister's work is generally not understood by his parishioners, and since it is possible for him to call a wide range of activities his "work" (for example, running errands for his wife—after all, she is a part of his flock, too), it is possible for a minister to create a relatively easy job for himself; some take advantage of that possibility.

If what has been said thus far is offensive, what now follows will be even more so. But it should be recognized that the ministry also provides certain psychological types with satisfactions that are not available elsewhere. Anyone who enjoys hearing "true confessions" will enjoy the ministry. People will tell ministers things they would tell no one else. Women will sit across the desk from a clergyman and without batting an eye tell him about sexual encounters that are mind-boggling; they will expect the minister simply to sit there and coolly evaluate their behavior. Another thing: because a person is a minister, women will sometimes treat him as if he were a eunuch—they will shower him with affections that between other people would be frowned on. There are some in the ministry today who enjoy these contacts with the opposite sex, which they can have in a thoroughly legitimate way. No one could accuse them of anything, for after all they are simply fulfilling the duties of their office.

It is not very pleasant to review such dimensions of the ministry, which can easily become the foundation for motivations that are strong, but not authentic. It is necessary, though, for motivation in the best of circumstances is always mysterious, and ultimately only God knows our motivations perfectly. Because some dimensions of the ministry can excite improper motivation, those who consider themselves called to the ministry need to examine themselves to make certain that they have not entered the work because of a motivation related to something just described. A minister who experiences an extremely high degree of discomfort in his work and who may be on the verge of a nervous breakdown should ask whether his own presence in the ranks of the clergy has been caused by impulses that are not entirely pure. For his own good and the good of his congregation, he should discontinue his attempt to fulfill a task that can be properly executed only by those who have been truly called.

It is also important to be aware of improper motivations for the ministry, for no minister is completely free from what has been reviewed. It is possible, for example, that a minister, whose original, strong, authentic sense of call diminishes at some point in his career, might fall back on one or more of the motivations just reviewed, to make up for the deficiency and carry him through. For example, a person who deeply loves to preach might stay with the ministry even though his original call has deteriorated. A minister needs to be aware of this possibility so that he will be able to monitor what is going on in his life.

Biblical Data and the Call

When one examines the Bible for direction concerning the ministerial call, the data are not entirely helpful for those who wonder if God is calling them to the ministry, nor is it all that helpful for those who have served in the ministry for some time and want to evaluate their sense of calling in the light of Scripture. The called people found on the Bible's pages cannot be directly compared to what we know as the ordinary minister of the Word.

One might examine the call of Moses, for example, in the hope of finding insights into the nature of calling. One writer concluded from the conversation between God and Moses at the burning bush that "there are no volunteers" so far as the ministry is concerned. Once, when I read that writer's devotional on this subject just before retiring for the night, I shuddered as I recalled I had volunteered to some extent as I moved closer and closer to

the ministry. Certainly I had never been confronted with anything quite as startling as a burning bush, and my protestations
concerning my own lack of qualifications did not compare with
Moses' declaration of his inability spoken while he stood without
his sandals in the presence of divine glory.

It is true that within the Bible, there are few, if any, religious
functionaries who stepped forward and urged God to accept them
for special service; surely there were some whose religion was
impure and tainted who tried that approach, but they were re-
buffed: Simon the Sorcerer is an example. Ordinarily, those who
functioned in the legitimate service of the God of Israel came into
their office through heredity, and those who really were the mov-
ers and the shakers in the Old Testament era were brought to
their special work because God demanded their services and assured them that He would qualify them: Amos, Samuel, Isaiah,
Jeremiah, and others.

And when one comes to the New Testament, he finds that
those who were really significant in shaping the life of the church
received their call in an inescapably recognizable way. The apostolic band illustrates this, especially when the most illustrious of
the apostles, Paul, is included. What a mistake it would be if
those who suspected that God was calling them to the ministry
would not act on their suspicion until they had received a Damascus Road experience! And what insufferable arrogance would attend the ministry of anyone who would claim that he had experienced something similar to what the apostle Paul experienced!

As we discuss the ministerial call, we must use the Bible with
extreme care. Surely, we must remember there is a sense in which
what we consider the ministerial office (as in organized churches)
did not exist in its present-day form during the time covered by
special revelation. The church during the apostolic era was a part
of the special work of God designed to serve as a foundation for
this age in which we presently express our several callings. At the
same time, the biblical data help us understand what the ministerial call is in this age, for it is the foundation for the church in
which ministers work today.

For our purposes, the revelation about Timothy and his office is the closest we have to something that can be used nearly as it stands when we think about the ministerial call. In the case of Timothy, there are obviously differences between his situation and ours that may not be forgotten, among them his special and close relationship with the apostle Paul; even so, when we read about Timothy, we are reading about a person whose function in the early church was significantly similar to the function of a minister in the church these days.

So far as the Timothy material is concerned, the most directly applicable to our thinking about the call today is the "man of God" material with which I Timothy is concluded and which reappears in II Timothy 3. The minister today, it must be conceded, is no modern counterpart of Moses, nor even of the apostle Paul, but he is merely a "man of God," which is in itself quite something. If the observation is made that not only ministers are "men of God," but all Christians should be that (women as well), this observation is certainly correct. For the minister today is really nothing more than an ordinary member of the church of Jesus Christ who is called to express His nature as "man of God" in an especially high degree.

Surely, he can learn from Moses and Abraham and all the great leaders of the church of all ages, but he may never simply assume that their prerogatives, dignity, and tasks are his today. A minister is a very little person, in comparison, a person with a narrow task: he is a man of God, with a specific call. In his case, as in all others in the church, it is extremely important that he does not think of himself more highly than he ought to think; he must, in fact, regard others as better than himself.

The Call and General Faith Development

Though the direct biblical data relating to the minister's call are not as extensive as we might wish, some principles derived from Scripture can certainly be developed. In the first place, it is very important that one's call be considered only within the context of maturity. In some instances, very young men—while they are still children in fact—will announce that they are going to be ministers. This could well be an authentic leading of the Lord. However, it is best to treat precocious announcements with a measure of skepticism; for the person involved and for whatever parishioners he eventually serves, it is best that the ultimate determination of one's call be made in connection with mature faith.

Although this is not the place to discuss fully the way faith matures, it is necessary to make some remarks about this subject. In the case of a child who has grown up in a covenant home and has been molded by Christian nurture from childhood, the maturation of faith occurs as a gradual movement from the faith that is natural for a child to adult faith. The faith of a child is real, but it is faith defined by the fact that the child is a child, and its distinguishing characteristic is that it reflects the faith of the parents. Throughout the teen-age years, the child moves through a "sundering" phase in which he severs his ties with his parents so far as his personality is concerned. What awesome and mysterious years these are! During them, ideally the child should move from a faith that depends on and reflects his parents' faith to an adult faith. This is a time of questioning—it has to be, no matter how painful this process may be. This is a time of rebelling even, and sometimes the rebelling is necessary in order that the child will arrive at a faith that is actually purer and better than his parents' faith. Finally, the child becomes his own person. He is a man, and the faith he has is the faith of a man. He is an adult, and the faith he possesses is that of an adult.

If a person comes to faith later in life, it is important to evaluate the call after a period of time has elapsed following his conversion. Often a person who is saved during the late teens or the twenties or even later immediately concludes that God is calling him to the ministry. It is easy to mistake the general feeling of relief, joy, and praise that a person experiences when he has been rescued from darkness and set in the marvelous light of life in Christ as the call to the ministry. It may well be no such call at all.

The Bible explicitly warns us about giving special spiritual responsibility to "novices," those who have just recently come to faith (I Tim. 3:6). It is difficult to avoid doing this, however, for, when a young man is saved after having lived an especially debauched life of sin and he announces that he wants to serve Jesus for the rest of his life in the ministry, one is inclined to encourage him to do exactly that. And often God does call people into the ministry who have been rescued from a particularly gross life of sin, and He may call them practically simultaneously with their call to salvation. Even so, because of the need to make sure that the ministerial call is authentic, the final evaluation of a person's call should be held off until the person has demonstrated that his call is not rooted in emotion, but is seasoned and true.

To be specific, if a person is converted later in life, he should not conclude that he is called to the ministry until he has spent some years in a regular church, hearing the proclamation of the Word and possibly taking up some form of ministry within the church such as teaching Sunday school. If he is serious about being a minister, he should very carefully test the call he feels he has, and that necessarily will take some time.

Those who fill the ministerial office must be among the most mature of Christian people, and consequently, it is important to recognize that the call in its most authentic form will be expressed in the lives of those who have benefited from a certain degree of maturity in every area of their lives, and especially in connection with their spiritual development. The very person who counseled Timothy against enlisting *novices* in the ministry of the church was himself a person whose personal experience involved an exceedingly quick movement from false religion to the religion of the Lord Jesus Christ. Even so, as a religious person, Saul the persecutor possessed an exceptionally high level of spiritual knowledge and discernment, and even in his case, his full entrance into his ministry did not occur until the Lord had prepared him with special instruction (Gal. 1:13-23). Maturity, or seasoning, is an extremely important element in determining the authenticity of calls.

Becoming Conscious of the Call

It is important now to spotlight what is involved as one's consciousness of his call develops within the context of a mature faith. So far as the call to the ministry is concerned, there is a development of one's consciousness with respect to it. It may be true that in some instances one's call can fall like a thunderclap into his life and his consciousness of what God wants him to do is immediately present. For most ministers, however, their becoming called to the ministry involves a development over an extended period of time. As it began, they may have been somewhat embarrassed about the direction their thinking was taking, but over the years, their call became the most dominant force in their lives. In any case, in this material, the feeling of being called into the ministry will be viewed as something that comes over a period of time, something that develops with the passing years.

And at this point, it is important to describe precisely what we are speaking of when we speak of the *call* to the ministry. Unfortunately, the idea of *call* has largely disappeared from our vocabulary, though there was a time in American life when it was talked about in connection with a wide range of human activities. The following statement regarding the way the concept of call operated during the Puritan period is enlightening:

> Directly related to the Puritan view of the prescribed institutional structure of society was an understanding of "calling" and "office." William Perkins characterized calling as "a certain kind of life, ordained and imposed on man by God, for the common good." The call was to the individual, but it was to serve in a social institution. God's calling to an individual to be a magistrate, for example, had meaning only insofar as the office of magistrate in the divinely ordained state served the commonwealth. The calling of a minister was to accept the office to preach the gospel in the church of God, and the calling of a father only had meaning as it related to an office in the family.[1]

1. Gordon Spykman, *Society, State, and Schools: A Case for Structural and Confessional Pluralism* (Grand Rapids: Eerdmans, 1981), p. 55.

Put in its simplest form, the call to the ministry as it is presently being discussed is the call to ministry of the Word and the sacraments; it is a call to a church office. There are of course a host of functions that surround and attend the ministry as it is presently expressed among us; for example, a minister is often required to express a prominent social role; ministers frequently decry the wide variety of activities they are expected to be skillful at performing. The ministerial call, though, as we think about it, is the conviction that one has been set apart by God to proclaim the message of His Word and administer the sacred sacraments, which Jesus has provided the church. In this connection, the inner conviction of the apostle most certainly carries over to the minister today: "Yet when I preach the gospel, I cannot boast, for I am compelled to preach. Woe is me if I do not preach the gospel!" (I Cor. 9:16).

The whole matter of preaching is worthy of prolonged discussion (and that is being done elsewhere in this volume); for now it should be noted that preaching involves the minister of the Word in an expression of extraordinary obedience. It is this obedience which sets preaching off from other forms of public address, and by means of this obedience, the minister is bound to proclaim the message entrusted to him by the Lord and that message alone. It has often been pointed out that the idea at the center of the biblical word for *preach* in the New Testament is the idea of *herald,* and a herald was merely a messenger who dutifully communicated the message his commander instructed him to bring to some other general, possibly even to the general with whom his commander was at war. Heralds are characterized by their absolute loyalty to the person who has sent them. And the call involves a similar obedience to the Lord who sends the minister with one message and one message only: the message contained within the Bible and personified in the person and work of the Lord Jesus Christ. The responsibility the minister has for the administration of the sacraments derives from his primary responsibility as a Word proclaimer, for the sacraments do not have an independent function—they derive their function from the Word of God for which they are a sign and a seal.

The person of the minister, then, must be seen in the closest possible connection with the Word of God. The apostle's words in I Corinthians 4 apply to ministers: "So then, men ought to regard us as servants of Christ and as those entrusted with the secret things of God. Now it is required that those who have been given a trust must prove faithful" (vv. 1, 2). Ministers are men in bondage to the Scriptures. Understand, this is what we are talking about in connection with the call. If it is clearly understood that we are talking about men in bondage to the Word of God and totally committed to proclaiming it, all of the other somewhat incidental elements that attend the ministry, which may give it a certain attractiveness to certain kinds of people, fall away. A minister is called to proclaim the Word of God, and his life is an expression of obedience to this one central task.

Now, of course, that is not the only thing the minister does with his life; it is not even the only thing he does effectively. The work of the minister most certainly must be complemented by the work of others within the fellowship. But at the moment, we are considering the ministerial *call* and this must be defined narrowly: *it is one's conviction that God would have him faithfully proclaim the Word of God.* The ministerial call is that and nothing more, and those who want to serve God in the ministry must make sure they have it; and those who have this call must make sure they obey it.

For our purposes, the development of one's consciousness of the call can be seen in connection with certain interior events that occur within the person being called. The call, after all, is an interior reality for a minister of the Word, and therefore consciousness of it grows in connection with a number of events that occur within a person. These events are deeply personal, and though they may occasionally be put on display by way of personal testimony, on their deepest level there is an inexpressible sacredness about them. Even so, it is necessary to talk about them if we are going to understand how the specific interior phenomenon we know as the *call* fits into a person's life.

"Conversion"

It is important to begin with conversion, for conversion is the fundamental prerequisite for the performance of any Christian service. When we speak of conversion these days, we most generally see it in relation to the experience that accompanies turning away from a lifestyle that is patently ungodly. We think of those who have been on drugs, those who have been enslaved by alcohol, and those who have lived in open and obvious rebellion against God. In many instances people who have been part of the current wicked scene are transformed by the powerful grace of God and turned into special servants of the Almighty. Today, Chuck Colson's book *Born Again* provides us with a classic case of such a turning.

But conversion must be viewed somewhat more broadly when we talk about it in connection with the ministry. Many who enter the ministry come from a background in which they have been exposed to the Christian faith from childhood. It is an inestimable privilege to be part of the covenant community and to grow up in a covenant home. Yet, coming from this background provides a special danger for an individual who contemplates the ministry. Such a person may never experience confession of sin and the steadfast turning away from sin that is part of conversion.

Even though growing up in a covenant community may have tended to shelter a person from gross forms of sinfulness, the covenant experience should enable a person to see the true nature of sin in general and to see sin in his own life very clearly. In fact, it is precisely the continual preaching of the Word of God that should take the scales from our eyes and enable us to see ourselves for what we really are.

In any case, a person serving in the ministry of the Word should be able to talk about his own conversion. It is true, of course, that some have difficulty describing a very specific time when this happened in their lives. Even so, a minister should be able to identify for himself, though he might not want to do so for others, when it was that he began to see himself as a miserable sinner whose only hope for salvation lay with the sovereign grace of God. He should be able to identify, further, when it was that he determined, with the help of God, earnestly to fight against sin in his life.

A study of the Bible leaves one with the unescapable conclusion that it is absolutely essential that each of us be able to say, "God, have mercy on me, a sinner" (Luke 18:13). It would be a mistake to pass over Jesus' story of the Pharisee and publican as an entertaining glimpse of His evaluation of the Pharisee sect; we must rather understand that if we wish to "return home justified," we must humbly confess our sins, too. And the apostle Paul insisted on calling himself the foremost of sinners (I Tim. 1:15). We may not fail to notice that when Paul stood before the cross, he did not view it as something that was of great value for certain people who were still in their sins, but he saw it as that which he himself needed desperately.

The truly called minister of the Word of God is a person who has himself drunk deeply of the fountain of life after he has thirsted mightily for the salvation that God alone provides; he is a person who has himself searched with desperate longing for contact with the Lord after he has felt disqualified for such fellowship. As he dispenses the medicine of life eternal, he does so as a person who himself knows that it is this medicine and this alone that has preserved him. Otherwise how can there be enthusiasm for the great task of gospel proclamation? After describing the believer's only comfort in life and in death as the certainty that he is not his own but belongs to Jesus, the Heidelberg Catechism asks how it is possible to enjoy this comfort; the answer begins with the statement that one must first know his misery. Only then can he experience the sweet refreshment of God's glorious salvation. And only then is there the necessary foundation for the minister's call.

"Centering on Christ"

Another essential component in the development of the ministerial *call* is the absolute necessity of the minister's having a personal relationship with the Lord Jesus Christ. Since Erroll Hulse discusses the subject of personal piety in the next chapter, I will make just a few brief comments here. It is the possibility of experiencing a personal relationship with God through faith in Jesus that is the distinguishing feature of the Christian religion. At the center of this religion is the Triune God, whose love endures forever, and this God has expressed His love fully in the person and work of the Lord Jesus Christ. As we are met by Jesus on the pages of the Bible, we discover Him as a person who delighted in experiencing personal relationships with His followers. Jesus' personality was one that turned Him outside of Himself toward others. Even when He was confronted by vast crowds of people, He had compassion on them (Mark 6:34) and unselfishly made provision for their needs. He often extended His hand of healing to lone individuals in great distress. He invited people to come to Him (Matt. 11:28) and assured them that they would find rest in His fellowship, doing His will. In the Gospel of John, the Jesus who invites people to come to Him declares that they must abide in Him as well (John 15:1-8).

It should be clear from this that *centering on Christ* involves seeking to know as much as possible about His person and His work. But there is more to *centering on Jesus*. While every Christian surely must have a personal relationship with the Savior, that is especially necessary for the minister. The ministerial office makes no sense if it is filled by someone who does not have a special relationship with Jesus. This should be very clear in connection with the matter of obedience and the call. The call is a call to special obedience; the called minister is a person who knows that Jesus is his Master. As has been noted, a preacher is a herald who carries out his duties in obedience to his commander. And for a minister, Jesus is the commander. If a person doesn't really know Jesus, he doesn't have a commander, and ministers who try to function as ministers without knowing the Lord act very strangely indeed.

Having one's faith centered on Jesus enables a minister to have a certain poise that he would otherwise not have—an imperviousness to the usual judgments people make about one another. As we think about this, it is certainly useful to think about the way the apostle Paul viewed his relationship with Jesus. Listen to him, for example, when he says, "I care very little if I am judged by you or by any human court; indeed, I do not even judge myself. My conscience is clear, but that does not make me innocent. It is the Lord who judges me" (I Cor. 4:3, 4). Yes, indeed, a minister knows that Jesus, his Savior, is the one who continuously appraises his ministry.

Having a personal relationship with the Lord Jesus Christ will enable a person to endure the injustices and hardships that accompany the ministry. There can be no question that ministers are often misunderstood, if not by their parishioners then certainly by non-Christians. If they are truly faithful to their calling, they will be required to experience danger at times. How can they do this unless they are following Jesus who, though He was reviled, reviled not again?

A personal relationship with Jesus—how important it is! A minister most certainly must be a person who can speak of his love for the Savior. He must feel himself united with Him through faith, and he must delight to speak with Jesus in prayer. It is the story of Jesus that the minister proclaims. A minister must be able to sing, without sentimentality, but with deep running reality:

> I love to tell the story of unseen things above,
> Of Jesus and His glory, of Jesus and His love.

A minister who is truly called loves to tell the story of Jesus . . . of Jesus and His love. And he loves to do that because he knows Jesus personally. His life, his faith, is centered on Jesus Christ.

"Fascination With the Bible"

One of the more humbling elements of the Christian faith is that it is rooted entirely in the Bible. We can talk about Jesus, for example, but our Jesus-talk is worthwhile only if it is talk that reflects the Bible's message about Jesus. The anchoring of the

Christian faith in the Bible can be very frustrating for religious leaders who are extremely creative, as many religious leaders tend to be. There is no room for invention in the Christian faith. The majestic religious ideas that we are capable of putting together and the intricate ways of salvation we are able to construct are less than worthless—they are detrimental for true religion and true spirituality. To be a Christian means that a person voluntarily limits his religious thinking to the Bible's material and voluntarily allows the Bible to function critically with respect to all of his religious experience.

It is important to emphasize this because it is a fundamental tendency of human life to invent religious edifices of one kind or another that become considerably more attractive than the biblical material. After man's fall into sin, he did not become less religious than he was before, but the religious dimension of his life was short-circuited; man became the great idol maker and idol worshipper. Even the people of God, who possessed God's true revelation, could not resist the idolatry of the nations that surrounded them—they worshipped worthless idols and became worthless themselves (Jer. 2:4). Our idol love must be curbed and destroyed. And this can happen only if our religion is biblical throughout.

That is why those who are truly called to the ministry of the Word of God must be men for whom the Bible becomes the center of their attention. Fascination for the Word—yes, this is necessary. The minister must come to the point early in his development where he recognizes that here at last is something in our world that is a direct word from God. From then on it is this Word that becomes central. A minister is a person who thinks about the Bible a lot, reads it a great deal, memorizes it, puzzles over it, and keeps coming back to it over and over again. How unfortunate that there are many seminarians who admit that they have never read the Bible through from cover to cover! If a person learns to be satisfied with a brushing acquaintance with God's Word, there can be no question that such a person is not truly called to the ministry. A minister is a person for whom the Bible is the most exciting book, and he willingly dedicates his life to living with it.

Fascination with the Bible, love of the Bible, obedient reading of the glorious book—these accompany the call to the ministry of the gospel. Those who don't like books and who aren't particularly interested in the Book of books are mistaken if they should ever think that God has called them to the ministry.

Examination of Gifts

What has been discussed thus far with respect to the call deals with elements of the Christian personality that all truly committed Christians possess in one degree or another. Conversion, centering on Jesus, fascination with the Bible—surely each of these must be found in all Christian lives. These are what we pray for when we pray for one another. But the developing consciousness of the *call* to the ministry must go beyond these, for the ministry of the Word is a specific function within the body of Christ, and the minister must have certain gifts in addition to those which all Christians have in common. It is somewhat dangerous to formulate a listing of the gifts required, but such a listing is necessary, so long as it is remembered that the list should not be absolutized. The Lord is able to use a wide variety of people in His ministry, and there are certainly cases of effective ministry by authentically called preachers of the Word who have been singularly ungifted. But such cases should be viewed as exceptional, and both the individual who thinks that God may be calling him to the ministry and the church that evaluates the ministerial candidate are obligated to examine him in terms of whether or not he has gifts.

To begin, then, we can assume that God endows those whom He truly calls to the ministry with the necessary intellectual capacity. Now, when we talk about the gifts of intellect, there is obviously a wide range among ministers. For our purposes, however, it is practical to assume that when God calls a person to the ministry, He will provide the person with intellectual capacities sufficient to enable him to handle the general course offered by an accredited seminary. This involves study in the original languages of the Scriptures, systematic study of church doctrine, and studies of the Old and New Testaments. This material confronts one studying for the ministry with material that demands a certain level of intellectual ability, and if a person cannot handle this material satisfactorily, we should assume that he is not being called to the work of the gospel ministry.

Closely related to intellectual gifts are the gifts of self-discipline. Self-discipline must be considered also in connection with the moral life of the minister, but it is also closely related to the way a person handles the formal requirements for the ministry. For it is possible that a person may well have the intellectual capacity to handle a seminary course, but not have the self-discipline that enables him actually to accomplish academic goals. This does not necessarily mean that a person is fundamentally undisciplined or lazy; it may simply mean that he is unable to express his ability of self-discipline with reference to academic activity.

The seminary experience not only provides those who are preparing for the ministry with the opportunity to study specific course material, but also provides a training ground in which they can develop abilities that they will be required to use as they do their work later on. For example, memorization is an important element in the performance of one's ministry, and for most people memorization demands self-discipline. Higher education provides students with the opportunity to develop their ability to memorize, and if a person discovers that he does not have the ability to do this, he is probably not called to the ministry of the Word.

Another important gift a minister should possess is the gift of communication. It is not necessarily eloquence that is needed—in fact, eloquence can sometimes be counterproductive for communication since it calls too much attention to itself. What is needed is an ability to attract people's attention as one speaks, and keep that attention, and succeed in transferring from the mind of the minister to the mind of the hearer a certain amount of information.

In connection with the *call* to the ministry, it is impossible to over-emphasize the importance of the gift of communication. If a person doesn't have this gift, there is no way he can be useful in the ministry of the Word. Now, we must remember that there are all sorts of other ways that the people of God serve one another within the church, and it is certainly no disgrace if a person is not able to communicate. If a person who thinks he is called to the ministry is in fact incapable of communicating the gospel but is not aware of this deficiency, the church should gently inform him of his lack.

A minister must have the gift of communication, but, again, it must be stressed that this gift is not a finished product that God presents to certain people; it is rather an ability that must be developed over the years. That is especially true nowadays when ministers communicate the gospel in a highly competitive situation in which people are exposed to many forms of communication. The way a minister communicates will necessarily change over the years; it will change during the course of a single day as he is required to communicate the gospel to different kinds of people. It will not do for a minister simply to adopt a certain way of doing his speaking and expect it always to be effective. Ministers who do this often attribute their lack of communication success to the hardness of the hearts of their people when in fact it is rooted in their own unwillingness to adapt to their audiences.

In any case, this gift is absolutely essential. And here is another one: the gift of judgment, or we might call it, the gift of wisdom. The exercise of the ministry as we know it today often occurs in a highly charged and complex situation. Gone are the days when the minister was an authority figure within the community who lived somewhat to the side of normal human events. Today the minister functions right in the middle of ordinary life. In some instances, a minister will be required to conduct his work as part of a staff. And always, if his church is of any size at all, there are all sorts of events occurring, as young people interact with one another, as children and parents interact, and as various groups and even factions in their churches interact with each other. Along with this, as a minister brings the Word of God into the lives of his people, he is dealing with that element of human life about which there are the strongest convictions. Religious conscience is the most tender and puzzling element in our lives, and ministers touch conscience all the time. Ministers these days are a part of the complex dynamic themselves, and with all of the other interactions, their congregations interact with them, too.

Against this background it is absolutely essential that a minister possess the gift of judgment, the gift of wisdom. He must have the ability to understand what is really happening among the people he is most closely related to, and he must be able to respond to the situation in such a way that does not make it worse, but better. Such judgment can be exercised only if a minister is able to maintain a certain degree of emotional distance from other people and from the circumstances in which he finds himself. The only kind of person who can maintain such distance is a person who is at ease with himself, has a proper amount of self-esteem, and possesses self-confidence.

Now, it is in connection with judgment that ministers have a special problem. The kind of person who has many of the gifts for the ministry is often a person who has great perception not only of himself but of others, and he is a person who himself needs a great deal of emotional support. Ministers are among the most sensitive of people, and they are exceptionally vulnerable, for they are always in a dreadfully exposed position. It is for these reasons that when ministers get involved in difficult situations, they often make those situations worse rather than better. Instead of bringing to the situation that which can lead to solutions, they themselves become part of the problem. Or worse, they can sometimes create totally new problems that make the existing ones pale into insignificance.

That is why a person who is to be a minister should have the gift of judgment. If one wonders whether he has the *call,* he should ask himself whether he usually makes matters worse or makes them better when he gets involved in a situation. In the Army it used to be and perhaps still is that an officer would not be promoted until he had been evaluated by his peers. Those who are preparing for the ministry should be evaluated by their peers, too, in terms of whether they possess the gift of judgment. And the church, when it evaluates candidates for the ministry should examine this element of their lives very carefully. Those in the ministry who are unable to express wisdom and judgment in their work cause the church a great deal of harm.

Evaluation of Attitudes

No discussion of the call would be complete, however, without giving attention to the attitudes that should be considered integral elements of the ministerial calling. The person called to the ministry of the gospel must possess the prerequisite qualities of faith such as those which can be described in terms of conversion, personal relationship with Jesus Christ, and deep interest in the Bible as the Word of God. In terms of matters such as these, the minister does not differ from any mature Christian person. And the gifts that have been discussed above are often found among other members of the body of Christ. Ministers have them, but they are by no means their exclusive possession. It is in connection with certain inner attitudes, however, that the peculiar, definitive structure of the call comes to its distinctive expression.

What are these attitudes? It is difficult to describe them with precision or identify them with neat labels. But they can be thought about and reflected upon, and those who think about their own call should think about these attitudes a great deal.

They are attitudes that relate to the ministerial call as a call to a special level of voluntary Christian obedience. *Obedience* is the key word, the key concept. If one is unwilling to view himself as being related to Jesus in a special bond of obedience, he should not consider himself called to the ministry. A minister must ordinarily express levels of self-discipline and self-sacrifice beyond those required of other Christians, and such levels can be achieved only if a minister feels himself in a special relationship of obedience to Christ. The words of Paul to Timothy are very useful in this connection: "Endure hardship with us like a good soldier of Christ Jesus. No one serving as a soldier gets involved in civilian affairs—he wants to please his commanding officer" (II Tim. 2:4). The idea of *soldiering* and the idea of *commanding officer* are extremely important for anyone who considers himself called to the ministry of the gospel. A person with the call is not a civilian; he is an enlisted man, a soldier, and the one person who is uppermost in his mind is his commanding officer.

As a called person, the minister of the gospel must express his obedience with reference to the flock of the Lord Jesus Christ. This is the supremely awesome dimension of the ministerial task: a minister is Jesus' earthly representative who must care for the flock that Jesus has purchased not with silver or gold, but with His own precious blood. "Guard yourselves and all the flock of which the Holy Spirit has made you overseers. Be shepherds of the church of God, which he bought with his own blood" (Acts 20:28). These words, spoken to the elders of Ephesus, apply with special force to those called to be ministers of the Word and the sacraments.

So then, those who feel themselves called are obligated to assess the state of their own souls to ascertain whether they have properly sensed the magnitude of their task so that they can be sure they will be able to exhibit levels of obedience that are necessary if a person is usefully to fill the ministerial office. And this process can be carried out by a self-examination designed to determine whether the minister is willing to do certain things required of those who have the obligation of expressing that special level of obedience to their commanding officer Jesus. Among the attitudes flowing from a sense of obedience to Christ that must be present in anyone called to the ministry are the following:

1. Self-discipline, not just in academics, but in all of life, from prayer and Bible study to proper habits of rest and exercise.
2. Self-sacrifice, a genuine willingness to endure hardship in terms of finances, peer esteem, physical comfort if the cause of Christ demands it.
3. Self-giving, not only to the powerful and wealthy, but also to the weak, the poor, to any who are needy in any way—an actual willingness to wash the feet of others.

4. Self-control, a sense of the Spirit's sanctifying work in one's own life, an awareness that Christ alone is one's Master.

There are probably other inner attitudes that could be presented as being necessary. But these may function as examples of what should characterize the minister of the gospel. It would, of course, be a mistake to suggest that no one should consider himself called to the ministry unless all the attitudes presented are perfectly present in his life. Alas, it is simply impossible for any person to approach the ideal all the time and in every respect. Even so, the attitudes discussed provide us with significant points of reference and can function as helps for those who are looking at themselves closely in order to determine whether God is truly calling them to the ministry of the Word. And thinking about this can be as useful for those who have been in the ministry and are seeking to determine the strength of their call.

The Call Over the Years

It is necessary that a person who works as a minister of the gospel be truly called by the Lord to this work, and it is possible for a person who is himself called to this work to talk about the call from various perspectives. Even so, it must be understood that the call to the ministry cannot be easily defined and delimited and identified—each individual who has been called will necessarily experience the call to the gospel ministry in a way that is peculiar to him. The *call* is not experienced in the same way at every point in a person's life. In other words, the *call* is not a hard, absolute entity that a person suddenly receives once and for all and that is that, an immovable point that is there, firm and steadfast, somewhere in the minister's soul, a constant that never changes.

It is possible to think about the way the ministerial call is experienced by remembering that it modifies as a minister passes through various stages of life. The initial call to the ministry may be experienced when a person is still quite young. As people speak to an individual who seems to have the gifts and attitudes described above, he may begin to wonder if the ministry is something that he should consider seriously. And it often happens that in these early stages there is a rebellion against the idea of the ministry because it is viewed as extremely restrictive and unrewarding. Then, there could well come a point when the young person is convicted of his call—possibly through a speech or a sermon, possibly through certain events that make it clear to him that God wants him in the ministry, possibly through the continued encouragement of God's people.

The initial experience of the call, however, should not be automatically viewed as an authentic call to the gospel ministry; rather, it provides the impetus for the individual involved to begin a process of preparation and testing. It is usually necessary for a person, once he feels himself called to the gospel ministry, to become involved in a period of intensive training that could last as much as eight years. This period of training should be viewed as a time in which God wants those who feel themselves called to examine themselves carefully, and some of the matters included in this present chapter could well help in that examination. In addition, the person who is preparing himself for the gospel ministry should willingly receive the evaluations of others—of family and friends and fellow students. If a person is truly called, the time of preparation can become a time for a deepening of the ministerial call, so that by the time the candidate is about to take up his work, he feels certain that God wants him to do this work and no other.

As a minister progresses through his career, he will experience his call in a number of ways and a number of degrees. Ministers are people, human beings—of course they are! But this means that they are subject to changes in their lives' circumstances. Many of them marry and raise a family and all of them have experiences that cause heart break. Ministers have their own emotions to contend with, their own natures. Ministers often drift into patterns of behavior and thought that are detrimental so far as their own spiritual life is concerned. They can sometimes feel themselves very alienated from other people and, yes, even alienated from God. Ministers go through mid-life crises, and they become emotionally and mentally unable to handle their work.

What all this means is that ministers themselves must expect that their own experience of their call will not be a constant support. From time to time, they will find that they must re-evaluate their own ministry and the calling they have. The material in this chapter is designed to help ministers evaluate just where they are with respect to their own call, and if they recognize there was a time when their sense of calling was considerably stronger than it now is, they should earnestly and deliberately rearrange their lives and reorganize their thinking so that they will again be able to experience the reality of the call.

As difficult as it is to talk about the ministerial call and as difficult as it is for a minister to evaluate his life in this regard, it is essential that there be a conscious awareness of problems surrounding the ministerial call. For it is actually impossible for a person without the call to function usefully in the gospel ministry. And this is why it is so necessary, if a minister's feeling of being called fades away, that he work at determining exactly what is happening in his life. There is evidence that some who have had a strong call to the gospel ministry at an early stage of their lives for one reason or another discover that it has left them. If this happens, a person should not doggedly continue his work—he will save neither himself nor those who hear him.

At the same time, one whose sense of call has deteriorated alarmingly should not quickly assume that he should leave the gospel ministry. It is important to remember that when it comes to the *call*, we are talking about an interior event that takes many years to develop fully and we should expect that under ordinary circumstances it remains for a person's entire lifetime; when it is not very prominent for one reason or another, its lack of prominence should be attributed to temporary circumstances that will be corrected with the proper remedies and with the passage of time.

The internal call, if authentic, will be confirmed by an external call from a congregation to do the work of the gospel ministry. If a minister whose own sense of internal call becomes somewhat threadbare at a given time nevertheless continues to be sustained by a strong and unmistakable ecclesiastical call to his ministry, he should assume that as he prays and continues to function in his office, the Lord will visit him anew, or from time to time, with a strong internal conviction that God has called him to be His minister.

The Call—A Reality!

When one reviews this chapter, the overall impression it gives is that one must be very careful with respect to the call, for some may think they have it and be mistaken. Unfortunately, the current situation with respect to the ministry demands that discussions of the call convey this note. But the fact remains that God does call men to the ministry of the gospel.

His action is what causes men to be called to the gospel ministry, a fact that must never be forgotten. For this reason any discussion of this subject demands that we develop an ability to examine the inner life of those who claim the call to see if God has assuredly called the person in question. One young man who felt called to the ministry declared in the publication of his denomination that he was indignant that the church would presume to test his call in terms of whether he had the prerequisite gifts. His indignation was misplaced. Those who claim that God has called them must cheerfully submit to examination.

The church may rejoice in these days that God is still building His church, and one of the instruments He uses is the ministry of the Word and sacraments. And so God continues to call men to the ministry of the gospel. He endows them with the gifts we have examined, and He creates through His Holy Spirit the prerequisite faith conditions in their hearts. It is God who creates the strength of the call within the man involved and brings him to the point at which he knows assuredly that he has that special responsibility of gospel proclamation, so that he finally must say, "Woe is me if I preach not the gospel."

In the light of God's sovereign calling to the ministry—which is experienced somewhat along the lines discussed in this piece—the call to the ministry of the Word is entirely positive, and, on balance, its impact in the life of the called clergyman is positive through and through. This does not mean that there are not elements of the call experience that are upsetting, even traumatic; but over the long term those who are called to the gospel ministry feel themselves to be among the most privileged of men.

And their task is easy. Those who have Jesus as their Master discover that it is true, as He said, that His yoke is easy and His burden is light. This is true of every Christian, but it is true to the fullest degree of those whom God calls and qualifies for the gospel ministry. There are, of course, descriptions of the Christian life in the Bible that suggest it is arduous. One thinks, for example, of the apostle Paul's frequent comparing of the Christian life to the running of a race; in Philippians 3:13, 14 the language he uses indicates that he is thinking of a highly trained athlete who is putting all of his strength into the last few yards as he throws himself toward the goal. Surely, such a figure of speech has a special application to the gospel ministry; even so, the work of the ministry is easy, for those whom the Lord calls, He also qualifies. Athletes at the height of their powers, at the moments of greatest exertion, experience their greatest exhilaration. The Master, Jesus Christ, is an easy Master—those who are truly called will testify to this.

Therefore, let whatever is said about the gospel ministry never be used to turn anyone aside from this great work. Those who suspect that they may be God's called men should not shrink from examining themselves with care to determine the reality of their call. If there is the slightest possibility that a man is called, he should eagerly begin the necessary preparation, knowing that as he does so, God will clarify what He wants him to do.

There must be special prayer on behalf of the people of God that God Himself will work mightily in the hearts of the people He has prepared for this special service. He is the one who calls. And He is doing that even today. There is such a thing as a special call to the ministry of the Word and sacraments. Those who have it should be among the happiest people in the world. Many of them are, usually. Possibly what has been written here will strengthen many in their sense of being called and give them the poise and the joy those who love them want them to experience all the time.

2

The Preacher and Piety

Erroll Hulse

When Moses came down from Mount Sinai, he was not aware that because he had spoken with the Lord (Exod. 34:29)[1] his face was radiant. The work of the preacher is illustrated by this phenomenon in the life of Moses. The work of the prophet envelops the preacher's person, and, therefore, the practice of preaching can never be divorced from the person of the preacher.[2] In this situation, the personality of the preacher is paramount. The gift of face, voice, presence, style is of immediate interest, but unless backed up by genuine fruit, all these are just leaves. Preaching is sacred eloquence through an ambassador whose life must be consistent in every way with the message he proclaims. The making of the person of the preacher is a vastly more complex and difficult matter than the making of a sermon, just as the making of the Concorde supersonic plane is vastly more intricate than the flying of it.

Preaching is not lecturing. It is not merely the presentation of scientifically accurate materials. Of course, the preacher is concerned with the world of exegesis and hermeneutics, with structure and flow, with simplicity and rhetoric; but without piety he will never be, and cannot be a preacher. Moreover, his effectiveness and power as a preacher will be directly connected to his

1. All citations are from the *New International Version* unless otherwise indicated.
2. John R. W. Stott, *I Believe in Preaching. The Preacher as a Person* (London: Hodder and Stoughton, 1982), pp. 265ff.

piety. Expressed negatively, if a glaring blemish of manner obstructs the message, how much more a moral inconsistency in the life of the preacher, as the Scripture says, "As dead flies give perfume a bad smell, so a little folly outweighs wisdom and honor" (Eccles. 10:1).

McCheyne, in writing to a missionary, asserted the matter positively when he said, "In great measure, according to the purity and perfections of the instrument, will be the success. It is not great talents which God blesses so much as great likeness to Jesus. A holy minister is an awful weapon in the hand of God."[3] This essential which we call piety requires explanation. What precisely is it? We must attend to that first. Then we will proceed to the other aspects as follows:

1. The meaning of piety, first, in English usage and, second, as conceived of in the New Testament.
2. The necessity of piety for the preacher.
3. The pressures upon, and breakdowns of piety.
4. The Lord Jesus Christ, the pattern and empowering source of piety.
5. The peculiar needs of seminarians and other specialists considered and encouragements provided.

1. Piety Defined: English Usage

Of prior consideration is the etymology of the terms *piety* and *pious*, how these words originated and how they have come to be understood. Our concern is not merely technical. Rather through our investigation I will illustrate the importance and relevance of piety for preachers by referring to leading Christians who have exemplified the godly life. My intention is to refer fairly often to eminent preachers, this being the most effective way of illustration for a subject of this kind.

The origins of our English word *piety* may be traced to Latin, *piare* (to appease) and to French *pius* (dutiful). The appellation

3. Andrew A. Bonar, *Robert Murray M'Cheyne: Memoir and Remains* (London: Banner of Truth, 1966), p. 281.

pietist was first applied to the followers of the German pastor and preacher, Philipp Jakob Spener (1635–1705). He began a movement at Frankfort in about 1670 for the deepening of piety and the reform of religious education. "Spener so completely drew around himself all that there was of religious movement in his generation, that his life is a history of the Lutheran Church during the latter half of the 17th century."[4] The work that made Spener famous was his *Pia Desideria* (1675) in which he provided a program for reform that in turn became the rallying cry of Lutheran Pietism. The stress was on the need for inward holiness, the avoidance by ministers of undue involvement with arid polemics (feeding people with stones and not bread), and a radical revision of courses for would-be ministers with a stress on introducing students to godly writers and encouraging a self-watch or moral surveillance for their lives, as well as an insistent emphasis on edifying rather than clever preaching.[5]

It does not put too much strain on our imagination to appreciate that such biblical emphases brought opposition and derision from the world. Thus secular dictionaries, while providing mostly helpful meanings of the word *piety*, also strike negative notes. Webster's declares of *piety* that it is devoutness, orthodox belief, and fidelity; and for *pious*, "marked by or showing reverence for deity and devotion to divine worship, marked by conspicuous religiosity, a hypocrite."[6] An examination of the general usage of *piety* and *pious*, past and present, reveals a broad meaning that can accommodate negative and critical elements.

This critical aspect, which emerges in the etymology of the term, is helpful inasmuch as it reminds us of the necessity to avoid and shun pseudo piety. It is salutary that in our pursuit of piety we be on our guard against any element that savours of hypocrisy or mere clericalism. By ministerial piety we do not

4. A. H. Murray, *A New English Dictionary on Historical Principles*, vol. 7 (Oxford: Oxford University Press, 1909), p. 842.

5. John D. Manton, "German Pietism and the Evangelical Revival" *Westminster Conference Papers*, (1969), pp. 8ff.

6. *Webster's New Collegiate Dictionary* (London: Merriam, 1975), pp. 869, 873.

mean any form of superiority complex, displayed either by inward pride or by outward prestige. In 1947 the holiness of the dominie in Holland was often defined by his clothes or his bicycle. He always wore striped trousers and rode a bicycle that was about two inches higher than everybody else's. One could identify him as he rode down the street. That is not what we understand by piety.

Our own definition of piety at this point is, that constant culture of the inward life of holiness before God, and for God, which in turn is applied to all other spheres of life and practice. Piety consists of prayer at God's throne, study of His Word in His presence, and the sustaining of the life of God in our souls, which in turn affects all our manner of living.

Martin Luther is an excellent illustration of piety as we have defined it so far. Veit Dietrich, his faithful scribe and companion, said of him, "No day passes that he does not give three hours to prayer, and those the fittest for study." Apparently he prayed aloud and that with compelling earnestness and deep reverence.[7] How could Luther keep that up together with all his preaching, and administrative duties, not to mention his prolific correspondence and writing activity resulting, in the course of his life, in one hundred folio volumes of approximately seven hundred pages each?[8]

Luther's piety may be likened to a fire, a fire of devotion before God. If coal be our symbol of burden and responsibility, then huge loads were deposited on that fire. One might think such loads would extinguish the fire, but in Luther's case, the opposite was true—the fire of piety only came to burn more heatedly and brightly. A life of devotion explains his accomplishments. We can be sure that Luther laid his preaching commitments, writings, burdens, problems, gladnesses, and griefs before God Triune during that prime time of communion.

7. James Atkinson, *Martin Luther and the Birth of Protestantism* (London: Morgan and Scott Marshall Publications, 1968), p. 250.

8. Gerhard Ebeling, *Luther. An Introduction to His Thought* (Philadelphia: Fortress, 1972), p. 46.

The meaning of piety in the New Testament. It is said of our Lord that He was heard "because of his reverent submission" (Heb. 5:7). The word *eulabeia* could be translated "piety" or "fear." The RSV translates *eulabeia*, His "godly fear" (Heb. 5:7). The same word occurs again in Hebrews 12:28, where we are exhorted to worship or serve God with "reverence and awe," but here again *eulabeia* could be translated "piety" or "devoutness." Simeon was described as *dikaioa kai eulabes*, righteous and devout (cf. Acts 2:5; 8:2; 22:12). Noah built the ark out of piety (*eulabetheis*, translated, "holy fear," Heb. 11:7).

However, the *locus classicus* for piety in the New Testament is found in the usage by Paul of a related word, *eusebeia*, meaning devoutness or piety. This he employs about a dozen times in the pastoral Epistles. Peter also uses the word in his second letter.[9]

This meaning invested in *eusebeia* is rich when we compare the references. For instance the term denoted spiritual power. There is power in godliness. If there is no power in a profession of piety (*eusebeia*), Paul says that profession is to be utterly rejected (II Tim. 3:5). Also this godliness or piety is to be exercised and developed as a way of life. Ministers like Timothy are to train themselves in piety, "For physical training is of some value, but godliness has value for all things" (I Tim. 4:7, 8). The source of all piety for us as we seek to conduct ourselves properly in the church of God is Christ. Declares Paul, the mystery of godliness is great, for it is seen best in the whole appearing and testimony of the Son of God in this world (I Tim. 3:16).

> He appeared in a body,
>   was vindicated by the Spirit,
> was seen by angels,
>   was preached among the nations,
> was believed on in the world,
>   was taken up in glory.

9. W. Gunther suggests that at first this word was used for non-Christian piety and only later was Christian content given to it in the pastoral Epistles and II Pet. *The New International Dictionary of New Testament Theology*, vol. 2 (Exeter, England: Paternoster, 1976), p. 94.

Piety has its genesis in our union with Christ and the divine power imparted by Him (II Pet. 1:3); yet again I must stress that it is a quality that extends from the place of exercise in the soul in meditation and prayer, to all practical departments of a man's life. Hence the apostle could without reservation point Timothy to his own example: "You know all about my teaching, my way of life, my purpose, faith, patience, love, endurance" (II Tim. 3:10). Piety includes all these attributes and cannot afford to be lacking in any one of them. Piety then is a way of life. This includes domestic life, the relationship of the man to his wife and children, for if anyone does not know how to manage his own family, how can he take care of God's church (I Tim. 3:5)? A life of piety replete with the virtues and qualifications that make it up is essential for any officer in the church (Titus 1:5-9; I Tim. 3:1-13). This leads us to our next consideration.

2. The Necessity of Piety in the Preacher

Since piety, then, is a way of life, communion with God and walking with God, we can readily see the necessity for a robust piety in ministers. They who are called to train others in godliness must be godly themselves. Not surprisingly does Paul say, "Watch your life and doctrine closely"—life first, and doctrine second, in that order. "Persevere in them," urges Paul, "for if you do, you will save both yourself and your hearers" (I Tim. 4:16). To Titus he wrote, "In everything set them an example by doing what is good" (Titus 2:7).

The enormity and complexity of the pastoral office is brilliantly set out in Richard Baxter's The Reformed Pastor, which J.I. Packer describes as dynamite![10] Besides what is involved in preaching, Baxter refers to evangelism, counseling, building up believers, pastoring families, visiting the sick, reproving and admonishing offenders and maintaining discipline, all of which, urges Baxter, must be carried on as follows: purely, diligently and laboriously,

10. Richard Baxter, The Reformed Pastor (Edinburgh: Banner of Truth, 1974), p. 14.

prudently and orderly—with plainness and simplicity, humility, severity mixed with mildness, seriousness, earnestness, zeal, tender love, patience, reverence, spirituality, earnest desires and expectations of success, a deep sense of our own insufficiency and dependence on Christ, and unity with other ministers! Only a robust devotional life, a pulsating piety, could possibly meet the needs of such an exacting office or provide the qualities of life it demands.

As we have already noted, preaching is not a mere elocutionary art. It is a proclamation in the name of God and by the authority of His Word. As such it is imperative that it be dynamic, for anything less is incongruous with its very nature. We can appreciate therefore the claim that, "The soil out of which powerful preaching grows is the preacher's own life."[11]

While the preacher engages in his busy vocation, which makes heavy demands on his time and energy reserves, he has to find the time earnestly to seek the mind of God as to what parts of Scripture he is to open up. That is only the beginning. The toils of exegesis and preparation follow. Piety is not in any way disconnected from these exercises. To use Paul's favorite expression, these exercises are performed "in the Lord" and certainly in His fear. Spiritual power is required as much in preparation as in the delivery of sermons.

Perhaps nobody has stated the matter better than Richard Baxter who said,

> Content not yourselves with being in a state of grace, but be also careful that your graces are kept in vigorous and lively exercise, and that you preach to yourselves the sermons which you study, before you preach them to others. If you did this for your own sakes, it would not be lost labour; but I am speaking to you upon the public account, that you would do it for the sake of the Church. When your minds are in a holy, heavenly frame, your people are likely to partake of the fruits of it. Your prayers, and praises, and doc-

11. Al Martin, *What's Wrong with Preaching Today?* (London: Banner of Truth), p. 3.

trine will be sweet and heavenly to them. They will likely feel when you have been much with God: that which is most on your hearts, is like to be most in their ears. I confess I must speak it by lamentable experience, that I publish to my flock the distempers of my own soul. When I let my heart grow cold, my preaching is cold; and when it is confused, my preaching is confused. . . . If we feed on unwholesome food, either errors or fruitless controversies our hearers are like to fare the worse for it. Whereas, if we abound in faith, and love, and zeal, how would it overflow to the refreshing of our congregations, and how would it appear in the increases of the same graces in them! O brethren, watch therefore over your own hearts; keep out lusts and passions, and worldly inclinations; keep up the life of faith, and love and zeal. . . . Above all, be much in secret prayer and meditation. Thence you must fetch the heavenly fire that must kindle your sacrifices.[12]

The overwhelming nature of pastoral responsibility so well outlined by Baxter, points to piety as the source from which so many needs will be met, for piety will always direct a man to prayer, not only concentrated private prayer, but prayer expressed in earnest dependence in heart upon the Holy Spirit.

Piety always upholds the preacher in his constant need to discern priority. Which tasks must be attended to first? There is always the necessity of wisdom in the fulfillment of responsibilities, as well as a gracious disposition that should characterize the execution of them.

The observation of the creation ordinance of a weekly cessation from work is not unrelated to piety, for a godly man will submit to the necessity of rest and recreation, there being nothing unholy in the stipulation of rest that God has ordained. In England I have observed that the lack of this principle has resulted in more breakdowns and consequent resignations from the ministry by able and proven men than any other single factor. This is usually called "overwork" but truly it is the sad outcome of men thinking

12. Baxter, *Reformed Pastor*, pp. 61ff.

that they can work without cessation. It is an unbalanced piety that does not cater for its own survival. This leads us to consider some of the pressures that come upon preachers.

3. The Pressures Upon and the Breakdowns of Piety

John Calvin's life illustrates vividly the variety of pressures that come upon the man of God, pressures that can combine to become so intense as to break even the spirit of the most intrepid and highly gifted men. Calvin knew what it was to suffer economic stringency, excessive pressure of work, bereavement, moral failure by his own family members, acute pastoral anxiety, the failure of a supporter and colleague, and perhaps worst of all, desperately poor and unreliable health. Concerning financial stringency, it is noteworthy that when at Strasbourg, Calvin had to sell his library in order to make ends meet, and when he commenced at Geneva, it took five months for his first remuneration to arrive. Concerning pressure and interruptions, shortly after his return from Geneva he wrote, "Since my arrival here I cannot remember having been granted two hours in which no one has come and disturbed me."[13]

Calvin's marriage to Idelette van Buren was a happy one, but they knew the sorrow of bereavement. The couple had only one son whom they lost soon after his birth. The Reformer was highly sensitive to loss. At the death of Courauld, his colleague in Geneva, his grief knew no bounds.[14] It was, however, moral and doctrinal failures that caused the couple most heartache. Idellete's daughter, Judith, fell into adultery. So grieved was the Reformer that he left the city for a few days respite. This was something he never did even at the height of other conflicts. Moral shame is particularly vexing to a soul in love with holiness.

13. Jean Cadier, *The Man God Mastered* (London: Inter-Varsity Press, 1960), p. 119.
14. T. H. L. Parker, *John Calvin* (Tring, England: Lion Publishing PLC, 1982), p. 120.

Pastoral anxiety, that is, the weight borne by criticism, gossip, opposition, division, strife, misunderstanding, bitterness, and negativism in those who should know better, can be enormous. This is by far the greatest strain laid on pastors. Calvin's experience endorses this claim. "Rather," asserted he in writing to Farel, "would I submit to death a hundred times than to that cross, on which one had to perish daily a thousand times over."[15] Such was the strain of the Geneva pastorate.

Bitter was that cup of woe drunk by our Lord, made more bitter at the time He had to drink it by the denials of Peter and the complete apostasy of Judas. There is something peculiarly painful in being let down by friends, worse still if they betray you (Ps. 41:9; 109:4, 5). Calvin experienced this form of trial too, as well as the grief of the apostasy of a close friend, Louis du Tillet who returned to the Roman church.[16] Castellio, trusted by Calvin to be rector of his college, proved to be a chapter of disaster and a sore embarrassment.[17] Although there were casualties, they were few in number compared to life-long reliable and rich friendships.[18]

Pastors who recognize the gift of health and are able to increase their efficiency by keeping themselves in a disciplined state of physical fitness are wise. Sometimes incipient ill health or body problems forbids this advantage as was the case with Calvin. "If only my condition was not a constant death struggle," he wrote. Gallstones and kidney stones, pleurisy, migraine, ulcers, arthritis, and finally consumption, were numbered among the bodily tribulations through which he persevered with a marvelous and heroic determination.[19] Calvin's piety, his personal relationship with the Lord Jesus Christ, was his line of defense against these pressures.

Having surveyed some of the pressures that came on one man who did survive, we ask the question, What are the main causes

15. *Letters of John Calvin* (Edinburgh: Banner of Truth, 1980), p. 59.
16. Parker, *John Calvin*, p. 84.
17. Emanuel Stickelberger, *John Calvin* (Cambridge, England: James Clarke, 1977), pp. 99ff.
18. Parker, *John Calvin*, p. 122.
19. Stickelberger, *John Calvin*, p. 86.

of breakdown today? We concern ourselves with the foremost enemies of ministerial piety, forces that the Adversary conspires to employ for the weakening of ministers, and if possible their destruction.

Breakdown due to a lack of self-denial. Walter Chantry in his little book *The Shadow of the Cross* devotes a chapter to the Christian ministry.[20] In this he drives the burning chariot of his zeal over the heads of erring pastors, but especially negligent, self-indulgent, and lazy pastors. Instead of criticizing the fury with which he drives, we do well to make quite sure that we are not guilty of the sins described. Nobody could deny that some of them are blatently obvious especially in the United States. An abundance of lawful creature comforts characterizes the North American scene more than most other places. The influence of a materialist, pleasure-loving, prosperous society can be so strong as to erode the piety of ministers. Gradually and unwittingly they conform to worldly standards and self-indulgence. In other words the world molds them more than they mold the world.

In Third World countries we go to the other end of the scale and find that the advantages of education can bring pastors into acute temptation. They sometimes have the opportunity to improve their living standards by part-time secular teaching or other secular employment. It takes resolute self-denial to stick to the relative poverty that their calling imposes on them. Likewise it requires determined self-denial for ministers who have to spend several years of study in a rich country, thereby becoming accustomed to a comfortable or luxurious lifestyle, to submit again to the poverty of their country of origin. Lack of self-denial at this point has caused some to defect from their holy calling. Consequently prayerful and careful thought must always precede a decision to move from an impecunious scene to one of plenty.

The exercise of self-denial is essential in the use of lawful pleasures and recreations. Jesus warned that "as it was in the days of

20. Walter Chantry, *The Shadow of the Cross* (Edinburgh: Banner of Truth, 1981).

Noah, so it will be at the coming of the Son of Man. For in the days before the flood, people were eating and drinking, marrying and giving in marriage, up to the day Noah entered the ark; and they knew nothing about what would happen until the Lord came and took them all away" (Matt. 24:38, 39). Now there is nothing unlawful about eating and drinking and marriage. There is nothing wrong with the usual activities in which we engage, providing they pass the test of Philippians 4:8—that is, they are true, noble, right, pure, lovely, admirable, and praiseworthy—but as soon as we overindulge, we commit sin. We are free to enjoy the many fine pleasures and lawful recreations that may surround us. However, the question must be answered, where does self-denial apply? Surely the pastor should be a model for others to follow. By discreetly cutting off or paring down lawful enjoyments and pleasures and replacing them with better activities that encourage and strengthen others, he leads the way and provides an example for his people. Which is more advantageous on a cold winter's night, visiting the fatherless and widows in their affliction (James 1:27, KJV) or watching a ball game on television?

The practice of self-denial for the Christian means that his feelings, desires, and comforts take second place to the Lord's will. Self-denial must be universal and constant. It often involves pain. When our Lord said that to follow Him requires self-denial and the taking up of "the cross" (Luke 9:23, 24), His disciples had no idea that He Himself would expire on a literal wooden cross of Roman manufacture. Our Lord's going to that cross was intentional even though it involved pain of the most excruciating kind. It was deliberate, calculated, intentional, irrespective of the pain involved. Do we practice self-denial in that way? Where are the pastors today whose lives show dedication of this order? Too often no difference can be seen between pastors and their easy-going neighbors who live exclusively for the pleasures of this world.

Self-denial applies to possessions as well. There is no limit to what can be spent on luxuries such as stereos, furnishings, and recreational equipment. A due sense of proportion is necessary. Covetousness, if not mortified, can become overwhelming. While traveling in the States recently I listened to the account of a pastor who was asked to resign because he had become preoccupied with making money when he was already rich. In wealthy societies ministers can fall prey to those who give them money to such an extent that they not only are exposed to luxury, but also become obligated to the donors, which is dangerous. It is wise to refer the donors to areas of genuine and urgent need and steer the case away from oneself.

There are many references in Scripture to fasting, yet fast days are very little known today. The pastors of the Puritan period testified of the delight and pleasure they found in days specially set aside for prayer and abstinence.[21] Do we ever write in our diaries what Thomas Boston did? "Being under some discouragements at home, Sept. 13, I began to be uneasy and discontent with my settling at Simprin—finding myself hereby carried off my feet as a Christian, I resolved to spend some time on the morrow in fasting and prayer."[22]

Self-denial by way of disciplined eating habits befits the minister. The commencement of disciplined habits is made easier by companionship. An agreement with a friend as to stipulations or rules as to what is to be done is conducive to success. A much improved work performance is often accomplished by avoidance of over-indulgence. In this context it is not out of place to raise the question of piety's demands in a world that contains both the starving poor and the grossly overindulgent, a subject that is discussed by Ronald S. Sider in his book *Rich Christians in an Age of Hunger.*[23]

Breakdown caused by nervous tension. Pastoral oversight can involve the pastor and his wife, and perhaps his children as well, in terrific emotional strain. Divisions, strifes, envies, and selfish ambitions breed disorders and evil practices of every kind (James

21. Peter Lewis, *The Genius of Puritanism* (Sussex, England: Carey, 1979), pp. 60ff.
22. Thomas Boston, *Works,* vol. 12 (Wheaton: Roberts, 1980), p. 84.
23. Ronald Sider, *Rich Christians in an Age of Hunger* (London: Hodder and Stoughton, 1980).

3:16). These can be a nightmare to the pastor and tax his nervous resources to the limit and result in a breakdown. Let no pastor be complacent and think that his church is immune. Problems come inexorably. Every precaution will not prevent trouble. Be thankful for times of peace, but prepare for war (Eph. 6:10–18). Some pastors are well equipped to ride storms. They are given a tranquil spirit. For everything there is a time and at night they sleep well. But others will wake at 3:00 a.m. or 4:00 a.m. regularly and worry and fret. They try different remedies, but nothing seems to help. Even fervent prayer does not solve their anxiety. Eventually they succumb. They break down. Many have resigned their pastorates, not because they could not preach, but because they could not stand the strain and hassle of church problems.

At the commencement of his ministry the pastor should come to terms with his calling to be a physician of souls. Moreover, the life-long progressive aspect of sanctification in those pastored must be fully reckoned with. The church local is a stone quarry, not the finished temple. Innumerable aches and pains will have to be treated in the Lord's infirmary, which we call the local church. A hospital for the infirm is not an inappropriate analogy. Think of the anxiety experienced by Paul in nursing the churches of Galatia and in correcting the maladies at Corinth. Remember him too imprisoned at Rome with little support and much discouragement. Whoever heard of a doctor grumbling because his patients are ill? To what is the surgeon called if not to tend the sick? Likewise spiritual physicians are called to tend those coming out of the realm of death and darkness. The pastor's calling is to deal with problems. His work is to anoint with the balm of Gilead. As a shepherd he must not only heal but also protect. Dealing with wolves is unpleasant and dangerous. A piety must be built that is sufficient for these strains and demands.

Breakdown due to moral failure. It is a morbid and depressing fact that when it comes to adultery, there are too many casualties among pastors. Ministers are just as vulnerable as others. No area, no country, no denomination is immune. The damage done in each case is irreparable: the breakdown, as far as ministry is concerned, final. This is a distasteful subject, but we cannot shirk it. The matter demands faithful treatment. Let him who stands take heed lest he fall. The only certain insurance against falling into David's sin is to maintain a pure heart, which of course is an integral part of piety. "Above all guard your heart, for it is the wellspring of life" (Prov. 4:23). Concerning bodily appetites Paul declared, "Well, I do not run aimlessly, I do not box as one beating the air; but I pommel my body and subdue it, lest after preaching to others I myself should be disqualified" (I Cor. 9:26, 27, RSV). Job said he made a covenant with his eyes, not to look lustfully at a girl (Job 31:1). He who can keep his heart as well as his eyes will be safe.

Breakdown due to pride and selfish ambition. Preachers, because of the nature and function of their office, are exposed to spiritual pride: ministerial pride, intellectual pride, and the pride of acclaim for their eloquence. Nothing could be more inappropriate. What do we possess that we have not received? The preacher's task is to uphold free and sovereign grace, the meaning of which is that salvation is not earned by merit, but bestowed through mercy. God has sovereignly come to us and freely enriched us in making us heirs of Himself and His Son. Gratitude and humility fill the heart of the recipient. Of all people the preacher himself should exemplify humility. Pride is the nature of the Lucifer who fell through that sin, and of Adam, who did likewise. Pride is deeply entrenched in fallen human nature. The preacher is no exception.

Let us look first at the temptation that comes through flattery. How many of us could say with Henry Martyn, "Men frequently admire me, and I am pleased; *but I abhor the pleasure that I feel.*"[24] Quesnal expressed this matter with much insight when he commented on that incident at Lystra recorded in Acts 14:13, 14, when the people prepared to make sacrifices for the worship of Paul and Barnabus. He wrote,

24. Charles Bridges, *The Christian Ministry* (Edinburgh: Banner of Truth, 1961), p. 153.

It is a very uncommon thing for men not to receive at least one part of the glory that is offered them. This is the touchstone, by which the fidelity of the minister of Christ is measured. We value ourselves upon rejecting gross commendation, and extravagant flattery, because we would not make ourselves ridiculous. But when the praise is fine and delicate, and the incense prepared with art, how seldom is it, that we do not suffer ourselves to be intoxicated thereby.[25]

Intellectual pride is a peculiar enemy and a particular danger for those with academic attainments. They love to be admired because of their learning and to be respected because of their great knowledge. Make way! Make way!—it is the language they like to hear. How tragic to be the victim of such pride for it is the chief sin of the devil who has every degree in the realms of intellectual attainment and cleverness. The Christian church in many cases insists on and certainly in most cases recognizes and applauds degrees for learning, but we need to remember that honors degree earned by Moses—forty years' learning of patience, humility, and meekness in the desert! For meekness he had no equal. Which academics today confer degrees for inward qualities such as humility? The question of motive is important. It is impossible for ministers to live for their own selfish ambitions. While it is not formally instituted, as in secular realms such as banks and building societies, some denominations have a ladder. Men proceed from the smaller churches to the larger ones. A proper estimation of one's own abilities and desire to use them fully is good (Rom. 12:3; I Tim. 3:1), but sheer egocentric ambition is self-worship, and damnable.

Breakdown caused by deviation from the truth and from reliance on the instituted means of grace. We have considered moral lapse as a cause of breakdown, reflecting on the frequency with which this has occurred. Both moral lapse and spiritual failure are, of course, directly related to piety. Piety is the guardian of the soul, not only the supporter, but also the nourisher of ministerial activity. Piety

25. Ibid.

includes as well a love for the truth. Just as God loves the truth and the ways of truth, so ought the minister.

To rely wholly on the truth that sanctifies (John 17:17) and cling only to the stated or appointed means of grace (Acts 2:42) when times are dark and barren is not easy. There have been periods of landslide in church history when the majority of evangelical ministers have embraced heresy of one kind or another. Remember those dark periods of rationalism and Unitarianism. Piety will preserve the minister in such times when there is almost irresistible pressure to compromise with a popular movement. The life of Christmas Evans illustrates the point. He succumbed to Sandemanianism, the dry and barren intellectual heresy of his day, and spent years in coldness and darkness, his ministry blighted miserably as he himself describes:

> The Sandemanian heresy affected me so far as to quench the spirit of prayer for the conversion of sinners, and it induced in my mind a greater regard for the smaller things of the kingdom of heaven than for the greater. I lost the strength which clothed my mind with zeal, confidence and earnestness in the pulpit for the conversion of souls to Christ. My heart retrograded in a manner and I could not realise the testimony of a good conscience. On Sabbath nights after having been in the day exposing and vilifying with all bitterness the errors that prevailed my conscience felt displeased and reproached me that I had lost nearness to, and walking with God. It had disastrous results among the churches. I lost in Anglesey nearly all my old hearers and we thus almost entirely took down what had taken fifteen years to raise.

It was a full, sudden, and glorious restoration to his former piety. He describes his return in a most moving way:

> I was weary of a cold heart towards Christ and his sacrifice and the work of his Spirit; of a cold heart in the pulpit, in secret and in the study. For fifteen years previouly I had felt my heart burning within as if going to Emmaus with Jesus. On a day ever to be remembered by me, as I was going from

Dolgellau to Machynlleth, climbing up towards Cader Idris I considered it to be incumbent upon me to pray, however hard I felt in my heart and however worldly the frame of my spirit was. Having begun in the name of Jesus, I soon felt as it were, the fetters loosening and the old hardness of heart softening, and, as I thought, mountains of frost and snow dissolving and melting within me. This engendered confidence in my soul in the promise of the Holy Ghost. I felt my whole mind relieved from some great bondage. Tears flowed copiously and I was constrained to cry out for the gracious visits of God, by restoring my soul the joys of his salvation and to visit the churches in Anglesey that were under my care. I embraced in my supplications all the churches of the saints and nearly all the ministries in the principality by their names. This struggle lasted for three hours. It rose again and again, like one wave after another, or a high, flowing tide driven by a strong wind, till my nature became faith by weeping and crying. I resigned myself to Christ, body and soul, gifts and labours, every hour of every day that remained for me and all my cares I committed to Christ. The road was mountainous and lonely and I was wholly alone and suffered no interruption in my wrestling with God.[26]

These are just a few of the possibilities of ministerial breakdown that may be traced to a lack of proper biblical piety. I turn now to consider Him who is the source of genuine Christian piety.

4. The Lord Jesus Christ, the Pattern and Empowering Source of Piety

In anticipation of the objection that Christ belongs to too different a category to be a pattern for us to follow, we recall that the great christological debates have taught us to respect the perfect unity of the two natures of Christ, divine and human. At the

26. *Reformation Today*, 29, pp. 29–30.

same time, we must avoid confusing them. That means it is our right and privilege to distinguish clearly between the two natures, as well as to observe their interaction. There are times when the divine nature is prominent. We see this in Jesus' prodigious miracles and also in some of His discourses when His "I am" utterances point to His unique and divine being. Yet at other times we observe Him hungry, thirsty, and fatigued. He was exposed far more than we are to physical strains and to enormous demands, and He found it necessary to have constant recourse to private prayer. It is heresy to advance the idea that He was a superman who did not know the trials that we know. The Scriptures declare otherwise. We have in Him one who has been tempted in every way, just as we are—yet was without sin (Heb. 4:15). The Scriptures encourage our following Christ as our pattern for holiness (I John 2:6), for patient suffering (I Pet. 2:21), and for love (Eph. 5:2). Ministers of the gospel are leaders and should, by way of example to the flocks they lead, be outstanding imitators of God (Eph. 5:1).

Having already explained that piety and holiness are all-embracing, we would do well to focus on just some foremost areas in which ministers should emulate Christ, namely, love, self-sacrifice, prayer and fasting, a humble and joyful service of others, and a faith to persevere. After concentrating on Christ as our pattern, we will consider Him as the one who empowers.

Christ, the Pattern of Piety

Love. The love of Christ for sinners of all kinds is proved by His compassion to heal and transform them. If ever there was an example of sovereign grace, it is seen in the healing of the demon-possessed man of Gadara (Mark 5:1-20). When we see the most depraved and wretched of fallen creatures, do we experience the compassion of Christ? Are we prepared to exercise any effort at all to reclaim seemingly futile and useless cases, drug addicts and the like? There is that love for mankind which motivates us in evangelistic endeavor and also that love for those already redeemed.

Love is not an abstract sentiment. It functions by intelligence and observation. Many factors are involved. Christ loved intelligently. For instance, Jesus looked upon the rich young ruler and loved him. He loved him for what he was as he was made in God's image, yet fallen and in need of redemption (Mark 10:21). Jesus loved with knowledge *(epignosis)*, discernment, and discrimination, which is the teaching of Philippians 1:9. Jesus loved John differently from the others (John 13:23). He loved Peter differently, which love included the will to restore Peter after his fall (John 21:15ff.). He loved His own, and loved them to the end. We must distinguish between a gracious and complacent love with which God loves His people, and that truly benevolent love of goodwill with which He loves all men. Jesus loved the Jerusalem sinners and wept over the calamity they brought upon themselves (Luke 19:41). We have in Jesus the pattern and empowerment for us to love as He loved and continues to love.

The practical importance of this in the pastorate can hardly be exaggerated. It is enormously difficult to love fellow believers during times of division or strife when issues of truth and principle that affect us intensely are at stake. Sometimes church members are guilty of tearing apart a local church. Self-will, bitterness, strife, jealousy, and stubbornness can take over. To love "the sheep" under such circumstances is extremely difficult. Yet God's love is always the pattern for ours (Eph. 5:1, 2; John 13:34, 35). He never ceases in His love for His people. Jesus loved His disciples in spite of their immaturity and their self-ambition (Matt. 20:24–28). It is important that pastors shine as examples of love—especially so when reproving and correcting wayward members of the flock (Gal. 6:1; II Tim. 2:24). The meekness and gentleness required in exasperating circumstances will only come from a life well ordered in piety.

Self-sacrifice. What did it mean for our Lord's disciples to forsake all their earthly prospects (Matt. 19:27)? How many ministers today think in these terms? How many young men aspiring to be ministers think of foregoing marriage? That would be regarded by most as pre-Reformation misguidedness! Yet our Lord spoke seriously of such a possibility. "Some have renounced marriage because of the kingdom of heaven. The one who can accept this should accept it" (Matt. 19:12).

Until the time of the Reformation, self-sacrifice in the form of renunciation of prosperity and marriage was regarded as the way to produce an hundred-fold. For instance, Antony, the father of the monastic system, took the words addressed to the rich young ruler as addressed to himself. He went immediately to distribute to the inhabitants of his native village his large, fertile, and beautiful landed estates, which he inherited from his father, reserving only a small portion of his property for the benefit of his sister.[27] In my experience I have known one man who, while he did not resort to a life of rigid asceticism as Antony did, gave wisely and with such generous endowment to the churches at large as to resemble some of these earlier examples of sacrifice.

We, however, fall far short with our subject if we stop here. The true meaning of self-sacrifice in our Lord was the giving of Himself. He expended His energies in the service of others and ultimately sacrificed life itself. He laid down His life for us. John said it was love that did that, saying, "And we ought to lay down our lives for our brothers" (I John 3:16).

The essence of this self-sacrifice is seen in the patient serving of others, not for the reward of gratitude from them, or praise from our fellows, but because Christ is our pattern. It is not at all inconsistent if we live humbly and acknowledge that everything we possess is a gift to be used for His glory, to work for the reward He gives (Matt. 25:34-36; I Cor. 4:5).

It is possible to give one's life by sacrificing it like William Tyndale (1494-1536), or burning it up on the altar of intense work like McCheyne (1813-43) or Thomas Halyburton (1674-1712). Whitefield and Spurgeon expended themselves well beyond their physical limitations, their lives being shortened considerably as a result. Whether we deliberately pace ourselves to

27. A. B. Bruce, *The Training of the Twelve*, (Kregel, 1979), p. 257.

attempt more good over a longer period within our given capacities or take great risks with our health depends on individual circumstances. Sometimes men see the brevity of their opportunity or an open door and give themselves accordingly. Those involved in scholarly labors like Bible translation must surely include in their reckoning the time span needed for their labors to be of maximum profit. Since no minister can know the future, the main point is to serve with a willing spirit of giving oneself to people, and wholly to consecrate oneself to God's will (Rom. 12:1, 2).

Prayer and fasting. The prayer habits of Jesus evoked from His disciples the request that He teach them just as John had taught his disciples (Luke 11:1). If John's praying was anything like his preaching, we can well understand why reference was made to it. We come directly to the question of whether the prayer habits of ministers today in any way resemble those of their Master.

One important feature of prayer is that it is expressing dependence upon God. Whether healing (Mark 7:34), or being baptized (Luke 3:21), our Lord prayed. This aspect of intercession is something we can develop until it is fairly constant. We read that Jesus rose very early in the morning while it was still dark, left the house, and went into a solitary place, where He prayed. Everyone was looking for Him. Eventually Peter and the other disciples located Him (Mark 1:35). The lesson that we can draw from this is that it is sometimes necessary to take drastic action to be alone and beyond the possibility of interruption for the purpose of determined intercession.

With regard to fasting, it is unlikely that anyone in the ministry today would follow Christ as a pattern for fasting and go into a wilderness for forty days (Matt. 4:2). We read of Anna serving God day and night in fasting and praying (Luke 2:37), but the very idea of fasting seems to have disappeared. Power over evil (Matt. 17:19), clarification as to guidance, liberty of spirit, power in preaching, discipline of mind, victory in crises, physical well-being, and growth in grace are advantages and benefits that accrue from the practice of fasting.[28] If congregations are to benefit in this way then it is obvious that they will require leadership.

A humble and joyful service of others. Washing the feet of guests was one of the most humble services rendered by servants in apostolic times. It was therefore fitly chosen by our Lord to represent that great abasement to which He was to subject Himself in being obedient to death.[29] Christ's present lordship over His church is based upon His humiliation (Phil. 2:6–11). In opposing the action of Jesus, Peter was striking at the very basis of this principle.[30] Not only redemptive teaching but also directly relevant practical instruction may be drawn from the washing of the feet (John 13:6–10): "I have set you an example that you should do as I have done for you" (v. 15). We conclude that our Savior intended that His disciples should perform towards each other every needful act of humble service, even the smallest and most servile. For such acts they should be ready and prompt.

Many occasions arise in the course of pastoral work that seem to be time wasting and to have no prospect of profit for church growth. For instance, we are sometimes called to meet the needs of elderly or sick people who have no influence in this world and certainly no means of rewarding the church. There must be a readiness to serve such in the name of Christ, not with resentment because of the sacrifice of time, but with joy. The spirit in which we serve is vital. When our Lord said, "Many who are first will be last, and many who are last will be first" (Matt. 19:30), He was surely referring to two kinds of service. There are those like Simon the Pharisee, efficient, respectable, correct, hardworking, but hard, legalistic, and ungenial. In contrast, there are those like Mary who serve with passionate devotion and joy. There is the spirit of the censorious elder brother, and there is the spirit of the prodigal who returns with a new heart. Not only should we serve

28. David R. Smith, *Fasting—A Neglected Discipline* (London: Hodder and Stoughton, 1954), pp. 51ff.

29. Jonathan Edwards, *Works*, vol. 2 (Edinburgh: Banner of Truth, 1974). p. 960.

30. Bruce, *Training of the Twelve* p. 346.

with humility and joy, but with zeal. A wrong motive vitiates everything. We have to be purged of vainglory and self-seeking. A great quantity of work is useless if at the end of the day it is revealed that we did all for our own glory. We should see then the necessity for constant piety by which the Holy Spirit endues us with joy in our service. That joy is our strength (Neh. 8:10). It is irresistible strength. It is something that baffles the enemies of the gospel. What can they say to those who find joy in the most humble and menial service of others?

Faith to persevere. Reference has been made to the tremendous pressures and temptations borne by those in the ministerial office. In addition to the conflicts that can take place within a church, there is the burden of barren times. There can be long periods of hard work without any visible evidence of success. After the romance of coming for the first time into a pastorate, plus the enthusiasm of novelty (a new minister in the town!), there can be the painful discovery of unsolved problems, and then following that, a possible dreadful period of fruitlessness in which nobody is added to the assembly for months or years. To add to distress some may leave out of dislike of the new pastor. Often men come into churches where traditions prevail, not Scripture. I know of one pastor whose flock shrank from 120 to 30 and then rose gradually to a present 90. Those who left did not agree with the discipline of a doctrinal and expository ministry. To persevere during the shrinkage period required enormous determination and tenacity.

Did our Lord know the heartache of rejection? He certainly did! The huge crowds that gathered could disappear like a morning mist. At one time, after being followed and then deserted by many thousands, He turned to the Twelve and said, "You do not want to leave me too, do you?" (John 6:67). It is worth pondering that He who had the power to regenerate did not actually see much fruit by way of large numbers of regenerate people under His preaching. That 500 could gather in Galilee (I Cor. 15:6) and 120 in Jerusalem testifies of limited success for the God-man who was sovereignly pleased to bestow from heaven what He did not choose to claim for Himself on earth.

Discouragement among ministers is prevalent and often severe. The majority confess to intense struggles in this area. We should ask if our Redeemer was Himself subject to discouragement. Literally the word means to deprive of courage or confidence. It would be inaccurate therefore to say that the Servant of Jahweh was discouraged. But this sadness is expressed (Isa. 49:4):

> But I said, "I have laboured to no purpose;
>   I have spent my strength in vain and for nothing.
> Yet what is due to me is in the Lord's hand,
>   And my reward is with my God."

Disappointment is described candidly but is accompanied with declarations of faith. He looked forward to eventual reward. "For the joy set before him he endured the cross, scorning its shame" (Heb. 12:2). He looked to the end result, the Holy City, a worldwide harvest. He knew the promise,

> It is too small a thing for you to be my servant,
>   to restore the tribes of Jacob and bring back
>   those of Israel I have kept.
> I will also make you a light for the Gentiles,
>   that you may bring my salvation to the ends of the earth.
>   (Isa. 49:6)

The exercise of faith in hard times of disappointment is an essential in the work of a pastor. Here too the Chief Shepherd is our pattern. The incarnate Son is Himself the man of faith *par excellence*. This is what it means when the Scripture says that He is "the pioneer and perfector of faith."[31] His was a faith characterized by complete trust in His Father and expressed in prayer as we have already seen. In looking to Jesus we see Him who is the supreme exponent of faith, one who exemplified what it is to live

31. Philip Hughes, *Hebrews*, (Grand Rapids: Eerdmans, 1977), p. 522.

by faith. He is both our example to follow and the one who empowers us, to which subject we now turn.

Christ, the Empowering Source of Piety

The very centrality of some subjects can have the effect of making them seem trite and commonplace. As we consider this important subject and some of the best known passages in Scripture such as John 15 (union with Christ) and Philippians 4:13 ("I can do everything through him who gives me strength"), it is worth recalling that the best preachers have concentrated on centralities and labored to perfect central themes over a lifetime. George Whitefield and the late Professor John Murray are examples of those who have followed this principle.

Our concern is to derive from Christ the spiritual power to live holy lives and to preach powerful sermons. The one is the support, pillar, and foundation of the other. This power can only be enjoyed as we abide in Christ. That means maintaining an intimate sharing partnership with the person of Christ continually. This unity or partnership is beautifully exemplified in the apostle Paul. From the time of his conversion it was as though Christ were alongside him all the way through, giving him the strength he needed at the crucial points. Do you remember the ordeal Paul experienced at Jerusalem? When it seemed that he would be torn to pieces, he was rescued in the nick of time by the command of the centurion. "The following night the Lord stood near Paul and said, 'Take courage! As you have testified about me in Jerusalem, so you must also testify in Rome' " (Acts 23:11).

What comfort those reassuring words must have been through the storms and dangers in the days to come! This partnership is again illustrated when during his final ordeal, when everyone deserted him, Paul testified, "But the Lord stood at my side and gave me strength, so that through me the message might be fully proclaimed and all the Gentiles might hear it" (II Tim. 4:17).

The word Paul uses for "gave me strength" is "empowered" (*enedunamosen*). The word *dunamis* suggests the inherent ability of a person to carry something out, whether spiritual, physical, or

88   *The Preacher and Piety*

political. Christ, the source of all our power, was Himself strong in speech and action (Luke 24:19)[32] The person of the Holy Spirit as indweller and empowerer is the gift of Christ to His people. Therefore the Christian life is described sometimes as a union with Christ (Gal. 2:20ff.; I Cor. 1:30; II Cor. 5:19ff.; Phil. 3:8ff.) and sometimes by the indwelling of the Holy Spirit (Rom. 8:11, 14; Gal. 4:6; I Cor. 2:12; 6:19).

It is imperative that we experience the power or enabling that Christ gives. William Hendriksen aptly translates Philippians 4:13, "I can do all things in him who infuses strength into me." Christ is our empowerer as liberator, for He delivers us from the terrors of the law, from sin, heaviness of mind, hell and death. He takes away the evils that vex us. But He also empowers us by wedding us to the law of the New Covenant, that is to love the mind of God as revealed in Scripture from the heart.

For our ministries to be effective it is imperative too that we experience the empowering of the Holy Spirit, as Paul says, "My message and my preaching were not with wise and persuasive words, but in demonstration of the Spirit's power" (I Cor. 2:4). "To me," asserts Professor Murray, "preaching without passion is not preaching at all."[33] Does he mean power as well as passion? D. Martyn Lloyd-Jones in a series of expositions at Westminster Theological Seminary in 1969 answered emphatically in the affirmative.

The last of that series was on I Corinthians 2:4 in which he described the greatest essential in connection with preaching as the unction and the anointing of the Holy Spirit.[34] It is easy to misconstrue this emphasis on power of the Holy Spirit—"You will receive power {dunamin} when the Holy Spirit comes on you" (Acts 1:8)—and construct a teaching whereby "an experience" is supposed to be the essential "open sesame" to a life of

32. Jesus' *dunamis* has its foundation in His being anointed; His *exousia* is founded in His being sent. *Dictionary of N.T. Theology*, 2:609.
33. John Murray, *Collected Works*, vol. 3 (Edinburgh: Banner of Truth, 1982), p. 72.
34. D. Martyn Lloyd-Jones, *Preaching and Preachers* (London: Hodder and Stoughton, 1971), pp. 304ff.

power. Because of this error, and out of fear of excess, many have shied away from all notion of power experiences. But that too is a mistake. We must make room for constant ongoing enablement by Christ through the Holy Spirit to live a life of piety and to preach powerfully. To dismiss "unction" as mere mysticism is misguided. It may be difficult to define what unction is, but we all certainly know what it is not! We do not have to read much further than Acts chapter 2 to know the results of it. Paul made it *(parresia)* an absolute priority. He asked the Ephesian believers to pray that he would be given boldness, the very experience of which is inextricably bound up with prayer and piety (Eph. 6:10-20).

5. Some Concluding Exhortations

I would encourage preachers of the gospel with two exhortations:

1. *The work to which you are called is a biblical one of high honor.* Paul writing to Timothy declared, "And the things you have heard me say in the presence of many witnesses entrust to reliable men who will also be qualified to teach others" (II Tim. 2:2). What does the future hold for us if men truly and properly called and equipped are not emerging to preach, pastor and lead the churches, and evangelize a lost world? What a high, noble, and honorable task is yours who preach! Daily the twelve apostles saw a living example of how to preach to the populace meaningfully. That example, Jesus, must be constantly before you as both example and source of piety. His life lived through you will empower His Word preached by you so that His kingdom will come. Your task is great, but your opportunities are even greater, as you proclaim to others the one with whom you walk day by day.

2. *Endless resources of truth are yours as you pursue your calling.* The truth of the gospel is a constant, thrilling, empowering source of inspiration. We sometimes call the truth God's whole

counsel (Acts 20:27) and sometimes the Reformed faith. It has become the vogue, even among some who pride themselves as Reformed, to devalue the Puritans. The Puritan movement covered a period of three generations, and therefore it is easy to seize on faults in exegesis and practice, but who would be so foolish as to discount all of Calvin's works because of the episode with Servetus? Those who feel themselves superior to John Owen, Thomas Manton, Richard Sibbes, or John Flavel should not underestimate the theological and exegetical abilities of those pastors, but should remember that the value of the Puritans' contribution lies mostly in their unrivalled ability to apply truth to experience and practice. We should therefore enrich ourselves from the past, always improving, always refining, always reforming—and thereby nurturing our own piety on the vibrant piety of Christians from earlier generations.

The preacher, like Moses, is to speak God's Word to God's people. To speak that Word accurately and powerfully, the preacher must first allow himself to be spoken to by that Word—both directly and indirectly. This is the life of piety.

3

The Preacher and Scholarship
James Montgomery Boice

Over the years I have developed a number of concerns for which I am nearly always ready to go on a crusade. One is the place of scholarship in preaching. We have a pernicious doctrine in contemporary evangelicalism—I do not hesitate to call it that—which says that if a minister is average in his skills and intelligence, he should take an average church. If he is above average, he should take a larger church. If he is really exceptional—if he is keen about books and simply revels in the background, content, and application of the Word of God—he should teach in a seminary. Ugh! I am convinced that those with the very best minds and training belong in the pulpit, and that the pulpit will never have the power it once had (and ought to have) until this happens.

When I say this I do not suggest that the pulpit should become a seminary lectern, though it would be better that than the sad stage prop it has become for many minister-entertainers. Obviously a sermon is not a lecture. It is exposition of a text of Scripture in terms of contemporary culture with the specific goal of helping people to understand and obey the truth of God. But to do that well the preacher must be well studied. To do it exceptionally well he must have exceptional understanding of (1) the Scripture he is expounding, (2) the culture into which he is expounding it, and (3) the spirituality and psychology of the people he is helping to obey God's Word. These understandings do not come merely from native abilities or mere observance of life. They

91

come from hard study as the preacher explores the wisdom of both the past and the present to assist him in his task.

I would be overjoyed if the chief accomplishment of this chapter would be to turn some young scholar away from a life of academic teaching to what I am convinced is a richer and far more rewarding life of using that same scholarship to teach the whole counsel of God within our churches.

One Preacher's Story

In trying to develop the theme of the preacher as a scholar I am aware that I might do far better had I achieved more in either of these areas. I would like to hear Martin Luther on the subject. (Who would not?) Or John Calvin! Or Jonathan Edwards! The only good reason for *my* writing on preaching and scholarship is that my thoughts are at least not yet well known.

My early training in grade school and high school was good, but it was not until college that I was awakened to the joys of serious study. And even that came slowly and not from the best of motives. In high school I had always been near the top of my class, which was high enough so far as I was concerned; I had no interest in being "number one." But when I left high school for Harvard University, which I did in the late fifties, I suddenly found myself in the company of people all of whom were brighter than I was and who were achieving far above my average. I had to study hard just to keep up or (in some courses) just to creep up out of the cellar. I worked hard just to be respectable. Out of that enforced mental application I found that I began to love the work I was doing and even began to take a personal delight in mastering some well-defined subject, however small.

Harvard taught me two things primarily. First, *the greater proportion of one's work should be with the original sources.* My field was English literature, and this meant studying the poetry, plays, novels, and essays themselves and not some other person's writing about them. The result of this was a love for the material. Second, *the student must give attention to details.* This meant details in the works being studied, as well as details in one's own work. One of my tutors was extremely helpful at this point, for he would grade my papers meticulously, making such notations as, "Where does Milton say that?" "Is this the most accurate word you could use?" "This is not good English idiom!" "Try moving this paragraph earlier in the essay." "What evidence have you given for this particular conclusion?" It was a tribute to this training that my grades moved up one rank group each year I was at Harvard.

When I came to Princeton Seminary I suffered sharp disappointment. Compared to Harvard, Princeton functioned on an inferior academic level. There were a number of good courses. Some of the professors were outstanding. But on the whole, secondary sources (often the professors' own books) were substituted for original works, and multiple assignments replaced what I had come to value as the joy of authentic study.

Moreover, we were passing by the books I most wanted to read. I had a problem at this point because the many routine assignments took up time that I needed to read the books of my choice. One of the evangelical students, now a worker with the L'Abri Fellowship in England, suggested that I keep a list of books I learned about in my studies and wanted to read, but did not have time for—and read them later. This was one of the most helpful suggestions I have received. I began to do that in seminary, generally even buying the books when possible, and I have continued to do that not only through the years of graduate study, but to the present day.

The chance to read widely and well came during my doctoral work at the University of Basel in Switzerland. Basel was the opposite of Princeton in many respects. Here there were no requirements, no papers—only a thesis and an extensive oral examination at the end. But this was ideal for me. I developed a pattern. From Monday to Friday during the normal working day, I would work on my thesis. (At first I learned German and read the pertinent German books, then broadened out to French and other texts. At last I organized and wrote the thesis.) At night I would read other books and pursue subjects of personal interest.

I started with works I should have read at Princeton: the three-volume *Systematic Theology* by Charles Hodge; the works of B. B. Warfield, particularly the collection of essays entitled *The Inspiration and Authority of the Bible*; J. Gresham Machen's *The Virgin Birth of Christ*; John Calvin's *Institutes of the Christian Religion*; James Orr's *The Christian View of God and the World*. I read material by conservative scholars: Donald Guthrie's *New Testament Introduction* (in three volumes); Alfred Edersheim's *The Life and Times of Jesus the Messiah*. I read works by the Basel professors: volumes of Karl Barth's *Church Dogmatics* (but not all); Oscar Cullmann's *The Early Church*, his *Early Christian Worship*, his *Peter: Disciple, Apostle, Martyr*, and *Salvation History* (then in German only). Most enjoyable was my reading of the classics: Augustine's *Confessions* (worked through in Latin under the tutelage of Bo Reicke, my thesis advisor); the writings of Josephus (nine volumes in the Harvard Classics); Epictetus; Tacitus; Suetonius; Herodotus; and Thucydides. Never in my life have I enjoyed any reading more than the reading of these ancient Greek and Latin authors.

After finishing my formal study and beginning to preach, which I have done from the pulpit of Tenth Presbyterian Church in Philadelphia since 1968, my attention shifted (among other things) to those who had been preachers before me. During my early years I worked through such collections as Alexander Maclaren's *Expositions of Holy Scripture*, volumes of Martin Luther's *Works*, and hundreds of sermons by Charles Haddon Spurgeon in *The New Park Street Pulpit* and *The Metropolitan Tabernacle Pulpit*. In some cases my work led to some original contribution in a field. One contribution of this nature was the commentary on Galatians in *The Expositor's Bible Commentary*.

Recommended Guidelines

Out of my experience, some of which I have just outlined, I have developed guidelines that I heartily recommend to any aspiring preacher.

1. *Get all the formal training you can.* Not everyone is in a position to do long years of formal academic training. Sometimes financial concerns hold one back. At other times a job opens up, and it seems wise to accept it. But these circumstances aside, if the possibility is present and the student has ability to do further work, it is good to get the training before taking up a ministry. For one thing, it is hard to do it later. Many ministers will confess that the pressures of pastoral work, demands of a growing family, and burden of administration have all but eclipsed serious reading or study from their schedule. Work toward an advanced degree if possible. One of my predecessors at Tenth Presbyterian Church, Donald Grey Barnhouse, used to advise young ministers that if they knew the Lord was returning at the end of four years, they should spend three of those years in intensified training and only then use the last year in full-time service.

2. *Never stop learning.* One advantage of pursuing advanced training before entering the ministry is that it disposes the mind to study and makes it easier to continue some form of serious work even in the midst of an active ministry. But whether or not such training has been possible, the work of preparation should continue in some form throughout the ministry. The ministry should not only be an educated ministry. It should be educable and self-educating. If it is, the preacher will continue to be fresh, alive, and interesting. If it is not, his material will soon run out and the sermons will become repetitious and boring.

In what areas should the preacher be sure to continue learning? The first and obvious area is the Bible itself. The preacher's life should be one long love affair with this book. He should master portions of it in exquisite detail and all of it in its general outlines. Moreover, his knowledge of the book should grow until the Bible becomes more precious to him even than life itself. This is one primary reason to preach expositorially, working through books of the Bible chapter by chapter, paragraph by paragraph, and sometimes even verse by verse or word by word, in the weekly preaching. (Geoffrey Thomas discusses this in more detail later in this volume.) This is vital for the people because it gives them a grasp of specific portions of Scripture, which thereby becomes theirs in a personal way. It is even more valuable for the preacher. He too masters specific blocks of material, including the difficult themes and doctrines he might otherwise pass by. Over a period of time, these detailed studies reinforce one another, and the minister's later preaching is enriched by the earlier expositions.

A second area for continued study is theology, both biblical and systematic. Here texts of systematic theology will be studied, but not necessarily as a discipline divorced from the minister's weekly expositions of a Bible book. Expository preaching will inevitably bring the preacher to themes that he has not previously considered in detail, and at this point a careful examination of the text may be enhanced by study of a selection of theology books dealing with its themes. (See Donald Macleod's thorough discussion later in this volume of the role of systematic theology in preaching.)

For example, I had been in the ministry for about seven years when my morning preaching through Philippians, the Sermon on the Mount, and John eventually brought me to the discourses of John 14–16, in which the work of the Holy Spirit is described. Strange to say, I had never done any serious preaching on the Holy Spirit before that time. But anticipating these texts, I was able to prepare for the exposition by studying James Buchanan's *The Office and Work of the Holy Spirit*, George Smeaton's *The Doctrine of the Holy Spirit*, W. H. Griffith Thomas's *The Holy Spirit of God*, Reuben A. Torrey's *The Person and Work of the Holy Spirit*, William Fitch's *The Ministry of the Holy Spirit*, and appropriate sections of the major systematic theologies. In the same way, the seventeenth chapter brought me to the doctrine of the church for which I prepared by working through James Bannerman's *The church of Christ* (two volumes), as well as other works. I would recommend that a minister plan such reading in advance, arranging his material so as to cover the great doctrines of the Bible during a fixed time early in his ministry.

A third area for continuing study is history, particularly the history of the major biblical periods. A great deal of work should be done in the background and history of the New Testament. This should include works contemporary or nearly contemporary with the period, such as Josephus' histories and the histories of the Latin writers. It should include modern studies, including the various lives of Jesus and the travels of the apostle Paul. Preaching from the Old Testament should be accompanied by readings in the history of the patriarchial, monarchical, and later prophetic periods.

A special word should be said about books or subjects particularly interesting to our congregations. I think here of contemporary novels that probe the consciousness of today's men and women. Again, there are scientific works dealing with the origin and value of life, genetic engineering, the cosmos and such things. In many of these areas a minister (unless he has specific training) will be dealing with arguments that he will have difficulty evaluating. He will have to be cautious. But his training in biblical disciplines will at least make him conscious of presuppositions and will guide him in weighing what he reads. Besides, a branching out to fields other than his own should be mind-expanding and stimulating. About ten years into my ministry I began to study the Book of Genesis and in preparation for that began to read such works as Robert Jastrow's *God and the Astronomers* and *Until the Sun Dies*; J. W. Klotz's *Genes, Genesis and Evolution*; J. Kerby Anderson and Harold G. Coffin's *Fossils in Focus*; Dan Wonderly's *God's Time-Records in Ancient Sediments*; Donald England's *A Christian View of Origins*; Robert C. Newman and Herman J. Eckelmann, Jr.'s *Genesis One and the Origin of the Earth*, as well as discussions of the same matters in commentaries by Henry M. Morris, Francis Schaeffer, and others.

The ministry is one discipline where knowledge in practically any field is useful. In fact, the more a minister knows, the more useful and more powerful his ministry may become. The preacher who is not continuing to learn is limiting himself unnecessarily.

3. *Set aside specific times for study.* In many cases a minister will fail in his scholarship, not intentionally, but as a result of many disrupting pressures upon him. This can only be overcome by

determination to win the time battle. As much as possible, the minister must control his schedule, making sure that he has solid blocks of time for serious work in it.

There are three major blocks of time a minister may use. First, there are his mornings. This is the ideal time for serious work, for, regardless of the threats to that time, most of the concerns that would interrupt it may be deferred to the afternoon. I have learned to schedule appointments and counseling sessions from the back of the day forward, beginning with an appointment at five o'clock, then four o'clock, and so on. This is generally most advantageous to the people involved, and it preserves the largest amount of uninterrupted time for me. Second, there are evenings. It is not as easy to do technical work in the evenings as in the mornings, but the evenings are an ideal time to read lighter or contemporary books. I have read all the Watergate books, as well as a selection of fictional and nonfictional best sellers, in the evening hours. The third major time block occurs during the minister's vacation. This is the time to take along some heavy theological works, Christian biographies, and books that will lay a foundation for the next year's preaching. In a typical summer I may read a volume or two of Saint Augustine from the *Nicene and Post Nicene Fathers* collection, a volume of John Owen, something of Jonathan Edwards, and a biography such as that of Charles Haddon Spurgeon or George Whitefield. I have used the summers to work through Thomas Watson's *A Body of Divinity*, *The Ten Commandments*, and *The Lord's Prayer*; Cotton Mather's *The Great Works of Christ in America* (two volumes); and the early volumes of Carl Henry's *God, Revelation and Authority*. When preaching on the minor prophets, I used the summers to work through the major commentaries on those books.

Two additional matters are worth mentioning. First, not only should the preacher have specific times for study, but he should also have a specific place to study, a place where he is interrupted only at the peril of the intruder. If possible, this should not be an office on the main corridor near the front door of the church where everyone who stops by during the week can stick his or her head in to say hello to the pastor. Ten of those interruptions will ruin the day so far as any serious work is concerned. If a pastor is to be a good pastor, there must be as much time when he is unavailable to his people as there is time when he is available to counsel them and visit in their homes.

Second, the minister must be rigorous in maintaining these uninterrupted times. I have learned that there is hardly a matter in the pastor's life that needs absolutely *immediate* attention. Nearly anything can wait an hour or two while the essential work of reading, study, and sermon preparation goes forward.

4. *Tackle some big problems.* Most people have a tendency to stay on tested ground or work in areas where they have already established some expertise. So we shy away from the truly great problems of Bible interpretation, theology, or ethics. This tendency should be identified and overcome. Working in difficult areas does not mean that we will master those areas or even come to firm conclusions in them. We may—in which case we will have something original to contribute, perhaps in an academic article or other writing. But even if we do not, we will at least have broadened our knowledge and may even have grown in a humility that will keep us from dogmatic utterances in areas where we possess no particular expertise. The bigger the problem, the more interesting and rewarding our study is apt to be.

A minister who will follow these guidelines will find that he can do much more in his study than merely extract outlines and develop applications from Scripture. He will develop a well-rounded knowledge of many things, focused by his love for the Bible, and will thus become a resource person for his congregation in a much broader way than by being merely a weekly pulpiteer. People will come to him for suggestions of what books to read either for their own personal study or for the preparation of classes they are teaching, and when confronted with a technical problem, they will turn to the pastor-scholar for assistance in sorting it out.

At some point the minister may want to consider making time for a public fielding of the congregation's questions. I have done that for many small groups in an informal way. I have also done it on a monthly basis as part of the Sunday evening services, requesting the questions beforehand. Seeing the questions beforehand allows me to check out matters about which I may be in doubt.

Scholarship in Sermons

There is a special area of the "preacher and scholarship" that concerns sermons themselves. Just how much scholarship should there be in sermons? How often should the minister deal with technical subjects? Should academic or scholarly matters even be visible at all? These questions are not easily answered because there are so many variables. Ministers will have greater or lesser ability to handle such matters. Some subjects will lend themselves to a scholarly handling; others will not. Above all, congregations will vary, and there will be different academic abilities and interests even within a single congregation. All we can say in general is that technical matters should at least be acknowledged and that they can sometimes be explored in detail.

I have found that the key element here is variety. A preacher will try for variety in preaching generally. He may follow a study of a New Testament book with the study of an Old Testament book, or the study of a long book with the study of a shorter one. He may vary book studies with doctrinal studies or studies of key personalities in Scripture. I would suggest that the same concerns need to operate where scholarly matters are concerned.

1. *Textual problems.* One area in which scholarship bears directly on the sermon is the text itself. What is the true text? To what extent should one acknowledge and deal with variants? Generally one does not need to deal with variants at all. Indeed, the preacher does not even need to spend much time considering them privately. This is because most are inconsequential. They concern variant word orders, spellings, or insignificant additions or omissions. But from time to time there are variants that bear upon the meaning of the passage, and these must be handled if

the text is to be treated honestly. I have found that this can usually be done in a portion of the message, perhaps prefacing the discussion with an acknowledgment that this is a technical matter that will not be of interest to everybody but will be of interest to some and in any case should be dealt with, simply because it is a problem.

When I was preaching through Galatians, Galatians 2:3-5 was one passage I felt obliged to deal with carefully. It represents a classic problem involving major variants from which several entirely opposing interpretations descend. In some manuscripts the words "to whom" in verse 5 are missing. In others the negative is missing. In some both are missing. Grammatically, the easiest sense comes from the omissions in which case the passage says, "But on account of the false brothers . . . we yielded for a time." That is, Paul yielded to the demands to have Titus circumcised for the sake of the false teachers who had infiltrated the Christian ranks. This seems contrary to the spirit of the passage as well as to everything Paul had been saying previously. We would expect him to have resisted the demands on Titus. However, if we retain the questionable words, verse 4 does not really end, and it is therefore hard to make sense of the passage. In discussing this problem I took as much as fifteen or twenty minutes to deal with it. But an ordered presentation kept up interest, and I was able to preface the discussion with a broader introduction to the issues and close with pointed applications.

2. *Problems of the higher criticism.* Higher criticism concerns the authorship of biblical books and the books' integrity. Again, as in matters of the lower criticism, there are issues that do not need to be raised, particularly if one is preaching from a conservative stance and the people are themselves conservatively disposed. Still there are questions that are in at least some persons' minds and do demand treatment. Did Isaiah write all of Isaiah? Are the early chapters of Genesis history or merely fanciful though instructive stories? Are the Gospel accounts of the resurrection of Jesus contradictory? If not, can they be harmonized? What about the ending of Mark's Gospel? These questions should probably

not be treated in most normal sermons on a random text or passage. But in a series of studies, particularly of an entire book, they should be dealt with, possibly in the introduction.

I sometimes do this as amplification upon more down-to-earth teaching that has already been presented. For example, I treated the factuality of Genesis on three separate occasions in a lengthy series on the first eleven chapters of that book. The first occasion was the second of the four messages on Genesis 1:1. I had considered the importance of studying Genesis in my first message, but in the second I asked, Is Genesis "fact or fiction"? I dealt with the matter a second time in reference to the Garden of Eden, asking whether Eden was a real place. The third time I raised the question was in a discussion of the fall. I titled that message "Is the Fall a Fact?" By that time, having raised the question of factuality in three different contexts, I was beginning to get the point across that whether the Book of Genesis is presenting things that really happened or not really matters.

Questions of authorship can generally be treated in the introduction to Bible books, although in the case of my studies of I, II, and III John, I held the discussion of the Johannine authorship of the whole until treating the two shorter Epistles. This was because the appellation "the elder" occurs only there and is a key part of the debate about the authorship of these letters.

3. *Scientific problems.* There are whole areas of the Bible in which scientific problems simply do not occur. There are other areas, such as miracles, where they lie in the background, but only in a general way. Not every discussion of a miracle should deal with the problem this presents to scientifically minded people, though at some point a frame of reference could be provided. A message on unbelief could deal with this quite independently of any specific studies of the miracles.

On the other hand, there are areas in which scientific objections must be handled forthrightly and in detail, if only because our age really is unusually concerned about such problems. I had to do this early on in the Genesis series. I did not start with it. My first messages (on Gen. 1:1) dealt with the nature of God and the creation. (It was here that I dealt with the factuality of Genesis.) But eventually the problem of evolution came up and was treated thoroughly. By the time I had finished, I had done studies of five competing views of creation: atheistic evolution, theistic evolution, the "Gap Theory," six-day creationism, and progressive creationism. I treated these as compactly as possible. Still the messages each averaged some fifteen pages in length and took about forty minutes to preach. They contained analyses of the size and complexity of the universe, evidence for an old (and young) earth and universe, fossil records, mutations, radiometric dating, and other technical matters. It is fair to say that one gentleman, who had been a member of the church for perhaps forty or fifty years, became exasperated with what he regarded as "non-spiritual preaching" and left the church. He has never been back! But others, particularly men with scientific interests, warmed to the treatment and declared that they had never been more interested in anything than in those studies.

In a less ambitious way I later dealt with evidence for the antiquity of man and the historical reliability of the table of names and peoples in Genesis 10. I used three messages to study the history and distribution of the Indo-European peoples, the nations that spread outward to the Orient and Africa, and the people of Semitic stock. The series placed the peoples of the West within this whole-world context.

First the Bible

I end with this qualification. Most of the above has been a polemic on behalf of scholarship behind and in preaching. But valuable and needed as this is, it is nevertheless a servant to and not a substitute for the plain exposition of specific texts of Scripture. Earlier I said that a sermon should be exposition of a text of Scripture in terms of contemporary culture with the goal of helping people to understand and obey the truth of God. To do this well involves sound scholarship, especially that which allows the Word of God to speak into today's culture and assists the listener in understanding the Bible in his framework. Still, it is not the scholarship we are preaching. Still less must we preach ourselves, as if the scholarly element in sermons could be used to gain prestige for the preacher. We are to preach the Word of God, knowing that only the Word contains within it the power necessary to break sin's shackles and turn a rebellious child of Adam back from the life of sin to the Savior. The minister, even in being quite technical, should never forget that his end is not chiefly to inform in such areas, but to confront his listeners with the need to hear and obey the Word of God. There is no message that cannot make its own contribution to this theme.

Anything a preacher has, including his scholarship, can be used of God when it is placed at His disposal. But if it takes the place of God's Word, it is worse than useless. It is evil and will harm both the preacher and his listeners. May all who take up this calling be, above all, ministers of God's Book.

4

The Whole Man
R. C. Sproul

The perennial bane of the student's existence is to be encumbered with assignments that fall under the rubric of "busy work," assignments with no apparent educational value save to keep idle hands busy and vacant heads occupied. Such was my plight as a seminary student enduring the role of guinea pig for a new curriculum designed to catapult our school to the level of a theological university. Ambitious reading levels were established, with quotas of twenty-five hundred pages per week, and term papers reached an aggregate total of two hundred pages per semester. The net value of the program was to induce a forced acquisition of the skill of speed-reading via skimming and scanning. (I once "read" a volume of Karl Barth's *Church Dogmatics* in twenty minutes. I also managed to "earn" an A on a critical book review of a work of Martin Buber's after reading only the table of contents. Buber said in his book exactly what I anticipated, artificially imposing existential categories of thought on the Old Testament prophets.)

Such confessions may result in the seminary's revoking my diploma for finding short cuts around the sheer volume of assignments. Happily the academic committee of the institution adjusted their quantitative goals and revised the new curriculum to more sober standards, thereby avoiding, at the eleventh hour, a mass student revolt. The crisis point of student unrest and agitation came when we were assigned the task of writing a twenty-five-page paper on "The Implications for the Image of the Minister in the American Culture Gleaned From an Analysis of Contemporary Cartoons." That was the superlative degree of busywork as far as I was concerned. Or so I thought. I diligently, though reluctantly, pursued the task of looking for cartoons depicting ministers in *Time Magazine, The Reader's Digest, Newsweek,* and other national publications. I paid attention to images of clergy in television programming and in the modern novel. After canvassing scores of cartoons and noting several television programs, I noticed that the images that emerged were ghastly. There was indeed a method to the professor's madness, which exploded my preconception of a busywork assignment. I suddenly realized that I was about to join the ranks of a professional group whose public image had deteriorated from that of respectable community leaders to inept and slovenly country bumpkins.

The caricature of the clergyman that was delivered by the media was that of the bald, overweight, sloppily dressed, inarticulate boob who veiled his inadequacies under the cloak of sanctimonius piety. Only once did a figure emerge who was depicted as virile, intelligent, compassionate, and walking with a praiseworthy degree of personal integrity. This exception was the priest portrayed by Tom Tryon in the Hollywood version of *The Cardinal.*

Martin Luther King was once asked a provocative question by a less-than-sensitive talk-show host. "Dr. King, is it true that Black people are lazy, over-sexed, and have rhythm?" I had to stifle a gasp that was forcing its way out of my throat in response to such a crass and demeaning question. The gasp intensified with King's immediate reply. "Yes," he said. "It is often true." Now my consternation turned to pure shock, until Dr. King qualified his answer. "What do you expect? For two hundred years white men have been caricaturing Black people as lazy, over-sexed, and rhythmic. After living in an environment of repeated caricature, people begin to live out the expectations imposed upon them."

The same thing can happen to the preacher. He will begin to look and act like the mirror-image projected and then wonder why the credibility of his office has eroded. Such a cultural reaction is a disaster for the church and its ministry. The preaching ministry requires *strength.* That strength must be physical, emotional, intellectual, and spiritual. The whole man must be a strong man if he is to survive the rigors of effective preaching.

The Physical Aspect of Preaching

We are aware that God answered the petitions of St. Paul with the words, "My grace is sufficient for thee: for my strength is made perfect in weakness" (II Cor. 12:9). Paul frequently noted his own weaknesses, citing especially the fraility of his body, his feeble eyesight, and his recurring bouts with chronic illnesses. So clearly do his physical limitations come across in his Epistles that we might easily overlook that in some respects Paul was a man of prodigious physical strength. How much physical strength is required to survive thirty-nine lashes, *five times?* (Many died under such beatings by the twentieth lash.) Or being beaten with rods three times? Three shipwrecks? One stoning? A night and a day in the sea? Or consider the rigors of travel in the ancient world. I would like to be as physically "weak" as the apostle Paul.

In my thirties I discovered that one of the difficult requirements of my ministry was its demand for physical stamina. My personal background was heavily invested in athletics, and so I benefited to some degree from the advantages of physical development. In spite of the training and my relative youthfulness, I found my most crying deficiency at the point of physical endurance. The remedy was jogging to improve cardiovascular efficiency, a truly ungodly price to pay. For once I emulated the apostle, pummelling my body to subdue it.

Though preachers differ in the expenditure of energy given in a sermon, it has been estimated that a half-hour address can use as much physical energy as eight hours of manual labor. Billy Graham, for example, has been cautioned by physicians against the danger of physical exhaustion due to preaching. It is possible, of course, to conserve energy while preaching by speaking in a monotone and squelching any temptation to be dynamic. The added benefit of this style is to conserve the congregation's energy as well, giving them the opportunity to catch up on their sleep.

Dynamic preaching requires physical strength and stamina. When the preacher's body goes out of shape, it will invariably affect the quality of his speaking.

We may fiercely resist the appropriateness of it, but it is difficult to gainsay the evidence that the preacher's physical appearance contributes mightily to his credibility. We are prone to dismiss such external considerations, seeking refuge in our certainty that ultimately our effectiveness rests in the power of the Holy Spirit. Yet our doctrine of providence declares that God uses means to accomplish His ultimate ends, and attention to externals is included among our God-given responsibilities. The preacher is a communicator and must be aware that he communicates with more than his mouth.

Communication is both verbal and nonverbal. For centuries preachers have been aware of the importance of gestures and stance to accent a point of their message. We have known that the externals of liturgy are capable of either enhancing or detracting from worship. We must be careful to avoid externalism and equally careful to avoid the error of neglecting the externals altogether.

A critical factor of external nonverbal communication involves the minister's physical appearance. We may argue vociferously that physical appearance should have absolutely no bearing on our credibility, but our arguments will do little to change the hard truth of the matter. We may protest that we ought not to be judged by outward appearances and decry the injustice of it, but the fact remains that we are so judged.

There are certain things about nonverbal communication that I wish my mother had taught me. My seminary curriculum did not include the sociological dynamics of how we dress. The Word of God can be preached, I believe, in a toga or a three-piece suit. The clerical robe can make us all equal, sidestepping prejudicial reactions engendered by civilian dress.

Recent studies have indicated via empirical methods of inductive research that dress patterns speak loudly, indeed scream nonverbal messages to people. These messages are clearly perceived and affect, at times dramatically, how our words are received.

Clothes have become far more than a means of shelter from the elements; they have become an art form, wielding the power of symbolic communication. Each of us dresses according to a particular style. We choose that style consciously or unconsciously, not so much for economic reasons as for aesthetic ones. We are attracted to clothes that we believe will express something about our inner personalities. The external is designed to express what we perceive or want others to perceive. In a word, we choose our dress patterns to project an image.

Often we project images of ourselves that contradict who we are. We give false messages nonverbally. These false messages confuse the hearers and frequently alienate them. How we dress may lead us into subtle forms of hypocrisy, which evoke resentment from those intuitive enough to penetrate the facade. We can dress ourselves down, demeaning our own dignity as we surrender to the negative caricature about ministers that the culture imposes upon us. Most of us, trying to be somewhat spiritually minded, or theologically preoccupied, never give much thought to the matter at all. We buy impulsively or strive to please the tastes of those closest to us and slip into a cavalier mode about the whole matter. We will pay rigorous attention to the details of the decor of the church and the nuances of the liturgy and utterly neglect the decor of the chief spokesman.

I said earlier that the gospel can be effectively preached in a toga or a three-piece suit. However, a three-piece suit may have cost St. Peter some credibility in Rome in the first century. We can verify this partially by appearing in the pulpit on Sunday morning in a toga.

The matter of nonverbal communication via clothing is made complex by regional and sub-cultural prejudice. A Presbyterian minister may wear cowboy boots in the pulpit in Phoenix, but not in Boston. A ministry to bankers may be enhanced by a starched collar, but not a ministry to college students. Our society is divided into micro sub-cultures, the lines of which are expressed by the subtle nuances of clothing styles.

The neophyte science of clothing engineering, as distinguished from clothing designing, has declared emphatically that all clothing patterns are a type of uniform. The policeman's uniform is as easy to distinguish as is that of the military officer or the football player. In these carefully defined micro-groups one can readily tell the players without a scorecard. Other uniforms also function in the culture with less clarity but real power of communication. There is a stereotype of the motorcycle gang member, the used-car salesman, the banker, and the physician. These stereotypes are reinforced daily in a multitude of ways. The cartoon exercise I noted earlier is one way in which a negative stereotype of the minister is so enforced.

A minister is called to be a leader. His is a position of leadership and authority, as well as one of servanthood. His is a holy office, an office of great but quiet dignity. God went to elaborate measures to detail the design of the priestly garments of the Old Testament, with clear awareness of the symbolic significance of the details. The clothing of the priest was neither garishly ostentatious nor salvaged from the missionary barrel. Our Lord's only worldly possession was a robe—a garment of exquisite taste and dignity—capable of versatility and beautiful, but not "loud." His robe fit His office as well as His body. He did not dress in the uniform of the used-chariot salesman.

There is a uniform of leadership in our society. Few clergymen are aware of its dimensions. The leadership uniform of our culture is dignified, quiet, versatile, and economic. It is easy to learn and provides a basis for a planned wardrobe that is economically sound. Those who are aware of it recognize it instantly in others. Those not consciously aware of it respond to it instantly by intuition.

While teaching a graduate course in seminary to eighteen ministers, I performed a simple experiment. At the beginning of the course, before the men had the opportunity to get to know each other or form opinions of each one's talents and gifts, I posed a hypothetical situation in which the seminary had submitted a proposal to a large charitable foundation for a grant of two hundred thousand dollars. The seminary wanted this class to select three of its members to visit the board of the foundation to make a presentation of the seminary's request. I then asked the class to select by secret ballot three of their members to present the proposal.

Before the vote was taken I wrote the names of three class members on a piece of paper and concealed it from their view. When the balloting was over, I dramatically produced the three names I had written and astonished the class by showing my list matched exactly the three men who had just been elected. The response of the class was one of wonder: "How did you know?" I felt like a magician who had pulled a rabbit out of his hat. But it was not magic; it was not done by mirrors. All I did was choose the three men in the room who were dressed in the uniform of leadership. Before I revealed my "magic" method to the class, I bounced the question back to them: "Why did you select these three men?" They stammered a bit until the consensus emerged that they really had no idea why they voted the way they did. When I explained my procedure, they groaned at the simplicity of it and were suddenly open to a discussion on the impact of clothes on first impressions of credibility.

The point is not that clothes make the man. The point is that clothes are a part of the complex process of communication. Clothes affect both the speaker and the listener. The effect can intensify when we probe deeper to the dynamic of reciprocity of exchange between the speaker and hearer. When an individual listener or a congregation responds to us by positive signals ranging from warm applause to the tilting of an eyebrow, our confidence is increased and our freedom of expression is enhanced.

The wise preacher considers the message of his clothes when he speaks. He must avoid the hypocrisy of sending a false message, as well as avoiding those forms of dress which are offensive to the hearts of recalcitrant sinners. It is not our call to *add* to the offense by placing unnecessary barriers to communication before our hearers.

Finally we must be conscious that every article of clothing we wear communicates a nonverbal message. The preacher can gain ground in his communication by carefully answering two questions: What do his clothes communicate? What does he want his clothes to communicate? If the answers to these questions are not the same, then change is in order. (For further discussion of the preacher's physical appearance, see "The Body in the Pulpit" by Gwyn Walters, in the present volume).

Preaching to the Whole Man

Emotionalism is anathema to the Reformed preacher. A cursory reading of Jonathan Edwards's critique of Enthusiasm with a capital "E," which broke out during the Great Awakening is evidence of this. Emotionalism stresses feeling without thought, passion without content as the head is bypassed by the heart. The opposite extreme, frequently manifested as an over-reaction to emotionalism, is intellectualism—an arid, reified stress on knowledge without love and thought without feeling. Intellectualism lives in Kierkegaard's comment on the nineteenth century European culture: "My complaint is not that the age is wicked. Rather that it is paltry, it lacks passion."

One need not embrace existentialism to gain passion. One cannot embrace Christianity without passion. A passionless faith is a dead faith, which justifies no one. Christianity is built on a balance of the mind and the heart, a correlation of passion and understanding. There is, in Christianity, a primacy of the intellect. There is in Christianity, a primacy of the heart. How can there be two primacies at the same time? Is this not a contradiction, or at best a dabbling in dialectics? God forbid. A contradiction would be present if we spoke of two primacies at the same time *and* in the same relation. What we have is a bona fide paradox whose tension can be resolved by close scrutiny. There are two primacies, but not in the same relation. There is a primacy of the intellect with respect to order and a primacy of the heart with respect to importance.

Understanding can never be in the heart without first being in the head. The channel to the heart is via the head. It is possible to have something in the head that never passes through the channel to the heart. It is possible to have a cognitive knowledge of God, an intellectual awareness, which does not issue in love. Satan knows there is a God; the demons recognized the sure identity of Jesus—but they hated Him. Thus one can have knowledge in the head with no affection in the heart.

The primacy of the heart emphasizes that the heart's response to God is the sine qua non of salvation. The great commandment is to love the Lord God with all the heart, mind, and strength. The disposition of the soul is the essence of justifying faith. One may make errors of reason in the totality of theology and still be redeemed. But if one's theology is impeccable while the heart is "far from Him," redemption is absent. There is a vital connection between head and heart that must be maintained. The heart does not beat in a vacuum. We will consider the intellectual primacy later, but now we focus on the emotional dimension of faith and preaching.

Preaching calls forth an emotional response. It is not merely an exercise in the transfer of information. The pulpit is the setting for *drama*. The gospel itself is dramatic. We are not speaking of the sense of drama as a contrived performance or as a make-believe world of play-acting. We are speaking of dramatic truth, truth that shatters the soul, then brings healing and sends the human spirit soaring. It must grieve the Holy Ghost when His dramatic Word is recited dispassionately. The preacher doesn't make the gospel dramatic—it already is. To communicate the gospel dramatically is to fit preaching with the content. Dispassionate preaching is a lie—it denies the content it conveys.

I urge students, when they read a biblical text, to look for the drama. Accent the emotive words from the text. Highlight the passion. For example, read the text below:

I am a debtor both to the Greeks and the Barbarians; both to the wise, and to the unwise (Rom. 1:14).

Where is the drama? What words should be accented in the reading of the text? Are there any emotive words in this verse?

The word that jumps off the page with drama is the word *debtor*. Does anyone feel the pressure of debt dispassionately? Think of human emotional reactions to the experience of debt.

There is a feeling of rushing weight that bears upon the soul. Paul uses an emotion-laden word here. He doesn't merely indicate that Greeks and Barbarians are included in his mission or even that he is concerned about them. He has a debt to pay. His obligation is intensified to the level of the debtor.

A rule of reading may also be illustrated by the text. When key words are set in contrast to each other, they should be accented. The reading of this text would go like this:

> I am a *debtor* both to the Greeks, and to the Barbarians; both to the *wise* and the *unwise*.

Drama in delivery is communicated by facial expression, bodily gestures, voice inflections, and above all the classic pattern of *pause, punch, pause.* Timing is crucial to drama. To read the words with even spaces of time between them is to kill the drama. The word *debtor* must be set off with the timed *pause, punch, pause.*

Drama is enhanced by vivacity of language. Jonathan Edwards apparently read his sermons from a manuscript in a monotone (often the death blow to dramatic preaching); yet people passed out under the dramatic weight of his preaching. Some attribute that exclusively to the sheer penetrating power of truth or the special attendance of the Holy Spirit on Edwards's preaching. There might well have been an added human factor involved.

Samuel Logan explores Edwards's understanding of the "affections" in the chapter "The Phenomenology of Preaching." Edwards was intimately familiar with the philosophical insights crossing the Atlantic from the pens of the British empiricists. Locke, Berkeley, and Hume concentrated their philosophical energy on questions of epistemology. They were concerned not only with the major question of how truth can be known, but with specific questions about how ideas are formed and retained in the mind. Hume's writings on memory images remain a classic. Edwards understood the link between memory retention and vivacity of mental images. The more vivid the picture, the stronger the mental sensation, the more powerful the affections raised, and the longer the memory retention. Consider the following methods of communication:

> The supreme being is given to a proclivity of indignation in the general direction of fallen humanity.

Or,

> Sinners in the hands of an angry God.

Does Edwards provide an abstract delineation of the peril of the unrepentant or does he strike at the heart with vivid imagery?

> O sinner, you hang over the pit of hell by a slender thread, like a spider over a burning fire; the flames of divine wrath thrashing about it ready to singe it at any moment and drop you in the pit.

Or,

> God's bow is bent, His arrow is aimed at your heart.

The accent is on nouns and verbs—on concrete images, the stuff of which drama is made. Edwards clearly knew how to preach.

Or hear Luther castigate the pseudo-intellectualism of fallen reason uninformed by faith. What does he say about reason? Does he speak of the inadequacies of abstract ratiocination or of "Frau Hulda, that whore, reason; the most evil mistress of the devil!"?

Vivid imagery is not necessarily flowery with a maudlin preoccupation with lyrical ornamentation. A sermon is not a poem. Twittering birds and scented lilacs are not what I'm talking about. The goal is not beauty, but drama, that the inherent drama of the gospel be not obscured. The drama need not be embellished to pierce the heart. Accented, yes. Contrived, no. Ignored, never. And Jay Adams's chapter, "Sense Appeal and Storytelling" develops this notion much further.

Perhaps the greatest catalyst to dramatic preaching is the extemporaneous sermon. This style of preaching releases the preacher from the barriers to communication that stifle so many sermons. Free from a prepared manuscript the minister's body and mind enter fully into communication. I recently was approached by a young pastor who asked me to observe him preaching and give him a thorough critique at the conclusion. Complying with his request, I both listened to and watched his sermon. The content was excellent, but an obvious barrier to communication was blocking the sermon from the congregation. Using a full length manuscript as a prop the minister broke eye contact with the congregation exactly 127 times during the sermon. (I counted.) The most obvious moments of rapt attention from the congregation came when the pastor related a painful personal experience to illustrate a point. Coincidentally the rehearsal of the personal narrative also marked the longest period of time in which the preacher maintained eye contact with his people.

After the service of worship the pastor asked for the results of my observation. I asked him, "How many times did you break eye contact with the congregation?" He thought for a moment and replied, "I guess about ten times." When I told him I counted 127 times he was aghast. More important, he was ready to listen to suggested changes. When I suggested he move toward extemporaneous preaching he was both terrified and confused. It meant preaching without the security blanket of the manuscript and conveyed the notion of poor preaching.

Extemporaneous preaching is not the same thing as "winging it" or "speaking off the cuff." Technically the meaning of the word, derived from the Latin *ex tempore,* carries either the notion of speaking "on the spur of the moment" or "as the occasion demands." I'm not speaking now about spur-of-the-moment preaching but "as the occasion demands" preaching. Effective extemporaneous preaching combines two elements: serious preparation and free-style delivery. It requires two vital factors: knowledge and facility of vocabulary or verbal skills.

It was Robert J. Lamont, successor to Clarence MacCartney as senior minister of the historic First Presbyterian Church in Pittsburgh, who taught me the rudiments of preparation for extemporaneous preaching. Lamont's system was to "plan" his next sermon the moment his last one was finished. He immersed himself in the upcoming subject, focusing his thoughts on it all week. In the interim he gave himself to serious research on his subject. He would do in-depth exegesis of the biblical passage for his sermon, checking the best commentaries to insure accurate understanding of his subject. His intellectual goal was to increase his knowledge of his subject. After the homework of research was finished he would construct a rough and brief outline of what he wanted to cover. Usually the outline was fixed in his head and sometimes put on paper if such a prop were needed. Illustrations came from the process of thought immersion and reading around his subject. As the moment of preaching drew near, he would fix in his mind the starting point, the conclusion, and the key points he wanted to include; then he trusted his mind and his verbal skills to add the flesh to the skeleton.

The free-style delivery flowed from the bedrock of his understanding of his subject, his personality, and his verbal skills. This method avoids writing out a manuscript or verbatim memorization of the sermon. The delivery comes "out of the moment" (*ex tempore*), but it builds upon hours of content preparation.

The spoken word differs clearly from the written word. The danger of prepared manuscripts is that few pastors can write in a spoken style. What works in writing almost never works in speech. The forms of communication are different. Preaching is a speaking skill, not a literary one. Memorization is also a barrier to effective communication as it squelches the dynamic of spontaneous communication and inclines toward the mechanical. Some things require memorization, but not public speaking. In part, perhaps (a quote or cited passage); in whole, however, the route of memorization is deadly.

Of course, it is virtually impossible to communicate to another person what one doesn't first understand himself. But understanding (which we will consider later) is only half the recipe for communication. Passion must be added to understanding for the magic of communication to take place. To simplify, *all* that is really needed for communication is an understanding of your subject and a desire to communicate it. If a person knows what he is talking about and *cares* what he is talking about, he will find a way to get his message across. If he is bored by his own subject, so will his congregation be. Understanding plus dramatic, effective, and, as Edwards would say, affective passion is the oldest and simplest formula for communication.

What about verbal skills? What about facility of vocabulary? Are these not vital skill factors? By all means. Facility of language is vital to enhance and enrich preaching. They sharpen one's ability to prick the mind and the heart. They are not absolutely necessary to communication, but they add substantially to the depth dimension of it. Preachers with weak vocabularies can communicate. Who hasn't been captivated by a passionate testimony of an unlettered, inarticulate speaker whose heart is so inflamed that his message gets through?

Dramatic preaching, over the long haul, however, must be fed by nutritional language. One danger of extemporaneous preaching is dull communication via falling back on repetitive patterns of speech—the hackneyed cliche, the empty platitudes, the same figures of speech over and over again. Christian "jargon" can flood into the bare outlines of the extemporaneous speaker, leaving his hearers' senses dulled by over-repetition. Variety of speech is as much a spice in preaching as it is in other areas of life. We are to add relish to our speech, lest our bland vocabularies inflict malnutrition upon our hearers. And we are to remember that it is the whole man whom we seek to nourish in our preaching.

The building of vocabulary is thus essential for the extemporaneous speaker (and even more for the nonextemporaneous speaker, as we have already seen in the case of Jonathan Edwards). Improvisation requires a prior mastery of technique. Freedom without focus is chaos. The free style of the extemporaneous delivery flows out of the prior mastery of linguistic technique, and there are no substitutes for mastery of this technique.

I enjoy two avocational hobbies that scream at me of the importance of technique. I play the piano and I play golf. My dream for piano playing, particularly in the mode of jazz, is to be able to experience the free-flowing art of improvisation. We have heard the exciting sounds emanating from the instruments of artists who depart suddenly from the melody line and venture all over the keyboard with fresh and imaginative patterns, and then come back home with sweet and harmonious resolution. How do musicians do that? How do their free-flowing departures end in harmony rather than cacophony? They are certainly not winging it. They are calling upon years of practice, practice, practice of tedious scales and runs, and mastery of harmonic relation to exercise the freedom of spontaneous and "impromptu" improvisation. An unskilled amateur or a free-playing baboon simply cannot do that. One can achieve mastery of technique and never capture the spirit of improvisation, but one can never capture the spirit of improvisation without first mastering technique.

Or consider golf. No essay of mine would be complete without incorporating at least one illustration from this sport created by devils and inspired by demons to torment the aspirations of frustrated athletes. I read the monthly articles published in *Golf* and *Golf Digest* searching with the lamp of Diogenes for the elusive "secret." Again and again the masters of the golf tour are asked the same question: "What do you think about while you are executing your golf shot?" The answers are monotonous. They all say the same thing. They focus their attention on their target. They visualize in the mind how they want the ball to fly and then just "go with the flow." They just call upon their bodies to make it happen. Their minds are not cluttered with a host of swing keys like keep the left arm straight, open the left hip coming through, or a myriad of other mechanical rules that invariably produce the malady of paralysis by analysis. When I look at the target and tell my body to hit the ball there, my body protests. It yells, "I don't know how." If I go with the flow, the flow takes me into the woods or the sand trap. What I lack is the prior mastery of technique that is so inbred it can be instantly recalled *ex tempore* by what golfers call muscle memory. My muscles suffer from a severe case of memory lapse because the techniques have never been mastered at the practice range. Freedom follows form. The preacher must master the forms to enhance the freedom of extemporaneous preaching so that the full impact of drama and emotion can take place.

The Intellectual Aspect of Preaching

We have earlier mentioned the primacy of the intellect in the Christian life and the vital importance of understanding the content we are seeking to communicate. Sound preaching incorporates the intellectual dimension at various levels. In sound preaching there must be a premium on accuracy. A negative value is attached to dramatic, dynamic, moving speaking if the content communicated is not true. May all preachers of falsehood be dull ones. Such a wish is fantasy indeed. Hitler could communicate. Satan is persuasive. Castro is dynamic. What does it profit the preacher if his skills are great and his content false? It profits him greatly in a society willing to pay for entertainment, but he faces the spectre of a future wearing a millstone around his neck, a garland placed there by an angry God.

God has chosen preaching as a means to save the world. The same God takes a dim view of false preaching. It is truth that liberates—it is in the truth of the gospel that its power is invested.

Jeremiah was frustrated by people's preference of exciting false prophets who told the people what their itching ears wanted to hear. Jeremiah was ready to turn in his prophet's card as he complained loudly to God,

> O Lord, thou has deceived me, and I was deceived; thou art stronger than I, and hast prevailed: I am in derision daily, everyone mocketh me. For since I spake, I cried out, I cried violence and spoil; because the word of the Lord was made a reproach unto me, and a derision, daily.
>
> Then I said, I will not make mention of him, nor speak anymore in his name. But his word was in my heart as a burning fire shut up in my bones, and I was weary with forebearing, and I could not stay (Jer. 20:7-9).

Even under the inspiration of the Holy Ghost, Jeremiah was given to redundancy. His economy of language was suspect. He wasted words. Why bother to add the words "and I was deceived" after saying, "O Lord, thou has deceived me"? It goes without saying. Or why call attention to the superiority of God's strength, which is obvious to anyone? Perhaps it is because redundancy is the stuff laments are made of. Jeremiah's pain for speaking the truth is so intense that he wants to make doubly sure God understands his cry. Here the Spirit indulges the prophet, not for God's sake, but for Jeremiah's.

God was acutely aware of the destructive influence of the false prophets. He did not need to be informed of the situation by Jeremiah. His reply to Jeremiah is succinct:

> I have heard what the prophets said, that prophecy lies in my name, saying I have dreamed, I have dreamed . . . yea, they are prophets of the deceit of their own heart; which think to cause my people to forget my name by their dreams. . . . The prophet that hath a dream, let him tell a dream; and he that hath my word, let him speak my word faithfully. What is the chaff to the wheat? (Jer. 23:25-28).

The preacher's responsibility is to be faithful. Fidelity, however, depends upon accuracy. The heart can be willing and the head weak. We may desire to preach the truth, but err in our understanding of what the truth is. Conversely there are false prophets who speak the truth "accidentally." Sincerity is a virtue, but not a substitute for truth. It is possible for us to be sincerely wrong and to sincerely mislead our people.

Accuracy is not so much a gift as it is a fruit. It takes painstaking labor to produce it. Here the pastor's mind must be busily engaged in study for his sermon preparations. Accuracy is a sober and terrifying responsibility. If we are not willing to pay the price of the discipline necessary to achieve it, we would be better to close our mouths and desist from preaching.

The anxiety of public speaking is usually felt at the level of concern we feel for people's responses to *us*. It is, of course, God's response that matters ultimately. The pulpit is a place where the fear of God must be paramount. I once asked a preacher if he was intimidated by the presence of a national celebrity in his congregation. He said, "No, why should I be? I speak in front of God every Sunday morning." The sentiment may be simplistic, but it is devastatingly true. If we were to take seriously the attendance of God at our services, our passion for accuracy in truth would surely be augmented.

Accuracy is related to both knowledge and understanding. Again, it is possible to have knowledge without understanding, but we cannot have understanding without knowledge. The goal that the wisdom literature of the Old Testament commends is *understanding*. "Wisdom is the principal thing; therefore get wisdom: and with all thy getting get understanding" (Prov. 4:7).

Understanding is, of course, crucial to teaching, as well as preaching. Every college student is aware of the professor who consistently lectures over the heads of the students. The professor is usually considered to be so brilliant that he simply cannot find a way to condescend to the level of his students. There are many possible reasons why a communication gap exists between the student and such a professor. The professor may simply overestimate the abilities of his students. He may be conscious of avoiding the error of underestimating them and committing the sin of talking down to them, and so he overcompensates. One possible reason, however, is not often considered. The professor may be a fraud. He may not understand his material himself and disguises the fact by conveying an unintelligible mass of technicalia. It is also possible that the professor has memorized or copied technical data he encountered in graduate school and is merely transferring it whole to his students without taking the time for necessary explanations. He is *transferring* information, not translating it. In effect the teacher is an errand boy, not a teacher—simply because he is not teaching.

If the teacher truly understands his own material, he ought to be able to communicate it to a five-year-old child. He may have to take longer to do it, and will certainly have to simplify his message to get the job done. The essence of effective teaching is found in the ability to simplify without at the same time distorting. That requires understanding. The deeper the level of understanding, the easier it is to communicate simply. Simple communication, however, is not simplistic communication. There are simple preachers and simple teachers who justly deserve the epithet of simpletons. They keep it simple because they have no alternative. They are speaking at the highest level of their own understanding. Here distortion is rampant, as our Christian bookstores bear ugly testimony—much of the "simple teaching" that attracts the public for its very simplicity is both simple and harmfully simplistic. Great teachers and great preachers are like icebergs. They only show on the surface about ten percent of what is actually there in substance. Understanding in depth promotes clarity, which is vital to communication.

Because good biblical preaching must be *from* the whole man *to* the whole man, understanding is crucial to the hearer as well. We are all students as well as teachers and preachers. Our own preparations must include the drive for understanding—remembering that we cannot teach what we don't first learn ourselves. The importance of the priority of understanding was impressed upon me as an undergraduate student in philosophy. It was apparent that many bright and intelligent students were stumbling hopelessly when they encountered courses in the abstract realm of philosophy. Often the problem was more one of method than of brains. I developed a method early on for preparing for essay examinations in philosophy. For example, if I were faced with an exam on Descartes I would ask myself several questions. What problem is Descartes trying to solve? What are his chief concerns? What is his starting point? What is his conclusion? What are the key points of transition from start to conclusion? Then the big question: Do I understand what he is saying?

I would restrict my memorizing to (1) the starting point, (2) the conclusion, and (3) a few *key* points of transition along the way. The bulk of my study focused, then, not on memory work, but on understanding. If I could understand Descartes and memorize a few key pegs, essay exams on him were easy. The system worked well until I encountered a few philosophers who plied their trade like the aforementioned professor, by giving verbal expression to their own confusion.

The art of clarification is polished by the use of illustration as, again, Jay Adams points out later in this volume. Businessmen tell me there are only three significant factors that determine the value of real estate. The first is location. The second is location. The third is location. Location, location, location. The same may be said for clear communication: illustrate, illustrate, illustrate. No teacher ever had a greater in-depth knowledge of his subject than Jesus. No one was ever a better illustrator.

Debates are fueled over the sources we use for illustration. Some contend that we ought never use personal illustrations as it calls undue attention to the speaker. Others argue that only biblical examples are appropriate for illustrative material. For better or worse, the research indicates that personal experiences pique the interest of listeners more than any other type of illustration. The theory is that no one has greater credibility about a matter than the person who experiences it. Jesus drew illustrative material from the Old Testament, but went beyond Scripture to employ examples from all of life.

A reservoir of illustrations helps the speaker to be a Renaissance man of sorts. He is called to speak to the butcher, baker, and candlestick maker. Such a task is made less formidable when one knows something about knives, flour, and tallow. The idea of a diversified field of knowledge was not invented by Erasmus or other Renaissance thinkers. Augustine, centuries earlier, admonished the Christian to learn as much as possible about as many things as possible. The broader the knowledge the deeper the reservoir of illustration.

The Spiritual Aspect of Preaching

Though others will plumb the greater depths of the spiritual dimension of preaching in this volume, we cannot speak of the whole man in preaching without considering the spiritual aspect. Preaching is far more than an art or a science—it is a spiritual exercise, a holy vocation. We recall at once St. Paul's declaration "And my speech and my preaching was not with enticing words of man's wisdom, but in demonstration of the Spirit and of power . . ." (I Cor. 2:4).

A close link between the preacher and the Holy Spirit must be maintained for effective preaching. The Spirit is the energizer, the dynamite (*dunamis*) of powerful preaching. We need the unction, the anointing of the Spirit, lest our words, eloquent or otherwise, bounce off recalcitrant hearts and evaporate. Ours is a commitment to word (*verbum*) and spirit (*spiritus*). The spirit comes through the word (*per verbum*) and with the word (*cum verbo*), but not apart from or without the word (*sine verbo*). The balance of word and spirit is ours to maintain.

It is a glorious sensation to feel the Spirit moving while we are preaching. It is exhilarating. I once preached for a graduate student who was also the bishop of a black urban church. The following day in class one of the other students asked the bishop, "How did the prof do preaching in your church?" The bishop replied, "Well, the prof got to preaching and the folks got to shouting, and then the Ghost came by."

I've never heard it stated more eloquently. When the Ghost comes by it transports our soul to the rim of ecstasy. But danger lurks here. A special caveat must be maintained lest we become sensuous preachers, depending on our own feelings to determine the presence of the Spirit of God. We are not called to preach simply when we feel like it; nor are our feelings the litmus test of the real presence. I was once called upon to preach at a communion service in a time of crisis for a Presbyterian congregation. Their beloved pastor of many years was lying in a hospital bed across the street, in critical condition, fighting for his life. I desperately wanted to bring a stirring message of comfort and hope to the frightened people. I yearned for the fullness of God's Spirit to fall upon the congregation. All week I wrestled and agonized in prayer pleading with God for that service. When the moment came I suddenly felt empty, totally void of the Spirit of God. I experienced that dreadful sensation of the awful absence of God. I was sure God had abandoned me, leaving me to fight through the dark night of the soul. My words sounded hollow in my own ears, and when the service ended and I walked to the door to greet the congregation, I had a fierce impulse to flee in embarrassment. Then, to my utter consternation, one member after another filed out, with serious expressions of wonder on their faces. They squeezed my hand and said, "We were overwhelmed by a sense of the presence of God. It was so thick it seems we could cut it with a knife." I listened dumbfounded to the litany of similar statements and was finally left standing alone at the door thinking like Jacob, "Surely God is in this place; and I knew it not" (Gen. 28:16).

We may, nay, we must assume the Spirit's presence when we preach. Yet we must not presume it. We must not cross the line from confidence to arrogance. Like the priests of antiquity we are called upon to weep between the porch and the altar (Joel 2:17).

Finally, the whole preacher must live his whole life *coram deo*. He must study, practice, dress, labor, speak, in the presence of God. All our preaching and teaching is done before His face, under His sovereign authority, and to His majestic glory. It is the Spirit who sings first *Soli Deo Gloria*.

PART TWO
THE MESSAGE

5

The Phenomenology of Preaching
Samuel T. Logan, Jr.

As one preacher put it, "If you aim at nothing, you'll hit it every time." Among the necessities of good, revived preaching (or, indeed, any other worthwhile endeavor), this must be at the top of the list—good planning. One must know what he wishes to accomplish and must plan all he does with this in mind; otherwise he will accomplish nothing. What one hits depends upon the care, the precision with which one aims.

Most good preachers consciously recognize the value of precise aiming in terms of the overall content of their sermons. They know that it is easy to try to do too much on one Sunday morning, that "congregational overload" constitutes a real danger, especially for a preacher whose orthodoxy is unquestioned and whose preparatory study has been thorough. Such preachers also realize that congregational overload is not necessarily a function of the *length* of the sermon, that it is more a function of the internal diversity of the sermon. A great sermon may very well be quite long (of course, what constitutes a "long" sermon varies from context to context, but in any context, it surely is possible to preach what would be regarded as a long sermon by one's congregation). But a sermon, to be great, to be effective, whether it is long or short, must be *focused*. It must not seek to do more than that particular congregation, regarded in the aggregate, can assimilate and act upon on that specific occasion. The aim must be precise and good preachers recognize this, often instinctively. (Both Glen Knecht and Sinclair Ferguson, elsewhere in this volume, deal with this matter of organizational unity in preaching.)

But few preachers seem to have taken the time to consider carefully the aims of their sermons vis-a-vis the primary medium used in the sermon, human language.[1] What precisely does the preacher want or expect the words he is using to accomplish? What can words accomplish anyhow? How does language work? The seemingly obvious choices available to the preacher are reflected in two major types of preaching to be heard in churches today—that which stores the heads of the congregation with doctrinally orthodox biblical understanding, and that which stirs the hearts of the congregation to works of evangelical obedience. Most would agree that truly biblical preaching does both, and most would probably also agree that these two must be maintained in a kind of symbiotic relationship for both heads and hearts to be ministered to appropriately. But why is this the case and how does it actually work? At what should the preacher aim in terms of the language he uses in the pulpit? What exactly should he seek his words to accomplish? This is the subject of the present chapter.

Before proceeding further, however, one obvious caveat must be stated clearly. The Holy Spirit, not the preacher, makes any given sermon effective, successful, even great. Such a statement may seem unnecessary, but it never can be. We can never hear too often of our total dependence on the gracious work of our sovereign God; we can never be reminded too frequently that the glory is His, the kingdom is His, and the work is His. Jonathan Edwards's thoroughly biblical warnings confront the preacher starkly: any externally good action may actually be undertaken for the glory of man rather than for the glory of God, and when it is,

---

1. Two other chapters in this volume are particularly relevant here. Gwyn Walters's chapter, "The Body in the Pulpit," reminds us that the words the preacher speaks are not the only ingredients in the total presentation that he makes. Jay Adams's chapter, "Sense Appeal and Storytelling," describes the type of language that can, as he puts it, transform an apathetic group of parishioners into an alert, interested congregation. The present chapter tries to put Adams's specific comments into a broader context. What, for example will be accomplished theologically by such a transformation as Adams describes?

it merits judgment rather than blessing.[2] Great preaching—either in prospect or in retrospect—may thus be more dangerous to the preacher than mediocre preaching because it poses more of a temptation to "worship the creature rather than the Creator." Warnings about this danger are not, therefore, unnecessary. The better the preacher becomes, the more relevant such warnings become.

This warning is not meant, however, to negate the biblical requirement that the preacher do the very best job he can. Paul's statement that God saves through the foolishness of preaching (I Cor. 1:21) does not legitimatize sloppiness or lack of preparation. Paul is talking in that context about the Corinthians' tendency to adopt secular values as their own, and he warns that the "world" and its wisdom are far from the kingdom of Jesus Christ. They are so far apart, in fact, that what seems wise in one appears foolishness in the other. But the fact that the preaching God uses to save those who believe appears foolish to the world no more legitimatizes homiletical sloppiness than the sovereignty of God legitimatizes ethical antinomianism. The Spirit does move where He chooses (John 3:8), but we are required to use every gift, every ability God has given us, as fully as we can. As Jesus chastised the servant who hid his talents out of ostensible reverential fear of his lord (Matt. 25), so the preacher who goes about his task carelessly will receive condemnation rather than commendation from his Lord. It is God's work, but in that work the preacher must be a faithful steward. Thus he must consider carefully the nature and function of the words he preaches.

1. The Historical Context

Twentieth-century discussions of the nature and function of language may be categorized in a variety of ways. One of the more

2. Jonathan Edwards, A Dissertation Concerning the Nature of True Virtue, in The Works of Jonathan Edwards, vol. 1 (Edinburgh: Banner of Truth, 1974), chap. 4.

helpful, perhaps, is suggested indirectly by Henri Bergson in *An Introduction to Metaphysics*. In that brief monograph, Bergson seeks to differentiate between two types of knowledge, the analytic and the intuitive.[3] In analytic knowledge, the intellect approaches the item to be interpreted from an external point of view, uses symbols to express its abstract, conceptual findings, and thereby, says Bergson, yields knowledge that is static and relative. Intuitive knowledge, on the other hand, "enters into" the reality being studied and identifies with it by a sort of intellectual sympathy, thus providing knowledge that is perfect and absolute.[4]

Bergson's concerns are clearly epistemological (and his evaluations simplistic), but his categorizations may be helpful in dealing with recent varieties of linguistic theory. Corresponding to Bergson's analytic type of knowledge are those approaches to language which value precision, accuracy, and objectivity most highly. An earlier (and extreme) example of this approach to language was logical positivism/linguistic analysis, largely an Anglo-American phenomenon in which the criterion for the meaningfulness of any specific use of words was the principle of verifiability. A. J. Ayer, in *Language, Truth, and Logic*, explains that principle as follows:

> The criterion which we use to test the genuineness of apparent statements of fact is the criterion of verifiability. We say that a sentence is factually significant to any given person, if, and only if, he knows how to verify the proposition which it purports to express—that is, if he knows what observations would lead him, under certain conditions, to accept the proposition as being true, or reject it as being false. If, on the other hand, the putative proposition is of such a character

3. Henri Bergson, *An Introduction to Metaphysics*, trans. T. E. Hulme (Indianapolis: Bobbs-Merrill, 1949), p. 21. For a more recent version of this (actually ancient) dichotomy, see James Barr, *The Bible in the Modern World* (London: SCM, 1973), p. 55.

4. Bergson, *Introduction to Metaphysics*, pp. 10–11.

that the assumption of its truth, or falsehood, is consistent with any assumption whatsoever concerning the nature of his future experience, then, as far as he is concerned, it is, if not a tautology, a mere pseudo-proposition. The sentence expressing it may be emotionally significant to him; but it is not literally significant.[5]

Language, Truth and Logic was originally published in 1935, and in the following decades, the "uncompromising" positivism (Ayer's own later characterization of his earlier work) was gradually modified. Among the modifications introduced was a substitution of the principle of falsifiability for the principle of verifiability. Antony Flew provided an excellent summary of what was involved in the newer approach:

> Let us begin with a parable. It is a parable developed from a tale told by John Wisdom in his haunting and revelatory article "Gods." Once upon a time two explorers came upon a clearing in the jungle. In the clearing were growing many flowers and many weeds. One explorer says, "Some gardener must tend this plot." The other disagrees, "There is no gardener." So they pitch their tents and set a watch. No gardener is ever seen. "But perhaps he is an invisible gardener." So they set up a barbed-wire fence. They electrify it. They patrol with bloodhounds. (For they remember how H. G. Wells's *The Invisible Man* could be both smelt and touched though he could not be seen.) But no shrieks ever suggest that some intruder has received a shock. No movements of the wire ever betray an invisible climber. The bloodhounds never give a cry. Yet still the Believer is not convinced. "But there is a gardener, invisible, intangible, insensible to electric shocks, a gardener who has no scent and makes no sound, a gardener who comes secretly to look after the garden which he loves." At last the Sceptic despairs, "But what remains of your original assertion? Just how does what you call an in-

5. A. J. Ayer, *Language, Truth and Logic*, 2nd ed. (New York: Dover, 1952), p. 35.

visible, intangible, eternally elusive gardener differ from an imaginary gardener or even from no gardener at all?"[6]

Flew then discussed the specific implications of Wisdom's parable:

> Now to assert that such and such is the case is necessarily equivalent to denying that such and such is not the case. Suppose then that we are in doubt as to what someone who gives vent to an utterance is asserting, or suppose that, more radically, we are sceptical as to whether he is really asserting anything at all, one way of trying to understand (or perhaps it will be to expose) his utterance is to attempt to find what he would regard as counting against, or as being incompatible with, its truth. . . . And if there is nothing which a putative assertion denies then there is nothing which it asserts either: and so it is not really an assertion.[7]

The meaningfulness of any given proposition or any linguistic construct is now seen to depend upon whether there are any specific conditions that would disprove what the proposition or construct is asserting. If such conditions cannot at least be imagined, then nothing meaningful is being said, no knowledge is being communicated, and there is therefore no way to arrive at a certain interpretation of the language under consideration.

Flew's understanding of falsifiability has itself been criticized from within the positivistic movement, and this suggests the continuing diversity within the overall tradition.[8] Nevertheless, it is clear that the basic emphasis has remained much the same. Ayer's principle of verifiability may have given way to Wisdom's and Flew's principle of falsifiability, and later positivists may argue for other principles, but all are concerned to establish and maintain

6. Antony Flew, "Theology and Falsification: The University Discussion," in *New Essays in Philosophical Theology*, ed. Antony Flew and Alasdair MacIntyre (New York: MacMillan, 1955), p. 96.

7. Ibid., p. 98.

8. R. M. Hare and Basil Mitchell, "Theology and Falsification: The University Discussion," in *New Essays*, ed. Flew and MacIntyre, pp. 99–105.

linguistic precision and to eliminate all hermeneutical confusion. In order to achieve this, a number of interpretive or hermeneutical principles (verifiability and falsifiability) have been introduced to regulate linguistic usage and thereby, it has been hoped, to achieve the desired goal. Such principles have sharply restricted language by defining its major function in terms of its ability to convey scientifically correct conceptual information, and it has been largely this fundamental emphasis on clarity that has constituted positivism's contribution to the modern philosophical scene.

But what has this abstruse philosophy to do with the practicing preacher? Quite a bit, for it offers one way of understanding the role of the language he uses in the pulpit Sunday after Sunday. Leaving aside the question of the detailed validity of the positivists' own specific assertions,[9] their emphasis is clear—and clearly contrary to Bergson's concerns. The positivists argued that the conceptual precision of a linguistic formulation is the central criterion of its value. In other words, if what the preacher says is meaningful at all, it is so because and to the degree that it conveys analytic, objective information. Thus, from this perspective, the primary function of the preacher's language should be to communicate propositional (shall we say orthodox?) truth.

Positivism as a distinct philosophical movement has been superceded by numerous other approaches to language, some of which, while rejecting its unique perspectives (such as the principles of verifiability and falsifiability), have retained its overall emphasis on objective distance and conceptual precision. Structuralism, for instance, totally discards the principles of verifiability and falsifiability and focuses on context as the source of meaning— but still the primary concern is conceptual accuracy in both the use and the interpretation of language.

9. For a critique of the positivist position, see Frederick Ferré, *Language, Logic, and God* (New York: Harper and Row, 1961), pp. 42–57; Philip Wheelwright, *The Burning Fountain: A Study in the Language of Symbolism* (Bloomington: Indiana University Press, 1968), pp. 61 ff.; and Langdon Gilkey, *Naming the Whirlwind: The Renewal of God-Language* (Indianapolis: Bobbs-Merrill, 1969), pp. 305 ff.

Henri Bergson would dissent, as have many other theorists in the twentieth century. They would say to the preacher, "Your task is not to tell your congregation about God; it is to cause them to know God—directly, immediately, rather than through the distracting abstractions of propositional theology." Though his subject is ostensibly literary interpretation, Richard Palmer, as the summary of his work on *Hermeneutics,* offers these theses (among some twenty-seven others):

> 5. The hermeneutical experience is an event—a "language event." Literature is robbed of its true dynamism and power to speak when it is conceived of in the static categories of conceptual knowing. As experience of an event and not as mere conceptual knowing, the encounter with the being of a work is not static and ideational, outside of all time and temporality; it is truth that happens, emerges from conceal-ment, and yet eludes every effort to reduce it to concepts and objectivity. . . .
>
> 18. It is not the interpreter who grasps the meaning of the text: the meaning of the text seizes him. . . .
>
> 23. To understand a text is not simply to bombard it with questions but to understand the question it puts to the reader. It is to understand the question behind the text, the question that called the text into being. Literary interpreta-tion needs to develop the dynamics and art of hearing, of listening. It needs to develop an openness for creative nega-tivity, for learning something it could not anticipate or fore-see.[10]

Palmer's emphasis typifies another approach to language, one that differs radically from the positivistic. The existential-phe-nomenological perspective received its fullest expression in Eu-rope by such scholars as Ernst Fuchs and Gerhard Ebeling who led the movement known as "the new hermeneutic." Instead of linguistic precision, they valued linguistic dynamism; instead of propositional, scientific accuracy, they preferred life-changing ex-

10. Richard Palmer, *Hermeneutics* (Evanston: Northwestern University Press, 1969), pp. 243, 248, 250.

perience. Ebeling put it this way: "It is to my mind not unimportant for the proper grasp of the hermeneutical problem whether we set out from the idea that a verbal statement in itself is something obscure into which the light of understanding must be introduced from elsewhere, or whether, on the contrary, we set out from the fact that the situation in terms of which and into which the verbal statement is made is something obscure which is then illumined by the verbal statement."[11] As James Robinson explained, "In dealings with the text *its* being interpreted by us turns into *our* being interpreted by the text."[12] Fuchs dealt with this relationship by insisting that the interpreter is at the disposal of the text, and Funk brilliantly described the situation in terms of the Humpty Dumpty question as to who is to be the master, the text or the interpreter.[13] The answer for the new hermeneutic, of course, the text.

The thrust of the new hermeneutic was, then, the attempt to understand how language, first the language of the New Testament and then the preacher's language, functions to elucidate the situations of its hearers. In the first place, the active, confronting, phenomenological potential of language meant that the words of the New Testament existed, for the new hermeneutic, primarily as proclamation rather than as information. Fuchs and Ebeling were insistent upon this fact, especially in setting their position off from the orthodox identification of God's Word with Scripture.[14] The original proclamation, which was later written down in the pages of the New Testament, was an act of interpretation of the situation into which the proclamation was spoken, and only if it is seen as such can the New Testament be properly understood.

11. James M. Robinson, "Hermeneutic Since Barth," in *The New Hermeneutic,* ed. James M. Robinson and John B. Cobb, Jr. (New York: Harper and Row, 1964), p. 94.

12. Ibid., p. 68.

13. Ibid., pp. 132, 143. See also Robert W. Funk, *Language, Hermeneutic, and Word of God* (New York: Harper and Row, 1966), p. 38.

14. Robinson, *New Hermeneutic,* pp. 86–88. See also Palmer, *Hermeneutics,* pp. 14–20.

Fuchs dealt more explicitly with the precise nature of the word event that occurs in the New Testament. He based his analysis upon the claim that the "essential feature" of language is its temporal quality.[15] "What is distinctive about language," he argued, "is not the content of the individual words, not the thought or the designation, but rather its uses, its application, its concentration upon the time and thus upon the distinction of the times."[16] New Testament words, then, tell what it is time for, and specifically, they tell that it is time for "true obedience to God in a new situation and for this new situation."[17] This is the entirety of the New Testament proclamation summarized in one sentence, and with this understanding of the purpose, function, and value of the New Testament message, as well as of Jesus Himself, it is not at all difficult to comprehend Fuchs' claim that "faith does not believe directly in Jesus, but rather it believes in Jesus' preaching."[18]

My purpose as an interpreter or as a preacher, according to the new hermeneutic, is to let Jesus' preaching happen again, to let the New Testament words enter the present situation anew so as to announce once again what it is time for, and thereby to interpret the present situation. Ebeling describes this process quite clearly:

> Proclamation that has taken place is to become proclamation that takes place. This transition from text to sermon is a transition from Scripture to the spoken word. Thus the task described here consists in making what is written into spoken word or, as we can now also say, in letting the text become God's word again.[19]

The goal of the preacher, then, is to use language in such a way that the members of the congregation are themselves, individually

15. Ernst Fuchs, "The New Testament and the Hermeneutical Problem," in *New Hermeneutic,* ed. Robinson and Cobb, p. 125.

16. Ibid.

17. Ibid., pp. 127–28.

18. Ibid., pp. 130–31.

19. Gerhard Ebeling, "Word of God and Hermeneutic," in *New Hermeneutic,* ed. Robinson and Cobb, p. 107.

and existentially, confronted by the invitation/demand that they "trust and obey," right here and right now.[20]

Positivist and phenomenologist—they present mutually exclusive alternatives to the preacher in terms of how he understands the language he uses in the pulpit. Or do they? Must one choose *either* analytic *or* intuitive language? Is there a way to see these as complementary rather than contradictory? I think there is. As a matter of fact, we must, as preachers, listen carefully to both positivists and phenomenologists if our aim, in our homiletical language, is to be fully biblical. The appropriate relationship between the two types of language may be stated thus: Analysis is the necessary but insufficient ground of intuition. That is, analytic language forms an essential foundation for intuitive, and intuitive language, based upon proper analysis, leads to the ultimate purpose of preaching.

What I am suggesting here is original only in the manner of its application to the homiletical goal of the preacher. Arthur Koestler, in his massive work, *The Act of Creation* (1964), applies similar insights to the problems involved in the fields of scientific and artistic creation and discovery. In Part Two of Book One, Koestler discusses "The Sage," and attempts to show just what is involved in what he calls "the moment of truth." He provides quite a number of examples to illustrate the act by which the mind moves from what is known to what is unknown, and, appropriately enough, he also uses the word *intuition* to describe this special activity of the mind.

One of the clearest examples provided by Koestler is that of Archimedes, who was confronted with the problem of determining the volume of a ruler's crown. Archimedes struggled and struggled with the geometric formulas that he knew, but it was all to no avail. Then one day, as he was taking a bath, he noticed that the water in the tub rose as he lowered himself into it. In an instantaneous flash of intuitive insight, he had discovered the answer to his problem: the volume of water displaced would be equal to the volume of the object displacing it, and all he had to do was to substitute the crown for his body. The question Koestler asks is how or why Archimedes saw the analogy between his body in the water and the problem on which he was working, and most of *The Act of Creation* is devoted to explaining what sort of mental processes are involved in such problem solving. He points out, for instance, that, as in Archimedes' case, the most frequent means employed is the search for and the discovery of some analogy with what is already known. But in the end, he does not really attempt to explain why a man's mind is able to discover just the right analogy.

Koestler does make one very essential point, however. He argues that one cannot even approach a problem, much less solve it, without first attaining some degree of knowledge relevant to the particular situation. Although Koestler spends hundreds of pages discussing the relationship between prior knowledge and the act of intuition, I will quote only a few of the most important passages:

> The statistical probability for a relevant discovery to be made is the greater the more firmly established and well exercised each of the still separate skills, or thought-matrices, are. . . . Ripeness in this sense is, of course, merely a necessary, not a sufficient, condition of discovery. . . .

> When the situation is ripe for a given type of discovery, it still needs the intuitive power of an exceptional mind, and sometimes a favorable chance event, to bring it from potential into actual existence. On the other hand, some discoveries represent striking *tours de force* by individuals who seem to be so far ahead of their time that their contemporaries are unable to understand them. Thus at one end of the scale we have discoveries which seem to be due to more or less conscious, logical reasoning, and at the other end sudden insights which seem to emerge spontaneously from the depth of the unconscious. . . .

> The moment of truth, the sudden emergence of a new insight, is an act of intuition. Such intuitions give the appearance of miraculous flashes, or short-circuits of reason. In fact they may be likened to an immersed chain, of which only the

beginning and the end are visible above the surface of consciousness. The diver vanishes at one end of the chain and comes up at the other end, guided by invisible links. Habit and originality, then, point in opposite directions in the two-way traffic between conscious and unconscious processes. The condensation of learning into habit, and the automatization of skills constitute the downward stream; while the upward traffic consists in the minor, vitalizing pulses from the underground, and the rare major surges of creation.[21]

In Koestler's case, the fulfillment of the process, that toward which everything else points, is the creative insight, the moment of discovery, the intuition. But even to have a chance of achieving that goal, the individual must be prepared, he must be ripe. The phenomenologists have seen correctly what the preacher should aim at—a dynamic meeting of his congregation with the inviting, demanding Word of God, a meeting that confronts and interprets each member of that congregation anew. But the positivists have seen correctly that language, to be meaningful, must be cognitive, accurate, precise. The biblical preacher must listen to both while turning, of course, finally to the Scriptures themselves for the model and for the guidelines for his preaching.

2. Preaching in the New Testament

There are, of course, far more ways to organize the message of the New Testament than there are to categorize twentieth-century language theory. Obviously, therefore, the way I am about to suggest can lay no claim to exclusivity or finality. It is just one perspective, a perspective, however, that I hope, will be thoroughly faithful to the entirety of the New Testament message, will draw together some of the emphases of both positivists and phenomenologists, and will provide some assistance to preachers as they seek to clarify the aim of their preaching.

21. Arthur Koestler, *The Act of Creation* (New York: Dell, 1964), pp. 108-9, 120, 211.

Jesus Himself was a preacher, and while we must always be careful about how we seek to follow His example (we are not, for example, to imitate His atoning death), His preaching may be instructive to us who would understand our responsibilities as preachers. The gospels suggest that Jesus' first sermon contained both information and confrontation: "From that time Jesus began to preach and say, 'Repent, for the kingdom of heaven is at hand' " (Matt. 4:17).[22] Immediately thereafter, we are told, "Jesus was going about in all Galilee, teaching in their synagogues, and proclaiming the gospel of the kingdom, and healing every kind of disease and every kind of sickness among the people" (Matt. 4:23).

Throughout His career, Jesus' ministry was characterized by this balance of word and deed, but not as though the two were entirely separate phenomena maintained in some quantitative dynamic tension. No, in His first sermon, when He announced the arrival of the kingdom, Jesus was not speaking as a reporter describing an event that had previously occurred, of which He thought His hearers were unfortunately unaware. His announcement of the kingdom constituted the arrival of the kingdom because Jesus was not just a messenger—He was the King. Thus, as He spoke, it *was,* the marriage between word and event being as perfect as that described in the opening chapters of Genesis.

Jesus' preaching might thus be classified as "performative discourse," for His words did what they announced.[23] One image suggested frequently in Scripture that might be particularly helpful here is the image of the judge who renders judgments. Jesus came to bring judgment, understood neutrally. That is, a judge may just as surely pronounce vindication on the innocent as he may condemnation on the wicked. Thus did Jesus. In announcing and accomplishing the arrival of the kingdom, Jesus was bringing truth and righteousness to bear on the human situation. In some

22. All Scripture quotations are from the New American Standard Bible.
23. See, on this entire subject, J. L. Austin, *How to Do Things With Words,* 2nd ed. (Cambridge: Harvard University Press, 1975).

cases this new dramatic presence of the kingdom meant vindication ("Blessed are the poor in spirit, for theirs is the kingdom of
heaven"), and in other cases it meant condemnation ("Woe to
you, scribes and Pharisees, hypocrites!"), but in all cases, judgment was both heard and experienced by those to whom Jesus
spoke.

Beyond this, Jesus' words of judgment altered even physical
reality. In the passage quoted above, Matthew describes in general
terms Christ's healing work. But time after time precise details
are provided. Blind eyes see, deaf ears hear, leprous flesh is
cleansed, dead tissue lives. Throughout His ministry, Jesus does
what He says in the most fundamental sense of that term. In fact,
when the disciples of John the Baptist approach Jesus, seeking to
discover for their master if He was actually the King, the anointed
one, Jesus tells them to look around and to report what they see:
"The blind receive sight and the lame walk, the lepers are
cleansed and the deaf hear, and the dead are raised up, and the
poor have the gospel preached to them" (Matt. 11:5). The point is
that something was actually happening when Jesus preached—the
kingdom was arriving *in His speaking;* judgment was being accomplished *in His preaching.* To be sure, the soteriological foundation
of our participation in the kingdom is Jesus' death and resurrection (without those events, we would experience only condemna-
tory judgment), but the kingdom itself and the judgment it en-
tailed happened as Jesus spoke.

But to stop here would be to commit the neoorthodox theological error and to leave unexplained how and why Jesus' preaching functioned as it did, neither of which the New Testament
does. Jesus' preaching was itself judgment because His preaching
was objectively, factually true. What Jesus preached was anchored
in the propositional bedrock of historical accuracy, and that is
why recognition and proclamation of the inerrancy of all biblical
affirmations is so crucial in the church today. The positivistic
perspective is helpful here. Unless Jesus actually *is* the King, His
announcement of the arrival of the kingdom of heaven is ludi-

crous nonsense, on the level, as C. S. Lewis reminds us, of some-one claiming that he is a poached egg.[24] Without the objectively true content, His words accomplish nothing, bring nothing to pass. With that content, His word is infallible and eschatolog-ically verifiable; it accomplishes what He purposes and prospers in that for which He sends it (Isa. 55:11).[25]

But we must go even further, still following Koestler's resolu-tion of the positivist-phenomenologist dichotomy. Unless Jesus' words actually accomplished exactly what the New Testament record says they accomplished, in all their supernatural, trans-rational scope, then we are confronting a fraud, not a king.[26] That is, if Jesus Himself were mistaken or if he consciously lied in Matthew 11 in His analysis of what His words had done, then perhaps the whole thing is a sham, and His words accomplished nothing. And further yet, if the words of the New Testament record are suspect at all, then they are suspect for all, and we have no way of knowing if a kingdom ever was or ever will be at hand. Koestler reminded us of the necessity of what he called "ripe-ness"; in doing so, he recognized indirectly the value of the posi-tivistic insistence on firm foundations. Creative insight doesn't happen in a void; neither does biblical preaching. For a judge's pronouncements to be valid, he must first actually be a judge. So with Jesus, and so the writers of the New Testament realized. "Many other signs," wrote John, "Jesus also performed in the presence of the disciples, which are not written in this book; but these have been written that you may believe that Jesus is the Christ, the Son of God; and that believing you may have life in His name" (John 20:30, 31). The believing unto life is John's aim, the "event" his words aim at; but he knows that if any such event is to be valid, and not just another exercise in psychological wish-

24. C. S. Lewis, *Mere Christianity* (New York: MacMillan, 1960), p. 41.

25. I am indebted to Mr. Kevin Vanhoozer of Cambridge, England, for sug-gesting some of these perspectives to me. On the subject of eschatological verifi-cation, see John Hick, "Theology and Verification" in *Religious Language and the Problem of Religious Knowledge*, ed. Ronald E. Santoni (Bloomington, Indiana: Indiana University Press, 1968), pp. 362–82.

26. Lewis, *Mere Christianity*, p. 41.

fulfillment, it must be based on facts, actual events as true as any positivist could wish.

So the foundation of what Jesus preached was ontological and historical truth. Because He *is* the Creator, He speaks and it is done; because He *is* the Judge, His Word never returns void but always accomplishes that to which He sends it; because He is the King, His announcement of the kingdom brings kingdom demands and opportunities immediately to bear on His listeners. Without the positivistic perspective on language, Jesus' words may be evaporated into the mists of first-century legend; without the phenomenological perspective, His words may remain historical or doctrinal and never become personal, which was their original aim; without Koestler's perspective, we may be inclined to adopt either the positivistic or the phenomenological attitude and miss the appropriate balance they provide together.

But what about the relationship between Jesus' preaching and our own? How can we appropriately transfer what was true of His preaching to our situation? Surely we must be careful, as was suggested above, not to arrogate to ourselves what belongs to Jesus alone. Proper transference from Jesus' example may be achieved by focusing specifically on one of the themes developed in the Gospels as they describe the establishment of the kingdom. The theme that I have in mind here is that of Jesus' *authority*, and one of the early passages that draws attention to this theme is Matthew 7:28, 29: "The result was that when Jesus had finished these words, the multitudes were amazed at His teaching; for He was teaching them as one having authority, and not as their scribes."

These verses occur at the end of the Sermon on the Mount and are obviously meant to apply to that entire discourse. What seems most to have impressed those who heard the sermon was the *authority* with which Jesus delivered it. The word used here and frequently throughout the New Testament is *exousia*, which suggests both sheer power and intrinsic right. That of which Jesus was speaking was under His rightful jurisdiction, and He had the might to back up what He said. Somehow in His preaching, Jesus communicated this, and His hearers were immediately struck with the degree to which His preaching thus differed from that of the scribes.

This authority was immediately reinforced in the next chapter of Matthew's Gospel when a leper approached Jesus with the words, "Lord, if you are willing, you can make me clean" (Matt. 8:2). What the leper was saying is that he learned well the lesson of the previous chapter—Jesus had both the right and the power to heal him—and the leper's response to Jesus was well founded, for Jesus spoke, " 'I am willing; be cleansed.' And immediately his leprosy was cleansed" (Matt. 8:3). Again and again the point is made in this middle section of Matthew's Gospel. The very next scene, in which the centurion mentioned both his own authority and Jesus', precedes the healing of the centurion's servant, the healing of Peter's mother-in-law, the calming of the winds, the healing of the Gadarene demoniacs—all of which provide further examples of Jesus' authority.

Perhaps the culmination of the theme, at least in this part of Matthew's Gospel, occurs in chapter 9 when the paralytic was brought to Jesus. The significance of the passage justifies quoting it in its entirety:

> And behold, they were bringing to Him a paralytic, lying on a bed; and Jesus seeing their faith said to the paralytic, "Take courage, My son, your sins are forgiven." And behold, some of the scribes said to themselves, "This fellow blasphemes." And Jesus knowing their thoughts said, "Why are you thinking evil in your hearts? For which is easier, to say, 'Your sins are forgiven,' or to say 'Rise, and walk'? But in order that you may know that the Son of Man has authority on earth to forgive sins"—then He said to the paralytic— "Rise, take up your bed, and go home." And he rose, and went home (Matt. 9:2-7).

At least three points need to be made about these verses. First, Jesus Himself identified the scribes' problem as an authority crisis. In verse 6 He specifically stated that He did what He did to demonstrate to them, and all the others gathered around, the scope of His authority. They had seen His physical miracles, they had heard His preaching, and now He was demonstrating that His authority extended beyond the here and now into eternity. Second, the scribes correctly recognized that in claiming to be able to forgive sins, Jesus was making the ultimate claim for His authority. Nothing is outside the scope of His authority, even spiritual realities—thus was Jesus asserting His deity. Third, in verse 5 Jesus subsumed both activities—healing body and healing soul—under one heading and asserted by means of a rhetorical question that, because might and right are combined in His person, all of creation must and will obey His voice. That is the essence of Jesus' authority.

Of course, what Matthew recorded is neither more nor less than was prophesied of the Messiah. Isaiah 40 and 61 clearly hold out the authority of the coming King as the hope of the Lord's people. The latter is worth quoting directly in this context along with its fulfillment in Luke 4:

> The Spirit of the Lord God is upon me, Because the Lord has anointed me to bring good news to the afflicted; He has sent me to bind up the brokenhearted, to proclaim liberty to captives, and freedom to prisoners; to proclaim the favorable year of the Lord, and the day of vengeance of our God; to comfort all who mourn, to grant those who mourn in Zion, giving them a garland instead of ashes, the oil of gladness instead of mourning, the mantle of praise instead of a spirit of fainting. So they will be called oaks of righteousness, the planting of the Lord, that He may be glorified (Isa. 61:1–3).

> And He came to Nazareth, where He had been brought up; and as was His custom, He entered the synagogue on the Sabbath, and stood up to read. And the book of the prophet Isaiah was handed to Him. And He opened the book, and found the place where it was written, "The Spirit of the Lord is upon Me, because He anointed Me to preach the gospel to the poor. He has sent Me to proclaim release to the captives, and recovery of sight to the blind, to set free those who are downtrodden, to proclaim the favorable year of the Lord." And He closed the book, and gave it back to the attendant, and sat down; and the eyes of all in the synagogue

were fixed upon Him. And He began to say to them "Today this Scripture has been fulfilled in your hearing" (Luke 4:16–21).

Jesus' claim here is one with His claim in forgiving the paralytic's sins. He, Jesus, has the *authority* to preach the gospel to the poor, to proclaim release to the captives and recovery of sight to the blind, to set free those who are downtrodden, and to proclaim the favorable year of the Lord. And it is in recognition of and obedient response to this authority that kingdom blessing consists, as both the centurion and the paralytic's friends realized.

Jesus possesses such absolute and unconditional authority both because of who He is and because of what He does. He is the eternal Word, one with the Father, Alpha and Omega; but He is also the Lamb of God who in His death and resurrection takes away the sin of the world. Possibly the most magnificent demonstration of His authority in the Gospels occurs in those electric words, "He is not here, for He has risen, just as He said" (Matt. 28:6). The apostle Paul affirmed the significance of Jesus' resurrection in terms of final authority when he wrote,

But now Christ has been raised from the dead, the first fruits of those who are asleep. For since by a man came death, by a man also came the resurrection of the dead. For as in Adam all die, so also in Christ all shall be made alive. But each in his own order: Christ the first fruits, after that those who are Christ's at His coming, then comes the end, when He delivers up the kingdom to the God and Father, when He has abolished all rule and all authority and power. For He must reign until He has put all His enemies under His feet. The last enemy that will be abolished is death. For He has put all things in subjection under His feet. But when He says, "All things are put in subjection," it is evident that He is excepted who put all things in subjection to Him. And when all things are subjected to Him, then the Son Himself also will be subjected to the One who subjected all things to Him, that God may be all in all (I Cor. 15:20–28).

The goal of all history emerges from Paul's analysis here as it does in other passages such as Philippians 2:9–11. And that goal is the final and complete and glorious recognition of the entire creation that indeed Jesus reigns as King of Kings and Lord of Lords forever and forever (Rev. 19). By His death and resurrection, Jesus has defeated the last enemy, the last challenge to His authority and has established His kingdom invincible and eternal. Thus the announcement made in His first sermon receives its ultimate substantiation and His authority its final legitimatization.

Jesus therefore had legitimate ground for His phenomenological preaching, because His preaching was designed to confront His hearers with an authoritative new situation and to demand a response from them. But do we have such a ground? Adequate ground must exist if our preaching is to be characterized by the power of truth, if we are to avoid the empty meaninglessness against which positivism has warned. How exactly do we move from Jesus' authority into our own pulpits today? Matthew 28:18–20 suggests an answer:

> And Jesus came up and spoke to them, saying, "All authority has been given to Me in heaven and on earth. Go therefore and make disciples of all the nations, baptizing them in the name of the Father and the Son and the Holy Spirit, teaching them to observe all that I commanded you; and lo, I am with you always, even to the end of the age."

The authority that belonged to Jesus, which was His by intrinsic right, that very authority He conferred upon His disciples. It was the authority both to speak and to do, to do by speaking. Their language was to function analogously to Jesus' own, bringing the kingdom to bear upon their hearers and thereby making disciples of all nations. Jesus' concluding promise, that He would be with His disciples even to the end of the age, was meant to reinforce the authority they had in His name. Because He was with them, they could speak and act with His authority.

Focusing upon the theme of authority in this way helps to place into proper context our gospel passage, which has been the source of endless and heated debate in the Christian church. Christ spoke to Peter in Matthew 16 and said, "You are Peter, and upon this rock I will build My church; and the gates of Hades shall not overpower it. I will give you the keys of the kingdom of heaven; and whatever you shall bind on earth shall be bound in heaven, and whatever you loose on earth shall be loosed in heaven" (Matt. 16:18, 19). Protestants have vigorously resisted Roman Catholic claims that this passage legitimatizes the papacy and have frequently read the rock upon which the church is to be built as Peter's confession in verse 16. But such an interpretation fails to deal adequately with the obvious parallel Jesus is drawing between "Peter" (*petros*) and "rock" (*petra*), and it fails to recognize appropriately the force of the commission Jesus gave to Peter in verse 19.

The passage really is a remarkable one, especially when viewed in conjunction with Matthew 28:18–20. Jesus was conferring upon Peter remarkable authority vis-a-vis His kingdom. But why Peter, and what does Peter's confession have to do with the matter? Jesus singled Peter out in Matthew 16 because Peter had just made the crucial statement about Jesus—"You are the Christ, the son of the living God"—and thus Protestant interpreters have been on the right track in concentrating on that statement. It was the *correctly confessing* Peter upon which the church was to be built, just as it was the correctly teaching disciples who would make disciples in Christ's name. Peter as an individual was special only in that he made the right confession at the right time, and the others did not. And when he became tempting Peter instead of confessing Peter in Matthew 16:22, Jesus saw him no longer as the rock of the church but as Satan.[27]

Two points must be made here. First, the importance of objective, propositional truth finds clear reaffirmation in these two passages in Matthew. It was only as Peter confessed the truth that

27. I am indebted to Dr. George Fuller, President of Westminster Theological Seminary, for suggesting to me this interpretation of Matthew 16.

he was the rock of the church; it was only as the disciples taught their hearers to observe what Jesus had commanded that they had any hope of making disciples of all nations. But secondly, real authority was being conveyed by Jesus to His followers, authority to bind and to loose *in heaven*. Jesus wanted His followers to recognize what they could do, and He wanted them to recognize what they should do. They had the authority to bring the kingdom to bear upon individuals in such a way as to provoke responses that would matter for all eternity. And that was what they should do. Their homiletical aim was to be not merely teaching about the kingdom; it was to be the actualization of the kingdom in the presence of their hearers. Surely in one sense Jesus had already brought the kingdom, and in another sense He will bring the kingdom at His second coming, but just as surely Jesus' followers who live between the already and the not yet, as they confess Him truly, as they preach Him fully, are bringing His authority to bear upon the situations into which they speak. And as we have seen, His authority is His rule, and His rule is His kingdom.

But the disciples were unique, weren't they? Their special gifts ended upon their death, didn't they? The miraculous and revelatory gifts did cease with the termination of the apostolic age, but the authoritative preaching ministry of the church continues.[28] Review quickly Paul's admonitions to Titus in Titus 1:5, 9 or to Timothy in I Timothy 3-4 and II Timothy 4. Clearly the preachers being addressed here, and all who follow them, maintain the authority that Jesus entrusted to the church in Matthew 16 and 28. But the statement must be made in this way and the earlier qualifications must be maintained. It is to the *church* that kingdom authority has been granted; individual preachers possess it as they speak on behalf of the church (which is, of course, what the ordination process is supposed to mean—it is the church's recognition that the individual being ordained has the kingdom authority to speak to and for the church). Such authority is not

28. For a full discussion of this point, see Richard B. Gaffin, *Perspectives on Pentecost* (Phillipsburg, N.J.: Presbyterian and Reformed, 1979).

infallible because we do have this treasure in earthen vessels and thus the earlier qualification is again seen to be crucial. The individual preacher's authority, indeed the entire church's authority, depends entirely upon the confession upon which it is based. If the confession resounds with the truth of the gospel, the authority will be that of the kingdom. But if the solidity of the confession wavers, the authority dissipates. Doctrinal orthodoxy is thus necessary to the authority of preaching.

It is necessary, but not sufficient—a phrase we used earlier to describe the relationship between analysis and intuition in both epistemology and language theory. The biblical preacher must take his aim from Jesus. His goal is not merely to tell about the kingdom, not merely to describe accurately its constituent parts. The biblical preacher must seek to build upon the objectively true facts about the kingdom and thus to bring Jesus' authority directly and immediately to bear upon his congregation where they live. Biblical preaching is thus preaching of judgment correctly understood. As he preaches with the authority that Jesus entrusted to His church, the preacher actualizes the kingdom in the midst of the people. The preacher not only speaks, he *acts* in Jesus' name; he looses and he binds; he makes disciples; he moves toward the fulfillment of Jesus' own prayer, "Thy kingdom come, Thy will be done on earth as it is in heaven."

An analogy might clarify a bit the nature of the preacher's task and opportunity. Particularly in the Reformed theological tradition, the exact nature of the efficacy of the sacraments has drawn much attention. In the Lord's Supper even more than in baptism, theologians have attempted to avoid both extremes, that of physical alteration of the elements of bread and wine, on the one hand, and that of pure memorialism, on the other hand. Thus Calvin's position on the Lord's Supper differed from both Luther's and Zwingli's. At the center of the Reformed position has been the conviction that the one who partakes of the Supper in a biblical manner is actually and specifically united to Christ through that partaking. Likewise, for those in the Reformed paedobaptist tradition, the child who is baptized according to the Scriptures thus actually becomes a member of the covenant community through that baptism. The sacraments are not just testimonies by those participating, but so long as they are observed according to biblical guidelines, they are actual events.

Such also is the biblical sermon. Many regard it simply as one Christian talking to other Christians, but it can and should be much more. Because of the relationship between Christ's authority and the church's authority, and because of the relationship between the church's authority and the preacher's authority, the sermon preached on the basis of a true confession of Jesus may be an event much as the Lord's Supper is an event. The two are not identical; preaching is not a sacrament, but their similarities and their mutual significance are two of the reasons why Calvin and others regarded faithful preaching of the Word and proper administration of the sacraments as the marks of the true church.

At least once more, however, the warning must be issued. Not just any preaching brings the kingdom to bear on a situation, but preaching that embodies the truth and aims at kingdom judgment in the name of the King. Neither analysis nor intuition alone is adequate. The one produces dead propositionalism; the other, vague and contentless moralisms. Biblical judgment can only be on the basis of truth and that must be the preacher's first concern. But biblical truth judges, challenges, confronts, and this must be the preacher's ultimate aim as he speaks for his church and for his Lord. (In saying this, I am wholeheartedly agreeing with what others, especially Geoffrey Thomas and John Bettler, say elsewhere in this volume.)

3. *Some Practical Guidelines*

To return to my initial statement, the preacher must know exactly what he is trying to do if he is to have any hope of actually doing it. This chapter is entitled "The Phenomenology of Preaching" because, as mentioned above, the ultimate goal of any specific sermon must be understood in these terms: as bringing the authority of Jesus to bear upon one's congregation in such a way as to elicit a response, a kingdom response (still recognizing and heartily affirming that it is the Holy Spirit who actually causes any such response). The response sought in this sermon may be kingdom rejoicing while in that sermon it may be kingdom repentance, but in every sermon, the preacher should be seeking to actualize some aspect of Jesus' kingdom authority for His people.

In specific terms the preacher should be able to state in one brief sentence what predominant response he is seeking to elicit in any given sermon. Certainly many emotions may be touched and many ideas explored, but each of these must be done in such a way as to move toward the one predominant response he wishes to elicit. One might even paraphrase the first sentence of this chapter to read, "The more you aim at, the less you're likely to hit." Or, to put it another way, to the degree that the one brief sentence described above evolves into a compound or even a complex sentence, to that very degree the likelihood of any response diminishes. Simplicity, clarity, precision of focus (none of which is synonymous with superficiality) characterize authoritative biblical preaching and facilitate its operations.

In setting the aim of his sermon, then, the preacher must realize what potentially may happen as he preaches (the kingdom may come to expression), and he must construct his exact purpose for that sermon with care. In this process, let it be said that of all the aids the preacher might use (including the present volume), outside of the Bible itself, the most helpful might very well be Jonathan Edwards's *Treatise Concerning Religious Affections*. This is both because of Edwards's solidly biblical foundation and because of his profound anthropological observations. That is, Edwards, in *Religious Affections* so brilliantly analyzes both Scripture and man that he provides invaluable assistance to the preacher who would bring kingdom authority to bear upon his congregation.

The core of Edwards's treatise involves his observation, frequently seen in his other works and sermons as well, that the root of all individual human behavior is the disposition or the affections. By "affections," Edwards has in view more than mere passions—he defines the affections in terms that incorporate much of what often are considered passions, but his focus is more particularly on the basic orientation of one's being, one's essential loves and hatreds, those movements of the soul toward some things and away from others. But let Edwards attempt the explanation himself:

> The affections and passions are frequently spoken of as the same; and yet, in the more common use of speech, there is in some respect a difference. Affection is a word, that, in its ordinary signification, seems to be something more extensive than passion, being used for all vigorous lively actings of the will or inclination; but passion is used for those that are more sudden, and whose effects on the animal spirits are more violent, the mind being more overpowered, and less in its own command.
>
> As all the exercises of inclination and will, are concerned either in approving and liking, or disapproving and rejecting; so the affections are of two sorts; they are those by which the soul is carried out to what is in view, cleaving to it, or seeking it; or those by which it is averse from it, and opposes it. Of the former sort are love, desire, hope, joy, gratitude, complacence. Of the latter kind are hatred, fear, anger, grief and such like; which it is needless now to stand particularly to define.[29]

Another distinction between passions and affections takes us back to the positivists' quarrel with the phenomenologists and to Koestler's apparent resolution of that quarrel. Edwards affirms,

> Holy affections are not heat without light; but evermore arise from some information of the understanding, some spiritual instruction that the mind receives, some light or actual knowledge. The child of God is graciously affected, because he sees and understands something more of divine things than he did before, more of God or Christ, and of the glorious things exhibited in the gospel. He has a clearer and better view than he had before, when he was not affected; either he receives some new understanding of divine things, or has his former knowledge renewed after the view was

29. Jonathan Edwards, A *Treatise Concerning Religious Affections* in *Works*, 1: 237.

decayed; I John IV:7. "Every one that loveth, knoweth God." Phil. I:9. "I pray that your love may abound more and more in knowledge, and in all judgment." Rom. X:2. "They have a zeal of God, but not according to knowledge." Col. III:10. "The new man, which is renewed in knowledge." Psalms XLIII:3, 4. "O send out thy light and thy truth; let them lead me, let them bring me unto thy holy hill." John VI:45. "It is written in the prophets, And they shall be all taught of God. Every man therefore that hath heard, and learned of the Father, cometh unto me." Knowledge is the key that first opens the hard heart, enlarges the affections, and opens the way for men into the kingdom of heaven; Luke XI:52. "Ye have taken away the key of knowledge." Now there are many affections which do not arise from any light in the understanding; which is a sure evidence that these affections are not spiritual, let them be ever so high.[30]

Affections, in distinction from passions, are grounded in knowledge, and, Edwards argues throughout his *Treatise*, genuinely gracious affections are grounded in knowledge of the truths of Christ's gospel. If analysis is not present, there will be no affections (only passions); and unless the analysis is true, the affections (intuition) will be spurious. Working with this basic psychological model (and developing it far more fully than I can here), Edwards then asserts the basic thesis of his *Treatise*: "True religion, in great part, consists in holy affections."[31] His exposition of this thought is, I would suggest, exhaustive, thoroughly biblical, and enormously helpful for the kingdom preacher who wants to work on the focus of his sermons. If what matters in ultimate terms is what one *really* loves or hates or desires or fears (each of these words being understood not as pure passions, but as Edwardsean affections), then the preacher speaking with the authority of his Lord must seek to create sermonic situations in which love for Christ *happens*, in which hatred for sin *happens*, in which desire for the blessing of God *happens*, in which fear of the

30. Ibid., pp. 281–82.
31. Ibid., p. 236.

consequences of sin *happens*. That is exactly how Edwards himself preached, and his most famous sermon, "Sinners in the Hands of an Angry God," is a perfect example of the last of these.

But Edwards does not leave us merely to draw the correct conclusion from the example of his preaching; he makes his point clearly and specifically:

> And the impressing of divine things on the hearts and affections of men, is evidently one great end for which God has ordained, that his word delivered in the Holy Scriptures should be opened, applied, and set home upon men, in *preaching*. And therefore it does not answer the aim which God had in this institution, merely for men to have good commentaries and expositions on the Scripture, and other good books of divinity; because, although these may tend, as well as preaching, to give a good doctrinal of speculative understanding of the word of God, yet they have not an equal tendency to impress them on men's hearts and affections. God hath appointed a particular and lively application of his word, in the preaching of it, as a fit means to affect sinners with the importance of religion, their own misery, the necessity of a remedy, and the glory and sufficiency of a remedy provided; to stir up the pure minds of the saints, quicken their affections by often bringing the great things of religion to their remembrance, and setting them in their proper colours, though they know them, and have been fully instructed in them already, 2 Pet. I:12, 13. And particularly to promote those two affections in them, which are spoken of in the text, *love* and *joy*: "Christ gave some, apostles; and some, prophets; and some, evangelists; and some, pastors and teachers; that the body of Christ might be edified in love," Eph IV:11, 12, 16.[32]

Biblical preaching enacts the kingdom of Christ, the reign of Christ, by eliciting, through the power of the Holy Spirit, gra-

---

32. Ibid., p. 242. It might also be noted what Edwards says in the preceding paragraph about the value of the arts in Christian experience. The implications, even for such diverse areas as church architecture and liturgy, are startling.

cious affections. That was God's aim in giving preachers to the church, and that is to be the preacher's aim as he speaks to the church. But Edwards has one more warning both to the preacher and to the congregation—the warning that, in addition to being grounded in biblical understanding, truly gracious affections must be focused on the King and His kingdom, on the Creator rather than on the creature. Among the temptations that confront the phenomenological preacher, even the solidly orthodox phenomenological preacher, is the temptation to reduce the kingdom of Christ to a kind of enlightened utilitarianism: "Repent, for you will benefit in the long run if you do!" No, the message of Christ had a different focus: "Repent, for the kingdom of heaven is at hand." To be sure, repentance will produce ultimate benefit to the repentant, but repentance is most fundamentally appropriate because of the nature of the King and His kingdom. Jesus *deserves* our worship and adoration and praise, and that fact provides that motivation behind the preacher's preaching and the congregation's response.

Edwards puts it succinctly:

> Whereas the exercises of true and holy love in the saints arise in another way. They do not first see that God loves *them*, and then see that he is lovely; but they first see that God is lovely, and that Christ is excellent and glorious; their hearts are first captivated with this view, and the exercises of their love are wont, from time to time, to begin here, and to arise primarily from these views; and then, consequentially, they see God's love, and great favour to them. The saints' affections begin with God; and self-love has a hand in these affections consequentially and secondarily only. On the contrary, false affections begin with *self*, and an acknowledgment of an excellency in God, and an affectedness with it, is only consequential and dependent. In the love of the true saint, God is the lowest foundation; the love of the excellency of his nature is the foundation of all the affections which come afterwards, wherein self-love is concerned as an handmaid. On the contrary, the hypocrite lays *himself* at the bottom of all, as the first foundation, and lays on God as the super-

structure; and even his acknowledgment of God's glory itself, depends on his regard to his private interest.[33]

The saints' affections begin with God and with the love of the
excellency of His nature, thus the preacher must remember as he
plans and executes his sermon.

This section of the present chapter is entitled "Some Practical
Guidelines." How might these observations of Jonathan Edwards
be regarded as practical guidelines? Possibly in the following way.
The preacher must begin his preparation by remembering the general aim of his preaching: to bring the authority—the majestic,
gracious, redemptive authority—of the King to bear dynamically,
"eventfully," upon his congregation (which is, in Edmund Clowney's words, preaching Christ). But this general, overall aim must
take specific shape as the preacher works through the text or the
topic with which he will deal in the particular sermon, and this
specific shape should be developed in accord with what Edwards
has to say about affections.

Suppose the text for a sermon were Jesus' own first public
preaching, Matthew 4:17. The general aim for this sermon might
be to demonstrate the nature and the present reality of Christ's
kingdom in such a way as to bring His authority to bear upon
that situation and to elicit the active response of repentance from
the members of the congregation. But as the preacher moved
toward specifying this aim, he might review carefully what Edwards says about affections, how they, to be genuinely biblical,
must involve correct understanding (in this case, of the nature of
the kingdom), but must go beyond understanding and must find
their focus in God Himself. Thus the preacher might choose as
his specific aim the elicitation of the affections of awe at the
majesty of the King and His kingdom and the consequent affections of unworthiness in His presence and praise that He has
nevertheless brought the kingdom to us in the person of His Son
Jesus. The result being sought is that the congregation respond by
turning anew *from* the kingdom of this world *to* the kingdom of

33. Ibid., p. 276.

Christ, and that, of course, is nothing more or less than the actualization of the kingdom, of the reign of Jesus in the midst of His
people. Certainly such a sermon would need to indicate very precise content for this turning, and, just as certainly, greater famil-
iarity with Edwards's *Religious Affections* would be of enormous
benefit to the preacher in constructing the sermon. But perhaps
these few suggestions will be helpful to the preacher who wishes
to make use of Edwards's insights.

4. Conclusion

The preacher's primary tools, once he steps into the pulpit, are
words. Choosing the right words, therefore, assumes critical importance in the homiletical situation, and such a choice must be
guided by the precise goal of the preacher. The positivists (and
others) have reminded us of the value, the necessity, of precision
and accuracy in language. The phenomenologists have responded
by pointing out that the real goal of dynamic, effectual speaking
(whether by the poet or preacher) must be the alteration of the
life of the hearer. Arthur Koestler has suggested that the latter
type of language both depends upon and fulfills the latter. And
Jonathan Edwards has brought all of this home to the contemporary preacher by analyzing human psychology in light of the biblical description of the nature of genuine Christian experience.
The cumulative evidence, therefore, is that the preacher must
build upon doctrinal orthodoxy in preaching phenomenologically, "eventfully."

But, of course, the primary reason the preacher must do this is
not because the positivists or the phenomenologists or Koestler
or even Edwards says so. It is because "the Bible tells me so." The
kingdom of heaven *is* at hand and biblical preaching both announces and furthers this fact. As he sees his task and his opportunity in relationship to the accomplishment of the rule of Jesus
over His kingdom, the preacher can do no else than bring divine
authority immediately to bear upon those who hear him. And
that, by the sovereign, gracious power of the Holy Spirit, is the
phenomenology of preaching.

I.
MESSAGE CONTENT

6

Preaching Christ From All the Scriptures
Edmund P. Clowney

May I invite you to inspect your Bible? Flex the binding; look closely at the signs of wear along the page edges. Unless your Bible is quite new or you are an unusual preacher, I will predict that you can find with your thumbnail where the New Testament begins. It is where the shiny gold has worn off the page edges in a decided line. Very likely you can pick out the Psalms or Isaiah by the worn edges, too.

You might make another measurement by looking over your file of sermons. In what proportion have you preached from Old and New Testament texts?

If we are going to carry Bibles and not simply pocket Testaments, we should surely be using the Old Testament more than we do. The missionary Bible of the apostolic church was the Old Testament Scripture. Our Lord in the synagogue of Nazareth (Luke 4), Peter at Pentecost (Acts 2), Paul in the synagogues of Asia Minor and Greece—these all preached the gospel from the Old Testament. During the time in which the apostolic witness to Christ was still being recorded, the Old Testament was the Scripture from which the church preached Christ.

Why do we use the Old Testament so little in our preaching? Some preachers might neglect the Old Testament because they do not preach from biblical texts at all. They prefer to preach, more or less biblically, on topics. Others feel that the Old Testament is too remote from contemporary life. But one great obstacle has been the uneasy feeling that Old Testament texts do not present the gospel with clarity. Christian preachers may well fear preach-

163

ing synagogue sermons, or becoming legalistic or moralistic in their pulpit ministry.

If we are to preach from the whole Bible, we must be able to see how the whole Bible bears witness to Jesus Christ. The Bible has a key, one that unlocks the use of the Old Testament by the New. That key is presented at the end of the Gospel of Luke (Luke 24:13-27, 44-48). It is found in the teaching of Jesus after His resurrection. When Jesus met the two discouraged disciples returning to Emmaus on Easter morning, He did not end their grief by revealing Himself to them at once. He did not bring recognition by saying "Cleopas!" as He had earlier said "Mary!" (John 20:16). Instead He rebuked them for their foolish sorrow. They could not believe in the resurrection even after hearing the women's report of the empty tomb. Why not? Because they were "slow of heart to believe in all that the prophets have spoken" (Luke 24:25b). They did not recognize that the Christ must suffer these things and enter into glory. Jesus began with the books of Moses, and proceeding through all the prophets He "interpreted to them in all the scriptures the things concerning himself" (v. 27). Their hearts burned within them as they saw how all the Scriptures focused on Christ. Only after that learning experience were their eyes opened to recognize the Lord in the breaking of the bread.

Later, the risen Christ continued His instruction, teaching "that all things must be fulfilled, which are written in the law of Moses, and in the prophets, and in the psalms, concerning me. Then opened he their understanding, that they might understand the scriptures" (Luke 24:44b, 45).

What did Jesus teach His disciples during the forty days between His resurrection and ascension? Apparently the coverage was extensive: Moses, the prophets, the psalms—these are the three major divisions of the Hebrew Scriptures. There was progression, too. The phrase "beginning at Moses and all the prophets" and the use of the verb *diermēneuō* indicate reasoned interpretation. Jesus did not present a course in "eisegesis." He interpreted what the Scriptures *do* say and opened His disciples' minds to understand it. Understanding brought conviction, a burning heart. Although Jesus Himself was their teacher, He did not assume that only He could so interpret Scripture. Rather, He blamed them as fools and slow of heart because they had not perceived the plain meaning of the Old Testament. Indeed, so clear is the message of the Scriptures that their misunderstanding must be accounted for by a mental block of some kind, a blindness to the truth expressed.

Do you wish you could have attended Christ's seminar during the forty days? Do you conclude ruefully that you haven't a clue as to what Christ's comprehensive, cogent interpretation of the Old Testament was?

Stop for a moment. Luke puts this spotlight on Old Testament interpretation right in the heart of his two-volume work on what Jesus did *and taught* both before and after His resurrection and ascension (Acts 1:1). Is Luke, then, describing secret teaching in Gnostic style? Does he picture Jesus as giving arcane instruction to a few disciples who are initiates? Of course not! What Jesus explained to the disciples about the Old Testament became the key for their preaching. Luke reports to us how the apostles used their new understanding in preaching Christ from all the Scriptures. Peter's sermon at Pentecost interpreted passages from Joel and from Psalms 16 and 110 (Acts 2:17-21, 25, 28, 34). Later Peter declared in the temple the fulfillment of "the things which God foreshowed by the mouth of all the prophets" (Acts 3:18). He quoted from Deuteronomy and added, "Yea and all the prophets from Samuel . . . as many as have spoken, they also told of these days" (Acts 3:24).

When Stephen made his defense, he surveyed the history of the Old Testament to point to Christ (Acts 7). Philip began with Isaiah 53:7 to preach Jesus to the Ethiopian eunuch (Acts 8:34); Paul traced God's redemption in the Exodus and reviewed the rulers God gave to Israel in order to point to the Messiah, the seed of David (Acts 13:16-41). Like Peter, Paul quoted from the psalms.

In all the preaching recorded in the Book of Acts we find the same themes reappearing. Plainly Luke did not think that we are left in the dark about Jesus' interpretation of the Old Testament.

What the Lord taught the disciples, they declared to the church. The whole New Testament interprets the fulfillment of the promises of God. Without the Old Testament the gospel message itself cannot be well understood. Quotations from the Old Testament are spread throughout the New; allusions are even more abundant. Look through a Nestle edition of the Greek Testament: the Old Testament phrases alluded to are in boldface type, and they are sprinkled on almost every page.

With this wealth of interpretive guidance, why should we be so uncertain about our use of the Old Testament? No doubt we have neglected what the Spirit of God has given us. The sweep and boldness of the interpretation in the New Testament has proved too much for us. We have become puzzled. Does the New Testament really interpret the Old, or does it only use the language, filling the old wineskins with new wine? Far from perceiving the principles used in the New Testament to interpret the Old, we often fall short of crediting the interpretations that are given. We would not dare to find Christ in passages where the New Testament does not expressly find Him, and we have difficulty with some of the passages where it does.

If our preaching of the Old Testament is to be renewed, we need that opening of the mind that Christ gave to His disciples; we also need to use the key that He gave for opening the Scriptures: that key is the witness of the Scriptures to Christ.

1. God's Structuring Promise

All the Old Testament Scriptures, not merely the few passages that have been recognized as messianic, point us to Christ. We are all familiar with messianic prophecy in the Old Testament. When Philip ran up to the chariot of the Ethiopian official and heard him reading from Isaiah 53:7, the evangelist began with that passage and preached Jesus (Acts 8:35). We have a good idea as to what Philip might have said. In the same way, we can understand that Psalm 22 is messianic since Jesus uttered its opening cry on the cross. Jesus Himself alluded to Psalm 110, and in its opening invitation to David's Lord to sit at the right hand of God we can recognize a prophecy of Christ's exaltation (Ps. 110:1; Mark 12:36; 14:62).

But what of the structure of the Old Testament as a whole? We may begin by asking, How do we have a written Old Testament? What accounts for this collection of seemingly diverse writings composed over so many centuries?

The Old Testament itself provides a clear answer. Scripture is given by God in the history of His covenant with Israel. Written Scripture appears first in Old Testament history as the text of the covenant treaty that God made with Israel at Sinai. Just as the speaking of the Lord from the mount provides the model of divine revelation, so the writing of the Lord on the tablets of stone provides the model of divine inscripturation. "And he gave unto Moses, when he had made an end of communing with him upon Mount Sinai, the two tables of testimony, tables of stone, written with the finger of God" (Exod. 31:18; cf. 24:12; 32:16).

The stone tablets are called the "tablets of witness" (Exod. 31:18; 40:20); the ark is called the "ark of the witness" (Exod. 25:16, 21, 22; 26:33; 39:55). The treaty form of the covenant explains the term "witness" or "testimony." The stipulations and promises of God's covenant with Israel are attested or witnessed by the written record. Duplicate copies are required for the same reason.[1] One copy is God's, the other copy is Israel's. Both are deposited in the ark. The lid of the ark is the mercy seat, the symbol of God's throne in the midst of His people. God's covenant testimony is stored under His throne.

If God were to be unfaithful to His covenant promise, the people could appeal to the witness that He Himself had given. If, however, the people were to be unfaithful, God's "testimonies" engraved in stone and written by Moses were in God's keeping as evidence of the terms of His covenant. Throughout the Pentateuch, and particularly in Deuteronomy, it is clear that Israel will

1. Meredith Kline, "The Two Tables of the Covenant," *The Westminster Theological Journal*, 22 (May, 1960): 133–46.

break God's covenant and that its sanctions will be applied (e.g., Deut. 30:1–3).

Scripture, then, is presented as God's covenantal witness. What is true of the first written words of God continues to be true of the rest.

For example, the institution of the prophetic office is modeled on Moses' ministry (Deut. 18:18). The prophets are God's mouthpieces, bringing God's Word, just as Aaron was Moses' mouthpiece, bringing his word (Exod. 4:12, 16). Further, the prophets serve to remind the people of God's covenant given through Moses. They reinforce the warnings and the promises. They also underscore the "witness" of God to Israel's unfaithfulness. The prophet Micah proclaims God's covenant controversy with Israel; God bears witness to His faithfulness and to Israel's covenant-breaking (Mic. 6:1–5).

Stern predictions of disaster are the prophesied outcome of Israel's covenant-breaking. Yet the prophets do not end with the doom of divine wrath. They regularly point beyond wrath to mercy. In Deuteronomy 30:1–10 we find an overview of covenantal history. The blessings God has promised will all be fulfilled; Israel will enter the land and drive out their enemies; God will set His name in their midst at the place of His choosing. But Israel will continue to rebel and the curses of the covenant will also be realized. The people will be driven from the land into exile. Then, after the blessings and the curses, God will gather His scattered people and circumcise their hearts to love the Lord with all their heart and soul, that they may live.

This structure shapes the whole of the Old Testament. The promised blessings are realized. Israel enters the land; the enemy nations are subdued under Joshua, the judges, and King David. Every man finds rest under his own vine and fig tree (I Kings 4:25). Solomon dedicates the temple and praises God for fulfilling all the promises that He made: "Blessed be the Lord, that hath given rest unto his people Israel, according to all he promised; there hath not failed one word of all his good promise, which he promised by Moses his servant" (I Kings 8:56).

But this glorious pinnacle proves to be the edge of a precipice. Solomon's wisdom becomes folly as he builds idol shrines for his heathen wives. Rehoboam, his son, is more foolish still; the kingdom is divided. The open apostasy of the northern tribes is followed by Judah as well; both go into captivity: Israel to Assyria and Judah to Babylon.

The prophets record this sad history and pronounce their mournful judgments. Yet the master-plan of Deuteronomy 30 holds. The judgment is not total or final, because God is a God of mercy and of unimaginable grace. He will not destroy *all* His people: a *remnant* will be preserved. He will not destroy them *forever*: a glorious future of *renewal* will come. The "latter days," the time *after* both blessing and cursing, will be the time when God will restore the tabernacle of David that is fallen down and establish a new covenant in sovereign grace (Amos 9:11, 12; Jer. 31:31–34; 32:36–41).

How can such a glorious finale be written to the history of God's covenant with a rebellious people? Only if God Himself intervenes to be the Savior of His own, not merely from their enemies, but from themselves.

God must come, because the plight of Israel is so hopeless that only God can save. Ezekiel sees a vision of the people in captivity. The prospect is appalling. He is in the midst of a great valley, a valley of the dead. Stretching away from Him in every direction are windrows of bones: not even skeletons, but scattered bones. Only the Spirit of God can give life to these bones and bring resurrection from the grave for this people (Ezek. 37:1–4).

God sees that there is none to deliver His people from their oppressors, and so He will put on the breastplate of His righteousness and the helmet of His salvation. He will come Himself to save them (Isa. 59:15b–21). The priests and leaders of the people are false shepherds who care nothing for the sheep. God Himself will come to be the good Shepherd who delivers His sheep (Ezek. 34:1–16).

On the other hand, God's promises are so great that only God can make good on them. Solomon could indeed praise God for having kept His promises by having given Israel peace in the land of their possession. But out of the sin and rebellion of Israel there emerges another level of divine promises. The mercy that will follow God's wrath will surpass all imagining. God promises not only restoration from captivity, but universal blessing. The curse on nature will be removed as God blesses the field and the forest (Isa. 43:18-21; 65:17). Creation will be transformed: the sun will give greater light, the animal creation will live in peace, and the knowledge of the Lord will cover the earth as the waters cover the sea (Isa. 11:6-9; 60:19-22; 30:23-26). To the restored of Israel there will be added the remnant of the nations (Isa. 49:6; 19:19-25; 66:19-21), and all the earth will flow to the mount of the Lord to praise His Name (Isa. 2:2-4; 25:6-8).

To accomplish such consummation blessings, fulfilling all the promises to Adam, Abraham, Moses, and David, God must redeem His people from their sins. This He will do, for in His coming He will not only subdue all the enemies of the people of God (Mic. 7:14-17); He will also subdue their iniquities underfoot "and thou wilt cast all their sins into the depths of the sea" (Mic. 7:18-20).

What coming of God can accomplish such marvels? It must be a coming in vengeance against the hostile powers: God is the Warrior who fights to deliver the poor and oppressed (Isa. 59:16, 17). It must be a coming in mercy to gather and lead the scattered flock: God is the Shepherd who redeems His people as He did in the time of the Exodus when He brought them out of Egypt and led them through the wilderness (Ezek. 34:10-16; Isa. 40:3, 11). It must be a coming in creation as God makes new the very fabric of heaven and earth (Isa. 65:17). God is the Creator Spirit who breathes new life and makes all things new (Ezek. 37:11-14).

But the mystery runs yet deeper, for promise seems set against promise. God's deliverance will be in judgment, in the great day of the Lord. Yet those who cry for that day do not know what they seek (Mal. 3:2; Amos 5:18-20). God will come, but who shall stand when He appears? In mercy God cries, "Ephraim, how shall I give thee up?" (Hos. 11:8), but in justice God pronounces doom on His sinful people. They are no people (*Lo-ammi*), those who can receive no mercy (*Lo-ruhamah*, Hos. 1:9, 6). If fire must renovate the earth to bring in a new order of life, light, and holiness, what can survive the holocaust of final judgment? The burst of glory from the presence of the Lord will consume every fallen sinner.

When that paradox was set before Israel in the desert, God foreshadowed its resolution. God was too holy to dwell in the midst of sinful Israel. He must consume them in a moment (Exod. 33:5). Should He then not dwell in their midst after all? Should He keep His distance and meet with Moses outside the camp (Exod. 33:7-11)? He could go before them in the presence of the angel, drive out their enemies and give them the land without dwelling in their midst (Exod. 33:1-3). Moses rightly saw in that scenario the loss of true salvation: "If thy presence go not with us, carry us not up hence" (Exod. 33:15). Moses prayed the right prayer, "Show me, I pray thee, thy glory" (Exod. 33:18). Communion with the living God is the meaning of salvation.

Salvation is *in* and *of* the Lord; we may possess it only as we have the Lord as our inheritance, and as we become the inheritance of God, and know as we are known (Exod. 34:9). God must come among us, dwell in our midst, and there reveal the light of His glory and the saving power of His holy Name. In symbol God gave that to Moses. He proclaimed His Name to Moses as the God of sovereign grace (Exod. 33:19; 34:6, 7). He did not do what He had threatened to do. He did not cancel the building of the tabernacle in the *midst* of the camp in favor of a tent of meeting *outside* the camp. Rather, God did, in a figure, dwell in the midst of Israel. The tabernacle with its furnishings provided both a screen to contain the holy threat of the Lord's presence and a way of approach by which sinners could come before Him through the shedding of blood and the mediation of the priesthood.

The life of Israel was built around that symbol. But what of the reality that was symbolized? The prophet Ezekiel sees a temple that holds the fountain of the water of life, watering a land that becomes a new Eden. Beside the river that flows from the temple, the tree of life again grows, with healing for the nations (Ezek. 47). But what sacrifice shall be offered when God comes? What dwelling will suffice when He comes, not in the symbol of the pillar of cloud, but in the reality of fulfillment?

And what of the fulfillment of God's covenant? If God comes, how can Israel come to meet Him? Who will have clean hands and a pure heart to enter the presence of the Lord (Ps. 24)? God is the Lord of the covenant, but what of the servant of the covenant?

God's justice is clear; His requirements cannot be compromised. It will not do for God to come only as Lord, even as Warrior, Shepherd, and Creator. To bring the salvation He has promised He must fulfill the part of the Servant as well as the part of the Lord of the covenant.

The tabernacle pictured the way of approach through the altar of sacrifice. But the blood of bulls and goats cannot atone for sin. The final and true sacrifice must be not merely the lamb of the flock, but the son of the bosom. The Passover threat against the first-born must be fulfilled against the representative Seed of the promise, the Isaac God has provided. Abraham's beloved son is the promised seed, but not yet the Son of God. The promise is "Jehovah-Jireh": the Lord Himself must provide the Son who is also the Lamb of God that takes away the sin of the world (Gen. 22).

When the prophets promise the coming of God, they are brought to see that God's Anointed must come: if God is the Shepherd, so is the Son of David, God's Prince (Ezek. 34:23). When the Servant of the Lord comes, He will fulfill the role of Israel (Isa. 49:3). He will also gather the lost sheep of Israel, restore the remnant of the people, and be a light to the Gentiles, God's salvation to the end of the earth (Isa. 49:6).

The name of the Messiah will be "Wonderful, Counsellor, the Mighty God, Everlasting Father, Prince of Peace" (Isa. 9:6). The house of David will indeed be as God, for as the mystery unfolds, God Himself comes in the tabernacle of human flesh. The Lord must come; the Servant must come. Jesus Christ comes, who is Lord and Servant: Immanuel, God with us!

The Old Testament, then, in its very structure is formed by God's promise: the promise to Adam and Eve in the garden (Gen.

3:15); the promise to Abraham (Gen. 12:1–3); the promise to Israel (Deut. 30:6); the promise to David (II Sam. 7:12–16). These are not mere episodes or occasional oracles. They mark the unfolding of God's redemptive plan. The promises of the Seed of the woman and of the Seed of Abraham are given in the Pentateuch; they present both the background and the purpose in the calling of Israel. Without them the perspective of blessing to the nations through Israel might be lost from view. Before the call of Abraham in Genesis 12, Israel is to read the table of the nations in Genesis 10. Israel must perceive its own calling in the light of God's purpose for the nations and of God's promise of the Seed to come.

For that reason the theme of blessing upon the remnant of the nations with the remnant of Israel (e.g., Isa. 19:19–25) is not a new twist added by more cosmopolitan prophets. It is the reaffirmation of God's original calling of His people, and a vision of the new form of the people of God in the wonder of God's own coming.

The focus on Christ in the Old Testament does not spring simply from the fact that Old Testament revelation is given in the framework of a history that does actually lead to Christ. Or, more pointedly, the history that leads to Christ is not a random succession of events. Neither is it simply history under God's providential control, serving His sovereign purpose. It is rather the history of God's own intervention in history, the history of His great work of salvation as He prepares for His own coming in the person of His Son.

The epiphany of the Son of God is not a divine afterthought, an *ad hoc* emergency plan developed to meet the unforeseen disaster of the apostasy of the elect nation. It is not the failure of Israel that necessitates the coming of Christ, as though an obedient people would have made a divine and incarnate Savior unnecessary.

No, the story of the Old Testament is the story of the Lord: what He has done, and what He has purposed to do. The Old Testament does not provide us with biographies or national history. It is the story of God's work, not men's. It speaks of men in the context of God's covenant with them. Since salvation is of the Lord and not of men, the issue is always faith. The heroes of the Old Testament, as the author of Hebrews plainly tells us, are men and women of faith. They trust in God, believe the promises, and look for the city that has foundations, whose builder and maker is God (Heb. 11:10).

2. Typology and Fulfillment

This God-centered and therefore Christ-centered nature of Old Testament revelation provides the ground and rationale of the typological interpretation of the Old Testament in the New. If God had not begun His work of salvation before sending His Son into the world, the Marcionite view of the Old Testament would be correct. We would then have in the religion of Israel only another example of the false religions of the world, and in the Yahweh of the Old Testament a tribal deity whose worship is idolatry. On the other hand, if God's work in the Old Testament is only continued and not transformed in the coming of Christ, then the new is subordinate to the old. Rabbinical interpretation of the Old Testament sought zealously to apply its texts to contemporary life. But they could not conceive of the transformation that Jesus brought, for they did not understand the partial, provisional and temporary character made evident in the old covenant by its anticipation of the power and glory of the new (cf. Matt. 22:29; Jer. 31:31-34; Heb. 1:1, 2).

Typology is grounded in God's design. It flows from the continuity and difference in God's saving work. There is continuity, for it is God who begins His work of salvation long before He gives His Son. Yet there is discontinuity, too. Salvation in Christ is not simply an improvement on Old Testament salvation. It is not just the final phase of God's dealings with His people. It is rather the ground of Old Testament salvation. God's call to Israel presupposes the sending of Jesus Christ. Salvation in Christ is the only real salvation, the only salvation with ultimate and eternal meaning. Abraham partakes of salvation because, by faith, he saw

Christ's day and was glad (John 8:56; cf. Rom. 4:3). To consider the old should in itself force us to see the need for the new; indeed, this is the message of the wisdom literature, as well as of the prophets.

If the real and final salvation is in Christ alone, in what sense can God begin His work of salvation before Christ? Obviously, by anticipating that final work. The anticipation takes place when God brings men into a saving relation with Himself by means of the future work of Christ. God reckons Christ's work as completed because of the certainty of God's own decree. Christ is the Lamb slain from the foundation of the world (Rev. 13:8, NIV; Eph. 1:4).

But God is pleased to bring men into relation with Himself by faith. He wishes them to know that He alone can save them; He requires them to commit themselves to Him in trust. To instruct faith, God provides a model, an analogy of His final and ultimate salvation. That model must show that God alone is the Savior. It must also avoid diverting faith from God Himself to an image separate from God.

The use of models, images, or symbols is part of God's design to anticipate the fullness of meaning that cannot yet be revealed. The blood of bulls and goats cannot make atonement for sin (Heb. 10:4). But the blood of sacrificial animals may convey significance. It may serve as a sign, a symbol that points beyond itself to the reality of Christ's atoning sacrifice.

Yet there are limits to the function of symbolism. This is dramatically depicted in the tabernacle. The sanctuary of God in the wilderness pictures His dwelling in the midst of His people. This symbol is developed as a master model, elaborated by rich architectural and ceremonial detail. The very throne of God is symbolized in the "mercy seat" (Exod. 25:17), the golden covering of the ark of the covenant. The cherubim of gold above it represent the heavenly guardians of the throne. But here at the heart of God's model of His dwelling there is that which cannot be modeled. The throne on the ark is empty. No image may stand in the place of God Himself (Deut. 4:15:24). This is not to say that there can be no image of God, for God has made man in His image (Gen.

1:27). Rather, the absence of any image at the center of Israel's worship shows that Israel does not worship a representation of God, but God Himself, the true and living God who has redeemed His people and brought them unto Himself (Exod. 19:3), in order that they might stand before Him (Exod. 19:17; 20:3), and that He might dwell in their midst (Exod. 34:9; cf. 33:3, 4, 15).

The mercy seat pictures God's throne as it is reserved for Jesus Christ, "who is the image of the invisible God" (Col. 1:15), "for in him dwelleth all the fullness of the Godhead bodily" (Col. 2:9). The God-man, the incarnate Lord, is not a mere symbol of God's presence, an image to represent Him. He is Himself the Lord, the second person of the Trinity. "He that hath seen me hath seen the Father" (John 14:9).

In the empty place between the cherubim God is present in the darkness, veiled from the sight of Israel, but dwelling in their midst. The golden wings of symbolism surround that which is not symbolical, the real presence of God. The symbol and the reality are closely joined, but are not identical. When Christ came, the reality came; God could be worshipped in the visible manifestation of His presence, "which we have seen with our eyes . . . and our hands handled, concerning the Word of life" (I John 1:1), for "the Word became flesh and dwelt among us (and we beheld his glory, glory as of the only begotten from the Father), full of grace and truth" (John 1:14).

Because the incarnate Lord is not a symbol of God's presence, but God Himself present with us, all the symbolism of the tabernacle points to Him and is fulfilled in Him. For this reason Jesus can tell the woman of Samaria, "Woman, believe me, the hour cometh, when neither in this mountain, nor in Jerusalem, shall ye worship the Father. . . . The hour cometh, and now is, when the true worshippers shall worship the Father in spirit and truth . . ." (John 4:21, 23).

The mountain where the Samaritans believed God should be worshipped was Mount Gerizim, the mountain that loomed up beyond Jesus as He talked with the woman. The Samaritans were wrong; as Jesus said, "Salvation is of the Jews" (v. 22). Jerusalem was the place where God had set His name. But Jesus removes Jerusalem along with Gerizim as the place for worship. How can He declare this? It is not simply on the ground of God's spirituality. Jesus does not contend that God cannot be worshipped in any one place simply because He is a Spirit and therefore cannot be confined to a place. If that were Jesus' point there would be no reason to speak of a coming hour when worship would be no longer at Jerusalem. (God is always a Spirit!) The coming hour is the hour of Jesus' death and resurrection (John 2:4; 17:1; 16:32; cf. 5:25, 28; 11:25). The earthly place of sacrifice must lose its significance when the true and final sacrifice is offered. Jesus has come as the true Temple (John 1:14). He said, "Destroy this temple, and in three days I will raise it up" (John 2:19).

Jesus does not call the woman to "temple-less" worship, but to worship in truth (John 4:24); He is the Truth, the true Temple, and the Spirit in whom worship must be offered is the Spirit that He gives, the water springing up to eternal life (John 4:14). The woman must therefore come to the Father through Jesus—"I that speak unto thee am he!" (John 4:26). In Jesus the Father seeks true worshippers, and finds one in a disgraced Samaritan woman by Jacob's well.

In Jesus, therefore, both the reality and the symbols of God's dwelling in the midst of His people find fulfillment. The key to the New Testament understanding of typology is found in the sense in which fulfillment comes in Jesus Christ. Leonhard Goppelt has pointed out the distinctive meaning that *typos* gains in the New Testament.[2] That meaning is clear in Romans 5:8 where Paul speaks of Adam as a *typos* of Him that was to come. Christ is the Man from heaven (I Cor. 15:47): not only the head of a new humanity, but the realization of the image of God in man (Heb. 2:6-9). Christ is not simply another Adam in the sense of being

2. Leonard Goppelt, Typos: *The Typological Interpretation of the Old Testament in the New*, trans. D. H. Madvig (Grand Rapids: Eerdmans, 1982), p. 199. See also his article *"Typos"* in Gerhard Kittel, Gerhard Friendrich, eds., *Theological Dictionary of the New Testament*, vol. 8, trans. Geoffrey W. Bromily (Grand Rapids: Eerdmans, 1972), pp. 252ff.

like Adam; neither is He a second Adam in the sense of beginning again another race, as though there were to be another cycle of history comparable to the one begun in the first Adam. Rather, Christ is Himself the fullness of the image of God; Christ is the *meaning* of created human nature. The completeness, the glory of created human sonship is uniquely manifested in the God-man. What defines the type in New Testament thought is not simply the surpassing glory of the eschatological dimension, not even the transformation by which the patterns of the Old Covenant are renewed. The heart of the understanding of "type" in the New Testament lies in the New Testament doctrine of Christ. Only in Christ as the divine Savior do we find the transcending and trans-forming fulfillment that creates a whole new dimension. That dimension in the Gospel of John is the "true," not in contrast to the false (although John makes that contrast, too), but in contrast to the shadow, the promise, the anticipation. Jesus is the *true* Vine (John 15:1), the *true* Son of God, the *true* Israel (Isa. 49:3; Rom. 15:8), the *true* Bread from heaven (John 6:32, 33). In Him the reality appears, and in Him that reality is given to His people.

The typical function of Old Testament history is not limited, therefore, to a few instances of graphically symbolic events: the exodus from Egypt as God opens a path through the waters of death, or the entrance into the land as God gives to His people their inheritance. Rather, the whole history of redemption before the coming of Christ has a symbolic dimension. God delivers His people, guides them, blesses them, judges them. Yet because God's full and final salvation has not come, His dealings with His people are always anticipatory. The land is not the new creation of God's final promise; victory over the Amalekites or the Ca-naanites is not victory over Satan and the powers of darkness; the fruit of the vine is not the fruit of the Spirit. Because God binds His people to Himself in living fellowship, their salvation is not *merely* a shadow, an outward husk to be discarded. Abraham by faith knows the Lord and can perceive the reality that lies behind and beyond the promises of temporal blessing. But the faith of the Old Testament saints gives us the key for understanding and interpreting the revealed history of their earthly pilgrimage (Heb. 11:13–16). They did not and could not find rest until the promise was fulfilled, not just in Isaac, but in Christ (Heb. 4:8, 9).

The New Testament proclaims the fulfillment of all the typical symbols of the Old Testament in Christ. The fulfillment is greater than the type: a greater than Solomon (Matt. 12:42), than Jonah (Matt. 12:41), than the temple (John 2:19–21) has come. The Son of David is greater than David: David therefore hails his Son as his Lord (Matt. 22:41–46). But, as we have seen, Jesus is not simply greater by a relative degree, but by a transcendent measure. John, the greatest of the prophets, baptized in water, but Jesus baptizes in the Spirit (Matt. 3:11, 12). In the Passover symbol, the people choose a lamb of the flock, but Jesus is the Lamb of God that takes away the sin of the world (John 1:29).

We may diagram the rationale of New Testament typology by basing it on the unfolding of redemptive history and its climax in Jesus Christ.

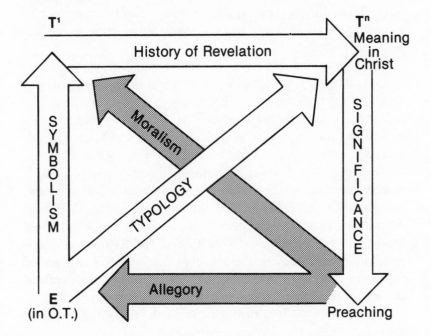

If we represent that history by a horizontal line leading to Christ, we may assume that all the truths of God's revelation are fulfilled in Christ. Truths may be emphasized in one period of redemptive history more than in another, but no truth is eliminated or forgotten. The meaning of any Old Testament symbol is the concept that is symbolized. In the biblical context the concept is affirmed or denied; it is related to other concepts in such a way that some statement is made. A truth is expressed. An Old Testament event, a ceremony, or a prophetic, priestly, or royal action may therefore symbolize, pointing to a revealed truth at a particular point in the history of redemption (truth to the first power: T^1). We may be sure that this truth will be carried forward to Jesus Christ (truth to the "nth" power: T^n). We may therefore connect the event, ceremony, or action directly with that truth as it comes to full expression in Christ. This line is the hypotenuse of the triangle it forms, and it is the line of typology. If the symbolism of an Old Testament incident or person is not perceived, or does not exist, no line of typology can be drawn. Nor can the event be a type in a sense different from its symbolic function in its Old Testament setting.

Since the exodus event, for example, is manifestly symbolic, we discover its typical meaning by perceiving its symbolic meaning in its Old Testament setting. It symbolizes God's deliverance of His people from the power of another lord so that they might be free to worship and serve Him as their only Lord and Master (Exod. 4:22, 23). Further, their deliverance is solely the work of God in a situation in which no deliverance is humanly possible. Much more is included in the details of the symbolism, including the ceremonial of the Passover, and the figure of the cloud. But an outstanding feature of the deliverance is that it is not only *from* death, but *through* death. The waters of the Red Sea threaten Israel with death before them just as much as the chariots of Pharaoh threaten with death behind them. Further, the depth of the sea in the Old Testament is the abyss, a synonym for the grave (cf. Jonah 2). It is through the depths that Israel is led to deliverance from the dominion of Pharaoh.

In Luke's account of the transfiguration of Jesus, we learn that Moses talked with Jesus about His "exodus" that He was to accomplish at Jerusalem (Luke 9:31). The truth of deliverance from the power of Satan into the liberty of the sons of God is to find its full accomplishment in Jesus Christ. Christ's miracles are indeed signs, but they differ from the miracles of Moses not only in being miracles of blessing rather than of judgment. They differ also in being signs that point directly to the Lord who performs them, and therefore to the realization of the promises that Moses' deliverance symbolized. Moses confronts Pharaoh, and the signs given to him from the Lord overwhelm the magic of Pharaoh's priests (Exod. 7:12). But Jesus confronts Satan and, having overcome the "strong man," is able to deliver those in captivity to him (Luke 11:19-22; Matt. 12:27-29). He not only casts out demons and delivers those oppressed by Satan; He forgives sins, and brings men and women from the kingdom of darkness into the kingdom of light (Mark 2:5-11; Col. 1:12, 13).

In His death and resurrection Jesus accomplishes His "exodus." He passes through the tide of death for us and enables us to sing the song of Moses and of the Lamb in the experience of resurrection joy granted already to those who trust in Him (I Pet. 1:3-5; Rev. 15:3; Exod. 15:2; Ps. 118:14; Isa. 12:1-2).

To preach the exodus event as an example of political liberation obviously does not do justice to the framework of God's covenantal promise by which He delivers Israel. God does not only strike off the yoke so that Israel may go free (Lev. 26:13). He frees Israel from the service of Pharaoh so that Israel may serve Him (Exod. 4:23). He brings Israel out of Egypt and bears them on eagles' wings unto Himself (Exod. 19:4). Yet even awareness of God's calling to Sinai and to Zion does not prepare us to preach the meaning of the exodus. We must perceive the reality of Christ's salvation as it is prefigured in the exodus event. Only in the fulfillment in Christ does the exodus have significance for us.

We must therefore complete the diagram by dropping a line from the *meaning* of the truth as it is accomplished and revealed in Christ, to the *significance* of the truth as it is perceived by us. This means that two other possible lines in the diagram are illegitimate. We certainly should not look back directly from our situation to the exodus in the Old Testament without considering the truth that was symbolized by the exodus. Sometimes this is done by allegorizing. The Old Testament events are made symbols for illustrating any significance that the preacher chooses to find in them. (This misinterpretation is indicated by the bottom, horizontal dotted line in the diagram.) The preacher can then read the account of Moses' sign and hold forth on rods that become snakes to warn against the misuse of authority, or to describe virtues becoming vices. His imagination is free of any constraint of Scripture.

A less blatant failure in scriptural interpretation is moralizing. (This is represented by the diagonal dotted line pointing back to the truth revealed at a particular point in the Old Testament.) The moralizing preacher does not arbitrarily seize on any element in the text that catches his fancy. He does take account of the meaning of the text in its original setting. He interprets for his hearers the significance that this truth has for them in their own lives and experience. But he completely fails to show how this truth comes to its full meaning in Christ, and only in Christ.[3]

The moralistic approach has sometimes been defended as interpretation pure and simple, proclaiming only what the text says and all that the text says, neither more nor less. But to ignore the dimension of promise in the Old Testament is to misinterpret it altogether. It is to forget the message of the primary Author of Scripture, the Holy Spirit. The Spirit of Old Testament Scripture is the Spirit of Christ who inspired the human authors to testify of the sufferings of Christ and the glories that should follow (I Pet. 1:11). (For a further discussion of meaning vs. significance in biblical interpretation, see Hendrik Krabbendam's chapter, "Hermeneutics and Preaching.")

Liberation theology at best offers an example of a moralistic interpretation of the exodus deliverance. It fails to appreciate the

---

3. I am grateful to the Rev. Richard Craven, who as a student at Westminster Seminary suggested the lines of "moralism" and "allegory" as part of the diagram.

significance of the exodus in the history of redemption. Indeed, it dismisses the orthodox interpretation as spiritualizing, as individualistic pietism that does not recognize that politics is God's work in the world. Pietism has been guilty of individualism and of ignoring the corporate view of the people of God that the symbolism of the exodus presents. But pietism nevertheless recognized the gospel and the centrality of Jesus Christ in whom our exodus is accomplished.

3. The Preaching of Christ Recognizes the Significance of the Old Testament

When the Old Testament is interpreted in the light of its own structure of promise and when that promise is seen as fulfilled in Jesus Christ, then the significance of the Old Testament can be preached in theological depth and in practical power. Preaching that does not center on Christ will always miss the dimension of depth in Old Testament revelation. It is in this dimension that the real significance of that revelation lies.

Without reference to Christ the covenant law of the Old Testament becomes legalism. A preacher may present a series of sermons on the Ten Commandments. Since he appreciates the Reformed creeds, he uses the Larger Catechism of the Westminster Assembly or the Heidelberg Catechism to guide his reflection. He is preaching, let us say, on the seventh commandment. His sermon has two parts: first, what the commandment forbids; second, what the commandment requires. He succeeds in describing a catalogue of vices in which lust finds expression; he also presents the central virtue of chastity that overcomes such sins. The sermon ends in warning, a call to repentance and to amendment of life for those who would be obedient to God's law.

No doubt the preacher will also enforce his warnings by examples from the Bible (David and Bathsheba) and from contemporary life. On the positive side, he may offer suggestions about the benefits of other interests and occupations to reduce the tempta-

tions to lust springing from idleness. He may counsel the avoiding
of lascivious films and TV movies.

Is this a caricature? Perhaps, to a degree. What biblically
grounded preacher would fail to connect the seventh commandment with our Lord's teaching? Certainly he will emphasize Jesus'
word that adultery is not only the outward act, but the inward
thought. As the commandment is carried forward into the context of Christ's teaching, however, its significance is at once deep-
ened. If the preacher recognizes this, he will be drawn into
preaching the heart of the law as Christ presented it. The issue is
then not simply the subduing of lust, but the expression of love,
the love that fulfills the law. What is that love, according to
Jesus? It is the love shown by the Good Samaritan, the love of
compassion, of self-denying, spontaneous, sacrificial mercy. That
love is modeled on the love of God in Jesus Christ. Love for
neighbor flows from love for God, and love for God is our response to His love for us.

Only at the cross do we know the real meaning of love—of
God's redeeming love. Only at the cross can our lusts be crucified. Only from the fountain opened at Calvary flows the blood
of cleansing and the living water of the Spirit. It is not only true
that the law should not be preached without the gospel. More
profoundly, the law itself cannot be understood without its fulfillment in the gospel. It is to a redeemed people that God gives
His law, and *God's* law, the law that centers on Him, requires
more of us than simple justice. It requires us to forgive as we have
been forgiven, to love as we have been loved by our gracious
Father in heaven.

The preacher must not divorce the catechism's analysis of the
commandments from the rest of the catechism. The commandments are there carefully placed in the context of redemption. As
preachers we must do the same.

Further, because God gives His commandments to His redeemed people, we must understand their twofold purpose: they
reveal His holy nature so that we may know Him, and they shape
our lives so that we may reflect His glory. Both sides of God's
purpose come to their realization in Christ.

We may ask, Why did God forbid adultery to His covenant people? The answer is not simply that God wished to provide stable family life for the sociological well-being of Israel. There is a deeper reason, one closely related to the very nature of God's saving covenant. God would emphasize and sanctify the reality of a jealous love. The love of the marriage bond, expressed in sexual union, is not to be shared with others who are not joined by that bond. The faithfulness of jealous love in marriage provides Israel with a model for understanding the faithful love that God's people are to show to Him, a response to His jealous, electing love for them. God reveals Himself to Israel as a jealous God: "For thou shalt worship no other god: for the Lord, whose name is Jealous, is a jealous God" (Exod. 34:14).

The constant biblical metaphor that compares idolatry to adultery is grounded in an analogy that God has appointed by His ordering of the marriage relationship. God will be known not only as the Father of Israel His son, but also as the husband and Lord of Israel His bride.

Without the analogy to God's jealousy for Israel's exclusive devotion we might suppose that any sexual liaison would be legitimate that was consummated with love. On the other hand, without the analogy to the jealous love of a husband for his wife, we might imagine that God would approve of acts of religious worship directed toward any deity whatever, since He alone is God and could therefore receive them for Himself.

But the analogy that permeates Scripture teaches us otherwise. God would have us know the intensity of a pure love that is exclusive in character, a commitment of the heart that is profaned if one turns from it to seek a relation of the same intimacy with another. The worship of the idols is not an indirect way of adoring the one true God who has revealed Himself to Israel. It is apostasy, turning away from the Lord; it is spiritual adultery. Solomon joins his heathen wives in worshiping Ashtoreth, the goddess of the Sidonians; Milcolm, the "abomination" of the Ammonites; Chemosh, of Moab; and Molech, of Ammon. When he does so he turns his heart away from the Lord (I Kings

11:1-13; cf. Exod. 34:10-17). No longer does he love the Lord his God with all his heart, soul, and might (Deut. 6:5).

Further, the sacrifices of the Gentiles are not at last offered to merely imaginary, mythical beings. They are offered to demons (I Cor. 10:20). For that reason Paul says, "Or do we provoke the Lord to jealousy?" (I Cor. 10:22). God is jealous, zealous for His own holy Name. He cannot tolerate the blasphemy of attributing to the powers of darkness the glory that is due to Him. Of course, what God requires is also that which delivers us from delusion, bondage, and destruction. Yet God must require it not merely for our sake but for His. God must be true to Himself.

The nature of God's jealousy for His Name and for His people is revealed in Jesus Christ. As we learn of the triune nature of God we are able to understand better the meaning of His holy jealousy. Jesus as the Son of God is jealous for the Name and glory of His Father. He drives the hucksters out of the temple: "Take these things hence; make not my Father's house a house of merchandise" (John 2:16). His disciples remembered the Scriptures, "Zeal for thy house shall eat me up" (John 2:17; Ps. 69:9). Jesus is consumed with jealousy for the pure worship of His Father in heaven. His jealousy is more than that of the true servant of God (like Phinehas, Num. 25:10, 11). His is the jealousy of the Son for the Name and honor of His Father.

So, too, the Father is jealous for His Son. His voice from heaven acknowledged His beloved Son; He has exalted Him above all creation in heaven and earth and given Him a Name that is above every name, that at the Name of Jesus every knee might bow and every tongue confess that Jesus Christ is Lord (Phil. 2:9-11).

God's commandment forbidding adultery should therefore be understood in its context: the unfolding history of God's redemption. Not just sexual purity, but covenant devotion is the underlying requirement of this commandment. For this reason the apostle Paul, when he describes the jealous love that a man should have for his wife, cannot help continually reflecting on God's jealous love for His people in Jesus Christ (Eph. 5:25-33). The great wonder and mystery for Paul is not the mystery of married love, but the mystery of divine love for which it provides a created analogy. Paul is no longer Saul the legalistic Pharisee whom Jesus met on the road to Damascus. He does not separate the commandments from the Lord who gave them or from His purposes in redemption. Marital faithfulness is the service of the Lord not simply because God has commanded it, but because it manifests love that springs from God's redeeming love. That vision of serving the Lord touches the deepest springs of motivation for the Christian. In loving others we manifest our love for Him who first loved us.

In christological perspective the law is not legalism, nor is covenantal history moralism. As we have seen, the Old Testament does not furnish us with a scrapbook of narratives useful for purposes of illustration. Rather it contains the record of God's ongoing work of redemption in the conflict between the Seed of the woman and the seed of the serpent. We dare not preach David's encounter with Goliath as an example of bravery to be emulated in our conflicts with the "giants" that assault us. Such an approach trivializes the Old Testament revelation. David's calling and enduement as the Lord's anointed has its deep significance in revealing the redemptive work of God. The Lord prepares us to understand something of the significance of Christ's final victory over Satan and the powers of darkness. The salvation wrought by David has typical significance that is not detached from its historical reality, but rather grounded in it.

In one other brief example, the poetry, as much as the law, of the Old Testament is grounded in the history of redemption. Many of the psalms are written in the first person plural. The people of God confess their faith in their Lord, ascribing praise to His Name and seeking deliverance from their enemies. The individual psalmist does not express merely private emotions. In many cases the psalmist is David, crying to God in full awareness that he is the Lord's anointed (II Sam. 22:51). Even when another inspired individual is the author of a psalm, it is written in the representative capacity of one called to serve the Lord.

The function of the psalms in God's dealings with His people is made clear at the beginning when the song of Moses is given by

God's inspiration (Deut. 31:19). The song is not a direct prophecy addressed to Israel; nor does it have the form of covenantal law, like the Ten Commandments. Rather, it has the form of response to God's revelation in praise. Yet it forms part of God's witness to Israel. Memorized and sung as part of Israel's heritage, it will "testify before them as a witness" when they prove unfaithful to the Lord their Rock (Deut. 31:21, 22). The later inspired songs of Israel have the same function.

When the Lord's people or the Lord's servants call upon His name, their songs are evidently written for worship and supplication, not for entertainment. As expressions of worship they are stamped by the distinctiveness of God's dealings with Israel, that is, by the history of redemption. The praises of God that describe His attributes do not have the motivation of such hymns among the polytheistic Gentiles. The inspired psalmist does not have the problem of a polytheist. Like a philanderer with many girlfriends the polytheist must convince the god whose favors he seeks that he is the winner among all the gods, at least for the moment.

Rather, the psalms of Israel are characterized by declarative as well as descriptive praise.[4] The Lord is adored for what He has done, as well as for who He is. He is the God of the exodus (Ps. 80; 81; 114), the God who redeemed Israel and made His covenant with David (Ps. 89). The history of God's salvation forms the basis for confession of sin and for petition for the renewal of God's saving mercies (Ps. 74, 80). The psalms also proclaim the fulfillment of God's promises when the Lord Himself will come again as the Redeemer, Judge, and Deliverer of His people (Ps. 96:10-13). The new song of salvation will be sung in that great day (Ps. 96:1; 98:1; cf. 144:9).[5]

In their theological depth the psalms are songs of God's covenant and of the hope of the covenant. Since God's great work of salvation will be accomplished by the Son of David, the psalms

---

4. On this distinction, and the contrast between the Psalms and ancient Near Eastern hymns, see Claus Westermann, *The Praise of God in the Psalms*, trans. Keith Crim (London: Epworth, 1966), pp. 15-51.

5. Geerhardus Vos, "The Eschatology of the Psalter," reprinted in *The Pauline Eschatology* (Grand Rapids: Eerdmans, 1953), pp. 323-65.

are explicitly messianic. Jesus confronts His enemies with passages from the psalms. They have not understood that David's Son must also be His Lord (Ps. 110:1; Matt. 22:41–46). They do not know that it is the stone rejected by the builders that God has made the head of the corner (Ps. 118:22, 23; Matt. 21:42, 43).

But it is not only in a few "messianic psalms" that the songs of Israel point to Jesus Christ. Indeed, we may perceive from plainly messianic psalms principles of interpretation that apply to many others.

Psalm 22, for example, is clearly messianic. The opening cry of the psalm is the cry of Christ on the cross, and the details of the sufferer's anguish are remarkably specific in their application to Calvary. The author of Hebrews cites Psalm 22:22 in reference to Christ (Heb. 2:11, 12). Not only the cry of abandonment, but also the vow of praise are Christ's own utterances. This is true not only because Jesus in His earthly ministry sang the psalms and in that way made them His own, but also because He fulfilled them. David as a righteous sufferer, persecuted because he was the Lord's anointed, prefigures the truly righteous sufferer, God's own Son and Holy One. Not just the first verse of Psalm 22 is Christ's; the whole psalm is His.

In addition to overtly messianic psalms (such as Ps. 22), there are other categories of psalms that no less unmistakably point to Christ. The "royal psalms," songs of Zion and of Zion's king, are pointedly messianic in the light of New Testament fulfillment. When the king of glory enters Zion, triumphant after subduing all his foes (Ps. 24), the scene that is pictured is fulfilled in Christ's ascension. The Lord who marches through the wilderness and enters into His holy hill, receiving and giving gifts to men (Ps. 68; 18) is the Lord whose way in the wilderness was prepared by John the Baptist (Isa. 40:3; Matt. 3:1–3). He who is the coming Judge (Ps. 96:13; 97:7; cf. Heb. 1:6) is the Savior who leads His people with Him in triumphant procession. His throne is established forever (Ps. 2, 110); He has universal dominion (Ps. 2; 72; 110). The King receives His bride and His household as the crown of blessing (Ps. 45). In Jesus both the psalms that exalt the King of David's line and the Eternal King are joined.

4. Conclusion

Only as we perceive the focus on Christ do we sense the depth of meaning in the Old Testament. It is precisely the discovery of this theological depth that will give our preaching practical power. Some would object to christological preaching of the Old Testament not because they dispute the possibility of making a case for it, but because they think it is just too complicated.

That objection will end the matter if we are unwilling to be workmen in the Word, laboring in the Word and teaching (I Tim. 5:17). It is much easier to build sermons out of wood, hay, and stubble than to be craftsmen using gold, silver, and precious stones (I Cor. 3:12-15).

Christological preaching calls for patient comparing of Scripture with Scripture, extensive use of concordances, and a lifetime commitment to Bible study, meditation, and prayer. Christological preaching is not contrived, however; nor are its lines obscure in the Bible. "Salvation is of the Lord" (Jon. 2:9) is the great text of the Bible and reminds us that we must not sacrifice the objective reality of what God does in salvation in order to stress the subjective reality of our knowledge of the Lord and experience of His mercy. If we mistakenly think that focusing on our experience is more practical or reaches men where they live, we will overlook the overwhelming gospel fact that salvation is God's work. We do not kindle faith by describing it but by describing Christ. Paul never tires of speaking of God's work; for him the *indicative* of what God has done always comes before the *imperative* of what we are to do (e.g., Col. 3:1-4).

Preaching Christ from all the Scriptures joins faith to grace. God is the Savior in Christ. The Old Testament believers trusted as they waited for that salvation to come. They are examples to us as *believers*—not apart from the objective facts of God's redemption, but as those who lived by faith.

The obedience of love flows from that faith relation. Like faith, love is kindled not by introspection, but by looking to Jesus, the Author and Finisher of our faith. We love because He first loved us; it is the love of God that is shed abroad in our hearts.

The Scriptures are full of moral instruction and ethical exhortation, but the ground and motivation of all is found in the mercy of Jesus Christ. We are to preach all the riches of Scripture, but unless the center holds all the bits and pieces of our pulpit counseling, of our thundering at social sins, of our positive or negative thinking—all fly off into the Sunday morning air.

Paul was resolved to know nothing at Corinth but Jesus Christ and Him crucified. Let others develop the pulpit fads of the passing seasons. Specialize in preaching Jesus!

7

Exegesis
Sinclair B. Ferguson

What is exegetical preaching? From one perspective all preaching that is truly Christian preaching is exegetical in nature. Exegesis is the explanation, or exposition, of a sentence, a word, an idea. As an exercise it depends on the prior existence of materials. It may be a creative discipline; but it does not create *ex nihilo*. In this sense the preacher is always an exegete simply because he is a herald, or ambassador, of Christ.

The preacher creates the *sermon*, he does not create the message. Rather he proclaims and explains the message he has received. His message is not original; it is given to him (II Cor. 5:19). Consequently, whether he preaches a topical, doctrinal, or textual sermon; whether he deals with a passage, or preaches systematically through a book, the exegetical principle will always be present: he is explaining and expounding the message that has already been given. Therein lies his authority and his confidence in the promise of God's help and blessing. The sermon is not the preacher's word; it is God's Word.

When we speak about "exegetical" or "expository" preaching, however, we customarily think not of preaching in general, but of a particular style of preaching.[1] In exegetical preaching the explanation of Scripture forms the dominant feature and the organizing principle of the message. *All* preaching should be based on the

---

1. Although the terms *exegetical* and *expository* are sometimes used to denote different things, in this context they are used as virtual synonyms.

apostolic *kerygma* and *didache*. *Exegetical* preaching is governed by the goal of expounding the meaning and significance of this "faith once-delivered" in terms of the actual way in which it has been delivered, namely the structure and content of the biblical revelation, in which truth is revealed not in the form of a series of theological or topical *loci* (God, sin, justification, sanctification; war, money, social ethics, etc.), but through history, parable, narrative, argumentation, poem, and so on. Exegetical preaching therefore sees as its fundamental task the explanation of the text in its context, the unfolding of its principles, and only then their application to the world of the hearers. As William Taylor, a notable expository preacher of a former generation, well expressed it, exposition is "the honest answer which the preacher gives, after faithful study, to these questions: What is the mind of the Holy Spirit in this passage? and what is its bearing on related Christian truths, or on the life and conversation of the Christian himself?"[2]

Two caveats need to be entered at this juncture.

1. The first is that exegetical preaching should not be confused with a homiletical running commentary on the text. The function of the exegetical sermon is not limited to furnishing information. Rather, it is dominated by a message and is intended to produce action as well as to impart instruction. Indeed, precisely because this is a function of the teaching of Scripture (grace leads to faith, indicatives lead to imperatives), it is also necessarily a dimension of exegetical preaching (and this is precisely why, later in this volume, John Bettler argues that all biblical preaching is applicatory preaching). The words of Jonathan Edwards about his own preaching are equally applicable to exegetical and to textual preaching:

> I should think myself in the way of my duty, to raise the affections of my hearers as high as I possibly can . . . . such

2. William Taylor, *The Ministry of the Word* (Grand Rapids: Baker Book House, 1975), p. 157.

preaching has been thought to have the greatest tendency to answer the ends of preaching. . . . Our people do not so much need to have their heads stored, as to have their hearts touched; and they stand in need of that sort of preaching which has the greatest tendency to do this.[3]

Exegetical preaching seeks to do this precisely because it is biblical preaching and recognizes that, as such, it will speak to the whole man, not exclusively to man as a cerebral being.

2. The second caveat is that exegetical preaching is not *merely* systematic preaching in the sense of preaching a course of sermons on a book of Scripture. Historically, many expository preachers have adopted the method of following the text of Scripture to the logical conclusion of preaching through entire books of the Bible. Here one may think of Chrysostom and Augustine, of Luther and Calvin, of Joseph Caryl and Thomas Manton, of Alexander MacLaren and D. Martyn Lloyd-Jones. It would therefore be relatively easy, particularly for a younger preacher, to assume that by preaching on the previous passage the previous week and the following passage the following week, he was expounding Scripture. But the core of expository preaching is not the connecting link between sermons; rather it is the style and content of a particular sermon. It is actually engaging in exegetically controlled exposition *this week,* not preaching on the following verses *next week!* It may be of the *bene esse* of preaching that it should be systematic as well as expository, but it is the *esse* of preaching that it should unfold the meaning and significance of the biblical text. It is this particular exercise that is the focus of our attention.

Systematic, exegetical preaching has many advantages. Indeed, such are its advantages that it ought to be the staple (if not exclu-

3. Jonathan Edwards, *Some Thoughts Concerning the Present Revival of Religion in New England* in *The Works of Jonathan Edwards*, vol. 1 (Edinburgh: Banner of Truth, 1974), p. 391. See also Samuel Logan's fuller discussion of Edwards's comments on the affections in his chapter in the present volume.

sive) diet of the preacher's ministry.[4] For one thing, it teaches the congregation how to read the Bible for themselves. Most Christians tend to use in their own Bible study the style of study presented to them in the pulpit. Models of study are necessary, and exegetical preaching is the best way to teach Christians exegetical reading of Scripture. Furthermore we live in an age (as did Chrysostom and Calvin) when the primary need *is* for our people to be instructed in the teaching and application of Scripture. Exegetical preaching serves that purpose, bringing the hearers under the influence both of the *content* of God's Word, and the *spirit* in which God's Word has come to us.

Furthermore, it is chiefly by the exegetical method of preaching that the individual pastor is most likely to grow as a student of Scripture, a man of God, and a preacher. One of the rather sad features of the community of preachers is that so few of us seem to exhibit continuing growth *as preachers*. Our congregations are little conscious that we ourselves increasingly love God's Word and feed on it, or that we are bringing from it "things old and new" with an excitement born of continued preparation for exegetical preaching.

This is not to say that the endorsement of a conviction about exegetical preaching will overnight revolutionize our pulpits. For such preaching is not the creature of a night. It is not the easiest or most natural of disciplines in which to engage. Nor should we ever forget that it is men sent from God (cf. John. 1:6), more than methods devised by these men, that God employs to build His kingdom.

---

4. Some great preachers like C. H. Spurgeon have, of course, expressed a strong antipathy for such systematic exposition. Note also W. G. T. Shedd's remark—which today seems overly sanguine: "The expository sermon should be occasionally employed. There is somewhat less call for this variety than there was before the establishment of Sabbath schools and Bible classes." *Homiletics and Pastoral Theology* (New York: Charles Scribner and Co., 1867), p. 137. Compare Pierre Charles Marcel's more recent remarks in which he lists ten reasons why *systematic* expository preaching is vital. *The Relevance of Preaching*, trans. R. R. McGregor (Grand Rapids: Baker Book House, 1977), pp. 74-75.

The Elements of Expository Preaching

There are six primary elements in the preparation for and preaching of exegetical sermons. They may be described as *selecting, understanding, crystallizing, structuralizing, concretizing, and delivering.*

1. Selecting

How are we to select a text or passage of Scripture for exposition? We have already noted that many expositors adopt a systematic form of preaching. To an extent this system obviates the need for selection, at least on a week-by-week basis. Indeed that is one of its main attractions to the preacher—he does not spend many hours of preparation before he even begins to deal with the text. But, unless the preacher is committed to series that last for years, exposition still requires selection. It takes place less frequently when entire books are to be expounded. But these also must be selected—and, once selected, the commitment is one of months rather than minutes. The choice of book (text) to be expounded systematically is therefore of immense importance to the preacher and in a profound sense to the whole ethos of the congregation's life. A *series* that "fails" may have far more disastrous consequences for the congregation than one sermon that fails! A right choice is therefore a matter of singular importance.

Our first principle must be to recognize (whether we preach from a single section, or through an entire book of the Bible) that the preacher operates with two horizons: (1) the text of Scripture and (2) the people of God and their environment in the world. He ought not normally to make his selection without consciously bringing these two horizons together. That, in the last analysis, is what all of his preaching is intended to do. His thinking must therefore begin here. The preacher's task is to communicate the whole counsel of God to His people. Over the period of his ministry the preacher must endeavor to discharge this responsibility faithfully. That is one horizon toward which he will work. As Donald Macleod reminds us later in this volume, the preacher must ask himself several questions: Am I covering the whole range of biblical teaching—Old and New Testament, historical and theological, poetic and prose, exhortatory and denunciatory? Am I covering the whole range of biblical doctrines—God and man, Christ and Spirit, sin and grace, heaven and hell? Am I dealing with all the applications of the gospel message—to individual, home and family, business and pleasure, man and woman, church and society, personal and civil? The expositor will be a man who engages in this kind of analysis of his own ministry, so that one element in his choice will always be that he is operating within the total framework of biblical revelation and doctrine.

Within that context the preacher will also, by necessity, be a biblical theologian.[5] He will be concerned to provide biblical depth as well as breadth. He will see his responsibility to focus on teaching that forms a central part of biblical teaching. He should not be deluded by the notion that his people need to hear the so-called "deeper truths" of the faith. Those truths in Scripture are none other than the fundamental truths of the faith, with all their implications rightly grasped.

But alongside this objective exercise, there is an exercise in spiritual sensitivity also required in the selection of preaching material. The preacher is not a systematic theologian whose exclusive task is to expound an inwardly coherent account of the Christian faith. He is a pastor, whose major task is to feed the flock of God. The context of the congregation therefore plays a major role in the selection of his material. Where are they in terms of the Christian pilgrimage? What are their situation, needs, lacks, pressures, composition? Of course our preaching is not to be *need-determined*, but it must be *people-oriented*, as Jesus Christ's was (cf. John 16:12).

At this point we see something of the value of systematic theology, when that theology enables us to see the interconnections between Christian truth. For those connections are not always the ones preachers tend to make. To give an obvious illustration:

5. I am thinking here of the comment that Calvin became a theologian in order to become a better pastor.

we find ourselves called to preach to people whose chief characteristic is lack of assurance. How does this govern our selection of biblical material? The natural instinct is to reply, "Preach a series of sermons on the nature of true assurance." But to do this is not only pastorally a questionable response; theologically it is a confused response. Why? Because assurance is not received by knowing about assurance so much as it is by knowing about Christ! In other words, the selection of material in such a context should be governed not by the nature of the problem so much as by the shape of the gospel, what Paul calls "the form of teaching to which you were entrusted" (Rom. 6:17). This is a principle of selection that lends itself to wide illustration.

One or two further general comments may be in place at this juncture. It is the present writer's conviction that under all ordinary circumstances an expository series should not be unduly prolonged. In this matter men's tastes and gifts differ very considerably. There are men who have such ability as preachers and find themselves in such circumstances that long series of expositions may be justified. But such men and circumstances are rare. It ought to be remembered in this context that the great series of sermons preached by Chrysostom, Luther, Calvin, and others generally included several sermons preached each week-day, so that the entire series was not prolonged to many years. People *need* breadth and variety in their spiritual diet, which is not necessarily the same thing as superficiality and novelty.

In connection with the exposition of individual passages, it is a commonplace observation that what first impresses us is most likely to make an impression on others through us. This should not, however, be taken to mean that we should preach on those texts which have made most recent impressions on us. There may be occasions when that is wise. But often younger preachers are tempted to make this the major rule of text selection. They in particular need to remember that there is a difference between our ability to *hear* the word clearly and our gifts and experience in *preaching* that same word clearly. Often the composition of a message from a text or passage that has meant a great deal to us will involve the passage of many months, even years, before we are able to use the material in such a way that we edify God's people rather than simply drag them through our own spiritual experience from text to text.

2. Understanding

Having made the selection of the book or passage to be expounded, we are now faced with the task of working with that text. What is our primary duty? Here we are faced with a fundamental issue that often sets apart theological education from the actual practice of ministry. For it is tempting for those involved in theological education to say, "The first step is to reach for the Hebrew Bible, or the Greek Testament." At the other end of the spectrum, it seems likely that some preachers enter their pulpits Sunday by Sunday not only *not* having consulted their original texts, but perhaps not even knowing where in the muddle of their studies their original language tools are to be found! It is tempting for them to say (and many have eager, well-instructed congregations large enough to confirm the conviction), that they are perfectly able to expound God's Word to their people from the English text.

To an extent this intramural debate between scholars and practitioners often centers on the wrong issue, for all practical purposes. On the one hand, perhaps many men do not gain a sufficient mastery of the original texts while at seminary to be encouraged to make regular use of them. Seminaries need to ask themselves, How is it that we train men for two or three years in the text of Scripture, yet fail to prepare them adequately? But on the other hand, it will not do for those of us who are practitioners to operate on the basis that an English text is altogether adequate for the task of exposition. We, for our part, should be asking, Should I not make use of all the tools available to me to give my very best to my people?

This focus on linguistics *simpliciter,* however, is a mistaken one in the current situation. Rather our concern should be the broader one of *understanding the text.* Such an understanding demands *some kind* of appreciation of the language in which that text is written, *however and wherever that appreciation is gained.* Consequently, whether we are capable readers of the original text, or whether we have simply enough grasp of the original tongues to proceed slowly through concordances, lexicons, grammars, theological wordbooks, and technical linguistic commentaries, our primary task is always the same—coming to an understanding of the meaning of the text to the best of our ability. Pure linguistics are of limited help for the composition of a sermon, but they are of fundamental help if it is our concern to interpret Scripture correctly. Furthermore, because of the very nature of language as a form of communication of concepts, the use of the original tongues and such aids as help us to read in them can sometimes be astonishingly illuminating. Sir Edwyn Hoskyns spoke wisely of burying oneself in a dictionary and coming up in the presence of God. One does not need to be a language expert to share that experience. But, if we share it, our hearers will undoubtedly be enriched as well.

It would be inappropriate in this context to proceed by listing a series of principles that should govern our exegesis. What should be recognized, however, is that our exegesis of Scripture must serve the ultimate goal of preaching. *Our* exegesis *as preachers* is not completed when we have analyzed the text. For that reason, it should not be limited to a grammatical exercise. As important—in some ways of greater importance—is engaging in an exegesis that uncovers both what the text *said* to the first readers, and what it *meant* to them. Out of the exegesis emerges the context and circumstances in which this Word from God was first spoken. It is here that the exegete is also the man of imagination. He does not "imagine" a context *de noveau;* but he must "image" the context in such a way that what is being said in the text takes on a three-dimensional significance. He sees that *this* text addresses itself to *that* situation. In a word the preacher-exegete grasps the dynamics that form the context of the text, statement, or passage.

Frequently this element in exegesis makes the difference between what one might call a surface exposition and a dynamic exposition in which hearers are caused to say, "So that is what this passage is saying; it is so clear to me now that I wonder why I never noticed it before." This may be called "depth exegesis," so long as we are aware that we are speaking here about the actual dynamics of the text, and not some spiritual, esoteric, allegorical sense that bears little relationship to the fundamental meaning of the passage.

Some illustrations may serve to underline this point. Two of Jesus' parables will serve to illustrate—partly because the material being expounded is so familiar that one might think it impossible for anyone to say, "So that is what the passage means; why did I not see that before?" The parables are those known customarily as "The Good Samaritan" and "The Prodigal Son" and are instances in which careful exegesis is obviously a larger discipline than merely the use of original languages.[6]

"The Good Samaritan." The "punch-line" of this parable is "Go and do likewise" (Luke 10:37). Accurate exegesis will take this to be the determining element in the structure of our exposition. Hearers are to be urged to imitate the Good Samaritan. But on what basis?

Christ's words emerge from the question He poses at the end of the parable? "Which of these three, do you think, proved neighbour to the man who fell among the robbers?" (Luke 10:36). Notice that our Lord's question answers the original *questioner,* but *not the original question.* The original question was "Who is my neighbour?" (v. 29). For that reason Jesus' answer is often taken to mean that whoever is in need is my neighbor. But that is not what he says. The neighbor in the story is not the man who fell among robbers, but the Samaritan. Jesus answers the question, "Who is my neighbour?" by saying: *You are the neighbor.* So

6. Modern scholarship has emphasized the importance of recognizing that parables have *one point* only. That, generally speaking, may be true; but it must be remembered that their *one point* is the consequence of a buildup of a variety of points essential to the parable. Cf. V. S. Poythress's review of Robert H. Stein: *An Introduction to the Parables of Jesus* (Philadelphia, Westminster Press, 1981) in the *Westminster Theological Journal* 44 (Spring 1982): 158–60.

long as I can answer the question "Who is my neighbour?" I can draw limits to my responsibilities. But that is the very reverse of what Jesus is saying. He is saying, there are no limits to your responsibilities, for *you* are the neighbor.

Here, then, we have an example of how careful exegesis of the text throws the dynamics of Christ's conversation, and the resulting emphasis of our exposition, into an entirely new light. It is not difficult to see that this presents us with a message at once more demanding and more revolutionary to our thinking than we would otherwise recognize. What at one level is an encouragement to "neighborliness" in the sense of seeing needs in others, is transformed into a challenge as to our own identity in relationship to the principles that govern the kingdom of God—namely to unreserved abandonment to the kingdom lifestyle.

"The Prodigal Son."   In this parable it is abundantly clear that the "one point per parable" principle keeps us from allegorization; but this principle also needs to be employed in such a way that not one of the nuances of Jesus' teaching is lost. Thus, the unity of the parable is not broken by the recognition that the figures—Father, Pharisee, sinner—are all equally recognizable, and that something is said here about each of them.

With that in mind, the details of the parable become highly significant. Take, as an illustration, the inability of the younger son really to believe that the father loves him and welcomes him as a son, rather than as a slave. Engraved in the prodigal's mind is his utter unworthiness to be a son any longer. By contrast, engraved in the elder brother's mind is the notion that his sonship has meant slavery (cf. Luke 15:29 vividly expressed in the NIV, "All these years I've *slaved* for you . . ."). While the younger son, even when his father falls on his neck in forgiveness, weeps, and kisses him, cannot believe that he is accepted, the older son has an altogether mistaken idea of what sonship is. There is a sense in which these two brothers share something in common. Neither of them has grasped who the father is. Ultimately this is Jesus' own condemnation of the Pharisees. They disgraced God, the Father;

they barred themselves from His kingdom, and would have barred others.

For those of us who are not particularly gifted as illustrators, or who lack that quality of imagination present in outstanding teachers and preachers, exegesis carefully done is our salvation! For here, in the dynamic of Scripture, in the imaginativeness of revelation properly expounded, is the arresting Word of God, which bears fruit as it instructs, searches, and challenges the minds of our hearers. Just as those who engage in academic teaching tell students that the *answers* in the exams lie in understanding the questions—if you understand the significance of the question you have the materials to answer it—so with preaching. If we understand the meaning of the passage, we have already the heart of the exposition and application.

3. Crystallizing

The third stage of preparation for exposition is what we may call the process of crystallizing. Crystallization is the process by which bodies with orderly arrangements of atoms, ions, or molecules are formed or enlarged, generally from the liquid state. The metaphor is appropriate, for what is involved in expository preaching, as we have already noticed, is more than the production of sound exegetical commentary. Rather at this stage we are moving from exegesis to the orderly arrangement of a single message. In exposition the principle concern is that *of unity*. That is a basic principle of all rhetoric, and certainly, as our Lord Himself indicates by His own example, of sacred rhetoric.

The question we are now asking, therefore, is, What is the *point* of this passage? Unity of course does not imply uniformity. The fact that the fundamental message of the passage is to be underlined does not mean that this message will be monotonously expressed. The crystallizing process may produce one large and beautiful crystal, but it is that, in turn, because it is composed of other crystals. We are therefore investigating the relationship between the parts and the whole, and seeking to bring those parts (furnished by our *exegesis*) together legitimately in relationship to the whole (the *message*).

For the expositor this is a very demanding but extremely fruitful discipline. Again, an example may make the point more lucidly than a prolonged discussion of the principles involved. One of the chief themes of Ephesians 3:1–13 is that of the wisdom of God. In discussing his own ministry, Paul sees that at the heart of it lies God's purpose to make known "through the church the manifold wisdom of God" (Eph. 3:10). But how does this theme crystallize in the context of the entire passage? It is fascinating to recognize how Paul speaks of various manifestations of God's wisdom in this context. As we hold the level of this passage up to the light, we recognize its multi-faceted beauty. For God's wisdom is seen here in three ways. First, God's plan to reveal His wisdom has been displayed *in Christ* (v. 11). But Paul also says that it is revealed *through the church* (v. 10). But notice that this little section ends with an application that at first glance is totally dislocated from the general context of wisdom. Paul encourages the Ephesians, on the basis of what he has already said ("So," v. 13), not to lose heart. How does what he has already said carry that implication? Precisely because they have learned about the amazing (*polupoikilos*—multi-colored) wisdom of God in Christ and through His people. *That same wisdom* they may expect to see displayed in the life of the apostle Paul also.

God's wisdom is therefore to be seen in three places: (1) in Christ, (2) in the church, and (3) in the sufferings of God's servants ("my sufferings for you, which are your glory," Eph. 3:13). Interestingly, in another (prison) Epistle, Paul indicates this principle in a very concrete fashion. To the Philippians he writes: "I want you to know brethren, that what has happened to me has really served to advance the gospel, so that it has become known . . . that my imprisonment is for Christ; and most of the brethren have been made confident in the Lord because of my imprisonment, and are much more bold to speak the word of God without fear" (Phil. 1:12-14). Multi-colored wisdom indeed!

What is the basic principle involved in this kind of movement from the general teaching of the passage to the recognition of a specific theme? It is the recognition of the principle of unity. Only practice enables us to be properly sensitive to the extent and limits of this principle. Yet it is not an esoteric principle. It is the principle of our ordinary speech. We say *something*. So too do portions of Scripture. We are therefore able to isolate what that "something" is, and recognize how it is built together as a unified "something." That is of advantage to us not only in the stage of crystallizing our message, but also in the stage that immediately follows.

4. *Structuralizing*

Thus far the pattern of our activity has been that of unpacking the text to be expounded and arranging it in its component parts. It's just at this point that an expository message demands different disciplines from those demanded by a running-commentary homily. For in expository preaching the material of the text is not only examined, it is also *restructured* in order to become a sermon. Whereas before the text was dismantled in order to unveil the heart of the matter, it is now brought together again on the basis of a new set of principles, the principles of sound rhetoric and communication governed by the identity of our hearers. To put the same point in different words, in preaching we translate the material we have gathered into a different medium from that in which it came to us. It was the Word of God *written*; it becomes the Word of God *preached*. We are no longer limited to the horizons of original exegesis—the horizon of the original speaker and that of the original hearer. Rather we are concentrating our attention on a third horizon, the contemporary hearer, in order to translate and interpret what was originally given to a different world altogether, and yet to do so without diminution or exaggeration of the message being preached.

How is this accomplished? The best way to accomplish it is along the lines already suggested. In the process of crystallizing the message we saw that the heart of the exposition was a composite center. We have already examined those various elements. Whereas earlier we brought them together to discover the essential message, we must now separate them once again in order to designate in our exposition the divisions of thought through which the core of the message is to be grasped. The analysis of how these parts are connected to the whole provides us with the division of thought involved. Again perhaps an illustration serves better than a series of vague principles.

Let us suppose we have chosen to expound Psalm 121. In our basic preparation we will have noticed a number of things. It bears the title "Song of Ascents." That title is shared by all the Psalms from 120 to 134; yet no other psalm bears this title. Our investigations set the actual use of this psalm probably in the pilgrim festivals of the Old Testament church. Although we may not know in precisely what context it was written, we do know that it served as instruction for the pilgrim. This in turn sheds light on the context of the psalm's use. Here we have what seems to be a younger, inexperienced pilgrim, facing his pilgrimage with some sense of apprehension, and receiving counsel either from the collective wisdom of others, or perhaps from the individual whose counsel is recorded in the rest of the psalm. The younger pilgrim is anxious about the dangers and hazards of the pilgrimage (v. 1): attacks from bandits, the possibility of sunstroke, the fear of lunacy ("the moon by night"). He wants to know where he can apply for help and strength. The answering voice points to the character and operation of God as the source of security and peace.

Now, our basic spadework, along with the more detailed questions of exegesis and etymology, has been intended to take us to the meaning of the text. But as in a carpenter's workshop there are pieces of materials lying around as the result of the cutting process, which he can use in the more creative process of his carpentry, so with exposition. Now our aim is not to put the material back the way we found it, but to create out of it something shaped for our own particular hearers. Out of these materials we may build the structure of the message.

There are several ways this can be done in Psalm 121. In any event, the psalm has a twofold division, in terms of the two speakers. We may choose a twofold division therefore for our message: (1) The Assertion of Untried Faith ("my help comes from the Lord . . .") *and* (2) The Assurance of Well-tried Experience ("He will not . . . the Lord is your . . ."). Again, focussing on the material from a different angle, we might restructure the psalm in terms of (1) The Fears of a New Pilgrim (What about my feet slipping, the noon-day sun blazing, the robbers, the moon, etc.?) and (2) The Encouragements of an Experienced Pilgrim ("God is a,b,c"; "God does x,y,z"). Similarly we might more directly speak of the fears of the disciple and the sufficiency of God, or the weakness of the disciple and the strength of the Lord. But in any of these divisions the principle is the same: we have restructured the psalm in a fashion specifically geared to communicate its message clearly and simply in stages to our hearers.

How we deal with those stages is often a matter of personal choice. We may lay out divisions very clearly; we may move along from one to another with less obvious division; we may build up a logical argument out of the materials. As we grow as preachers so we ought also to grow in variety of approaches.[7] But the underlying principle will be that of restructuring for the purposes of communication.

5. Concretizing

The next stage of preparation is one of the most important and difficult for expository ministry; but it pays rich rewards. We have been largely engaged in the process of analysis and synthesis thus far. Now we have reached the vital stage where we must bring together the biblical horizon with the horizon of the late twentieth century. We have to ask, What does *this* (e.g. Ps. 121) have to say to *these* (Mr. X, Miss Y in my congregation)? For this stage we may employ the metaphor of setting in concrete. It is the final stage in relating biblical exegesis to the hearer. It involves *making concrete* in our world what we have "melted down" from the world of Scripture and then crystallized by careful analysis.

7. In this connection, a study of Jesus' various preaching "styles" is illuminating.

What is the process by which this is done? We begin with the biblical text and explore its message. From its message we have brought out a number of basic principles. It is these basic principles that we must now take and translate into our own world. Yet we cannot abandon biblical controls at this point. We must also ask of the passage, What was the biblical writer doing with these principles? We cannot simply unravel the principles and then employ them in any fashion that appeals to us. Such exposition would have abandoned proper biblical controls. Instead we must endeavor to use these basic principles in a fashion that remains faithful to the actual use of the original writer. Can we do for our context what he did for his context?

While this is a rigorous procedure, it is not merely an academic one. For the question, "What was the author doing with these principles in his time?" will itself be highly suggestive for the exposition and application we may also make in our own time. The danger at this point is to leave the text and turn to applications *that do not arise directly out of the exposition.* In Pauline terms the "therefore," which links exposition to application, is absent; the application does not arise *directly* out of the exposition. But if we follow this more rigorous effort to pursue application along the lines of the application inherent in the passage, the effect will increasingly be that our application is not merely an appendage or an interesting personal observation, but actually arises out of the Word of God itself. The consequence will be that the hearer will the more clearly sense the weight, thrust, and light of *God's* Word (which is the point that both Samuel Logan and John Bettler make elsewhere in this volume).

Although perhaps Psalm 121 is of too general a nature to illustrate this principle most pointedly, "concretizing" may nevertheless be demonstrated from such a passage. We noticed that the psalm contains a tacit acknowledgment of the weaknesses and fears of the young pilgrim-believer. Those are clothed in the context and lifestyle of a young disciple in the ancient Near East. But what do his fears amount to? What are the fundamental fears, which in his case, have taken *Near Eastern* flesh and blood? Judging by the response of the second voice in the psalm, the younger pilgrim is afraid (1) that God may desert him; (2) of various dangers on the way (sun, moon, robbers)—fear of circumstances, fear of the night; and (3) that he may not be able to make it home at the end of the journey—he may lack the necessary perseverance to overcome the obstacles. It does not take much imagination to see that the horizons of Psalm 121 and those of young twentieth-century converts are not very far apart. Similarly, the counsel needed will point in the same direction: God is the covenant Father ("Lord") of His people; God is the one who watches and keeps. God is the one who rules over circumstances; God is the one who governs both our beginning and our ending. The answer to the pilgrim's anxiety then, as now, is to be found in the revelation of and trust in the character of God. Indeed, in this short psalm we may even pick up leads that will help our less imaginative spirit to preach in the imaginative power of the Spirit in Scripture—God as the guardian of the slipping foot, the watching parent, the shade of protection, the bodyguard of His people.

This is not to say that the use of other biblical material, or even extra-biblical material, for illustration is wrong. Rather it underlines the fact that when we stick to the text with the most rigorous expository intention, we will find more than enough material for exposition, illustration, and application. The more rigorous we are initially with ourselves at this point, the more likely we are to be encouraged with a sense of the absolute adequacy of Holy Scripture for the work of expository preaching. It is this, perhaps supremely, which leads to a style of expository preaching of which it can be said, as John "Rabbi" Duncan did of Jonathan Edwards's, the doctrine is all application and the application is all doctrine.

6. *Delivering*

When Demosthenes was asked what he regarded as the chief element in rhetoric, he reputedly responded, "First, delivery; second, delivery; third, delivery" (See Lester De Koster's discussion of rhetoric here). At first sight it might seem that the connection between exposition and delivery is fairly tenuous. After all, expository preaching is a form of communication rather than a definition of the style of delivery. But precisely because it is *biblical* exposition, the content of the preaching has an influence on the manner in which we deliver it.

Paul twice described his preaching as *phanerōsis;* that is, there was an unveiling or exposing of the message in its inherent reality and power. In Colossians 4:4 he appealed for help in prayer that he may thus preach. In II Corinthians 4:2, he contrasted deceitful preaching with "the open statement [*phanerōsis,* 'exposition'] of the truth." Although he did not preach himself, but Christ (II Cor. 4:5), by such exposition, he wrote, he did commend *himself* to every man's conscience in the sight of God (II Cor. 4:2). He was thinking about his motives in the delivery of God's Word. But notice that those motives were intertwined with the manner of delivery. It is an open manifestation and exposition of the truth. By this he commended himself as one whose ministry was controlled not only by a particular preaching *style,* but by the *message* itself. His exposition of it dominated his presentation of it. The content of the gospel dominates the style and the spirit in which the gospel is preached. To this extent, the medium *is* also the message "heard" by others.

This, supremely, should be the hallmark of expository preaching. It should express a spirit that has been led captive to the truth expounded. For lack of this, congregations may be sent away from the regular diets of worship still hungry, even though the Word is, indeed, formally expounded. For God has so ordained it that His people should be fed and nourished by the exposition of His truth through the lips, lives, and personalities of His human servants. It is peculiarly in this way that He ministers to whole men and women, and makes broken men and women whole. It is for lack of this—a spirit that is dominated by the teaching expounded and is in harmony with it—that the needs of men and women are not met.

We can never rest content with exposition that is formally "correct." Unless exposition breathes the Spirit of the truth expounded, it is incorrect and itself needs healing and correction. It may be that this, among other reasons, is a chief cause of the preaching-counseling tension so current in North American churches today. In many instances spiritual health could be preserved at a much earlier stage were preaching directed to whole men from whole men whose disposition and whose message were intertwined.

Andrew Bonar was asked one Monday morning by his friend Robert Murray McCheyne on what theme he had preached the previous day. When he replied, "On hell," McCheyne further asked: "Did you preach it with tears?" How else could it be for those who expound the message of Him who Himself wept over Jerusalem in the course of His ministry of expounding the heart of the Father (*exēgēsato*, John 1:18)?

8

Hermeneutics and Preaching
Hendrik Krabbendam

It is impossible to cover the full range of implications of a full-orbed biblical hermeneutics for preaching in the brief compass of one chapter.[1] The present writer set out to do just that, but had

1. The table of contents of a properly constructed biblical hermeneutics may well look something like this:

Introduction
1. The concept of hermeneutics
2. Trends in hermeneutics

Chapter I: The starting point of hermeneutics: the phenomenon
    of Scripture
1. The nature of the biblical text
2. The meaning of the biblical text
3. The significance of the biblical text

Chapter II: The centerpiece of hermeneutics: the interpretation
    of Scripture
1. The approach to Scripture
2. The language of Scripture
3. The genres of Scripture

Chapter III: The goal of hermeneutics: the understanding of Scripture
1. The nature of understanding
2. The acquisition of understanding
3. The transmission of understanding

This table of contents is predicated upon the conviction that biblical hermeneutics should not just concern itself with the interpretation of Scripture, admittedly its centerpiece, but also with the phenomenon of Scripture as its starting point and the understanding of Scripture as its goal. It is my intention to argue in a larger, projected, volume that the treatment of all three issues as equally essential for a full-orbed hermeneutics is historically justifiable, etymologically proper, biblically warranted, and organizationally a boon.

to abandon the attempt in favor of the much more modest objective of dealing with two fundamental issues against the backdrop of an equally basic assumption.

The basic assumption pertains to the nature of the biblical text and will simply be stated in order to save a maximum of the allotted space for the discussion of the two fundamental issues. The first of these issues concerns the *meaning* of the biblical text and pertains to *exposition,* and the second concerns its *significance* and pertains to *application.*[2] They will be formulated in the form of two theses, which subsequently will be developed.

The basic assumption is that the Scriptures of the Old and New Testaments constitute a truly and fully divine-human book, the one uncompounded product of God as the divine author and the human writers as agents, in which the divine and human factors or elements do not exclude, suppress, or supersede each other.

The first thesis is that the biblical text has a *single meaning* determined by the will of the author as expressed in the text with a view to a specific public and can be reproduced from it in consultation with its context and in accordance with its purpose.

The second thesis is that the biblical text has a *manifold significance* that is squarely based upon the meaning of the text and can be formulated by means of universal principles and patterns to be gleaned from it with a view to any public.

The remainder of this introduction consists of a number of comments intended to leave no doubt about the content of the basic assumption. This, then, will be followed by the body of this chapter, which will unpack and account for the two theses.

On the one hand, Scripture displays the unmistakable imprint of the divine in its unity, inerrancy, trustworthiness, perspicuity,

---

2. For the importance of the distinction between meaning and significance, see E. D. Hirsch, Jr., *Validity in Interpretation* (New Haven and London: Yale University Press, 1967), pp. 8, 38, 57, 62, 127, 141, 216, 255, and *The Aims of Interpretation* (Chicago and London: The University of Chicago Press, 1976), pp. 1–13, 79–86, 146. See also Walter C. Kaiser, Jr., *Toward an Exegetical Theology* (Grand Rapids: Baker Book House, 1981), pp. 31–32.

and authority. Scripture in its totality and in its parts is God's truth, which originates with Him, takes shape under His superintendence, and is designed to accomplish His purpose.

On the other hand, Scripture equally displays an unimpeded humanity. It bears the marks of the various historical situations and cultural settings. It is presented in various languages and literary genres. It is made up of various building blocks, as data from oral tradition, information from written sources, and insights from interviews. While it is and remains God's truth, it is simultaneously thoroughly human. It arises from the human situation, is embedded in the human environment, and addresses the human predicament.

All this, incidentally, should encourage biblical hermeneutics to list, analyze, and evaluate the attributes of Scripture that comport with its divine author, and to engage in historical, cultural, language, and genre studies, as well as source, tradition, and redaction research[3] in recognition of the humanity of the biblical writers. This, in turn, should serve the twofold objective of shedding light upon the full meaning and the significance of the biblical text as the locus, if not the substance, of God's truth for man.

1. The Meaning of the Biblical Text: The First Thesis

This section sets out with a general evaluation of the key issues mentioned in the first thesis and a detailed discussion of a feature that comes to light in the process of this evaluation. It concludes

3. It is the present writer's opinion that the historical-critical method is rooted solely in the Enlightenment. The stage for it was set when rationalistic scholarship began to differentiate, and eventually create a rift, between Scripture and the Word of God. From that moment on, Scripture became fair game for source, form, tradition, and redaction criticism. Conservative scholars may do well to demarcate their position clearly by substituting research for criticism. It has been said that the historical-critical method is equally rooted in the Renaissance/Reformation movement by virtue of its insistence upon free, unencumbered, historical research. There is, however, the decisive difference that the latter sought to liberate historical studies from the domination of the medieval church, while the Enlightenment decided to "free" itself from the authority of Scripture as the eternal Word of God.

with some inferences from this detailed discussion for the interpretive enterprise as the prerequisite for biblical preaching.

1. The Single Meaning and Its Recognition

The biblical text has only one, single, and unchangeable meaning that is determined by the intent of the author as expressed in
the text by means of linguistic symbols. This is a significant con-
tention, for it precludes any kind of multiple meaning, whether in
the form of the Jewish mystery sense, the medieval fourfold
sense, the Protestant deeper sense, or the Roman Catholic *sensus
plenior*. But it seems unassailable. Even the recognition that the
biblical text is authored by God through human writers does not
alter this fact. To assign an intended meaning to the divine author
different from that of the human writers would violate not only
the notion that Scripture is a single uncompounded product, but
also the concept of its unimpeded humanity. When God used
human writers to produce Scripture as His Word, He therewith
adopted voluntarily and by definition the total range of possibilities and limitations inherent to their humanity. To make an exception in the case of intended meaning not only seems arbitrary,
but also invites a rift between the divine and human factors and
opens the way to one type of mechanical inspiration or another.

But beyond this, it appears that the case for a multiple meaning
cannot be substantiated from Scripture. Even the probably most
celebrated argument in its favor, based upon a comparison of
Hosea 11:1 and Matthew 2:15, falls short of the mark. At first
glance it seems that Hosea 11:1, which identifies the son who is
called out of Egypt as the nation of Israel, is reported by Matthew
2:15 to refer beyond that to Christ as well. One phrase seems to
carry two meanings, the first one presumably intended by both
the divine author and the human writer in one context and immediately revealed, the second in retrospect reserved by the divine author for a later context and temporarily withheld. However, this interpretation is predicated upon the assumption that
inherent to the word *fulfil* is the notion of intended predictive

prophecy that eventually becomes a reality. But this is hardly necessary, as a quick reference to James 2:21-23 convincingly shows. James declares with the word *fulfil* that Abraham's obedience, as evidenced in his willingness to sacrifice Isaac and reported in Genesis 22, was a necessary *implication* of his faith that, according to Genesis 15, was counted to him as righteousness. Similarly, Matthew conveys with the term *fulfil* that God's calling of Christ out of Egypt was a further *application* of the phrase originally coined by Hosea. In this application Matthew capitalizes on the analogy between Israel and Christ to underscore in the framework of his Gospel, addressed to the Jews, that Christ in a real sense is the Israel of God.

All in all, intended meaning should be sharply distinguished both from its possible implications and from its applications. This distinction will clear up a lot of difficulties and go a long way toward showing that the intended meaning of the divine author and the human writers is always and by definition the same in any passage of Scripture.[4] It also proves to have rewarding implications for the interpretive process.

First, it will never be necessary to be dependent for the meaning of the text upon a criterion outside or beyond the text, whether a revelation added to it (Jewish mystery sense and Protestant deeper sense), a conceptual scheme imposed upon it (medieval fourfold sense), or an ecclesiastical authority over it (Roman Catholic *sensus plenior*).

Second, it will pave the way toward adopting the methodology of the New Testament writers in their use of Scripture, including their quotations of, references to, and observations about the Old Testament, as sufficient, necessary, and authoritative models. Opposition to this is, on the face of it, astonishing. The church is

---

4. Just as God and Hosea intended to identify the son in Hosea 11:1 as the nation of Israel, so God and Matthew intended to apply Hosea's phrase further to Christ. For further discussion of the relationship between intended meaning and inspiration, see Bruce Vawter, *Biblical Inspiration* (Philadelphia: Westminster Press, 1972), pp. 115ff.

called upon to follow in the footsteps of Christ and the apostles in all areas of faith and practice unconditionally and unreservedly. Why would an exception be made in their use of Scripture?

A word of caution, however, is in place. The emphasis upon authorial intent as the exclusive determinant of the meaning of the biblical text does not require the interpreter to search the hidden recesses of the author's mind. That would condemn him to an unverifiable leap into the unknown and mire him in subjectivism and relativism. No, as the first thesis emphatically states, the intent of the author comes to expression in the text. Therefore, the focus of the interpreter must be on the text. That is where he will find the intended meaning. The text is its own validation point. This is fundamental for the second key statement made in the first thesis.

The meaning of the text is to be discovered, recognized, and validated by means of the grammatical, syntactical, and semantic study of the text, which ought to account for the total linguistic structure in general and for every linguistic component in particular. This, in turn, is complemented by historical, geographical, and cultural research that should shed all possible light on the background, setting, and modes of expression of the text. It finally culminates in genre and context analysis, which aims at bringing out the particular traits and assists in establishing the purpose of the text.

All this spells adventure. The search for meaning may often appear tedious. At times it may seem never ending. At other times it may appear to be a dead-end street. But suddenly it will be suprisingly and richly rewarding. This should stimulate the pursuit of meaning and make it exciting.

By the same token it spells limitation. The meaning of the text does not transcend the laws and boundaries of the language of the original readers in which the text is composed. Nor does it go beyond the characteristics and particularities of the environment of the original addressees from which the text emerges. Nor is it to be sought outside the purpose of the text or the scope of its traits. This is an invitation to self-restraint in attaching meaning to the text.[5]

In short, the interpreter should pursue all the clues of the text, aided by all possible pertinent research, to the limit, but he should never go beyond the limits of the clues in his pursuit of the meaning of the text.

Of special importance is the study of genre and its traits and of the text and its context. The issue is the relationship of the whole and its parts.[6] On the one hand, the whole is greater than the sum of its parts. On the other hand, the parts are the constituent elements of the whole. Consequently, the meaning of a particular text as part of a larger whole, ultimately all of Scripture, can never be isolated from the meaning of that whole of which it is a part. Nor can the meaning of the whole stand in isolation of the parts that make up the whole. To ignore this fact is to upset a fine balance, which will lead either to a fragmentation of meaning, when the unifying whole vanishes from sight, or an imposition of meaning, when the parts are denied their integrity.

Although this means that the parts are understood through the whole and the whole through the parts, it does not justify the conclusion that the interpreter is trapped in an unavoidable vicious circle. Far from it! Indispensable for the recognition of meaning is an often laborious, at times painstaking, but then also at other times suprisingly smooth process in which initially provisional and tentative constructions of meaning are corrected, revised, suspended, rejected, or confirmed and validated by the presence or absence of freshly appreciated or further recognized clues in the text or context.[7]

5. This self-restraint is not exercised by allegorical interpretation, which imports meaning from outside the text to serve interests that are often contrary or even inimical to the text.

6. Hirsch, *Validity*, p. 77, suggests that the hermeneutical circle is better defined in terms of genre and its traits than of the whole and its parts. It seems preferable, however, to subsume both genre and its traits and the text and its context as specifics under the genus of the whole and its parts.

7. This should not come as a surprise. After all, it appears that all of the learning process displays this very same pattern.

One of the most significant clues to help this process along is that of the explicitly stated purpose of the text within the framework of the larger context. A case in point is Genesis 22. The text expressly states that God instructed Abraham to sacrifice his son for the purpose of testing his faith (Gen. 22:1) against the backdrop of a context that has the multi-faceted promises of God as an ever-recurring theme (Gen. 11:27–25:11). Consequently, this should determine the direction of the interpretation of the many sparkling features of this chapter. Accordingly, it should be taken to convey that Abraham, although oblivious of God's purpose, but nevertheless abandoning himself to God's promise and the provision contained in it,[8] demonstrated that he feared God by displaying supreme love for Him, unquestioning obedience to Him, and unreserved trust of Him (Gen. 22:12). This implies, negatively, that this chapter does not intend to foreshadow the substitutionary atonement of Christ, and therefore should not be understood or presented that way. In fact, careful analysis of the chapter and its context indicates that such interpretation transcends the limits of any available clue. This is not to say that a message on this chapter may not contain a reference to the substitutionary atonement, but only as one of the many, and on a par with all other possible *applications* of the universal principle enunciated by Abraham, "The Lord will provide" (Gen. 22:14), and not as presenting the *meaning* of the text.

2. The "Hermeneutical Circle" in Its Broadest Parameter

If the understanding of the whole is essential for the understanding of the parts and the understanding of the parts is constitutive for the understanding of the whole, it should be the first order of business to develop a well-defined view of Scripture in its totality, as the largest, all-encompassing whole, by means of an analysis of the major constituent parts, not in the last place in their relationship to each other. This is of paramount importance. It is not just that everyone approaches Scripture with some view

8. This is further corroborated by Heb. 11:17–19.

of the whole, whether consciously or not, and therefore might as well be forced to make a well-informed, well-reasoned, and well-founded choice. Nor is it that it may function as a model for the study of less extensive wholes. It goes well beyond that. From it will crystallize a number of basic interpretive principles, which together will form and function as a kind of global interpretive framework from which the meaning of all of the parts will be construed, unless and until, of course, it is corrected in the process and by means of the examination of the parts.

Thus it appears to be no mean issue. Unless an interpreter has a proper and all-encompassing view of Scripture, he is bound not to see what is in the text and bound to see what is not in the text. This is tantamount to being victimized by the traditions of man, which would encumber him with tunnel vision, blinders, unreliable contact lenses, or whatever figure of speech seems preferable, so that he is forced to bend, distort, add to, or subtract from Scripture to a greater or lesser degree. The implications for preaching hardly need to be emphasized!

The present writer has grown into the conviction, through an analysis that spans more than two decades, that Scripture is essentially covenantal in nature, more precisely that it is a covenant edifice that steadily rises over the centuries with the Adamic, Noahic, Abrahamic, Mosaic, Davidic, and New Covenants as the constitutive and successive stories.

The term *covenant*, which is to be defined as bond-relationship,[9] represents the constant that is indicative of the fundamental continuity throughout the Testaments. The concept of the rising edifice honors the steady progress that is made in the gradual unfolding of the Testaments. The combination *covenant edifice* conveys that the earlier stories are fully foundational for the later ones and, conversely, that only in the later ones do the earlier ones come fully into their own. In short, the relationship between the

9. See the excellent article on the subject of the covenant by J. J. Mitchel, "Abram's Understanding of the Lord's Covenant," *The Westminster Theological Journal* 32 (1969): 24ff., esp. 29, 43–48. He concludes that covenant, shorn of all its modifiers and concomitants, is basically bond-relationship.

covenants is one of neither monolithic unity nor radical discontinuity, but rather progressive continuity. All this points to the
broadest parameters within which the interpretive process must
take place.

But it must be fleshed out. Typical of the bond-relationship
between God and man, which is one of nonparity, and is initiated
by God's sovereign love, reflective of His moral excellence, and
befitting the position and predicament of man, are the two major
concomitants of law and promise. The promulgation of the one is
never quite without the other. Still, each of the several covenants
has its own emphasis. The covenant with Adam, before the fall,
emphasized law. Following that, there was a threefold emphasis
upon promise in the covenant with Adam after the fall, the covenant with Noah, and the covenant with Abraham. This, in turn,
was followed by a focus upon law in the covenant with Moses
and promise in the covenant with David. The covenant edifice
received its capstone in the new covenant in which promise and
law, although each with its own function, appear equally central.[10]

To construe a sharp contrast between law covenants and promise covenants is totally unacceptable.[11] The facts that the promulgation of the one is never without the other and that they are

10. A comparison of Gen. 15:18 and 17:1 quickly shows that in the covenant
with Abraham the emphasis upon promise does not exclude law, while a similar
comparison between Deut. 5:1–21 and 30:6 makes it equally evident that in the
covenant with Moses the emphasis upon law does not remove the promise from
sight. In Jer. 31:31ff. the Lord, finally, promises to write the law on the heart of
His people. A closer connection between the two can hardly be envisioned.
11. D. R. Hillers, *Covenant: The History of a Biblical Idea* (Baltimore: Johns
Hopkins Press, 1969), pp. 46–71, 98–119, construes a difference between two
types of covenant, representing two different traditions and points of view. The
covenants at Sinai and Shechem (Josh. 24) emphasize the law; the covenants of
Noah, Abraham, and David, the promise. The latter type began to become
predominant when the earlier type failed to reach its objective. M. G. Kline, *By
Oath Consigned* (Grand Rapids: Eerdmans, 1968), pp. 22–25, speaks about a
radical contrast, a radical opposition, and a sharp distinction between law-cov-
enants and promise-covenants, which are ratified by human and divine oaths
respectively. O. Palmer Robertson, *The Christ of the Covenants* (Grand Rapids:
Baker Book House, 1980), p. 60, correctly rejects this approach.

coessential in the new covenant already militate against this. But beyond this, such a construction misses the fine tapestry that the successive covenants, each with its own emphasis, present. The emphasis upon law invariably occurs against the backdrop of man's presence with God, while the promise comes into the foreground against the backdrop of man's bankruptcy before God. This stands to reason. The presence of God demands holiness. The bankruptcy of man requires provision.

But there is more to the tapestry. The promulgation of law exposes man's bankruptcy and therefore evokes the subsequent promulgation of promise. Conversely, the promulgation of promise aims at man's presence with God and therefore calls for the subsequent promulgation of law. The two strands are intertwined from the beginning. They are always found in each other's company. They purposely set out to serve each other's cause by preparing the ground for each other. They leapfrog over each other. No wonder they merge at the end.[12]

In addition to this it should not go unnoticed that in the successive promulgations of law and promise, of promise and law, there is an ever-increasing fulness of expression and sharpness of focus. The structure of law and promise, therefore, appears to be identical to that of covenant. Just as there is not one monolithic covenant but a number of covenants as successive stories of the covenant edifice, so there is not one law and one promise, but a number of successive, ever more pointed, promulgations of law and promise. Furthermore, just as with the various covenants, the earlier promulgations of law and promise are foundational for the later ones, while only in the later ones do the earlier come into their own.

But the covenant edifice must be fleshed out some more. It becomes increasingly clear not only that the Triune God stands behind it, but also that He is ultimately intent upon reaching a threefold objective. Since both features come to their fullest ex-

12. This merger takes place in the person and work of Christ, who is the new covenant personified (Isa. 42:6; 49:8). See specifically Isa. 51:4-5 and Luke 1:69, 72, 74-75.

pression in the new covenant as the culmination point of the covenant edifice, this will now be the focus of the further discussion.

First, the new covenant is rooted in the Triune God. It is promised by God the Father (Jer. 31:31–34), personified in God the Son (Isa. 42:6), and personalized by God the Holy Spirit (Isa. 59:21).

Second, the threefold objective is spelled out in terms of the threefold promise of a new heart or regeneration, a new record or justification, and a new life or sanctification (Ezek. 36:26, 25, 27).

Third, each person of the Triune God cooperates toward reaching the threefold objective in a specific way. God the Father holds out the prospect of all three (Ezek. 36:26, 25, 27). God the Son procures the *new heart* through union with Him in His crucifixion and resurrection (Rom. 6:3–6, 11), the *new record* through His substitutionary atonement on the cross (II Cor. 5:21), and the *new life* through communion with Him as the fountain of holiness (John 15:5; Phil. 4:13). God the Spirit secures *regeneration* by means of the Word (John 3:5; I Pet. 1:23), *justification* by sealing the believer with His indwelling presence (Eph. 1:13–14), and *sanctification* by means of the Word, fellowship, and prayer (Rom. 15:16; Acts 2:42–47; Eph. 4:12–16; I Tim. 4:5).

Fourth, each one of the three objectives has its own specific function. Regeneration and its consequent entrance into the kingdom of God is the experiential starting point; justification and its consequent peace with God, the legal cornerstone; and sanctification and its consequent fellowship with God, the crowning piece of man's bond-relationship with his God.

In summary, Scripture appears to give an account of the successive covenants, their components, concomitants, and history. Together they constitute the essence of the ongoing, ever-progressing bond-relationship between God and His people. In it He binds Himself to them by means of an increasingly pointed set of promises and binds them to Himself by an increasingly pointed set of laws. He ultimately anchors it in the threefold promise of the new heart, the cleansed record, and the holy life, which are produced by the incarnate Son of God and implemented by the

Holy Spirit. He ultimately aims, as the content of that threefold promise indicates, at joyful and unblemished obedience to
His law.

3. A Network of Fundamental Interpretive Principles

All this yields some fundamental principles of interpretation
that suggest a global framework from which the meaning of all of
Scripture is to be discovered.

In its broadest sense the interpretation ought to be covenantal-
historical, safeguarding both the fundamental continuity and the
unmistakable progress evident in Scripture. In the light of what
already has been argued, however, this can be translated into
three major principles.

First, the earlier is to be recognized as both foundational for
and seminal to the later. This means concretely not only that the
later rests on the earlier, but also that in the later the earlier
comes into its own. If this is recognized the integrity and rights of
both will be honored. The meaning of the later will not be imposed upon the earlier, nor the meaning of the earlier regarded as
on a par with the later.

To illustrate, the truth of Genesis 15:6 that Abraham's faith
was counted to him for righteousness is foundational for and
gives rise to the doctrine of justification by faith as Romans 4:2-5
indicates. If the interpreter were to adopt the principle just stated,
he could not possibly hold that of the two passages Genesis 15:6
would give the more complete formulation of the biblical teaching on justification. This would be to reject the bloom for the
bud. At the same time, he could not possibly read the Pauline
doctrine of justification by faith into Genesis 15:6 either. This
would be to force the bloom into the bud. However, this latter
procedure is precisely the one followed by most interpreters. The
passage is generally understood as saying that Abraham was
counted righteous (justified!) by faith, in apparent distaste for the
unpalatable alternative conclusion that Abraham's faith itself
constituted his righteousness before God. Ironically, the debate
over Genesis 15:6 appears to center upon the relative merits of
two equally unacceptable interpretations. The one is biblical, but

cannot be maintained textually in the light of the wording of the passage. The other one seems favored by the passage, but cannot be maintained contextually in the light of the totality of Scripture. The solution is to view the passage from the vantage point of the immediate context (Gen. 11:27–25:15) with its emphasis upon the double theme of God's promises and Abraham's faith. Against this backdrop Genesis 15:6 appears to teach that Abraham's faith, precisely because it is an unconditional embrace and appropriation of the promise of God, for all intents and purposes "equals" righteousness. It neither defines its nature nor indicates the instrument of its reception. Only in subsequent covenant history, in which more and more "new record" information is made available, does it become evident that this righteousness is a God-righteousness (Ps. 85:11), a Christ-righteousness (Jer. 23:6), and a faith-righteousness (Hab. 2:4). All these strands, finally, come together in Paul who displays the full tapestry of justification in Romans 3 and 4 against the foundational and seminal backdrop of Genesis 15:6, which naturally gives rise to what follows.

All this serves to demonstrate that to read the later into the earlier is to violate the integrity of the text and to obscure its unique message. One, indeed, can ill afford to lose sight of the explosive truth that faith is the unconditional embrace of the promise of God and as such for all practical purposes "equals" righteousness. Early and universal recognition of this fact would have dramatically changed the course of ecclesiastical history!

Second, the covenantal-historical method is trinitarian in character. This does not just arise from the trinitarian involvement that has been sketched already in broad outline. It is also in recognition that the self-revelation of the Triune God belongs to the warp and woof of the covenant documents. From the account of creation in Genesis 1 to the call for Jesus' return in Revelation 22, the Scriptures are replete with data about the Father, the Son, and the Holy Spirit, references to their persons, descriptions of their work, and accounts of their words. Adoption of the trinitarian method of interpretation cannot but yield handsome dividends. For one thing, it opens up new vistas upon Scripture. The structure of Isaiah 40–66 is a case in point. Careful analysis reveals that the writer groups his material along trinitarian lines. He completes the cycle twice, first by way of introduction and then by way of further elaboration. So do Isaiah 40–41 and 45–48 focus upon God the Father, Isaiah 42–43 and 49–57 upon God the Son, and Isaiah 44 and 58–66 upon God the Spirit. In addition to this, full awareness of the trinitarian character of God's self-revelation will minimize, if not eliminate, the grave danger on the part of the interpreter of overlooking, ignoring, or toning down any part of God's truth with regard to any one of the persons of the Trinity.

Third, the covenantal-historical method is threefold in its scope. As such it not only reflects the threefold promise of the new covenant pertaining to regeneration, justification, and sanctification, but also gives the appropriate emphasis to each unit of this triad within the framework of its function.

From this perspective, it would be inappropriate to declare that the doctrine of justification is the *articulus stantis et cadentis ecclesiae*. Such a declaration might be understandable in the heat of the Reformation battle, but no less fraught with inherent danger. It seems an invitation to take justification as the centerpiece, if not heart, of the gospel, to which other truths are subservient or function as appendages. It should not go unnoticed, however, that it is just as impossible to enter the kingdom of God without regeneration and to enjoy the fellowship with God without sanctification as it is to be the recipient of the peace of God without justification. All three are equally necessary and indispensable, and are equally benefits of the new covenant. Likewise, all three are equally promised by the Father, produced by the Son, and implemented by the Spirit. And all three are equally gifts of the gospel. If one is present, all are present. If one is missing, all are missing. All three, therefore, must receive equal emphasis and attention: regeneration as the experiential launching pad, justification as the forensic platform, and sanctification as the productive crowning piece of the Christian before his God. If there is a hierarchical order at all, the nod should probably go to sanctification as the crowning piece. Statistically, it receives more biblical attention than the other two combined.

In summary, the covenantal-historical method views the earlier as both the foundation and the seed for the later, is trinitarian in character, and has a threefold scope. All this suggests a framework of interpretation, the importance of which cannot be overestimated. This can probably be demonstrated most convincingly by way of a series of contrasts.

If the covenantal-historical method of interpretation is correct, the dispensational method is unacceptable. Its construction of the radical breach between the dispensation of law and grace would not comport with the notion of steady progress in continuity. If law and promise are equally significant concomitants of covenant, an exclusive, or even special, emphasis upon the one could only come at the expense of the other and therefore ought to be ruled out as improper. If the earlier is foundational for the later, the popular typological approach in which the later is read into the earlier must be rejected. It violates the integrity of the earlier with its own unique message. If the proper interpretive method is trinitarian in character, the exclusively or even predominantly Christocentric interpretation must raise serious questions. It is bound to narrow the focus of the biblical message, consciously or not. In fact, the rigorous application of it may well have crippling effects. Luther's Christocentrism serves as a warning. If that had prevailed, the Epistle of James might well have been dismissed from the canon! If biblical interpretation has a threefold scope, an improper or even central emphasis upon one of the three benefits of the new covenant will only obscure the other two and, therefore, cannot be condoned. It would impair the full biblical message of salvation.[13]

13. The Protestant Reformation may well have had a disproportionate emphasis upon the doctrine of justification, as also its hymnology seems to indicate. Luther is known to have made it the centerpiece of his theology. While Calvin had an enlarged scope, inasmuch as he in his *Institutes* gives a systematic treatment of two benefits of the gospel, justification and sanctification, still it is questionable whether his treatment of sanctification is as thorough as that of justification; it is further quite conspicuous that a separate treatment of regeneration is totally missing. All this points to a basic weakness. After all, the new covenant emphasizes a threefold benefit. This, however, is not the place to discuss at length its implications.

All in all, the thesis seems defensible that the failure and down-fall of the church always goes hand in hand with a deficiency in the understanding of the full-orbed covenantal-historical content of Scripture and a corresponding deficiency in preaching its message. It is easy to see how deadly this can be, not only because preaching is the primary God-ordained means of grace (Acts 2:42; Rom. 10:14-15), but also because there is no acceptable substitute for the whole counsel of God (Acts 20:25-27).

But this leaves the most fundamental question still undecided. Why should the covenantal-historical method with its concomitant three interpretive principles be preferable to any other method, specifically those with which it has just been contrasted? In other words, is there a ready-made criterion that determines the correct method of interpretation?

The answer is in principle simple. There is no such identifiable, a priori criterion. The methodology must be construed from the biblical text itself by paying painstaking attention to the aggregate of pertinent clues. Its subsequent validation depends upon its ability to do full justice to that very same text, so that it always and in every instance speaks for itself.

All this seems to favor the covenantal-historical method over any other approach. It appears both to flow forth from and to accommodate the total biblical text. As such it seems to provide the only interpretive framework from which the meaning of all of Scripture can be discovered, recognized, confirmed, and validated without warping, wresting, molding, ignoring, underestimating, overestimating, curtailing, suppressing, or truncating any of its totality or parts. In other words, inasmuch as it appears to be scriptural, it can be counted on to assist Scripture in having the final word and the full say.

2. The Significance of the Biblical Text: The Second Thesis

This section begins with a determination of the relationship between meaning and significance with a view to preaching and in the light of a pertinent, recent, hermeneutical controversy. It continues with the proposal of a method to be used in order to arrive at the significance of the text. It concludes with the presentation of a number of examples aimed to show persuasively that the suggested method is proper, if not indispensable, in order to reach the desired objective.

1. The Relationship of Meaning and Significance

According to a well-known definition, preaching is the communication of God's truth by man to man.[14] This suggests that preaching is more than a lecture that confines itself to a presentation of the meaning of the text. It is not exhausted by a narration of data, whether they pertain to God or man, to persons or things or events. However competent and skillful such narration may be, it too often has the earmarks of irrelevance. No, preaching as the communication of truth implies by definition an encounter with the reality of God in His person, His works, and His words. As such it is always compelling. It demands. It directs. It promises. It offers. It energizes. It electrifies. The list of possibilities is endless. But it always forces the issue. Thus man responds. He submits. He conforms. He objects. He rebels. He ignores. Once again, the list is potentially endless.

In other words, in preaching, God's truth is integrally brought to bear upon the life of the hearer. The bottom line, therefore, is that both the meaning of the text and its significance are transmitted. Preaching as communication of truth encompasses not only exposition, but also application.

The second thesis is concerned with the quest for significance or application. The nature as well as the sufficient and necessary conditions of significance have always been interests of a properly construed hermeneutics and, of course, are an essential concern for homiletics.

Significance has been defined as the relationship of meaning to someone or something else, any person, any situation, or any

14. This definition of Phillips Brooks is quoted from John R. W. Stott, *Between Two Worlds* (Grand Rapids: Eerdmans, 1982), p. 266.

predicament.[15] The meaning of the text, as has been argued, is one, constant and unchanging. It can be discovered by appropriate hermeneutical procedures. The significance of the text, on the other hand, is manifold and constantly changing. It is manifold because the persons, situations, and predicaments to which the text can be related are manifold. It is constantly changing because the persons, situations, and predicaments to which the text can be related are never the same.

This gives rise to two questions. What is the relationship between meaning and significance, and how can the significance of the text be determined? Both key issues are addressed in the second thesis, which endeavors to show that significance has a firm anchor point and a predictable structure. This subdivision deals with the first issue.

The significance of the text is squarely based upon and is to be derived from the meaning of the text. If the interpretation fails to reproduce either the proper or full meaning of the text, the search for its significance will be either sidetracked before it starts or seriously hampered. Conversely, if the asserted significance is not anchored in the meaning of the text, it cannot be said to set forth its truth. (This is essentially the same point made by Samuel Logan in "The Phenomenology of Preaching" in the present volume. His terms "analysis" and "intuition" correspond roughly with my terms "meaning" and "significance.")

That will now be illustrated with an analysis of a recent controversy between two methodologies. The first one has been designated as the "exemplary" method and is centuries old. The second one, which was developed as a backlash against it, is the so-called "redemptive-historical" method and emerged during the last half of the century.[16] This controversy lends itself well to our purposes because the focus of the former is the significance of the text, and the focus of the latter, its meaning. This is reflected in the various charges and countercharges. From the opposition's

15. Hirsch, Validity, p. 8, Aims, pp. 2–3.
16. For an excellent discussion of this controversy, see S. Greidanus, Sola Scriptura (Toronto: Wedge Publishing Foundation, 1970).

point of view the exemplary method is seriously flawed in the area of exposition, while the redemptive-historical method is seriously lacking in the area of application. The irony is that neither assessment is without justification. At the same time it is hardly surprising that the debate ended in a stalemate and mutual frustration. The fundamental issue of the relationship between meaning and significance was never really joined. The opponents addressed each other on different levels, which prevented proper communication.

The exemplary method, as has been correctly observed,[17] approaches Scripture as a kind of "picture gallery," consisting of a massive collection of "examples" intended to fit every possible human predicament and life situation. As a result, this method is not averse to moralizing, psychologizing, spiritualizing, and at times even allegorizing the text. One does not need to endorse this method to recognize that it is motivated by the desire to show that the text contains truth that makes a difference in everyday life.

Proponents of the redemptive-historical method object to the exemplary method, however, on three counts. First, it regards the biblical text as illustrational rather than foundational, gleaning from it surface parallels between the "then" and the "now" across the centuries rather than viewing it as the basis for biblical teachings that prevail throughout the centuries. Second, it approaches the biblical text as an aggregate of splintered fragments rather than a well constructed organic whole, shifting the focus away from the history of salvation, with its many unique phases, to the order of salvation in a rather monotonous uniformity. Third, it interprets the biblical text atomistically rather than synthetically, emphasizing the disconnected individual features at the expense of its thematic structural cohesiveness.[18]

This threefold objection seems to be well taken. But the most damaging criticism is still unsaid. What in the final analysis is the

17. Ibid., pp. 9–10.
18. See B. Holwerda, *Begonnen hebbende van Mozes* (Terneuzen: Littooij, 1953), pp. 87–96, esp. 94.

function of the text in the exemplary method? Is it essential and necessary for the message that allegedly arises from it? It appears not. In moralizing, psychologizing, and spiritualizing, the text is used as a launching pad to transmit "lessons." Similarly, in allegorizing, the text functions as a Pandora's box to produce "timely truths." But in either case not only does the text in its unique situation, with its unique content and its unique purpose, vanish from sight, but also nonbiblical "texts," as accounts about people and of events in church history, could easily render the same service.

All this is not to say that the "lessons" and "timely truths" in view are necessarily unacceptable or unhelpful. But it is to say that in this methodology the text itself is practically silenced and not allowed to speak its authoritative message.

The redemptive-historical method, as the two component elements already indicate, has a twofold theme. For one, it calls for the person and work of Christ, both before and after His incarnation, to take center stage. He is the compendium of all the activity of God. He is the content of all revelation. He is the scope of all of Scripture. He is the reference point of all interpretation. This is not to deny that there is more to the Christian message than the incarnation, the crucifixion, resurrection, and ascension of Christ. But it is to say that nothing can be disconnected or isolated from Him without losing its Christian character. Everything stands or falls with Christocentricity. But there is a second underlying theme that is possibly even more fundamental. Christ is all that He is as the center of history. In Him is the unity, continuity, and progression of history guaranteed, if not personified. History is the story of that one, continuing, and progressing Christ. Thus a heavy emphasis is placed upon the person of Christ in His three-fold office of Prophet, Priest, and King, as He marches through history from creation to His incarnation and then on to His return, ever speaking, ever acting, and ever directing.

All this explains the insistence upon the Christocentricity of Scripture, the emphasis upon the Christocentricity of interpretation, and the passion for Christocentricity in preaching. Scripture is Christocentric because it gives a full-bodied account of all phases and facts of Christ's triumphant procession through redemptive history in either direct or indirect—through the mediation of others—word, deed, and rule. Accordingly, Christocentric interpretation pinpoints the phases and brings out the facts, indicated by the biblical text, by means of a thematic analysis of all its elements in their cohesiveness, while Christocentric preaching makes a presentation of these phases and facts as part of the grand sweep of history.

When done properly, the redemptive-historical exposition of the biblical text is supposedly at the same time its application. This is apparently guaranteed by a threefold fundamental identity in spite of an equally real difference. The same Christ speaks, acts, and rules in every phase of history, even if He reveals and manifests Himself ever more fully. The same march constitutes the essence of history, even if He progresses from stage to stage and its contours become proportionately more evident. The same people march with Christ through history, even if they enjoy an increasingly rich revelation of Christ and find themselves at an increasingly advanced stage of His march. However, in Christocentric preaching exposition does not equal application only by its emphasis upon the grand sweep of redemptive history, which has the identical structure and characteristics throughout its course, but also because Christocentric preaching itself is a part of redemptive history, a part of the victory march of Christ through which He sweeps His people along. One does not need to subscribe to the redemptive-historical method in order to acknowledge that it is prompted by a desire to display Christ's triumph in all its details with a view to full participation in it.

Adherents of the exemplary method, however, express their misgivings in two areas. While they hasten to endorse the reality of the history of redemption, they charge the exclusively redemptive-historical method with being restrictive, if not reductionistic, both in its Christocentric interpretation and in its possible applications.

This twofold charge should not be dismissed lightly. When a preacher in the redemptive-historical tradition proposes to capture the truth of Acts 2 in terms of the following theme, "The

Feast of the Spirit is the Feast of *Christ*," by virtue of Luke's statement that the Spirit was a gift of the ascended Christ (Acts 2:33), it is difficult to deny that there is a problem. Why was it veiled from his view that Acts 2 is the classic chapter of the outpouring of the Spirit, the manifestations of His presence, as well as the manner in which His presence is secured? What other conclusion can be drawn than that the interpretation of Scripture from an exclusively Christocentric perspective is bound to obscure God's full trinitarian self-disclosure and emphasis? This restrictive tendency, which withholds the precious truth of Acts 2 from the congregation, becomes alarming when it is understood from Romans 8:9b that the presence of the Spirit is a matter of life and death.

Further, when another preacher in the same tradition describes the twelve stones of Joshua 4:19–24 exclusively as a "Monument of God's Saving Might in History," with a reference to Joshua 4:24a, and urges his hearers, by way of application, to be alert to God's saving might through similar monuments in the history of Scripture and of the church, again some nagging questions arise. What made him overlook, or blinded him to, the explosive truth that the ultimate aim of Joshua's monument, according to Joshua 4:24b, is the fear of the Lord? What else could it have been but the same restrictive interpretive method that seems to have eyes for one thing only and consequently ends up with curtailing the applicatory possibilities of the text? This reductionistic trend, which compromises the full truth of Joshua 4, becomes even more objectionable when it is recognized from Scripture that the fear of the Lord is the beginning of wisdom and the very soul of godliness.

It seems that a well-constructed covenantal-historical methodology, which honors God not only in His trinitarian self-disclosure, but also in His threefold objective of regeneration, justification, and sanctification, would immediately have recognized the full meaning, as well as significance, of both Acts 2 and Joshua 4.

It is ironic that all this in the final analysis leads to a fundamental criticism similar to that of the exemplary method. What is the function of the text in the redemptive-historical method? It has been astutely observed that the focus of this method is not first and foremost the text, but rather the various facts and stages of unfolding redemptive history. The text functions somewhat as a "window" through which the phases and facts of Christ's march through history are witnessed.[19] It is hardly surprising that the text as text, therefore, is frequently curtailed in its scope, ignored in its purpose, or even violated in its nature, as it is ultimately made to serve the cause of what may be described as "aesthetic contemplation." Indeed, preaching in the redemptive-historical tradition is often comparable to a ride in a Boeing 747 high above the landscape with its hot deserts, its snowpeaked mountains, its wide rivers, its dense forests, its open prairies, its craggy hills and its deep lakes. The view is panoramic, majestic, impressive, breathtaking, and always comfortable. But there is one problem. The Christian is not "above" things. He is in the middle of things. He is trekking through the landscape. As such he experiences heat, or cold, or pain, or failure. Sometimes the journey

19. Greidanus, *Sola Scriptura*, pp. 191–95, 212. He charges both the exemplary and the redemptive-historical method with descending to the fact-level below the text, as both endeavor to preach the original facts behind the text. The exemplary method looks for the original facts in the conduct of the people described. This, then, becomes either a positive or a negative ethical model. The redemptive-historical method defines the original facts as the redemptive-historical acts of God in Christ. These, then, become the objects of the attention of God's people. Greidanus holds that both methods lose sight of the biblical text and substitute *sub Scriptura* for *sola Scriptura*. C. Trimp, "The Relevance of Preaching," *The Westminster Theological Journal* 36 (1973): 1–30, esp. 17–30, insists, from within the redemptive-historical tradition, that the relevance of preaching is bound up, indeed given, with the *sola Scriptura* principle. Regrettably, however, he does not reply in this context to the charge of Greidanus that precisely in the issue of *sola Scriptura* his tradition is below par. Further, when he begins to explain "how the Reformation's *sola Scriptura* principle implies, seals, and guarantees the relevance of preaching," he is somewhat disappointing. Statements like the following may show that preaching is relevant, but are too general to produce relevant preaching: "The relevance of preaching is principally given in Him who in the garb of Scripture is present and active in the church"; "All relevance, which is not at the same time a preaching of the Christ of Scripture, is pseudo-relevance"; "In the ministry of the Word He, i.e. the Spirit, pushes His way through and woos nothing less than the hearts of men"; and, "The Spirit's work is so concrete and relevant that everyone . . . 'hears them speaking of the mighty deeds of God' (Acts 2:11)."

seems interminable, or monotonous, or cheerless, or impossible. At times the traveler loses his sense of direction, or his strength to continue, or his hope of success, or his will to endure. At other times, he lacks wisdom, or expertise, or resources, or support. At all times he is engaged in battle. That is why "aesthetic contemplation" is simply not sufficient fare for the Christian on his way through life. All by itself it is a starvation diet.

This is not to say that there is no truth factor in redemptive-historical preaching. A panoramic view is uplifting and from time to time necessary. But it is to say that it does not begin to address the fulness of life and therefore, as a method, is doomed to ultimate sterility.

In conclusion, the picture looks rather grim for both methodologies. In spite of its laudable aim of concrete application, the exemplary method fails to arrive at a well-construed significance because it is not anchored in the meaning of the text. In spite of its equally laudable goal or proper exposition, the redemptive-historical method fails to arrive at the full meaning of the text and its corresponding significance. Both operate with a grid that is imposed upon the text and not warranted by it. Both, in summary, fall short of producing the truth of the biblical text consisting of its proper and full-orbed meaning and, based upon it, its consequent proper and full-orbed significance.

2. Biblical Significance and Universal Principles

Is it possible to arrive at a proper and full-orbed application of the text based upon an equally proper and full-orbed exposition? The answer to this question is decidedly in the affirmative. This is not to say that the application of the text is always immediately available. The reason is simple. Textual truth is wrapped up in a variety of cultural forms that often differ radically from those familiar to present-day man. It is situated in a variety of historical settings that often do not correspond to those of the modern hearer. It is couched in a variety of literary genres with which today's society is not necessarily conversant. It is expressed in a variety of linguistic peculiarities that may well be foreign to contemporary man. All this explains why the relevance of the biblical text has often been lost to twentieth-century man. It is ironic that preaching that is intent on setting forth textual meaning is often dry and deadening because it does not come to grips with the hearer. On the other hand, preaching that endeavors to be lively and meet the hearer where he is, is often devoid of well-presented biblical truth. But this does not need to be so. There is a way to insure that the truth of the text is transmitted in its full meaning and relevance. It is the way of universal principles and patterns to be gleaned from the text. As will be shown, this is the model that Scripture itself holds forth.

In order to recognize and reproduce these principles and patterns, the help of linguistic, cultural, historical, and other pertinent studies should first be enlisted to the fullest. They will often shed a surprising, if not indispensable, light on the text. A sampling of illustrative material will support this.

A recent study suggests that the verb *baptized* in the phrase "baptized for the dead" (I Cor. 15:29) should be taken figuratively as "to be fully engaged in," or "to be submerged in," which lexicographically is quite legitimate. This suggestion seems to make a good deal of sense against the backdrop of the widespread custom of the day to take meticulous care of the dead by means of libations, sacrifices, and memorial meals on their behalf. There even appear to have been graveworkers' guilds that would provide these and similar services. Paul, then, would ask a rhetorical question. Why would people be submerged in the care for the dead, if they do not rise? If this interpretation would be correct, it certainly would end the confusion about I Corinthians 15:29.[20]

Similarily, it is essential for the meaning and application of Matthew 8:28–34 to know whether Christ's journey into the land of the Gadarenes constituted an attempt to foreign missions or was part of his ministry to lost Israel. Both geographical and historical studies indicate that the countryside of the Gadarenes at one time was part of the commonwealth of Israel from which it

20. J. van Bruggen, *Het lezen van de bijbel* (Kampen: Kok, 1981), pp. 43–53, esp. 51–53.

seceded for economic reasons. The passage, therefore, does not record the "First Failure in Foreign Missions" but is the written report of "One of Christ's Biopsies of Israel in the State of Its Lostness." The situation appears depressing. Intimate involvement with the swine, a symbol of uncleanness, indicates the total lack of interest in separation from sin.[21] The terror-inspiring presence of the demoniacs on the crossroads of the land points, further, to the domination of Satan. But what is worse, deliverance from the demonic domination, which once again guarantees the safety of daily living, and closely connected with this, the end of a forbidden involvement, which once again brings the beauty of holiness into view, are met with a fear-struck hostility.

Of equal, if not greater, importance than these "auxiliary" studies, which illumine features or even the structure of the text, is the search for the main purpose, the general thrust, or the unifying theme of the biblical text, ultimately in its widest context. This will prove to be invaluable in discovering its meaning and settling on its significance.

By way of illustration, an examination of the Gospel of John in the light of the stated purpose with its three themes of Christ's deity, faith, and life (John 20:31) discloses the structure of John 1–11, which otherwise might have gone unnoticed. Following the first chapter, with its emphasis upon Christ as the Word, John the Baptist (who leads up to Him), and the disciples (who eventually go forth from Him), John gives an introduction to deity, faith, and life in John 2, 3, and 4, spells out their essence, in John 5, 6, and 7, and presents their implications, in John 8, 9, and 10. These three cycles culminate in John 11, in which all three themes come together in the account of the raising of Lazarus. Only the threefold recurrence of the three themes in their interrelationship already holds out a promise of powerful application.

Once the "auxiliary" studies have been completed and the gen-

21. According to Lev. 20:22–26, esp. 25, God makes the distinction between clean and unclean foods to symbolize the necessity of separation from unholiness. In II Cor. 6:14–18 the same truth is set forth, but then in connection with a different symbol.

eral purpose or unifying theme(s) has (have) been determined, the stage is set to harvest the universal principles and patterns from the biblical text. This is to be done by means of an outline of the text in the framework of its context and in terms that are applicable to all times and all people in comparable situations. Factual outlines that present the details of the text can be of great help in bringing the contours, structure, and content, and therewith the meaning, of the text into sharp focus. But they are only an intermediate step toward the ultimate goal of an outline couched in universal terminology.

The benefits of such an outline are multiple. First, it achieves a thus far elusive objective. Exposition is indeed application. This merger of meaning and significance insures that the preaching ministry can proclaim a message that constitutes God's Word for its day.

Second, the more detailed the outline becomes, the more concrete the universal principles turn out to be. The more general universal principles of the major divisions in the outline indicate the large structure and the broad parameters of God's truth and the Christian's life. The more specific universal principles of the subdivisions in the outline disclose the finer points and the more concrete issues of God's truth and the Christian's life. The total network of universal principles covers the total tapestry of God's truth and the Christian's life.

Third, the outlines of earlier revelation bring into view universal principles that set the stage for, are foundational to, and form the framework for the universal principles displayed in outlines of later revelation. Sometimes the earlier principles are introductory or preparatory for the later ones; at other times they are fleshed out or enlarged by them.

Fourth, frequently universal principles are found in clusters, the combination of which form whole patterns. To isolate these patterns in their totality will yield maximum understanding of the message of the biblical text.

Fifth, many universal principles are easily detectable. They either lie on the face of the text or appear fully formulated as general statements that transcend specific situations. Christ's great commission to the disciples (Matt. 28:19) illustrates the former category; similarily God's commandment, "You shall not murder" (Exod. 20:13) demonstrates the latter.

Sixth, other universal principles do not so easily come into view. They must be mined like nuggets out of a gold mine. This is mostly the case with historical material and predictive prophecy, as well as the so-called ceremonial sections of the Old Testament, since time and culture gaps, as well as change in economy, have to be taken into account. The more strenuous the efforts on the part of the interpreter, however, the greater the rewards!

3. One Illustration and the Biblical Model

An example will now be given to illustrate what has been said thus far. It will consist of a factually as well as universally worded outline to incorporate the intermediate step recommended to reach the ultimate objective. Then some comments will be added so as to remove any doubt about the procedure followed and the results achieved:

Genesis 11:27–25:11 With Special Emphasis Upon 12:4–20.

I. The Life of Abraham

Introduction: 11:27–12:3

  a. Command to enter Canaan

  b. Promise concerning the land, the nation, and the world

1. Abraham and the promised land: 12:4–14:24

  a. Abraham and the king of Egypt: 12:4–20

  b. Abraham and Lot: 13:1–18

II. The Father of All Believers

Introduction:

  a. Command to claim his inheritance

  b. Promise concerning his inheritance, his descendants, and the world

1. The promised inheritance

  a. Beyond the parameters of the promise without God's command

  b. On the foundation of the promise in obedience of faith

c. Abraham and the kings of the East: 14:1–24	c. Action by virtue of the promise in love for the brothers
2. Abraham and the promised child: 15:1–21:34	2. The promised offspring
3. Abraham and the promised future: 22:1–25:11	3. The promised future

The twofold theme of the narrative of Abraham's life is that of God's promise and Abraham's (un)belief. The material could have been presented from a different perspective and with a different theme. But it was not. Apparently God wished to convey that both promise and faith are indispensable for the child of God. The twofold theme, as the outline suggests,[22] has three variations, pertaining to the land, the child, and the future. The story of Abraham's flight into Egypt is an instance of the first variation.

A sketch of this chapter in universal terminology will once again demonstrate that in this way exposition is at the same time application and, furthermore, that the concreteness of the application for everyday life goes hand in hand with the detailedness of the exposition.

It appears that God's promise and God's command often stretch the believer to the breaking point (the command to leave everything and everyone for a totally unknown land). However, a combination of dependence upon God's promise and obedience to His command will invariably meet with His blessing (safe arrival in the land). This blessing, in the meantime, will always be accompanied by a time of testing (famine in the new land). The tendency will be to lose sight of God's promise and to embark upon an uncharted course to secure survival (flight into Egypt). Such course of action will lead to greater distress (the threat

22. The threefold division of the narrative of Abraham's life, which appears to run parallel to the threefold promise to Abraham pertaining to the land he was to inherit, the descendants he was to receive, and the worldwide future he was to have, is suggested by the phrase, "After these things," which marks the beginning of the second and third section (Gen. 15:1; 22:1).

posed by Pharaoh). If a man does not recognize his original error and fails to turn back from it in genuine repentance, his irresistible Adamic tendency to be totally irresponsible (Gen. 3:12) will emerge to stave off disaster. In case of need, he will cheerfully sacrifice his wife to save himself. If it comes down to the choice of having her violated or himself killed, he will opt for the latter (request to Sarah). The method of approach will have a semblance of righteousness (technically he was her brother). On the other hand, if his wife in faith does not indignantly give in to her, humanly speaking, equally irresistible womanly tendency to dominate (Gen. 3:16b),[23] but submits to the technically legitimate demands of her husband in spite of the possible consequences, the corner is in principle turned. Disaster may loom larger and larger (removal to Pharaoh's harem). Nevertheless, obedience to God's command in dependence upon His promise (I Pet. 3:6) will ultimately produce God's blessing, even if it requires His intervention (it eventually did!). Incidentally, a man often fails his first real test (Abraham did), unlike his wife (Sarah did not). How heartening it is to know that man's faithlessness (the father of all believers!) cannot nullify the faithfulness of God, because He cannot deny Himself (II Tim. 2:13) (and He did not!). It is equally heartening to recognize that the biblical text is very relevant in a very searching way in very concrete situations without having to succumb to moralizing, psychologizing, spiritualizing, or allegorizing.

Ultimately, however, no methodology may make a claim upon the interpreter unless it can be demonstrated to have its anchorage in Scripture itself. This, then, is the final order of business,

---

23. The irresistible tendency to be irresponsible on the part of the man is indicated by Gen. 3:12 and is exhibited throughout Scripture, not in the last place in Gen. 12:11-13. The irresistible tendency to dominate on the part of the woman is predicated upon a specific exegesis of Gen. 3:16, especially of the phrase, "Your desire shall be to your husband." It seems that Susan T. Foh, "What is the Woman's Desire," *The Westminster Theological Journal* 37 (1974): 376ff. esp. 380-82, has conclusively shown, with a reference to Gen. 4:7, which uses the same phraseology, that it is the woman's desire to "control her husband," "to contend with him for leadership," and "to usurp his divinely appointed leadership."

which in this context will be confined to only two lines of, it is hoped, persuasive argument.

First, it appears that Scripture itself in both the Old and New Testaments customarily gleans universal principles and patterns from previous Scripture and presents them as God's Word for the day. Not one type of literature is excluded. Universal principles are derived from historical events and narratives (Gen. 22:14; Ps. 126:5-6; Rom. 4:1-5; James 2:20-25), from legal promulgations and accounts (Ezra 9:10-12; 10:10-12; 13:1-4, 23-27; Mal. 3:8-10; I Cor. 9:9; Eph. 6:2-3), from wisdom literature like Proverbs and Psalms (Rom. 3:10-18; 12:20; Heb. 12:5-6; 13:5-6), and from prophetic pronouncements (Matt. 2:18; 13:14-16; Acts 28:26-27; I Cor. 1:19; Heb. 8:10-12; 10:16-17).

Second, possibly even more telling is the "allegorical" and "typical" use of Scripture by the Bible itself. An examination of the pertinent data quickly shows that this is not at all comparable to the popular ancient allegorical interpretation that reads meaning into the text from outside the text and serves outside interests, or to the modern typological interpretation that introduces meaning into the text from later Scripture and serves the interests of later revelation. In fact, the "allegorical" and "typical" use of Scripture, as found in the Bible, has nothing to do with meaning whatsoever. Its focus is always and exclusively the domain of significance.[24] More precisely, in the "allegorical" and "typical"

24. Note the sharp distinction between allegorical and typological interpretation and the allegorical and typical use of Scripture. The former is an activity of the fallible interpreter who basically assigns meaning to the text from beyond the text. The present writer rejects this approach as an unacceptable attack upon the integrity of the text. The latter is simply a given in the infallible Bible, which aims at radiating significance from the text beyond the text. The present writer, of course, embraces this as an authoritative model. The whole subject matter is admittedly difficult and has produced a stream of inconclusive, and at times confusing, literature. It seems, however, that the failure to distinguish between interpretation and use, and all that this entails, lies at the root of much of this inconclusiveness and confusion. John Goldingay, *Approaches in Old Testament Interpretation* (Downers Grove: Inter-Varsity Press, 1981), pp. 97-115, openly admits that both allegorical and typological interpretation introduces meaning from elsewhere: allegory, to biblical texts; typology, to biblical events (pp. 103, 107, 112). This is supposedly made possible by analogies and correspondences,

use of Scripture the biblical text is always honored in its unique character and original meaning, while its significance is derived from it, indeed, by means of universal principles and patterns! The only passage, Galatians 4:24ff., where the term "allegorical" actually occurs, is a case in point. Paul detects a universal pattern in Abraham's life, as to the way his two sons came into existence and with regard to the relationship his two wives sustained to him and to each other, which he applies with great force and effectiveness to the situation he faces in the Galatian congregations. Just as Isaac came into existence by virtue of the promise through the free woman Sarah, and Ishmael through the flesh by means of the bondwoman Hagar, so the believers trace their origin as a result of the promise to the Jerusalem above, which is free, and the Judaists through the works of the law to the present Jerusalem, which is enslaved. Furthermore, just as Sarah's insistence was correct that Ishmael and his mother should be expelled because he persecuted Isaac, so the church is duty bound to remove the Judaists and to distance itself from their spiritual mother because they are inimical to the faith as it is in Jesus.

What is noticeable here is more than a general analogy or an interesting parallel. Paul extracts a universal principle from a biblical text that is foundational and therefore has compelling applicability.

A second passage, I Corinthians 10:6ff., in which the word *type* occurs, depicts the same methodology in connection with the "typical" use of Scripture. A perusal of the record of the desert journey shows Israel to be a nation involved in evil cravings,

specifically between the Testaments, as well as intensifications from the Old to the New Testament (pp. 98–101). As long as the allegorical and typological interpretation, which has as its main focus the relationship Old Testament texts (allegory) and events (typology) sustain to the New Testament Christ event and *vice versa* (pp. 109–15), honors the *biblical* analogies, correspondences, and intensifications, it will be legitimate (p. 106). But this structure does not undo the damage. Not the text, but the interpreter appears to have the last word. Goldingay, indeed, also states that typology studies biblical events out of an interest in their symbolical significance! But without further elaboration on his part, it is difficult to draw any conclusions from that (p. 107).

idolatry, sexual immorality, and grumblings. God's judgment consisted of death meted out in a variety of ways. According to Paul, all this is not incidental to the desert journey. It opens a window upon a universal pattern of God's dealing with His people. The way of evil cravings, idolatry, sexual immorality, and grumblings is the way of death in one way or another. Paul's solemn warning is that this applies at all times to all people everywhere (I Cor. 10:11-12). In short, it is a universal principle!

What has been argued thus far should go a long way toward the recognition that the determination of biblical significance by means of universal principles and patterns is not just a matter of the individual interpreter's personal taste. It appears to be a biblical model that should be acknowledged as authoritative. What is good enough for Christ and His apostles ought to be good enough for the church of all ages.

In summary, it is nearly instinctively sensed that this methodology is superior not only to the exemplary method, which tends to bypass the original, intended meaning and easily ends up with an unfounded, mistaken or nonobligatory application, but also to the redemptive-historical method, which tends to narrow the approach to and the scope of the original, intended meaning and easily leads to an ethereal, aesthetic contemplation or a truncated application.

In conclusion, it seems that the convenantal-historical method, as outlined above, is best suited to bring out the single, proper, and full meaning of the biblical text by means of "auxiliary" studies, is in harmony with its purpose, and is most effective to open up the way to its manifold, proper, and full significance by means of universal principles and patterns.

9

Preaching and Systematic Theology
Donald Macleod

"Theology without proclamation is empty, proclamation without theology is blind."[1] So wrote Gerhard Ebeling, and if what he says is true—and surely it is—then the connection between theology and preaching is an intimate one. The theological process does not exist for itself. It exists only as a preparation for preaching. If it does not issue in proclamation, it is an abortion, or a still-birth. To change the perspective, if our theology (or any detail in it) is not preachable, its claim to being a theology at all is exceedingly doubtful. James Denney was surely right when he said, "I don't care anything for a theology that doesn't help a man to preach."[2] A true theology will seek articulation, claim a place in the liturgy of the church, and assert its right to walk with the people of God in the valley of the shadow of death. If it is content to be silent or to be confined to the groves of academia, it has lost its prophetic character, and with that its integrity.

It is equally true, however, that theology is essential to preaching. Without theology there is no preaching, at least not in the New Testament sense. Preaching is a message as well as a method. It is even arguable that preaching is a message rather than a method. The right message poorly proclaimed is preferable to a nonmessage well proclaimed. Paul saw his own function as being to declare the word of the cross. He had to proclaim the facts:

1. Gerhard Ebeling, *Theology and Proclamation* (London: Wm. Collins Son and Co., 1966), p. 20.
2. Quoted by Alexander Gammie, *Preachers I Have Heard* (London: Pickering and Inglis, n.d.), p. 163.

Christ died, Christ rose. But he had also to proclaim the meaning of those facts. Uninterpreted, they were useless and meaningless. Interpreted as Christ's vicarious suffering for sin and as the attestation of His divine sonship and lordship, they were the saving power of God.

Paul defines the role of the preacher in even more stringently theological terms in II Corinthians 5:20. The ambassador of Christ is given the task of expounding to the world the message, "God made him who knew no sin to be sin for us that we might be made the righteousness of God in him." It is not enough that the preacher does not contradict that message. It is, unfortunately, quite possible to be completely nonheretical and yet at the same time totally unfaithful to the preacher's mandate. The great theological, christological, and soteriological themes must sound forth clearly. Otherwise, there is no preaching. "It is through the truth that souls are saved," wrote B. B. Warfield. "It is accordingly the prime business of the preacher to present this truth to men, and it is consequently his fundamental duty to become himself possessed of this truth, that he may present it to men and so save their souls."[3]

We may remain with Warfield for a good summary definition of systematic theology: "It is nothing other than the saving truth of God presented in systematic form."[4] It utilizes what biblical theology has discovered regarding the distinctive contribution made to our understanding of the great doctrines by each successive era of revelation. It also makes use of what historical theology has to say on the questions raised by former generations, the challenges posed by heretics, and the contributions made by the great theologians. But systematic theology is more comprehensive than either biblical or historical theology. It seeks for the over-all biblical and historical view, collating all the relevant biblical passages and the contributions made by academic and polemical discussion. It is final and normative in a way that its sister disci-

---

3. B. B. Warfield, *Selected Shorter Writings,* vol. 2, ed. John E. Meeter (Phillipsburg, N.J.: Presbyterian and Reformed, 1973), p. 180.
    4. Ibid., p. 281.

plines are not. It seeks the final view of Scripture, rather than the transitional one of the Old Testament or even the Book of Acts. Similarly it not only describes the views of fathers and heretics (in the manner of historical theology), but also evaluates them in the light of the rule of faith.

Systematic theology, then, has four characteristics:

First it is *thematic*. Its interest is not in a particular text or a particular book or in an author or personality, but in the doctrinal themes of Scripture. Second, it is *comprehensive*. It draws upon *all* that Scripture and historical theology have to say on particular topics. Third, it is *normative*. It regards its own conclusions as representing not what a particular biblical author thought or what certain theologians believe or what it may be inspiring for the church to accept, but the truth. Fourth, it is *systematic*. It seeks to arrange its topics in the best possible order, to analyze and synthesize individual doctrines as lucidly as possible, and to relate them as coherently and cogently as possible to the life of both the church and the world.

Systematics and Exegesis

When it comes to the relevance of this kind of study to the work of preaching, the first question we have to ask is, What should be the relationship between the exegesis of a specific text and the whole of systematic theology? In general, the answer is that each text must be seen in the light of the whole system of revealed truth. This means two things.

First, the system of truth elucidates each text. In practice, this is what is meant by *the analogy of faith*: "The infallible rule of interpretation of Scripture is the Scripture itself; and therefore, when there is a question about the true and full sense of any Scripture, it must be searched and known by other passages that speak more clearly" (Westminster Confession 1.9). Take, for example, the directive given by Paul in Ephesians 5:18, "Be filled with the Spirit." The only way to expound this is by taking account of the whole doctrine of the believer's relation to the

Spirit: the facts that (1) every believer has been filled with the Spirit (Acts 2:4; I Cor. 12:13), (2) believers may be filled repeatedly (Acts 2:4; cf. 4:8), (3) the Lord promises that in every emergency the Spirit will teach us what to say (Luke 12:12), (4) there is an *abiding* in Christ as well as a receiving of Christ, and (5) the ideal condition for a Christian is to be full of the Holy Spirit (Acts 6:5). Unless we draw upon the whole doctrine we cannot possibly elucidate Ephesians 5:18.

The same is true at many other points. The text "Believe on the Lord Jesus Christ" requires us to draw on the whole doctrine of faith. The text "Now are we the sons of God" requires us to draw on the whole doctrine of adoption. The text "Holy, holy, holy, is the Lord of hosts" requires us to draw on the whole doctrine of the divine holiness. In all such instances, the exposition proceeds by way of bringing to bear on a single passage all that Scripture has to say on a particular topic. (This does not mean that we should preach from any individual text all that the Bible says on, for example, the divine holiness. We must select those aspects which are most relevant to the context.)

Secondly, the system of doctrine *exercises control* over the exposition of a particular passage. Precisely because there is a system, and because truth is one, dogmatics lays down parameters that our exegesis must never trespass. At some points, this is a matter of crucial importance. Take Psalm 6:5, for example: "There is no remembrance of thee in death. In Sheol, who will give thee thanks." No exposition of this (or similar passages) must ever contradict the doctrine of the immortality of the soul or suggest that the intermediate state between death and resurrection is anything other than a conscious state. Systematic theology exercises a similar control on our exposition of a passage like John 3:5, "Unless one is born of water and of the spirit, one cannot enter the kingdom of God." Any suggestion of baptismal regeneration is immediately ruled out by what the rest of Scripture tells us of the spiritual nature of salvation. The same principle applies to II Corinthians 5:21, "God made him who knew no sin to be sin for us." We hold to the doctrine of the sinlessness of Christ, and that immediately rules out the idea that vicarious suffering involved the Lord in any moral or spiritual pollution. *Made sin* can never become *made sinful*.

Another passage that raises christological problems is Colossians 1:15, "He is the image of the invisible God, the first-born of all creation." All that the church learned in the Arian controversy forbids us to tolerate any exegesis that compromises either the preexistence or the deity (creator-hood) of the Savior. As a final instance, we may take the notorious crux, Hebrews 6:4ff.: "For it is impossible for those who were once enlightened and have tasted the heavenly gift and been made partakers of the Holy Spirit and have tasted the good word of God and the powers of the age to come, if they fall away, to renew them again to repentance." *Prima facie* this passage suggests that true believers can commit apostasy. Dogmatics alerts us, however, to the fact that such an interpretation is untenable, and closer examination of the passage itself confirms that it is pointing in the direction of another doctrine altogether—the doctrine of temporary faith.

More cautiously, that each text must be seen in the light of the whole system of revealed truth also involves a third principle, namely, that we should not build a doctrine on one single passage. "That," said A. A. Hodge, "is like balancing a stool on one leg."[5] In matters theological as well as judicial, we must hold to the principle, "By the mouth of two or three witnesses, let every word be established." This has often been forgotten, especially in connection with eschatology. Men have built the doctrines of the rapture, the first and second resurrections, and above all the doctrine of the millennium virtually on single passages (I Thess. 4:17; Rev. 20:4; 20:5). These doctrines suffer from the additional disadvantage that they contradict the overall view of Scripture. But even if they did not, their slender textual basis immediately renders them suspect.

Systematic theology does, however, create certain dangers for the exegete and expositor. One is the temptation to suppress and

5. Quoted by C. A. Salmond, *Princetoniana: Charles and A. A. Hodge With Class and Table Talk of Hodge the Younger* (Edinburgh: Oliphant, Anderson, and Ferrier, 1888), p. 167.

play down the doctrine of a particular text in the interests of our own system. For example, those who hold to the Calvinistic doctrine of election may, because they mistakenly fear for their own position, do less than justice to the breadth of God's love as declared in John 3:16 and I Timothy 2:4. Similarly, and just as mistakenly, we may minimize the emphasis on working out our own salvation (Phil. 2:12), washing our own robes (Rev. 7:14), and purifying ourselves (I John 3:3). Again, because of an aversion to decisionism, we may be reluctant to call for decision (no man ever became a Christian without deciding to become one). Yet again, because of a legitimate recoil from the histrionics of certain evangelists, we may fail to insist on the need for an *immediate* response to Christ. *Now* is now—where men are. It is not tomorrow or the near future. The three thousand at Pentecost were not only *awakened* by Peter's sermon. They were brought to decision and to baptism.

The same danger exists in other areas. The New Testament contains many warnings as to the danger of apostasy. These must not be muted in the interests of the doctrine of the perseverance of the saints. Indeed, these warnings, solemnly applied, are one of the means God uses to keep His people from the complacency and carelessness out of which apostasy is born. Sometimes we are equally fearful (and equally unfaithful) with regard to the doctrine of justification. It is indeed the very foundation of the gospel that men are justified by faith, apart from the works of the law. But this must not mean that our hearers never hear the message of Matthew 7:21, "Not every one who says to me, Lord, Lord, will enter the kingdom of heaven; but he who does the will of my Father who is in heaven." Indeed, all his life the preacher must wrestle, theologically and homiletically, with the fact that salvation involves not only justification by grace, but also entering by the strait gate, walking the narrow way, and doing the words spoken by the Lord.

The second danger is closely related to the first. Rather than let the text speak its own message, we sometimes can embark on the apologetical exercise of showing how it can be reconciled with some favorite doctrine of our own school. Here again a passage like John 3:16 suffers most. Too many sermons give the impression that the preacher's overriding concern is to qualify and contract the love of God rather than to show it in the glory of its self-renunciation, magnanimity, and extravagance. But other passages and other doctrines suffer too. The free offer of the gospel to all men indiscriminatingly is muted or withheld as the preacher tries, instead, to show how much an offer can be reconciled with the sovereignty of God. The gratuitousness of justification is obscured as we spend our strength trying to show its consistency with the imperatives of sanctification and end up frustrating the grace of God. The solemn reality of judgment and hell is forgotten as the sermon speaks instead of the love of God and insists incontrovertibly that His judgment must be consistent with that. The preacher faces a text that declares that those who are born of God do not sin (I John 3:9) and spends his strength showing that they do. The text's insistence on the anomalousness and the monstrousness of sin in the life of a Christian is forgotten.

The principle to be applied in all such instances is surely this: after determining the actual message of the text by comparing Scripture with Scripture (systematic theology), we must let the text speak its own truth. All necessary reconciliation, all correcting of imbalances, will come as other facets of truth are emphasized in the course of preaching the whole counsel of God.

One other danger deserves a mention. It is very tempting when a doctrine is laid down in a text to try to bring out in one sermon all that systematic theology has to say on this particular subject. This is almost always unwise. It is better to concentrate on the two or three points relevant to the doctrine that are suggested by the text itself. Otherwise, the sermon will be diffuse and lifeless. (Even at the purely human level it is the constraints and limitations of our materials and medium that stimulate rhetorical strength, and Glen Knecht instructs us well in the next chapter about the need for a carefully focused sermon). "It is a common delusion of inexperienced speakers or writers," says John A. Broadus, "to think that they had best take a very broad subject so as to be sure of finding enough to say. But to choose some one aspect of a great subject is usually far better, as there is thus much better opportunity for the speaker to work out something fresh and much better prospect of making the hearers take a lively interest in the subject as a whole."[6] Alexander, whom Broadus quotes, states the principle succinctly: "The more you narrow the subject, the more thoughts you will have."[7] The more fundamental and hence the more clearly revealed a doctrine, the more important it becomes to observe this rule. It is impossible to cram the whole of Christology or the whole of justification into a single sermon. We must limit ourselves to the perspectives and emphases of our particular texts.

The classic example of the danger is Hebrews 2:4, "How shall we escape if we neglect so great salvation." One could write as many volumes as the combined dogmatics of Barth and Berkouwer and still not have fully expounded the greatness of the salvation. If we confine ourselves to the context, however, we find that it is great because it offers a great Savior, the Son of God; and, following from that, that it is great because it offers an authoritative revelation (1:1), a complete purging of sin (1:3), and a mighty, living leader (1:3). To go beyond the context is to court homiletical disaster.

The Shaping of a Sermon

What role does systematic theology play in the shaping of a sermon? One's immediate response is to confess reluctance to allow dogmatics to determine the structure of our preaching. The text itself will normally provide not only the theme but also the divisions of the sermon (see again Glen Knecht's comments on this). It will also provide momentum, as we move through the successive phases of its teaching. Above all, the context and life-situation of the text will almost always indicate how the doctrine of the text is to be applied. To abstract the text from its existen-

6. J. A. Broadus, *A Treatise on the Preparation and Delivery of Sermons* (London: James Nisbet and Co., 1874), p. 90.
7. Ibid.

tial setting in Scripture and impose on it instead the dynamics of mere literary style (alliteration) or of dogmatics is not only to jeopardize the liveliness and the relevance of our preaching, but to abandon the role of expositors. We must be faithful not only to the doctrines of the text but to the pastoral perspective that underlies it. To preach Philippians 2:5–11 is not only to preach Christology but also to plead for an end to all obsession with our own rights; to preach II Corinthians 8:9 means not only to proclaim the marvel of the incarnation, but also to lay down the biblical theology of Christian giving; and to preach Galatians 2:19ff. is not only to declare the doctrine of definitive sanctification, but also to relate it in the closest possible way to the charge that the doctrine of justification by grace gives an encouragement to sin. Not only the doctrinal points but the contours and application of the sermon arise from the text itself.

Despite what is often said as to the unsystematic nature of the oriental mind, there are however some texts that are most naturally divided according to the categories of systematic theology. The doctrinal part of the message of Philippians 2:5ff. can be divided, for example, in terms of (1) the preexistent Christ, (2) the humiliated Christ, (3) the exalted Christ. A sermon on John 3:1ff. would deal with regeneration, one of the great themes of dogmatics, and within the bounds set by the passage itself, could deal with (1) the author/agent of regeneration, (2) the nature of regeneration, (3) the results of regeneration, (4) the necessity of regeneration. Here the contours of systematic theology correspond to those of the text itself. The same is true of Romans 3:24–25, one of the great biblical statements of the doctrine of justification. It states (1) the meaning of justification, (2) the source of justification (grace), (3) the grounds of justification (the sacrifice of Christ), and (4) the means of justification (faith alone). If confined within these parameters, however, these would not be easy sermons to preach. They are too exclusively didactic. It would be imperative to find some balancing practical perspective (in the biblical context) so that the teaching was related constantly to the needs, interests, questions, doubts, or even indifference of the congregation.

On other occasions, systematic theology could give the sub-headings (the subordinate contours) of our sermons. For example, a sermon on Acts 16:31 would have to concentrate on the meaning of faith and relate it in the closest possible way to the person and work of Christ. It could therefore organize this part of its material around the threefold division of the mediatorial work—faith in Christ as Prophet (submitting our intellects to Him), faith in Christ as Priest (bringing our sins to Him) and faith in Christ as King (accepting His lordship and leadership). The rest of the sermon could be devoted to expounding the promise, "thou shalt be saved."

A similar approach could be taken with a sermon of which one of the divisions was the nature of repentance (for example, Mark 1:15, "The time is fulfilled and the kingdom of God is at hand; repent and believe the gospel"). The section on repentance could very well borrow from dogmatics and expound it as (1) a change of mind, (2) a change of mood, and (3) a change of direction.

On a few rare occasions there may be a straightforward overlap (in content, not in language) between the sermon and the theological lecture. This would be true, for example, if on the basis of Genesis 1:26 we were trying to expound the doctrine of man as the image of God. The preacher would have to draw copiously and carefully on what systematic theology has to say on the subject. He could hardly escape utilizing the idea of the twofold image, distinguishing between the moral image (which has been lost) and the natural image (which is an integral and inalienable fact of human nature). Bearing in mind, however, that the object of the exercise is homiletical, not academic, the practical application would have to be kept clearly in mind. The doctrine of the image is the great symbol of the dignity of man: hence the gravity of homicide; and hence, more strikingly, the gravity of slander and libel.

Covering the System

Should a preacher cover all the major sections of systematics each year? There are at least three principles to be borne in mind in trying to answer this question. First, the Lord has charged us to search the Scriptures. This suggests that our primary concern should be not to cover the relatively human system, but to give the people a comprehensive acquaintance with God's written revelation. It would be pedantic (at least) to begin our ministry with Genesis 1:1 in the morning and Matthew 1:1 in the evening. But it is the Bible, in all its divisions, that we are to traverse: the Old Testament and the New, the Gospels and the Epistles, the historical and the didactic, the ethical and the doctrinal, the experimental and the theological. This is the only way to ensure a balanced diet.

Second, we have been directed to declare the whole counsel of God. This includes more than doctrines—at least in the strict sense of systematic theology. But it does mean that we are charged with proclaiming *all* the doctrines and our pattern of biblical exposition must take careful account of that.

Third, we must maintain a biblical proportion and balance. The temptation always exists to preach too frequently on our favorite doctrines and on denominational or party distinctives. With regard to the doctrine of the divine sovereignty—and its associates, predestination and election—we should bear in mind the wise words of Charles Hodge: "This doctrine is to all other doctrines of Scripture what the granite foundation is to the other strata of the earth. It underlies and sustains them, but it crops out only here and there. So this doctrine should underlie all our preaching, and should be definitely presented only now and then."[8] This "only now and then" applies even more forcibly to party distinctions that cannot claim such foundational status as the sovereignty of God. No preacher, whatever his convictions, has the right to be constantly harping on the millennium, the rapture, the Sabbath, tithing, infant baptism, or the doctrine of hell.

On the other hand, there are some doctrines so important that to preach them once a year is not nearly enough. Attention to biblical proportion will mean that we cover some of these repeat-

8. Charles Hodge, *Princeton Sermons* (Edinburgh: Banner of Truth, 1979), p. 6.

edly—in some instances, every Lord's Day. This is notably true of the doctrine of the person of Christ. His deity stands out on every page of the New Testament; it is the one doctrine that commands the undivided assent of Christendom; it is the foundation and presupposition of all our worship. Consequently, the church should be steeped in it, and Edmund Clowney discusses this fact at some length earlier in this volume.

There are other doctrines scarcely less important. Of justification by grace alone through faith Luther said that it was "the article of a standing or a falling church." Of the doctrine of the atonement Paul said, "I determined not to know anything among you save Jesus Christ and him crucified" (I Cor. 2:2). Of the grace of love the same apostle said that without it we are "sounding brass and tinkling cymbols." Such statements should give us pause. Do these doctrines have the prominence in our preaching that they have in the New Testament?

Clearly, every preacher needs a sense of theological proportion. All revealed doctrines are important. But some are absolutely fundamental and primary. How are we to identify them? There are at least four closely related criteria. First, there are some things "which are necessary to be known, believed and observed for salvation" (Westminster Confession 1.7). The confession does not define these, but it recognizes that, as a category, they exist. Without the hearing of certain doctrines, faith is impossible (Rom. 10:11).

Second, there is the fact, also recognized in the Westminster Confession (1.7), that some doctrines "are so clearly propounded and opened in some place of scripture or other, that not only the learned, but the unlearned, in a due use of the ordinary means, may attain unto a sufficient understanding of them." The criterion here is the fulness of revelation. Some aspects of truth are made so plain that no ambiguity or uncertainty surrounds them: and the plainness is a hallmark of their overriding importance.

Third, and closely related to the clarity factor, there is the principle laid down by John Stott: "Any subject on which equally devout, equally humble, equally Bible-believing and Bible-studying Christians or churches reach different conclusions, must be

considered secondary, not primary, peripheral not central."[9]
There are many subjects in which we have so little light that good
men see them differently—the millennium, the extent of the
atonement, infant baptism, church order, and many others. They
must, of course, be preached: but with the modesty, charity, and
sparingness that become their relative unimportance.

Fourth, and most important, Scripture itself gives very clear
guidance as to which doctrines are fundamental. The list is surprisingly long. For example, we have the central affirmation of the
Old Testament, "Hear, O Israel: The Lord our God is one Lord"
(Deut. 6:4). We have Paul's statement as to "the first things" of
the Christian tradition: "I delivered to you first of all, that which
I also received, that Christ died for our sins according to the
Scriptures; and that he was buried, and that he rose again" (I Cor.
15:3f.). In the apostle's view, the doctrines of particular atonement and the resurrection of Christ were clearly of foremost importance. So was the lordship of Christ, which was the key element in the message preached to the Colossians: "As you have
received [by tradition] Christ Jesus as Lord, so walk in him"
(Col. 2:6). Conversely, the apostle John declares the doctrine of
the true humanity of Christ to be fundamental: "Every spirit that
confesses that Jesus Christ is come in the flesh is from God: and
every spirit that does not confess Jesus is not from God; and this
is the spirit of the antichrist" (I John 4:2f.).

And so one could go on. According to Galatians 1:8ff. the
doctrine of justification by grace alone through faith alone is absolutely essential. According to I Corinthians 15:19, the resurrection of the dead is fundamental. According to John 3:1–15, the
new birth is fundamental. According to I Corinthians 13, love is
fundamental. According to many recurring summaries of domini-
cal and apostolic preaching, faith and repentance are fundamental.
And according to the most basic biblico-theological perspectives
(especially the concept of "the promise"), initiation by baptism in
the Holy Spirit is fundamental.

9. John R. Stott, *Christ the Controversialist* (Downers Grove: Inter-Varsity
Press, 1970), p. 44.

Preaching that maintains a biblical sense of proportion will give prominence by repetition and by weight of emphasis to all these doctrines. The problem of maintaining the precise balance of Scripture is complicated, however, by certain factors in our particular pastoral situations. For example, there is controversy. We may find ourselves in situations where some doctrines are contradicted and threatened and in order to defend them we have to resort to what in normal circumstances would be an unbalanced emphasis. This was true, for example, of Athanasius in his battle with the Arians, of Augustine during the Pelagian and Donatist controversies, and of Luther at the time of the Reformation. We may find ourselves in similar situations because the church still has (and always will have) the problem of false prophets. It may be the charismatic movement or dispensationalism or perfectionism or antinomianism or agitation against a single doctrine such as the perseverance of the saints. At such times, controversy gives an importance to particular doctrines that they would not have in ordinary circumstances.

Again, we may inherit congregations that suffer from various kinds of theological weakness or imbalance. It is not altogether impossible, for example, that they have had a surfeit of doctrine to the exclusion of the practical and the ethical. For a time, the preacher in such a situation would have to give an otherwise undue prominence to the emphases of the Sermon on the Mount and the Epistle of James. Congregations today are more likely, however, to be suffering if not from the total absence of theology from their diet (which would be true in many instances), at least from the absence of certain doctrines. Professor John Murray maintained, for example, that such doctrines as the judgment of God, the high demands of the Christian vocation, and the need for constant self-examination were virtually absent from preaching today and urgently needed to be reinstated.[10] In particular situations, the free offer of the gospel may have suffered long years of neglect. In others, the church may be suffering from the

10. John Murray, "Some Necessary Emphases in Preaching" in *The Collected Writings of John Murray*, vol. 1 (Edinburgh: Banner of Truth, 1976).

exaggerated monergism of Barthian theology, with its tendency to minimize the human response to the gospel. God's action in salvation is everything. Man's response in faith and repentance is nothing. Men are asked to believe that they are saved, rather than to believe in order to be saved. In more orthodox churches, the same situation has been created by fear of hyper-evangelism and especially of "decisionism." In such circumstances, it becomes particularly important to insist upon (and to define clearly) the bilateral nature of the covenant of grace: "To escape the wrath and curse of God due to us for sin, God *requireth of us* faith in Jesus Christ, repentance unto life, with the diligent use of all the outward means whereby Christ communicateth to us the benefits of redemption" (Westminster Shorter Catechism, answer 85).

Another factor that must affect the theological balance of our preaching is the maturity or otherwise of our congregations. If we have a well-taught people, with a comprehensive theological knowledge, we may give them strong doctrinal meat. On the other hand, the congregation over which God sets us may be ill taught. This may be true even though they have been Christians for many years and are active, zealous, and self-assured. Many churches are in the condition described in Hebrews 5:12: "For though by this time you ought to be teachers, you have need for someone to teach you again the elementary principles of the oracles of God, and have come to need milk, not solid food." Such people need basics, not the five points of Calvinism or the intricacies of Christian experience. They have never properly understood the fundamental doctrines concerning God, sin, and salvation.

Should the System Be Obvious?

Should the presence of systematic theology be obvious to the congregation? Of theology, yes. "If it is bad to preach over people's heads," wrote Dr. James Stewart, "not to preach to their heads at all is worse."[11] We are teachers. *Didache* is our business, and our preaching must therefore be unashamedly theological.

This is true even—if not indeed especially—in evangelism. Biblically, there can be no such thing as untheological evangelism. The *protevangelion* of Genesis 3:15 is richly doctrinal. Who is the seed of the woman? How did He bruise the Serpent's head? What was involved in the bruising of His own heel? The same is true of the seminal revelation of the covenant of grace given in Genesis 17:7, "And I will establish my covenant between me and you and your descendants after you throughout their generations for an everlasting covenant, to be God to you and to your seed after you." Evangelism means introducing this God to our lost race, proclaiming His promises and making plain His stipulations.

The same theological character of evangelism is clear in the New Testament. Our Lord's preaching began, as Samuel Logan reminds us earlier in this volume, with the message, "Repent, for the kingdom of heaven is at hand." Any faithful exposition of that has to wrestle with the theological questions, What is the meaning of repentance? And what is the meaning of the kingdom being imminent? Peter at Pentecost, Paul at Philippi, Paul at Athens—all are theological. In I Corinthians 1:18 Paul defines his basic message as the word of the cross; in I Corinthians 15:3f. the basic affirmations of the evangelical tradition are the death and resurrection of Christ; in II Corinthians 5:18ff., the ministry of reconciliation consists in explicating the astonishing statement that "God made him who knew no sin to be sin for us, that we might become God's righteousness in him." John's summary of the gospel is even more intimidating in its profundity: "For God so loved the world that he gave his only begotten Son that whosoever believeth in him should not perish but should have everlasting life" (John 3:16).

Evangelism, as defined in Scripture, is a battle for the mind. Its very essence is the affirmation and explanation of truth: "To call

11. James Stewart, *Heralds of God* (London: Hodder and Stoughton, 1946), p. 152.

upon men constantly to 'come to Christ' and to repeat perpetually the words of Paul to the jailor, 'Believe in the Lord Jesus Christ' without at the same time telling them who Jesus is, and what it is to come to Him, and believe on Him, is the merest mockery," wrote William M. Taylor. "It is using the name of Christ as if it were some cabalistic charm, and reducing the Gospel message to a mere empty formula. If, therefore, we would be effective preachers, we must be ready to give an answer to him that asks us, 'Who is Jesus, that I may believe on Him? and what was there in His dying that has any relation to me?' "[12] To make even the feeblest attempts to answer such questions is to engage in theology.

Equally, theological preaching is the primary means of pastoral care. The flock is to be fed—indeed, pastors must never forget that it is possible to kill them not only with heresy, but with starvation. Only the truth can sanctify them (John 17:17). To change the perspective, if they have not girded their loins with the truth, they lack an essential part of the armor of God (Eph. 4:14). Doctrine cannot be set against experience: "Christian experience," wrote Charles Bridges, "is the influence of doctrinal truth upon the affections"[13]—a point made strongly also by Jonathan Edwards, as Samuel Logan reminds us in the present volume. This is why, time and again, when the biblical writers were faced with problems in the realm of experience and practice, they appealed to Christian doctrine. Take, for example, the Lord's dissuasion in John 14:1, "Let not your heart be troubled." The exhortation rests on an entirely theological foundation: believe in God, believe in me, in my Father's house are many mansions, I go to prepare a place for you, I will come again and receive you to myself. Ultimately, "Let not your heart be troubled" rests on the indescribably glorious foundation, "Where I am, there you will be also."

12. William M. Taylor, *The Ministry of the Word* (London: T. Nelson and Sons, 1876), p. 83.
13. Charles Bridges, *The Christian Ministry* (Edinburgh: Banner of Truth, 1961), p. 259.

We find this same approach frequently throughout the New Testament. Paul's exposition of Christian liberality in II Corinthians 8:9 culminates in an appeal to the incarnation: "For you know the grace of our Lord Jesus Christ that though he was rich yet for our sakes he became poor, that we through his poverty might become exceeding rich." He confronts the problems of the church at Philippi in the same way. There is strife, vanity, pride, and touchiness. The answer is again to place the whole situation in the light of the incarnation: Let this mind be in you which was also in Christ Jesus who, being in the form of God, emptied Himself by taking the form of a servant, the likeness of men and the cursed death of the cross.

The rest of the New Testament follows the same pattern. The writer to the Hebrews, faced with growing apostasy among those to whom he is writing, urged them to cling to their confession and to pray for preserving grace. But he based his plea on the theological fact that we have a great High Priest—great because He is the Son of God, great because He has passed through the veil, and great because He can be touched with the feeling of our infirmities (Heb. 4:14). Similarly the apostle John (and, behind him, the risen Lord), conscious that many believers were already experiencing the woes implicit in the seven seals, began his apocalypse by describing the vision of the throne and Him that sat on it (Rev. 4:2). All that follows has to be seen in the light of the sovereignty of Him who is at once the august Lord and the slaughtered Lamb.

Theologically, nothing is to be held back. What God has revealed was not intended for academics and theological colleges, but for the people of God. If a thing is not biblical, it must have no place in our preaching. If it is biblical, we have no right not to teach it. We must wrestle with the great themes, even if they throw us. We cannot plead height or depth or complexity. We are stewards of the *mysteries* of God, and it would be an absurd defense that we kept some things back because they were too *mysterious*. "Never fear," said Phillips Brooks, "to bring the sublimest motive to the smallest duty, and the most infinite comfort to the smallest trouble."

The pattern given in the New Testament was clearly followed by the great preachers of the succeeding centuries. Their proclamation did not lack theology and their sermons are still treasure-troves for the students of doctrine. One might even say that apart from the Scriptures themselves the best quarry for theologians is the homiletical output of the great preachers. Athanasius preached his *Orations Against the Arians*. Augustine preached his views on man, sin, and grace. Luther and Calvin preached justification by faith alone, the bondage of the will, and the sovereignty of God in salvation. Two of the best volumes in Goold's sixteen-volume edition of the works of John Owen are sermons. Edwards crammed his sermons with doctrine. Wesley's sermons became the virtual theological standard of Methodism.

We cannot choose between popular preaching and theological preaching. The theology given in revelation—the only theology we have any right to hold, let alone proclaim—is theology for the people of God. Yet, in the preaching of theology, there are certain pitfalls to be avoided. Theology should not be taught from the pulpit the way it is taught in a theological seminary. The theology should be the same. The method of communicating it should not. Three particular pitfalls should be noted.

First, we must avoid the use of jargon in the pulpit. Theology has its own technical terminology, appropriate enough to academic discussion, but presenting barriers to comprehension when used in public proclamation. The problem is not a simple one. Much of this terminology (for example, *justification, predestination, regeneration, repentance*) is taken directly from Scripture, and as such it is not only permitted, but required that the pulpit use it and explain it. The same is true of certain words like *trinity* and *incarnation*—embodied in the church's confessional tradition. But we should be very hesitant about introducing the language of the schools to the pulpit. It is fatally easy for those newly released from seminaries to be totally unaware how specialized the terminology of these institutions is. Words like *ontology, hermeneutic, eschatology,* and *existential* may be the everyday speech of academics, but it is mumbo jumbo to the world outside.

The second pitfall is the temptation to pepper sermons with quotations. These may be useful and even necessary in academic discourse. In the pulpit, quotations are seldom appropriate. They constitute an unnecessary display of learning, their style lies unconformable to that of the spoken word, and they interfere with the momentum of the message. These, doubtless, were the factors that led the Westminster Assembly, in compiling its *Directory for the Public Worship of God,* to lay down that only sparingly should we cite "sentences of ecclesiastical or other human writers, ancient or modern, be they ever so eloquent." The skillful use of aphorisms can be very effective, but extended quotation is only a distraction.

The third thing to avoid is *exhaustive* presentation of the subject. This again is perfectly appropriate in academic discourse. Here every possible facet of a truth may be drawn out, every available argument may be marshalled, and every conceivable objection may be answered. In the pulpit, such procedure is totally inappropriate. At the risk of being facetious, one may suggest that *four* of everything will suffice. Beyond that, the audience is often exhausted and lost.

Thomas Chalmers focussed on two further crucial differences between the way theology is handled in the seminary and the way it should be handled in the pulpit. First, in the pulpit the overriding concern must be to apply doctrine in a hortatory and practical way. The aim is not academic exposition, but practical influence. "The Christian revelation," wrote Chalmers, "does not end with the intellect, but begins with it. The *credenda* are not the landing-place, but only the stepping stones to the *agenda.*"[14] In other words, the pulpit aims to make people personally and actually Christians.

Second, the preacher must drive the doctrine home to the individual. In systematics, we have a distant and general exposition of Christianity—the doctrine "as it bears upon the mass of the species," said Chalmers. In preaching, the perspective is totally differ-

14. Thomas Chalmers, *Select Works,* vol. 8 (Edinburgh: Thomas Constable and Co., 1856), p. 239.

ent: "Isolate each of your hearers and make him feel that the matters wherewith you are charged are addressed specifically and individually to him."[15] Each must be made to apply the truth to his own conscience, precisely as Peter urged upon his hearers at Pentecost: "Repent and be baptized *every one of you* in the name of Jesus Christ" (Acts 2:38).

Use of Confessions and Catechisms

What use should the preacher make of the confessions and catechisms of the church? The first answer to this probably is that we should use the documents as aids to exegesis. They often provide excellent outlines of biblical topics. This is especially true of such key areas of Scripture as the Ten Commandments and the Lord's Prayer. The catechisms of virtually all Christian traditions contain expositions of these. Their use is not confined to these limited areas, however. For example, within the Westminster tradition, a sermon on conversion could hardly bypass answer 87 of the Shorter Catechism: "Repentance unto life is a saving grace whereby a sinner out of a true sense of his sin and apprehension of the mercy of God in Christ doth with grief and hatred of his sin turn from it unto God, with full purpose of and endeavour after new obedience." Answer 14 of the same catechism catches much more accurately than the King James Version the meaning of John's definition of sin as in I John 3:4: "Sin is any want of conformity unto, or transgression of, the law of God." (The King James Version has simply, "Sin is transgression of the law.")

Where, in brief compass, can we get a better definition of faith than in the following words: "Faith in Jesus Christ is a saving grace whereby we receive and rest upon Him alone for salvation as He is freely offered to us in the Gospel" (Shorter Catechism, answer 86)? Similarly, what better commentary can we have on the words, "Take heed how ye hear" (Luke 8:18) than the answer given by the Westminster divines to the question, "How is the

15. Ibid., p. 247.

word to be read and heard, that it may become effectual to salvation?" (Answer: "We must attend thereunto with diligence, preparation and prayer; receive it with faith and love, lay it up in our hearts and practise it in our lives.") And anyone wrestling with the practical problems suggested by Paul's exposition of the Lord's Supper in I Corinthians 11:22–34 will surely find suggestive guidelines in the Shorter Catechism's treatment of the same theme: "It is required of them that would worthily partake of the Lord's Supper that they examine themselves of their knowledge to discern the Lord's body, of their faith to feed upon him, of their repentance, love, and new obedience; lest, coming unworthily, they eat and drink judgement to themselves" (answer 97).

The Westminster Confession is equally useful as an expository aid. For example, its exposition of Christian liberty (Chapter 20) is quite magnificent and sheds brilliant light on such a text as Galatians 5:1, "Stand fast therefore in the freedom with which Christ has made you free." The same is true of the chapter on assurance, which steers a skillful course between encouraging presumption on the one hand and making a virtue of doubt on the other. But from the pastoral and preaching point of view, the outstanding section in the Westminster Confession is probably to be found in paragraph 5 of the chapter on justification (Chapter 11). This deals with what is often an urgent pastoral problem— What about the sins we commit after justification? The confession gives superb guidance: "God doth continue to forgive the sins of those that are justified: and although they can never fall from the state of justification, yet they may by their sins fall under God's fatherly displeasure, and not have the light of his countenance restored unto them, until they humble themselves, confess their sins, beg pardon, and renew their faith and repentance." These last few sentiments delineate most movingly the steps in a backslider's recovery.

The confessions and catechisms of the non-Anglo-Saxon traditions are equally valuable. Suppose we are preaching on John 16:7, "It is expedient for you that I go away"; where can we find a better exposition than in the answer given by the Heidelberg Catechism to the question, "What benefit do we receive from

Christ's ascension into heaven?" "First, that in heaven He is our Advocate in the presence of His Father. Secondly, that we have our flesh in heaven, as a sure pledge that He, as the Head, will also take us, His members, up to Himself. Thirdly, that He sends us His Spirit, as an earnest, by whose power we seek those things which are above, where Christ sitteth on the right hand of God, and not things on the earth."

The same catechism contains an excellent definition of faith: "It is not only a certain knowledge, whereby I hold for truth all that God has revealed to us in His Word; but also a hearty trust, which the Holy Ghost works in me by the Gospel, that not only to others but to me also forgiveness of sins, everlasting righteousness and salvation, are freely given by God, merely of grace, only for the sake of Christ's merit."

Besides using catechisms and confessions as guidelines in expounding particular topics, it may sometimes be profitable (or even necessary) to explain *well-known* creedal phrases. The number of these in general circulation will obviously vary enormously from place to place and the propriety of commenting on them must be a matter of individual pastoral judgment. Any affirmation of the deity of Christ, however, could hardly ignore the word *homoousios;* and any preacher who keeps his ear to the ground will surely be asked, What do we mean by our Lord's descent into hell, by the perseverance of the saints, by "elect infants dying in infancy," by the internal testimony of the Spirit, and by the affirmation that man is "wholly defiled in all the faculties and parts of soul and body."

More occasionally, it may be appropriate to indicate defects in our catechisms and confessions. Within the Westminster tradition, the greatest blemish is probably the statement that the Word of God is *contained* in the Scriptures of the Old and New Testaments (Shorter Catechism, answer 2), which strongly suggests that there are areas of Scripture that are not the Word of God. Reservations may also have to be expressed with regard to the summary of the divine attributes given in answer 4, the definition of effectual calling in answer 31, and the definition of sanctification in answer 35 (which omits all reference to *definitive* sanctification). So far as the confession itself is concerned, the preacher may have to distance himself from the exegetical statement (added to the doctrine that Christ alone is Head of the church) that the pope is the Man of Sin. The reason that such statements cannot be passed over silently is that their very inclusion in the catechisms and confessions gives authority and currency to the distortions they reflect, and if uncorrected these will become endemic to the theology of particular traditions. In the case of the allusion to the pope as the Man of Sin, the distortion also adds fuel to the fires of religious bigotry.

Should we preach on catechisms or confessions as such? Only in the most exceptional circumstances. Our mandate is to preach the Word. To resort instead to expounding a human document is to confuse our people by blurring the distinction between what is normative revelation and what is to be judged by that revelation. Even when creeds are inerrant (a claim that can be made for the Apostles Creed, for example), their proportion, balance, and selection of topics will not be that of Scripture. Furthermore, confessions and catechisms present doctrine abstracted from its existential context—the life-situation of Scripture—and thus obscure its practical relevance or tempt us not to apply it at all.

Two final points may be made in connection with creeds and confessions. First, these documents represent the collective wisdom of the Christian centuries. Consequently, anyone who is preaching under their stimulus and within their parameters can be absolutely confident that he is not preaching a private opinion or introducing doctrines that threaten the peace and unity of the church. Many allege, of course, that to have the preacher bound to a confession is an unbiblical curtailment of his freedom. This can only be true, however, when the confession itself is sectarian, rather than catholic or comprehensive. In a well-ordered church, the only restriction imposed by a creed is that it prevents the undermining of fundamental doctrines. In fact, a confession should be seen as a charter of freedom. It lays down plainly the deviations that the church will not tolerate. With a proper theological standard the preacher knows his precise position. Where his creed speaks, he is bound (unless he can show that his creed is wrong); where his creed is silent, he is free to express his own judgment. For example, a minister bound by his ordination vows only to the Westminster Confession can have absolute confidence that his conscience is not bound on such matters as libertarianism, premillennialism, smoking, or the immediate imputation of Adam's sin. Indeed, men committed to the same confession can debate many issues most vehemently and vigorously, as the differences between Rutherford and Boston, Candlish and Crawford, Thownwell and Hodge, and Warfield and Kuyper clearly demonstrate.

Second, creeds and confessions furnish the preacher with an invaluable indicator of the relative importance of the various doctrines. The preacher must be "most in the main things" and these "main things" may not be the doctrines we like most and those we have studied most fully. They are very likely, however, to be those contained in our confessions and catechisms—doctrines on which the communion of saints is in agreement and that the deliberate judgment of the church regards as nonnegotiable. "Whenever you find vital piety," wrote Charles Hodge, "there you find the doctrines of the fall, of depravity, of regeneration, of atonement and of the deity of Christ. I never saw or heard of a single individual, exhibiting a spirit of piety, who rejected any one of those doctrines."[16] These doctrines are the very core of confessional theology.

Conclusion

The burden of this chapter has been that we must preach all the theology we know. The Bible is the people's book, and all its doctrines, from the Trinity to the beatific vision, belong to the individuals, learned and unlearned, who constitute the community of faith. We have no right to keep anything back. Even the proclamation of such truth, however, can be vitiated by our own attitude, and it is upon this that we must dwell in conclusion.

16. Salmond, *Princetoniana*, p. 30.

First, we must preach with authority. This is not a matter of self-righteousness or self-assurance. It is an authority, both internal and external, born of the confidence that what we are proclaiming is the Word of God. So long as our theology is based on the exposition of Scripture, we can announce as confidently as any Old Testament prophet, "Thus saith the Lord!" Barth quotes Luther's great claim, "I and every man who speaketh Christ's word may freely boast that his mouth is Christ's mouth" and adds, "Doctrine is not sinful or culpable; nor does it belong to the Lord's Prayer when we say, Forgive us our trespasses; for doctrine is not our doing, but God's own word which can neither sin nor do wrong."[17] This is one great reason that preaching needs dogmatics—to make as sure as we possibly can be that what we are proclaiming is the Word of God. To quote Barth again, the great role of dogmatics is to criticize and revise the church's Sunday sermon (the preaching of which is the church's supreme task): "Starting from the question how man spoke about God in the church yesterday, dogmatics asks how this should be done tomorrow."[18]

Second, even when dealing with the profoundest themes of revelation, we should strive for lucidity. The alleged depth of our doctrine often proceeds from our own darkness. "Any fool can lose himself in a philosophic fog," writes Hamish Mackenzie. "It takes a first-class mind, great purity of heart and much labour to achieve simplicity."[19] We have no right to avoid biblical topics on the ground of their profundity. If we did so we would not open our mouths at all. Our calling is to explain and illuminate every theme in the church's prescribed syllabus, Holy Scripture. But we must do so with all the directness and clarity at our command.

Above all, we have to preach lovingly. This is especially true when we have to handle controversial and polemical subjects. The *odium theologicum* is proverbial. Our sermons should be models in

17. Karl Barth, *Church Dogmatics*, vol. 1 (Greenwood, South Carolina: Attic Press, 1962), p. 107.

18. Ibid., p. 86.

19. Hamish Mackenzie, *Preaching the Eternities* (Edinburgh: Saint Andrew Press, 1963), p. 93.

the loving treatment of those from whom we differ. But the principle applies universally. We must "truth it in love" (Eph. 4:15—love for the God who commissioned us, love for the truth He gave us, love for those to whom He sends us, and love for those who reject us and in rejecting us, reject Him.

II.

MESSAGE FORM

10

Sermon Structure and Flow
Glen C. Knecht

The revived preacher possesses but one instrument, but having that he needs no other. He has a tongue of fire, the very weapon given to the church on Pentecost. His tongue, energized by the Holy Spirit, is the means of articulating to the world the truth of God in such a way that hearts are changed and heaven comes to earth. One encounter in a lifetime with a true tongue of fire is all that is needed for the converting work of God to be done in a human soul. Having had that encounter, one will never be the same again.

William S. Arthur was right when he said that the tongue of fire is the chief symbol of the church, and as such ought to be cherished and cultivated as the choice gift of God in the body of Christ. The preacher is heir to this gift and privileged to wield this mighty weapon Sunday after Sunday. *How* he wields it is the subject of this chapter.

It is tempting to let the burning heart express its warmth and light as it will. The heart has a force of feeling and a fluidity of expression that is arresting both to speaker and hearer. Why not then abandon all effort at structure in the interest of the free flow of the fiery tongue? Why not let the burning heart simply set forth its message without regard for the shape, for after all, fire has no shape? If the preacher feels the subject intensely, is that not after all enough? Can he not rely on his burning heart for the communication of divine truth?

The answer of this volume is no! Why? Because God is a God of order. He did not create everything all at once, but in sequence.

275

He grouped things in classes and created like things on the same days. He revealed Himself in stages and brought all things to readiness before He gave the crowning piece of His revelation, the Lord Jesus Christ. Full of ardor, God is also full of order in what He does.

We must copy God in this order, realizing that the source of His order is His love. It is because He loves us that He adapts His work and His words to our condition and speaks to us in such a way that we can understand and apply what we learn of Him. Our ardor to proclaim His Word and to see the fruit of His Spirit's work in the world is also an ardor of love. It is because we love Him and others that we preach. Our love makes us translate our ardor into order when it comes to the proclaiming of the Word of God.

Giving order to substance is an act of loving the hearer and loving the author of the revelation. It is the second mile that is the mile of love. "Good thoughts abound," Pascal reminds us, "but the art of organizing them does not." The difference between the first and second mile preacher is that one has powerful thoughts issuing from a burning heart, and the other, having the same truths and as full an ardor, adds to his love the strenuous effort of molding them into a shape that will be helpful and retainable to those who listen. The proposition of this chapter is this: The revived preacher loves his hearers when he orders his sermons in a way that draws them to the truth, feeds their minds and hearts, and calls them to respond appropriately to the Word of God.

1. Order: "Heaven's First Love"

In creation God built His world according to His own order. Thus, a sense of order is built into the nature of things even from such phrases as "the evening and the morning were the first day." The predictability of the creation, the rhythmic movement of the heavenly bodies, and the change of seasons are reminders of the God of design.

The writer to the Hebrews notes this desire for order in God when he cites His command to Moses: "For when Moses was about to erect the tent, he was instructed by God, saying 'See that you make everything according to the pattern which was shown you on the mountain'" (Heb. 8:5). "According to the pattern shown you" is a mandate for order. While the Bible does not contain such a sermon pattern itself, we can turn to the experience of the church, the principles of human psychology, and the general knowledge of rhetoric to help us develop the pattern most useful to us in this time.

Clear advantages to good order emerge on reflection. Think first of what good structure means to the preacher. With a solid organization of his material he meets his hearers confidently. He knows where he is to go: the end is clearly defined. Like the taxi driver pulling away from the curb with the destination fixed in his mind's eye, he can move deftly and surely through whatever obstacles may confront him.

The preacher's heart can follow the movement of a good order. There is only an imaginary dichotomy between the head and the heart. The heart also has a logic and it is not opposite to the logic of the mind. With a definite plan there are clear banks for the stream of human emotional force. One cannot always predict at which points the heart will overflow, but a good plan makes possible those sudden surges of feeling and harnesses them toward their appointed end.

The mind of the minister is aided by his structure as well. If he is proceeding without manuscript, his thoughts will easily suggest themselves to him when his plan is clear and natural. If he is using notes or even the total text, he will be freer from these knowing how his plan unfolds.

Timing is an important part of preaching. Today's audiences are accustomed to fast-paced radio and television so that attention spans are short. The preacher must think in terms of several three-minute presentations as he moves through his plan, rather than of one lengthy unity. But how are these clips of thought tied together? How can they accumulate the meaning and the power of the message if there be no structure that is sound and sequential and that moves toward a climax?

A sound structure enables the minister to practice the most important of homiletical skills, the art of omission. "Good preaching," Andrew W. Blackwood was fond of saying, "is knowing what to leave out and then having the courage to leave it out." The plan, if constructed well and followed with discipline, will reject certain of the illustrations or ideas or quotations that had seemed fitting in the gathering of materials. "But where shall I put it? It doesn't fit anywhere." Then leave it out. Save it for another day. It has no place if it is not exactly on the mark and if it does not advance the progression of thought within the plan you have adopted. The elements of a plan ought to trip each other like dominoes in that one suggests the next. But if the gap is too great or the point is placed off to the side, there is no movement toward the goal. The plan itself is a disciplinary tool for the preacher.

Think of the advantages of a good structure to the most important part of the sermon, the hearer. When he senses the presence of a good structure he can rest in the pilgrimage that the minister is leading. He gains confidence in the dominie's knowledge of the terrain and in his ability to take him through its pitfalls and around its obstacles to the desired destination. The people will not always see the elements of the structure, and they may not be able to recite the plan itself, but they will profit nonetheless from the existence of that plan in the mind of the minister and in the shape of the sermon.

The plan must not call attention to itself as clever or profound. The purpose of the plan is to help the people see past it to the truth being set forth. The structure is the frame of the painting, which contains and draws attention to the beautiful without distracting from it. Frames help us to focus our attention to separate the art from all else. So structure aids hearers by setting the revelation of God in an orderly and limited arrangement with which they can deal on a given occasion. A well-ordered sermon is a sign of love to the congregation.

Even regenerate people do not naturally take to the hearing of the Word of God. They must learn to hear and digest sermons from their minister. How shall they be trained? Not the least of the ways is to present to them week after week messages that are well built for clear recollection and ready restatement to others. As they hear different styles of structure they will come to identify them in their own minds and mentally to adjust to them. They will come to recognize the Robertsonian sermon, the more typical three-point sermon, or the Puritan approach of finely shaded presentation of truth resulting in several headings. They will listen for what is required of them in the final section and be ready to respond to the call of the Spirit on that day.

A sound structure communicates more than the thought of the sermon alone. It expresses to speaker and hearer that the body of truth we have is an orderly revelation. It is consistent and integrated, and forms a symmetrical pattern of thought and action. Many a Christian exists on little nuggets of wisdom and knowledge from here and there unrelated to an overarching pattern. Hearing the logical exposition of God's truth according to sound structure reveals to them a system of doctrine that is orderly and self-consistent. Such an order is a breath of heaven, a sign of the love of the God of the sound mind.

If structure is so worthwhile, we should not be surprised that it is also difficult to achieve. To take what one has gathered from his exegetical, theological, and literary sources, and from his personal experiences and mold that material together into one coherent and unified thrust is an arduous task. Such labor requires comparing Scripture with Scripture, choosing what is relevant and what is not, weighing the importance of different aspects of the truth, deciding about the sequence of the ideas, and fashioning the remaining elements into a shape that is suitable for its holy purpose and aim. This requires deep concentration and strenuous effort, and sometimes agony.

This is the part of sermon preparation that asks the most of the minister. For these hours let him have the deepest quiet, the most sustained spirit of dependence on God, and the most creative and imaginative forces he possesses at work upon the subject. Let him in these moments be grateful for the privilege of standing before the people as a herald of God. That in itself will unlock the creative strengths within him. Let him seek the mind of God as to what He would have said from this text on that day in that place. Let him confess his own sins and apply the truths to his own heart before ever they should be brought to bear on others. Out of the struggle, the gratitude, the self-examination, and the prayer there emerges a sense of structure. But more of this in a moment.

2. Intuition: Key to Order

Among the many wise words from the pen of James Stalker are these: "Originality in the preaching of the truth depends on the solitary intuition of it."[1] The intuition of a passage is what it means to you after you have pondered it and worked with it and prayed over it. An intuition is original in the sense that it is uniquely yours. You have arrived at it yourself. While your statement of the truth might closely resemble what others have found, nevertheless it is yours. Your intuition of a passage is your particular statement of that interpretation at this time in your own spiritual pilgrimage. This original grasp of the text or passage is the key to your structure.

Thus originality is itself a key in preaching. I don't mean invention, for there is very little to be said that has not been said before, and preaching is often reminding. But by originality I do mean the flow of truth through you as it would not flow exactly through any other minister of the gospel. A man's sermon ought to have his own soul in it and his own fingerprints on it in the way that a great oratorio speaks of its composer in every line. If originality is so crucial, it must be cultivated and studied by the aspiring preacher. We must be ourselves, for that is the way to Christian originality. Whatever ultimately is in the sermon must first be in the preacher, as both Erroll Hulse and Geoffrey Thomas remind us elsewhere in this volume. If originality is to be

1. James Stalker, *The Life of St. Paul* (Old Tappan, N. J.: Fleming H. Revell, 1950) p. 47.

found in the message, it must be cultivated in the man. I stress this because everything conspires to keep us from being ourselves. We may have the image of another minister before us, and we can be seized by that image in such a way as to forfeit our own unique style and gifts. When we labor under such a shadow, we fail to tap the resources of who we are. We may even labor under the broader, collective shadow of what we've been told is the ideal preacher—and this can stifle our originality as well.

The relief from such tyranny comes through a new grasp of the deep responsibility on us as ministers of the gospel. If we see the awesome task we have and the great answer we shall have to give for our words or lack of them, we will be wooed away from the lack of originality due to the imitation of others. Whatever it takes to shed this pattern, we must do it and, in the freedom that is ours, begin to find the creative gift that God has given to each of us uniquely.

So the call to originality is a call to the minister to be himself— joyously, thankfully, and creatively. But even that can be taken too far, so that one becomes haunted by his own image, as he might by a pulpit master. He is addicted to being different and cannot use the friendly helpers of sermonic tradition that point in some useful directions. He rejects the right plan merely because it *does* contain three points. This is to be angular, not original, and prevents originality by denying that part of him that he shares with the rest of the human race.

Discovering the intuition of a passage brings a man right up against himself. His own inner life is exposed. He is not here against the devil as much as he faces himself. He is his own antagonist. For something within him would conceal the text, would handle it as another man would, would run from the text and seize a tangential truth. But he must not yield to these opponents of his own original intuition. He must be himself, under God, and grasp the solitary intuition of the passage as he sees it displayed in front of him on the screen of his inner life. That is his and that will be the embryo of his sermon.

But we are seeking to unfold the mystery of the intuition of a passage. We have made the point that it is uniquely one's own.

But what exactly is that intuition? Assuming that one has studied the major words in the passage, has pondered deeply the cross-referenced passages, has reaped the fruit of the study of others on this portion of the Word of God, has read the parallel readings in doctrinal studies, has made his own personal application of the text to his life, and has prayed over the relevant way to bring this Scripture close to the consciences and the hearts of his hearers, now he comes to the most exciting part of the process.

The minister should select from the pages of notes that he has made (and they ought to be abundant notes), the most salient elements of truth from the text or passage. He should put down on one sheet the things that simply must not be excluded. These are the facets of the subject as they have come home to him during the ruminating and study period. There is something sacred about this stage of work, for one is already selecting and omitting, if only in a preliminary way, the spiritual food his people will receive on the Lord's Day.

When the listing has been made prayerfully in one's words, then the minister must turn to his period of deepest meditation upon the meaning of Scripture. He might choose to walk in a lonely place or to be alone in the prayer closet or walk about his study with the Bible open. The important thing here is that he be undisturbed in these moments and that he be able to place all his concentration in a relaxed way upon the passage before him. He must read and reread it. He must get beyond the surface of it, get into the center of it. What is the controlling idea here? What weaves all these words together into a whole? What is at the heart of this passage? What is deeper and more unifying than any of the aspects written down thus far? Now he is approaching the intuition of the passage.

The intuition may be summarized in a few of the words of the passage itself, as for example, the paragraph of Romans 12:14–21 finds its intuition, I believe, in the closing words: "Do not be overcome by evil, but overcome evil with good." More often, however, it seems that the intuition is found in words of one's own making that express the underlying truth of this section of Scripture as it has come through him.

One way to crack open the inner meaning of the text is to surround it with questions. Talk to it and ask what truth it holds. Talk with God and ask Him what He wants to say through this word. Be very grateful for the chance to unfold the truth found here. Never search for it because Sunday is coming and a sermon must be preached. But with an attitude of expectation and hope, and a spirit of wonder, listen to the voice within for the apprehension of the intuition of the passage. Thus the heart of the sermon is the preacher's intuition of what the passage is saying. A sermon is unfolded from the interior of the text and the inner life of the man. It comes from the depths of Scripture and life and its intuition does not lie upon the surface. Sermons constructed this way reach to the depths of others' souls. "Deep calls unto deep."

Having the solitary intuition of what the passage is saying is the big step in preparation, but there is more work. One needs then to formulate the proposition of the message out of this basic intuition. It may be the same as the intuition, or it may not. Propositions are preachers' attempts to construct brief statements of what God wants to communicate through this passage to the hearers that day. If the intuition was framed in the very words of Scripture, then the proposition will necessarily be different. The preparing of a proposition is a vital step in the building of a plan. This step must not be hurried or skipped, for then there will be no basis for a plan.

The proposition should be not more than one sentence, lest it be too cumbersome and involve the sermon in more than can be covered. Its words should be well-chosen and memorable, with a minimum of adjectives and adverbs. Choose the nouns and verbs that make a sentence strong, but, most importantly, let it state the intuition in no uncertain terms. For example, the proposition for a sermon on Romans 12:14–21 might be: "The Christian overcomes every evil by the victory of love." It takes practice to be able to state truth in strong and simple language, but that is what makes good preaching. No one should be discouraged if propositions do not come easily. The harder they come the more valuable they will be, for they represent struggle, prayer, and love for the people.

It is not necessary that in every case the proposition be stated in the sermon. Often it will be given toward the end of the introduction. There the people will come to listen for a sentence that is deliberate and clear and from which everything else flows. Sometimes it will be helpful to restate the proposition a few times throughout the message, perhaps between headings. The uses of the proposition will vary according to the sermon. Its usefulness is in the mind of the preacher as he prepares and goes on to deliver his message. It is for him a unifying factor—a constant reminder of his precise aim in this message. The proposition captures the preacher's intuition of the passage and forms the essential link in his mind with the structure of the sermon. With the intuition and the proposition in mind the preacher is ready to proceed to the ordering of his sermon.

3. The Orderly Plan: "Drawing Them to the Truth"

The thesis of this chapter is that the revived preacher loves his hearers when he orders his sermons in a way that draws them to the truth, feeds their minds and hearts, and calls them to respond appropriately to the Word of God. The drawing of the hearer to the truth is done through the development of an orderly plan. It has been said that the orator draws men after him with golden chains that issue from his mouth. The preacher's golden chain is his plan, which link after link leads the hearts of his people nearer and nearer to the truth.

What are the parts of that plan? Preachers in different ages have enumerated them in varying ways. I use here the schema of Robert L. Dabney because it summarizes much of Reformed practice and has proved useful to me in regular pulpit ministry.[2] The message begins with an *exordium,* which is an element of the introduction. The function of the exordium is to introduce the speaker and his thoughts on this occasion. It sets the stage for the message with the unfolding of a single thought that leads the

2. Robert L. Dabney, *Sacred Rhetoric* (Edinburgh: Banner of Truth, 1979), pp. 137-67.

hearer into the mind of the speaker. Brief, compact, informative, and interesting, it is a vestibule into the thought of the speaker.

The *explication* introduces the passage of Scripture to be expounded on this occasion. It may describe its setting or its peculiar relevance for this time. It may deal with misunderstandings relative to this text or suggest some of the questions raised by it. It may explain some of the important words or themes or show how this text has its thought expounded or seemingly contradicted in other parts of the Word of God. The text is the central element of the explication. The *proposition* may be announced at the close of this section, showing the great truth that rises out of this part of the Word of God. It is usually stated in one carefully chiseled sentence, containing a subject and a predicate. For example, think of Horace Bushnell's statement: "Every Man's Life a Plan of God."

The *argument* follows. Here the body of thought takes shape with assertions about the text and the proposition. This is the heart of the sermon in that the great truths found in the passage are dealt with in depth. The message stands or falls with the force and the fullness of this element. The *application* may follow the argument as a separate section of the sermon, or it may find its way into the body of the argument itself (which is the way John Bettler, later in this volume, argues it should be done). The purpose of the application is to bring the Word of God to bear upon the specific questions and situations of the lives of those present in such a way that its force and relevance cannot be missed. The *conclusion* seeks to lift the one grand dominating truth expressed in the proposition into a place of prominence to be appreciated and grasped by all present. These elements of an orderly plan will be treated more fully below.

Armed with his passage, his intuition of its meaning, and his proposition, the preacher is ready to develop his plan for drawing the hearts and minds of the people to the truth at hand. In many ways this is the crucial part of the creative process of sermon preparation. It is like the moment when the architect, cognizant of cost, function, location, and resources available, ponders his sketch. The question then is, "With what plan shall he lift up the subject that has gained such a deep entrance into his being?"

Some things must be avoided. The preacher must resist the temptation to give a purely intellectual argument. Likewise he must refuse to cater to men's self-interest by erecting a plan that shows men how to reach their own goals. The preacher is a herald of the living God. What he is called to do is to think in generalizations. He has already made one such generalization—his proposition. Now he must discover from the passage before him the headings that will undergird and amplify his proposition. They must arise from the text. Unless they are in the text, they should not be included in the sermon. They must be found, and it is the preacher's task to discover them.

One way to do this is to ask the question, "What generalizations are involved in or flow from this one main truth?" The human mind is gifted with the ability to generalize and the preacher must become a master of this art. That does not mean to become broad in the scope of the message. The sermon must remain as limited in focus as the proposition and the text call it to be. The process of generalizing is the making of assertions about the truth involved in the sermon idea in such a way that its meaning is led out into the open where all can grasp it. Thus in preaching from Revelation 22:14, one formulates the proposition, "Eternal happiness depends upon the right to eat of the Tree of Life," and then generalizes about the tree of life in Scripture: in Eden, on Calvary, and in paradise. Each of the pictures of the tree reveals a different aspect of the broad truth expressed in the proposition. One tree depicts the forfeit of the right to life, another shows God's provision for access to the tree, and a third portrays the tree of life in its eternal setting in the garden of God with fruits and leaves for the healing and nourishing of the people of God. Or take Romans 16:25-27 as an example. The proposition might be, "The Christian life is for the glory of God." One might bring out of such a text and proposition the following assertions: The Christian lives for the glory of God's power; the Christian lives for the glory of God's authority; the Christian lives for the glory of God's wisdom. Each of these headings rises out of the passage itself.

Generalizing leads to making assertions about the truth to assist the people in loving and responding to it. (That is why the preacher always puts the truth as beautifully as he can). These assertions we might call the headings of the sermon. They are important for they convey the content of the idea of the sermon in manageable units. While they too are generalizations, they are not as general as the sermon topic or the proposition. Often these headings make up the framework the people take with them by which to recall the thrust of the message for their own hearts and for others.

There are dangers in the formulation of these headings. They can dissipate the force of the message by so dividing the impact that they squander the strength of the sermon into three disparate, miniature sermons. None of the parts truly says what the text or the proposition contains. The headings, thus, may conceal the point of the sermon, rather than display it, by distracting from the unity, rather than building it. A sermon has one central thrust, and the headings are for the making of that one thrust, not the weakening of it. The preacher may guard against this by being sure that each of his headings leads toward the truth of the proposition, rather than away from it.

At the risk of stereotyping the making of headings, let me suggest some of the common features often found in the division headings. I do this to assist a beginning preacher or a friend who finds my approach difficult to follow. I beg forbearance and ask the reader not to fashion his headings along this line at the expense of his own creative freedom. Still it may be helpful to state that often the first heading treats the definition of the topic; the second, motivation; the third, execution; and the fourth, fruition.[3] Some such description may be helpful. May it not injure!

We have seen in some measure how these headings are related to the proposition, but now we must ask how they are related to

3. William Evans, *How to Prepare Sermons and Gospel Addresses* (Chicago: Bible Colportage Association, 1913), pp. 91–101.

each other. What are the different types of relation between headings within the body of the sermon? We may call this relation "movement," since the sermon progresses from one division to the next. There are several types of movement within the argument of the sermon. Let me suggest a few of them. A sermon may have "the blade" as its first heading, then "the ear," and the last section may present "the full corn in the ear." That is, this type of movement is one in which gradually the hearer is taken into the fullness of a doctrine or a command of the Word of God.

Another way of understanding movement within a sermon is to think of an increase in depth as a message progresses, like the vision of the water of life in Ezekiel 47. There one begins by showing the surface meaning of the passage and then going beyond that to unfold the deeper meaning and finally the ultimate generalization of that theme. Or he may occasionally use different areas of application of the text, stating its propositions clearly and forcefully early, and then using the headings to bring that principle to bear upon the various arenas of human life. One might also deal with the headings from an historical point of view, describing the meaning of the passage in its various contexts and making a common generalization about what God is saying in this word. For example, he might explicate "The just shall live by faith" in its settings in Habakkuk, Romans, and Galatians. Sometimes he might use concentric circles as models of the relationship between headings. That is, beginning either at the center or on the periphery, one can move through the various levels of life to examine and apply a text. For example, Romans 12:1 (remembering that "body" refers to the total person in this passage): To begin, one might point to the need for the dedication of the body to God (as flesh), then move to the consecration of the emotions and the mind, and finally to the conscience and the will. The sermon would thus conclude at the very center of human life.

Sometimes it might be useful to arrange headings as a builder erects a home. First foundation is laid in a strong basic statement on which everything else rests. Then the living quarters rest upon it. This is the day-by-day-relevance of the truth for life. Finally, the roof of joy and aspiration and eternal life is erected on top of the structure, thus making a home for the soul in one of the rich truths of the Word of God. One is limited only by his imagination in the conceiving of ways of relating headings to each other to lead the truth of the text and make it available and lovable to the person in the pew.

May I say what must seem obvious? This work takes time, for the plan is not conceived and developed at once. It may seem to come early in the process, presenting itself in too facile a way. But the subject has to be well-digested before arranging is possible. Wait on the Lord, and He will give you the desires of your heart. That is why sermons must not be left to Saturday, but must be the product of a period of study, reflection, struggle, and rumination over the text and the truth. Most preachers are not geniuses, and the sign of their humility is their willingness to recognize this fact and allow time for the creative process.

When headings emerge and press for acceptance, they must be put to the test. Ask tough questions of these candidates for holy ministry! Are they concise and attractive? Are they consistent with each other and progressively marching toward a consummation? Are they trite? Do they yield the element of unexpectedness to the hearer? This test is one reason to refrain from printing the headings in the bulletin or engaging in a pre-Sunday sermon planning session with church officers. The element of pulpit surprise is part of the expectation the minister wants to foster in his people.

Are the headings unified around the proposition, clustering like fruit on a branch? The human mind has in it a desire for unity. Do they please the mind in this way? A common flaw is to crowd the essence of a text into a sub-point of one of the headings. Such a situation reveals that the headings are not well conceived. The truth of the proposition ought to come shining through in each of the headings. Are they mutually exclusive, or do they overlap in content? If there is alliteration, is it forced and fancy rather than nice and natural? Better to ban that burden than to have it become the weight that bends the whole outline into banality.

Are there the right number of headings to do the work that needs to be done? Ought the two points to be three, or the three four, or two? A change is necessary when one has difficulty saying to himself precisely what he wants to cover under each one of the divisions. Having the right number of headings for the text and proposition will help to proportion the emphasis of the sermon properly. Simplicity in the divisions is a crucial test. The simpler the headings the more useful they are to the preacher and the hearer. They need not be elementary or lack profundity, but to be simple they must be lean and clear and well stated.

Sometimes the headings need to be arranged differently from the order in which they first presented themselves. The first and the last places are the most important, while those things in the middle are often the most substantive and illuminating. Think of the headings as waves washing upon the shore, each one carrying the thought of the passage further into the mind and heart of the people, each one closer to the goal. Be sure that the last heading is not neglected. Often preachers spend their time and strength on the earlier parts of the sermon and the last division lacks careful thought. Consider the time given in the pulpit to the headings and see if this is the case. Remember how the wine the Lord Jesus made was described: "The best was saved for the last." The motto of the designer of sermons is the same as that of the long-distance runner, "Finish Strong!"

Shall the divisions be announced early in the message? I suggest that be done only when they would otherwise be difficult to follow, and that should be rarely. That means, of course, that if they are not so announced, they must be lifted up as the message unfolds. Early announcing tends to eliminate the sense of natural growth and artistry. Such announcement may also be a subtle temptation to pride oneself in the sound of his divisions, though that is seldom the case. Yet whatever calls attention to the preacher must distract from his message.

In this section I have tried to show that an orderly plan draws the hearer's mind and heart toward the truth. It does that in part by indicating that the truth is important enough for the preacher and his congregation to take great pains in its apprehension and application. Headings developed in the form of assertions flowing from the proposition make the hearer aware of the breadth and fullness of the truth involved. He is, therefore, led to see the truth as a significant reality toward which he is being drawn.

4. The Process of Particularizing: "Feeding the Mind and Heart"

Thus far we have discussed the skill of developing these generalizations which we call propositions and headings. But these alone will not feed the souls of people. While we need them, we also need the particulars that will help people realize how the general truths expressed fit their own experience.[4] This is a point emphasized in the preceding chapter by Donald MacLeod.

Each generalization, therefore, must be given feet to walk into people's lives. This is done by imagery, illustration, explanation, enumeration, and personal witness. It is this process of developing specifics for our assertions or headings that fills out the sermon and makes it useful to feed minds and hearts. This is covering the outline with the flesh and blood, muscle, and heart it needs. Thus, if the preacher is asserting in one of his headings that the Christian life is a portrait of God's wisdom, he must bring that down to the specific of saying that God has supplied the Christian with everything needed for refreshment, guidance, maintenance, and protection in the midst of a hostile environment. Then he will go on to point out how wise God is in giving Scripture, the Holy Spirit, the church memory, and conscience to the believer as the guardians of Christian life. The Christian assimilates the truth best when it reaches him in generalizations that have been refined into particulars. Neither generalizations nor particulars alone will feed his heart. He needs the blend of them found in an adequate group of headings expounded effectively in particular statements.

4. Henry Grady Davis, *Design for Preaching* (Philadelphia: Fortress, 1958), pp. 242–64.

The transition is a bridge from one generalization to the next in such a way that we are led from one truth into another without breaking the flow of thought. In fact each transition contributes to that flow by showing how one assertion is related to the next. As a bridge is real and solid, so must a transition be. It is a real thought, not just a leap over a chasm. Obscurity in meaning and interruption in flow come from making leaps with no bridges. On the other hand, boredom comes from using the same transitions always, e.g., "In the second place." Such a transition serves neither the preacher nor the hearer. One way for the minister to assist himself in building transitions is to form a summary sentence after the discussion of each heading. That will stimulate him into making a proper approach to his next major assertion. If a transition cannot be made without awkwardness, he is faced with a flaw of structure. He should see if he has the proper number or arrangement of divisions with respect to the chosen text. Transitions are important to the flow of the sermon, for in the feeding of the mind and heart we are concerned about the sense of evenness and connection that runs thoughout the delivery of the message. Nor do we wish to lose our hearer at any point in the pilgrimage. There are enough obstacles to the reception and assimilation of the Word of God. We must not add breaks in thought to them.

The act of writing the sermon in full before preaching it will enhance the flow of the sermon, especially if the preacher keeps before him the image of one of his people with whom he is sharing the excitement of his discoveries. Yet the greatest key to the flowing of the sermon is the movement of the preacher's own heart. When he is stirred to the depths of his being by the truths that have been shown him in the study, then his heart will be moved while he writes. And as he speaks, if the heart is moved, the sentences will flow. That is why it is essential that prayer accompany study time and precede preaching time (see again both Erroll Hulse and Geoffrey Thomas on this point). When the preacher's heart is moved, his hearer is greatly aided.

The flow of the sermon is also encouraged by the generous use of connecting words. In writing we have learned to be sparing of them, but in speech they are invaluable, holding the discourse together, reminding of and recalling what has gone before. "Both . . . and," "either . . . or," "on the one hand . . . on the other hand," "if . . . then." These can rarely be overdone in the effort to smooth out the flow of the preached Word.

Without repeating himself excessively, the minister should learn to build upon what he has already said. He should recapitulate without repeating. He may use words like, "assuming this to be the case," "remembering what we saw here, let us turn our attention to." These references backward and forward tie the message together in the mind of the hearer and assist him in receiving the flow of ideas. Making application of assertions within the body of the sermon will also enhance the flow of the message. Application tends to touch the emotions, while the points themselves may be mainly directed to the mind. The involving of the emotion with the mind in the listening process catches the hearer up in the message. The emotions pull the mind along and the mind the emotions. It is this sense of being carried along with the preacher in the unfolding of truth that the worshipper experiences in the flow of the message.

The sermon will flow more gracefully if the minister resists the temptation to enumerate in too great detail. That can be tiresome in the hands of all but a very few. Suggest a series of activities or sins or prayer needs by naming a few in the group, but not all. Suggest without exhausting. When the hearer's mind jumps ahead of yours in the search for truth, he loses the leadership of the preacher's mind and begins on his own course.

In particularizing the truth of the message, the preacher should adorn his sermon with nuggets. That is, he should look over his plan and the way he hopes to make it specific to the people and see if there are not some gems of beauty with which he might enhance it. These are the verses of Scripture that illustrate and reinforce what he is saying, for example. He should follow Jesus' own use of Scripture and see how He did just this—using little-known portions of the Scripture to illustrate great truths. To adorn a message is to give insights, or hints of insight along the way, so that the people are provided with food beyond what they realize they are receiving. It was Cotton Mather who "crowded his sermons with matter."

Having done these things in the development of his plan from the skeleton of headings to a full outline of particulars, applications, and adornment, the preacher must now look over the salient points he hopes not to exclude from the final work. He should review it to see if in fact some of these major thrusts have been omitted. This is an important step and a risky one for he may be tempted to bring in what does not actually belong. But if he has simply lost track of a particular thrust, and it fits naturally under one of the headings, then it has a right to stay and to be used in its own place.

Then, the preacher must check that he has used the right sequence in the specific ideas that are included in his plan. Sequence in biblical ideas is important. For example, the good should be placed before the bad to hold interest. In expounding the tenth commandment, it is better to describe Christ's call to contentment first and then to move to the description of the sin of covetousness. The human heart is fascinated by the explication of evil, but will tire quickly of the exposition of good. In general, the natural should be placed before the spiritual, as Jesus did with Nicodemus. Since Nicodemus could not follow the natural lessons, Jesus said he was not ready for the spiritual truths. We must seek God's order of things, watching how He arranges and then following His example.

Feeding the mind and the heart of the believer is the God-given task of the preacher. The process of developing the particular ways in which the truths of the passage will enter the lives of the people is a skill that will require the lifelong work of the preacher to develop.

5. Opening and Closing the Sermon: "Calling Them to a Right Response"

Preaching is more than setting truth before people. It is also persuading them to receive the truth, to act upon it, to be comforted by it, to share it with others. It is asking for action, trust, and faith. Preaching *is* phenomenological, as Samuel Logan reminded us earlier. Though the persuasive element runs throughout the message, it is more prominent in the preacher's mind in the opening and closing sections. We shall deal with those in some detail here.

The conclusion of the sermon is the final engagement of the mind of the speaker and the mind of the hearers in that particular discourse. It is the decisive conflict. Humanly speaking, eternity hinges on the effectiveness of the preacher's conclusion. He must give it his all. Here his proposition is clearly in mind—it is the one great luminous truth that must be mounted high for all to see in its most comprehensive statement. The whole of it must be seen at one time. So the preacher concentrates his efforts to make one point only at the conclusion. It will not be new, but will be the gathering up and holding forth of all that he has asserted thus far. He must decide what he wants the hearer to do with the truth. If he wants a lesson learned, then let him summarize and recapitulate what has been taught. If the preacher is eager for them to feel the reality of God's love or some other great spiritual truth, then let him draw a striking verbal picture of the truth in action or in display. But if the preacher desires the response to be one of decision, then he must appeal to great Christian motives or to Christian character or example as the driving force of his conclusion.

While conclusions must not be drawn out, they are more likely to be unduly brief, so that they seem hurried and unworthy of the argument that has preceded them. Let the conclusion have enough body to be a significant part of the whole and occupy enough time for the hearer to realize that something important is being asked of him in these closing moments of the preaching of the Word of God. The conclusion is to be a kind of climax of the preaching event. Someone has likened it to the final tap the mason gives to the brick that nestles it firmly into place. The preacher will have to take care not to give that tap too early in the message. To change the figure, if we reach the crescendo of the movement too soon, there will be no sense of culmination left for the concluding words. Instead, we gradually build toward the conclusion in such a way that the truth stands out, dominating everything in mind and heart. Then the hearer will hold in his heart forever the memory of those closing moments when the Word of God was all in all to him.

The style of the conclusion is ordinarily not oratorical. Rather it is persuasive style at its keenest, not always in appeal, but always in earnest, serious, and loving tones. Here the souls of the preacher and the people are joined at the feet of the author whose Word has been expounded that day. The conclusion is the key to drawing the hearer to the appropriate response to the Word of God.

The opening of the sermon consists of the exordium and the explication. People in worship do not normally need to be arrested at the beginning. They have come to hear the Word of God expounded. The preacher may assume their interest, though he will have to work to hold it. But the exordium should be varied. The previous week's message might be reviewed to indicate continuity in pulpit work and the expectation of every-Sunday participation in worship. The preacher must avoid saying things like, "As I was thinking what to preach about this week." That ranks with, "Unaccustomed as I am to public speaking." Rather, the congregation must be gripped; they must be *engaged,* by the occasion, the need for the lesson, the longing of the human heart, or the preacher's own overwhelming conviction that this is what needs to be said in this hour. In the exordium, the hearer begins to trust the preacher and yield him the audience he needs, so rapport and trust should be built in these opening sentences.

The explication is to set the text forth in public view as the authoritative Word from God for this occasion. It may be displayed in its context as the Puritans did. Its meaning may be stated and its misinterpretations attacked. But whatever else is done with the text at this point, the preacher is primarily to lift up its essential truth. In so doing, he will make it clear that he is not an inventor of truth, but an expounder of it and that it is the Word of God and not of men that will be held forth in the ensuing moments.

The introductory section, consisting of these two parts should not be long, for the people are anxious to get into the meat of their spiritual meal. Still the opening section is there to whet the appetite and lead into the subject. It prepares the hearer for what is to come. Such moments act as transitions from the thoughts of men to the thoughts of God. With the right sort of opening word the people can catch up to the place the preacher has been for days or weeks. The introduction assists him too, for in these moments his heart once again warms to his theme and the sentences begin to flow as he anticipates revealing the momentous ideas he has found in his study.

In drawing his hearers to a proper response to God's Word, where should the preacher place his concrete, specific words of application? I have already mentioned that applying assertions as one goes along tends to involve mind and heart together in the pursuit of the truth. Normally this seems to be the best timing of applications (again, as John Bettler argues so strongly). But no two sermons are alike, and sometimes when the whole truth is set before the people in all its splendor, one will find that moment to be the ideal time to apply its force to the heart and mind. Therefore, with each sermon as it is being prepared, the preacher should prayerfully consider the best placement of the concrete application, remembering the need for variety, the ability of the people to recall assertions, and the particular features of the topic under discussion.

Often the preacher will want to follow the Puritans in their particular applicatory preaching. We are addressing people in all kinds of trials and conditions. Some are regenerate and some are not. Some are backsliders and some are growing rapidly. There are new Christians and those who have walked with Christ before you were born. One size cannot fit all. Therefore, sometimes (never do anything always), we will be drawn to address the different groups of our hearers directly, one after another. There is unusual power in doing this the right way. Great wisdom, tact, and restraint are called for, along with great love. Perhaps the group that will benefit the most from such directed and particular application will be the young. They will not soon forget the day when their pastor spoke pointedly to them and urged them to give their time and attention to things that last forever. At the end of the letter to the Ephesians Paul did this, addressing, in turn, wives, husbands, children, fathers, slaves, and masters. We still turn to these particular applications for valuable instruction. So will our people long remember the application of the Word of God that we made to them week by week.

In this section we have been dealing with structure and speaking about the skill of putting a message together that will be an effective instrument in the hands of God. Such care in the design of the sermon is not in order to produce a work of art to be admired, but the fashioning of a tool that will do what it is called to do—lead the people to a fitting response to the Word of God. That response is submission to and love for the glory of God in the face of Jesus Christ.

6. The Sensing of Order: "The Process of Listening"

It is utterly important for the preacher to remember the gate through which his sermon will reach the minds and hearts of his people. The gate is the listening process. This has been brought home to me vividly. Many times after the sermon is over, I have come upon the bulletins of those who have used the bulletins to take notes and have then left their bulletins with the notes in the pew. Often their hearing did not correspond with what I thought I had said. I have had to ask, Why? I have concluded that I saw the structure of the sermon through *my* eyes and they heard it through *their* ears. They heard a flow of sounds coming to them, and they tried to make some notes about what the points were. But they did not always discern them accurately. Their mistakes have aided me in my struggle for effective structure in preaching.

Sermons come to hearers in streams of words. There are no pages, no punctuation points, no capital letters, no underlinings. All hearers have are words and gestures forming impressions. What we perceive as an outline, they sense as continuity, or the lack of it.[5] The flow of the sermon is really, therefore, the quality of this continuity. As a preacher I am faced with the task of developing and maintaining this continuity in order to aid my hearer, remembering all the while that I am appealing to the listener, not to the reader (which is a point made earlier in this volume by R. C. Sproul).

So the question we face as preachers as we design and fill out our messages is, How will this sound in the ears of my people? Will they understand here that I am making a generalization and that I intend to make it specific for them? Will they see that I am illustrating this truth here and that my purpose is to help them realize this truth in daily living? I cannot use just any words—I must clothe my thoughts with arresting and attractive language. I must seek variety. I shall be interested in how words sound and go together, as well as in their meaning and function. I will pay close attention to the transitions for they will draw the hearer from one concept to the next without losing interest. I will seek to use many connecting words, realizing that these form the mortar that holds the bricks of thought together in tight and solid arrangement. I will seek to show the point of my illustration, tying it closely into the truth it displays, so that my hearer is not fascinated by it rather than induced to give entrance to the spiritual reality I am illustrating.

Remembering that the message enters through the ear gate affects everything the preacher does in ordering the message. The hearer's memory becomes all important. He cannot go back and review. He must hold before him the things said and try to see the order in them and gain the overall impression by putting ideas together. Thus, design becomes utterly important in the enabling of the hearer to retain and relate the things he has heard. The preacher has the great responsibility of introducing his text, his proposition, and his headings in such a way that he makes very clear to his hearer that these are crucial building blocks in the message. Each one must be set forth with clarity and emphasis, or

5. Ibid.

they will not stand out in the stream of language that enters the ear gate of the hearer.

Knowing this the preacher will construct his sentences differently. Many books will call him to short sentences, but that practice will interrupt the flow of preaching. Most of his sentences should be long. They are not heard as long sentences, but as satisfying groups of words conveying one thought. Some sentences will be short for emphasis, but the sermon that is interesting to the listener is the one that is a blend of short and long sentences. The short sentences set forth the major assertions to be made and the longer ones expound, make specific, and apply those short statements of Christian truth. When we speak, the new element in the sentence should come toward the end of the sentence. It will remain with the hearer and form a basis for yet another insight in the next sentence.

Since my entree is the human ear, I must enter there, but I am not confined to appealing to that one sense. I must gain access through the listening process to the whole person. We must help our people to see the empty tomb with words that image it (see Jay Adams's chapter). We must appeal to their visual sense with descriptive nouns and a minimum of adverbs and adjectives. We must get them to taste the sweetness and delicate flavor (like a trace of honey) of the manna in the wilderness—a taste of which men would never tire. The breakfast on the beach ought to be preached with the smell and the texture of fish broiled by Christ Himself accompanying the truth portrayed. We should make it possible for our hearers to feel the roughness of the cross or the welts raised on the back of the apostle when he endured the beatings for Christ. The whole person is sitting before us, and he is equipped by God with more than one gate by which reality may enter and grip him.

Through the ear, however, we must gain entrance initially for the truth of the Scriptures. The ear is the corresponding symbol to the human tongue with which we began this chapter. If the symbol of the church is the tongue, then the paramount image of the preacher is the human ear. There is his target. Everything stands or falls with the impression made there. Structure and flow aimed for the ear are different from any other kind of structure and flow. So the preacher enters the ear that he may gain entrance to the most important gate of them all—the gate of the heart, leading to the emotions, the conscience, and finally the will, where the inner spring is, where life is bent and changed and directed to the will of God.

7. Conclusion

I am not calling here for a triumph of form over substance, of structure over content. Such a victory would lead to a concealing of the gospel. What I am saying is that there is no real conflict between ardor and order. In fact, the passion for communicating truth in preaching must lead us to a concern for structure. The person whom we are addressing has a God-given sense of order. Our proclamation of the truth must conform to that or fail to find entry with power.

This will be borne out as we construct sermons, week by week. When we begin the work, the order of the sermon is ours to develop and shape. But after it is formed, the structure of the sermon, humanly speaking, determines what possible function it can have in the life of the hearer. Therefore, from a human standpoint, the fashioning of the proper design for the sermon at the right point in its development is all-important. So we must translate our earnest zeal into a useful order, that we may move the mind and heart.

Thus we will also come to see that every message has a structure of some kind. The question is whether it is a careless and haphazard form, hurriedly conceived, or whether it is the product of thoughtful application of love and skill to the material God has given. We must dedicate ourselves to developing sermons with structure that comes from a loving heart and a disciplined mind, fashioned by artistic skill and inflamed by holy imagination.

We must remind ourselves of the diligent and sacrificial labors of others who rely on design and structure for effectiveness: the playwright, the architect, the composer. How assiduously they give themselves to the perfecting of their arts in order to communicate something to others! They know that excellence can only come from long labor, and it has no cheaper price tag for you. "Shall I offer to the Lord that which has cost me nothing?" We cannot make a profound impression upon the human mind unless, along with the eternal message, we master the temporal form with which we will convey it to our hearers. In this chapter I have not addressed the all-important element of the unction and anointing of the Holy Spirit upon the preaching of the Word. I would not denigrate the utter necessity for the Spirit's blessing to make a sermon effective. What I have tried to show is the requirement God makes of us preachers, that "we be not workmen that need to be ashamed. . . ."

The artists of this world seek for an earthly crown—the honor of others or of their own hearts, but we have been called to be the oracles of God. Shall we not then set aside our distaste of order and our foolish reluctance to study structure and, in the name of the God of order, devote ourselves to the preparation and delivery of messages that, sharp and trim as swords, shall pierce human hearts, lay bare consciences, and be to men and women the instruments of new life?

11

The Preacher as Rhetorician
Lester De Koster

This chapter deals with rhetoric as history and its potential for pulpit eloquence. The pulpiteer draws, or should draw, upon all the resources that can hone the skills the preacher yields to proclamation of the Word of God. These resources lie in the living rhetorical tradition. Our aim is to sample that tradition here.

Use of oral language is not incidental to being human. Language is, rather, of the essence of *humanitas*. In the long tradition of the liberal arts, words are the tools employed for sculpting the lineaments of culture upon the human soul. Nor is it incidental that the centrality of divine revelation both in creation and in redemption lies in the Word. What distinguishes man from animal, said the ancients, is the use of words.

Every effort to trace man's ability to use words back to natural origins gets lost in the mists of our beginnings. What accounts for speech is the biblical report of man's endowment with God's image—the image, that is, of the God whose Word made the heavens and the earth and comes clothed in flesh and symbols. The gap between the "bow-wow" of the animal and the lisping speech of the child is never bridged by evolutionary theory—though few seem to make use of that striking fact to affirm creation. Even Plato was so puzzled by the child's acquisition of speech that he postulated the pre-existence of the soul. Hearing the child learn to speak is observing a miracle at close hand. Unhappily, in a way, speech comes so naturally that few invest in it the time and effort required to make art of nature. Many must be the teachers of speech who wish that their students had not come by the use of oral expression quite so effortlessly.

The community-effecting character of language is illumined at Babel, for when God wished to divide man into men, He did so simply by confusing His gift of speech. And, again, when He chose to annul for the church the dispersion of Babel, God permitted the tongues of the apostles to be heard in the languages of a divided world at Pentecost.

Language may not quite be, as the philosopher Heidegger put it, "the house of being," but man and word are correlative. The art of rhetoric aims at using words well. Indeed, the ancient rhetoricians looked to rhetoric as guiding language in humanizing the soul through the power of speech—much as today the patient of the psychiatric counselor finds talking a form of self-liberation.

The beauty, mystery, and power of words have long fascinated the observant. And seeking the essence of language has become a contemporary passion, involving such names as Martin Heidegger, Eugen Rosenstock-Huessy, Franz Rosenzweig, Martin Buber, Jean Paul Sartre, and various schools of contemporary linguistic philosophy. Indeed, for a period—which seems to be nearing the end of its course—modern philosophy was so acutely mesmerized by the vehicle of language as to dissolve all categories into *how* words *mean*. (For a further discussion of this matter, see, in the present volume, Samuel Logan's chapter, "The Phenomenology of Preaching.")

Preaching involves rhetoric or, no less, preaching is the exercise of the ministry's oral subordination of self to the language of divine revelation. The more effectively this subordination occurs, in terms of the range of trained capacities the preacher places at the disposal of the Word, the better channel for proclamation his pulpit becomes.

We will do our brief survey of rhetorical history with an eye to suggesting what the preacher can derive from theorists of the past, the better to serve the Word in the present. Still more, we will hope to make the mines of ancient rhetorical wisdom intriguing enough for exploration on the minister's own—not, to be sure, on the assumption that these resources are unknown, but rather in the conviction that they are infinitely rich. We will turn, then, to the effect of the Reformation upon pulpit rhetoric, and conclude by suggesting additional readings.

Ancient Rhetoric

Lamech lectured his wives (Gen. 4:23), and Homer put speeches into the mouths of his heroes. Man spoke before formulating theories about his performance. Theory followed upon practice and, in its turn, perfected practice.

Plato was suspicious of oration because he, like Socrates, was dubious about the claim of the Sophists to teach the use of words without (as he saw it) wisdom, but Aristotle took speech seriously enough to compose an enduring treatise on rhetoric. It is called his *Rhetoric*.

With characteristic conciseness, Aristotle defines rhetoric "as the faculty or power of discovering in the particular case what are the available means of persuasion" (1.2). It is a definition that has held good for over two thousand years.

The great practitioner-counterpart of Aristotle as theorist was, of course, Demosthenes—last spokesman (and martyr) for the political liberty that both eloquence and rhetoric presuppose. Like its sisters, the art of rhetoric flourishes best in the atmosphere of freedom, even if that be the relatively restricted liberty of the Greek city-state. Athens fell, and Demosthenes in due season fell also before the onslaught of Alexander, ironically enough the pupil of Aristotle. But left to the ages were the amazing power of the orator and the subtle analyses of the philosopher. What can the ministry today learn from them?

First, Demosthenes perfected in practice the principles codified by Aristotle. The preacher determined to perfect the capacities for effective speech that he places at the Word's behest does well to peruse at least the "Orations on the Crown"—Demosthenes' final and fateful struggle to alert Athens to the liberties it had frittered away. In times and places where rhetoric was taken seriously across the centuries, these orations (of Demosthenes and of his opponent Aeschines) were memorized and delivered under competent criticism. In our times when opening the mouth enjoys eulogy as song and speech, and frequently reaps fabulous financial rewards, he who would nonetheless cultivate a fastidious appreciation of an oratory empassioned by commitment to a cause will keep Demosthenes' orations to hand.

Second, the preacher takes note that Aristotle attributes the power to persuade to three confluent means:

1. Appeal to the head, via fact, argument, logic.
2. Appeal to the heart, via the emotions.
3. Appeal subtly emanating from the character of the speaker.

Aristotle regards the third as the most important. Derived from it is the proverb, "What you are speaks so loudly I cannot hear what you say." Happily the speaker is not necessarily stuck with the limitations of what he is, though it is obvious that the influence of, say, the saintly John Henry Newman in the pulpit awesomely echoes the Aristotelian dictum. Aristotle suggests that the orator may carefully, but very unobtrusively, suggest the audience (often called the "judge" by ancient writers—for it is they who make or break the speech, if not the speaker . . .) carefully, I repeat, give the listeners to understand that the speaker is (a) competent and well informed, (b) of high character and ideals, and (c) devoted to the interests of the listeners. One will discern the practice of this ancient advice in countless sermonizings via the electronic media.

Third, though Aristotle wishes that all audiences were made up of philosophers, so that reason alone would always prevail, he recognizes that emotion does in fact color judgment, and sometimes overwhelms sobriety. So the *Rhetoric* becomes a penetrating definition and then sustained analysis of a dozen forms of human emotion—with an intricate listing under each of ways in which it may be aroused (by one speaker) or allayed (by his opponent).

If, as Calvin writes, the psalms trace out every emotion of which the soul is capable, Aristotle's *Rhetoric* is one of the Psalter's pagan counterparts. Modernity did not discover the emotions; it merely exploits them. The preacher determined to mold feelings to divine purposes will find Aristotle an inexhaustible resource.

Fourth, no less so is the *Rhetoric* useful in the suggestion of perspectives from which subjects may be approached—what Aristotle called "the topics," and one translator, Lane Cooper (I think the best), calls "the hunting ground" for rhetorical ideas.

In short, Aristotle's *Rhetoric* bears out to this day the encomiums it has enjoyed over the centuries, from experts as great as Cicero, to Voltaire's "I do not believe there is a single refinement of the art that escapes him," and Thomas Arnold's " . . . its immense value struck me again so forcibly that I could not consent to send my son to a University where he would lose it altogether"—a determination hard to be satisfied, it is likely, in our own times, when the appreciation of freedom and the exercise of its arts both wane together.

The emergence of the homily in the pulpits of the church introduced a type of oratory not quite congenial to any of the Aristotelian categories, and sermonizing found its theoretical elaboration in St. Augustine, himself a teacher of rhetoric, and enjoyed further refinement at the Reformation.

Meanwhile, Aristotle's *Rhetoric* continues to tower high above today's popular speech texts, and forms with Quintilian's *Institutes of Oratory* the foundations of Western rhetorical theory. A ministry bent upon affording the Word of God the best of rhetorical vehicles will make Aristotle a well-worn companion.

The Rhetoric of Rome

Roman rhetoric is summed up in two names: Cicero, both theorist and practitioner, and Quintilian whose *Institutes* established the pattern for liberal education through the Reformation—and no doubt suggested to Calvin, for reasons we will explore, the title of his own *Institutes of the Christian Religion*. What is to be learned from these?

Marcus Tullus Cicero (often called Tully across the intervening centuries) was the unique combination of practical statesman and urbane humanist. He reigned supreme among Roman orators, like Demosthenes, in the decline of political liberty—and, also like Demosthenes, Cicero finally lost his life to plain speech, at the hands of Antony's brigands.

Unlike Demosthenes (whose prescription for oratorical power consisted in the famous "practice! practice!! practice!!!"), Cicero wrote at least three treatises on rhetoric, in studied prose, while reigning as exemplar supreme of the power of the word in human affairs. What he says is an ongoing interplay of theory with practice, which cannot be summarized here. Some indication of how profoundly all great oratory resides in conscious art is suggested, for one example among many, by Cicero's minute study of speech rhythms (to which Roman audiences were particularly sensitive—often hooting and stamping speakers off the platform if their cadences fell out of pattern). Practically, the preacher may learn from Cicero the following:

First, the means of persuasion suggested by Aristotle—head, emotions, character of speaker—can appear in another form. Cicero prefers this trilogy: conciliate, instruct, move. Or, again, persuasion through appeal to the affections, to the understanding, and to the passions. Omitted, it is obvious, is stress upon the character of the speaker. This is not because Cicero is unaware of this powerful influence, but because he probably believes that this means is beyond immediate control—we are who we are.

Second, as vehicles for these forms of persuasion are the three styles of oratory made famous by Cicero: the plain style, the middle style, and the sublime or exultant style. The plain style instructs and will be interspersed with the middle, more emotional, style throughout the early parts of the speech. The middle style ingratiates, by the use of figures, illustrations, even on occasion carefully calculated humor. Then at the climax, the sublime style triumphs, "sweeping all before it." The reader will be reminded of the anti-Nazis who came away converts under the magnetic oratory of Adolf Hitler. Cicero counts rhetorical triumph among the highest of human attainments—as did St. Augustine—one in which words are used not so much to communicate as to capture, the audience not so much illumined as possessed.

Third, in lieu of stressing "character" Cicero lays emphasis upon winning the affection of the "judge." Quintilian is later to say that if an audience likes you, it will find it easier to believe, and harder to disbelieve, what you say. The role of the middle style is to ingratiate, to win the "judge's" confidence not only, but to win its affection.

Fourth, some indication of Ciceronian influence across the centuries is revealed by Calvin's determination in both speaking and writing to use only the "plain" style (he is thinking of Cicero's definitions), capable as he was of at least the middle style on the pulpit (being the victim of asthma) and the exultant style via his pen.

Style is always adapted to purpose, and purpose underlies "invention," that is, the formulation of ideas. It was commonplace by Cicero's time to divide the construction of a speech into five stages: invention, arrangement (of the ideas invented), wording (the ideas in language suitable to audience and purpose), memorization, and delivery. The plain style is not first of all concerned, then, with wording. Plainness or simplicity is a function of purpose. Some modern handbooks like Rudolf Flesch's *Art of Plain Talk* and *Art of Readable Writing* focus prescription for intelligibility chiefly on word and sentence length. One can even work out some kind of intelligibility quotient by discovering the ratio between syllable count and sentence length.

It is not likely that so artificial a technique would have appealed to Cicero. Wording comes late in composition and ought to be subordinate to the intent of the speaker. The vehicle ought not define the passenger. Let the speaker know both well and passionately what he wants to convey, and wants to happen as a result—and wording will take care of itself.

What Cicero has in mind, probably, is what the late Alfred North Whitehead called "style." The last of the "Aims of Education," Whitehead says, is development of

> the most austere of all mental qualities; I mean the sense for style. It is an aesthetic sense, based on admiration for the direct attainment of a foreseen end, simply and without waste. Style in art, style in literature, style in science, style in logic, style in practical execution have fundamentally the same aesthetic qualities, namely, attainment and restraint. . . . But above style, and above knowledge, there is something, a vague shape like fate above the Greek gods. That something is Power. Style is the fashioning of power, the restraining of power. . . . With style you attain your end and nothing but your end. . . . Now style is the exclusive privilege of the expert (*Aims of Education*, Mentor, p. 24).

Only those who lack style, Cicero would tell us, need bother about word and sentence lengths—but that might include more of us than we like to suppose.

Fifth, the preacher learns from Cicero that the genuine orator has a goal, persuasion; he has a means, language; and he has a technique, delivery. The measure of his expertise is how well he molds an audience to his purpose—or, for the ministry, how well a congregation is molded according to the purposes of divine revelation.

Sixth, the rhetorically artistic journey begins, for the Ciceronian, with narration (in the pulpit, doctrine)—bringing the audience to one mind with both speaker and itself. If, to achieve this, sentences are short and languages colloquial, these are dictated by antecedent intent. And that intent is the all-important creation (in the most artistic sense of the term) of one audience-personality out of many audience-persons. And more, the creation of such a corporate personality brings into existence seeing with the eyes of the speaker, feeling with his emotions, and sharing communion through his perspectives. "Communication" is, after all, creating community.

Nonrhetorical techniques for stimulating audience unification abound in our times, like the common mouthing of song or pledge or prayer; prelude and musical performance; rising and sitting in unison, and the like—often the more sentimental, the more employed. The Ciceronian orator disdains, of course, such artificial, pseudo-artistic devices. Indeed, from Cicero's perspective, the more a speaker leans upon such "unartistic" crutches, the more rhetorically lame he confesses himself to be.

Only after he has molded his listeners into a corporate body by his own eloquence will the classic orator demonstrate his achievement by eliciting audience response—as when Demosthenes taunts Aeschines with a "tool of Alexander," and gets the sophisticated "judge" to shout its agreement with this risky charge of treason.

Finally, for our purposes, what Cicero teaches is that powerful speech has its origin in passionate conviction, focused upon a precisely envisioned oratorial objective, molded by a "style" that obliges every syllable and every gesture to pursue the predetermined end. To attain such skill (and, in the preacher's case, to offer it to the Word for its proclamation) Cicero recommends intensive study of all the elements of oratory, of the speeches made by experts in the craft, and a lifetime devoted to the whole world of knowledge.

It is the course he himself pursued, raising Roman oratory to the highest pinnacle it achieved.

Quintilian

Rhetoric becomes pedagogical with Quintilian, in the first century of the Christian era. His *Institutes of Oratory* sets eloquence as the goal of education and underlies pedagogical practice from his own era to beyond the Reformation. Quintilian's twelve-part work is a compendium of rhetorical theory set down by a master hand.

The liberal arts tradition, still at least nominally the staple of collegiate education, is rooted in Quintilian's *Institutes:* "We are to form, then," he writes, "the perfect orator, who cannot exist unless as a good man; and we require in him, therefore, not only consummate ability in speaking, but every excellence of mind" (Preface).

"The art of speaking," this pedagogue goes on, "depends on great labor, constant study, varied exercise, repeated trials, the deepest sagacity, and the readiest judgment" (2. 13). But all this is in vain unless "the orator be, above all, *a good man*" (2. 16).

Quintilian's *Institutes* scheme to form the good soul by way of the liberal arts. Underlying the liberal arts is the assumption that words are tools by which souls are sculpted, and these arts guide the verbal tools into the creation of the "good man, speaking" (Johann Sturm's pedagogical ideal in Strasbourg in the mid-sixteenth century). Fifteen centuries after Quintilian, whose influence never waned across the years, Calvin perceived that the underlying assumption of these *Institutes* is in conflict with St. Paul's depreciation of eloquence in his first letter to the Corinthians— and Calvin decided to write another *Institutes* pointing a better way to the formation of the good man—confirming his humanity by deed rather than in word. To this we will come soon.

Fundamental to the liberal arts, meanwhile, as Quintilian expounds them, and unchanged across the centuries, is the *trivium:* grammar, logic, and rhetoric. Grammar, including literature, arouses the powers of comprehension; logic formulates the power of judgment; and rhetoric leads to artistic expression of all that is being learned. No impression without expression.

Vestiges of the Quintilian schema linger on in the "orals" that complete doctoral programs to this day—only what can be orally expressed has been truly mastered. The *res* comes to expression in the *verbum*—the reality of education reveals itself in the words of eloquence.

But Quintilian has subtly shifted the classical emphasis. Eloquence now crowns a liberal education rather than the hero of oratorical victories. Such an education, as Newman was to argue eighteen centuries later in his *Idea of a University,* is an end in itself, its own goal. Rhetoric merely completes the pedagogical circle. The speaker himself will decide, Quintilian says, whether or not he has spoken well; he need show no results to justify his self-analysis. Power of oral expression need not aim at a career on the hustings or in the courts. Rhetorical excellence does not posit the risk of life in oratorical commitment to freedom of speech when political liberty has become unpopular. Quintilian, whose ideal ever remains Cicero, nonetheless tames oratory and domesticates eloquence in ways Cicero declined to follow himself.

Rhetoric becomes fossilized, a museum piece, wreathed in ivy, paraded in cap and gown, and practiced in the ivory tower. Quintilian makes rhetoric go introvert and play for sentimental stakes. *Belle lettres* supplants the ferocity of Demosthenes and the polished intransigence of Cicero. In consequence, oratory speaking truth to power appears thereafter more in the pulpits than on the tribune, sounding forth a new Word on the lips of courageous bishops. For all that, Quintilian calls the tune in education for fifteen centuries and more. What comes to matter rhetorically is progress through a curriculum, meticulously outlined in the *Institutes* from elementary school through finished speaker, an orator better acquainted with the literature of culture than with the struggles for free speech.

But, all this being granted, what may be learned, now, from Quintilian? Much in many ways, not least in felicity of expression. Quintilian is master of what he seeks to teach, and he writes with a certainty that imparts a serenity of style and liveliness of wit. Even more than Cicero he explores every facet of the speaker's art, every aspect of his performance from invention through delivery. Because he believes that the educated man must take all knowledge as his province, Quintilian outlines a broad course of preparation for the culminating power of eloquent speech. His survey of Greek and Roman literature requisite to a humane education remains as noteworthy criticism. But these things require perusal of the *Institutes* themselves.

For us, here and now, Quintilian provides the following: First, a sense of the scope and range of knowledge and training that skilled speaking requires. If, on the one hand, eloquence crowns liberal education, on the other hand, eloquence presupposes it. Talk may be cheap, but sustained oratorical power exudes, as

Aeschines said in derision of Demosthenes, the smell of the lamp. Better, replies Demosthenes, than the odor of other spirits on the lips—and Quintilian sides with Demosthenes. The road to rhetorical excellence is long and arduous. The Gettysburg Address reflected something of the firelight that illumined the youthful Lincoln's slate late into the night.

The unschooled may display passion, employ tricks, even attract the credulous; the demagogue may substitute chicanery for art; but the great pulpiteer who year after year opens new channels of trained capacity for the Word of God to enter the world has invested heavily to attain his eminence. The history of preaching from the age of the early Fathers to the masters of the modern pulpit confirms the causal relation between broad learning and oratorical excellence.

Second, Quintilian affirms unequivocally what Aristotle and probably Cicero left open: goodness is basic to eloquence. To obtain good fruit, a higher authority teaches, the tree must be made good (Matt. 12:33).

Aristotle had insisted that the character of the speaker is one of the elements, perhaps the most important element, in persuasion. But Aristotle at least permits the suspicion that what the audience may skillfully be led to assume about the speaker's virtues may not reflect the reality; what matters, in the *Rhetoric* is that the "judge" be given the impression that the speaker is informed and competent, of high character, and bent upon the hearer's good. So long as these play their persuasive role, Aristotle can be read to suggest, isn't that enough? Rhetoric is not, after all, ethics. On this Aristotle has another treatise.

Cicero maintained a high personal ethic and was, though not always consistently, enamored of the Stoics. But the student of his speeches in the courts may wonder if the end did not sometimes govern the means. Nor does he, like Aristotle and Quintilian, play upon the power of character in attaining persuasion. As suggested above, he may have seen through Aristotle's possible ruse, without endorsing Quintilian's alternative.

But in Quintilian there is no equivocation. Great speaker, good man. It is interesting, and can be profitable, to ask if Quintilian

would have counted Hitler a great orator. Effective, yes; gifted
with a style that moved easily through Cicero's three stages, yes;
mesmerizer of half a nation, and it among the best educated of
peoples, yes; absolute master of his craft, yes—but a "good" man?
Who would affirm it? Did Hitler hypnotize himself as he trans-
fixed his audiences? Or was he watching himself perform? Was
his oratory, like the gigantic pageantry that environed it, only
histrionic? Was it all a stage, himself ever at the center? What is
the preacher to learn from these things? A good deal, it may be, if
he can answer such questions in the light of the ancient rhetoricians—who would, I think, not have taken Hitler into their company. Churchill, of course; Roosevelt, indeed! But Hitler and
Mussolini, also a powerful propagandist, would have been viewed
by the classical rhetoricians as criminally guilty of abusing the art
of rhetoric in precise proportion to their successful prostitution
of it.

Third, in keeping with his own prescription of integrity, Quintilian agrees with Cicero that the speaker cannot really convey
any emotion or recollection he does not, at the moment of delivery, himself experience or relive. With vivid illustration, Quintilian details how the speaker must assume the character of those
whose feelings or thoughts he describes. The orator must, as it
were, be simply reporting events he "hears" or "sees" as vividly at
the moment of delivery as if he were "there"; he must arouse
emotions by deeply experiencing them himself. No counterfeits
will move the "judges."

But let us ask how, as a final illustration of how Quintilian's
paragraphs come alive with unexpected turns of insight, will a
man of integrity respond, say, to a falsehood that has misled an
audience against him? May the "good" man counter lie with lie?
With an air of innocence Quintilian answers, it is the role of
oratory to lead the audience along the path of truth, but if the
audience has been taken on a false detour away from that path,
what then? There they are, off the track, mired in falsehood. To
get them back to the path might it not be necessary (and entirely
justifiable) to contrive another detour? One imposture may have

to be countered—for the time being—with another—the good unsullied by such rescue.

We have but touched on the most prominent among the classical rhetoricians. If, now, we have left the impression that "old" and "new" are merely categories of time but not of value, and that the ancient writers and orators are as "with it" for today's ministry as tomorrow, we have attained our own rhetorical purpose.

St. Augustine

We turn now to the greatest of the Christian rhetoricians, both as theorist and as orator. Profoundly schooled in the writers and practitioners we have been discussing and their many contemporaries not here mentioned, Augustine supplied the basis in theory for the homily, or sermon, already heard in the church for more than three centuries by Augustine's time.

We have already observed that the sermon finds no place, really, among the types of speech discussed by Aristotle and generally accepted by the pagan rhetoricians. Nor does Augustine try to fit preaching into the Aristotelian pattern. By Augustine's time, the sermon had been established by the great Fathers who were well aware of what they did. When Augustine comes to giving the sermon, or homily, a rhetorical description, he simply treats it as its own genre. And so the sermon is.

Like so many Christian thinkers before and after him, Augustine compares the church's use of classical wisdom with the gold and silver carried off by Israel out of Egypt. There is no truth, he says, as did Calvin after him, but from God; let us use all we can absorb and be glad. It is not surprising, then, that Augustine's relatively brief work on the rhetoric of the sermon, entitled *On Christian Doctrine,* quotes copiously from classical writers, especially from Cicero.

But the church enlists a new resource, of which Augustine takes account, in the creation of eloquence—the Bible. And to stress the extent to which the Bible can be the pulpiteer's rhetorical well, Augustine again and again illustrates rhetorical principles from Scripture. The three styles, for example, which he takes over from Cicero—plain, middle, exulted—Augustine illustrates by quotations from the Bible.

Where, however, Quintilian insists that the orator must be good, Augustine insists that he must be wise—and wisdom consists in knowledge of the Word, experience of reconciliation, and companionship with God. Moreover, the word of the pulpiteer is never quite wholly his own. His art lists more toward transmission than invention. Or, rather, his invention seeks ways to convey a word that has already found him. Augustine therefore focuses the five steps commended by the classical writers—invention, arrangement, wording, memorization, delivery—upon exegesis and application of truths derived from divine revelation. The ministry searches the Scriptures through the "topical" perspectives of Aristotle, in search of ever more effective ways of proclaiming these to church and world.

The first and larger part of Augustine's treatise deals with the interpretation of the Bible, in terms of his hermeneutical principles. And while Augustine, too, wants the pulpiteer to take all knowledge as his domain, he requires that the preacher be, above all, conversant with the Bible—and like the great exegetes of all ages, Augustine himself knew the Bible pretty much by heart. He writes,

> Now it is especially necessary for the man who is bound to speak wisely, even though he cannot speak eloquently, to retain in memory the words of scripture. For the more he discerns the poverty of his own speech, the more he ought to draw on the riches of Scripture, so that what he says in his own words he may prove by the words of Scripture; and he himself, though small and weak in his own words, may gain strength and power from the confirming testimony of great men. For this proof gives pleasure when he cannot please by his mode of speech. But if a man desires to speak not only with wisdom, but with eloquence also (and assuredly he will prove of greater service if he can do both), I would rather send him to read, and to listen to, and exercise himself in

imitating, eloquent men, than advise him to spend the time with teachers of rhetoric; especially if the men he reads and listens to are justly praised as having spoken, or as being accustomed to speak, not only with eloquence, but with wisdom also. For eloquent speakers are heard with pleasure; wise speakers with profit. And, therefore, Scripture does not say that the multitude of the eloquent, but "the multitude of the wise is the welfare of the world" (Wisdom 6:24).

He goes on to illustrate from Paul (Rom. 5:3-5; II Cor. 11:16-30) and Amos (6:1-6) that in the Bible wisdom and eloquence are combined.

Accepting from Cicero the duty of the orator "to teach, to delight, and to move," Augustine approves Cicero's elaboration: "To teach is a necessity, to delight is a beauty, to persuade is a triumph." But, with an eye on influencing behavior, he maintains that teaching ranks first in importance for the Christian orator: "To teach is a necessity. For what men know, it is in their own hands either to do or not to do. But who would say it is their duty to do what they do not know?"

Giving pleasure is not a necessity, nor is persuasion always so—though Augustine yields to those "who are so fastidious that they do not care for truth unless it be put in the form of a pleasing discourse." Please them if possible, remembering, however, "what does it profit a man that he both confesses the truth and praises the eloquence, if he does not yield his consent, when it is only for the sake of securing his consent that the speaker in urging the truth gives careful attention to what he says?"

> The eloquent divine, then, when he is urging a practical truth, must not only teach so as to give instruction, and please so as to keep up the attention, but he must also sway the mind so as to subdue the will. For if a man be not moved by the force of truth, though it is demonstrated to his own confession, and clothed in beauty of style, nothing remains but to subdue him by the power of eloquence (from Book IV).

Cicero would not have said it otherwise.

For Augustine, as for the church at large, pulpit discourse is moral pedagogy. Its text is the Bible, its audience the congregation, its goal obedience, its end the maturing believer. This defines the nature of the homily, the role of the sermon. Nothing of the passion and finesse of classical rhetoric need be lost, but all is refocused.

The commitment and power of a Demosthenes, the analytic of an Aristotle, the poise and urbanity of a Cicero, and the scope of a Quintilian are indeed, like the jewels of Egypt, placed rhetorically by Augustine in the service of the people of God. The power of the spoken word surges into the world now from pulpit as well as podium; moral as well as political behavior comes under the sway of eloquence, requiring no less rhetorical training than commended by the classic treatises.

The Reformation

We leap a millennium, now, to rhetoric at the Reformation, limiting ourselves largely to the influence of Calvin. And we ask, again, what may the preacher hope to learn from Geneva?

Calvin was schooled according to Quintilian's prescription. He was among the countless thousands subjected to the liberal arts for sculpting goodness upon the soul, and he had been well trained in eloquence to prove the attainment of *humanitas*. Calvin quotes more extensively from Cicero than from any other of the ancients and for a time no doubt joined in the universal effort to emulate him. His first publication, a commentary on Seneca's "De Clementia," was in the classical mode.

But at some time never recorded, Calvin stumbled over a roadblock that Augustine (whom he came to know well-nigh by heart) nimbly leaped. That roadblock set before the youthful humanist (I surmise) two hurdles: (1) Does eloquence evidence the possession of a truly humanizing training? (2) Is the goodness requisite to eloquence attainable via the liberal arts?

Though I know of no textual evidence for my intuition, I suspect that these questions confronted Calvin in some reading of Paul's first Letter to Corinth. There the apostle says, simply, "For Christ sent me not to baptize, but to preach the gospel: not in wisdom of words, lest the cross of Christ should be made void. . . . my speech and my preaching were not in persuasive words of wisdom, but in the demonstration of the spirit and of power: that your faith should not stand in the wisdom of man, but in the power of God" (I Cor. 1:17; 2:4).

The exact time, and nature, of Calvin's "conversion" from nominal Catholicism to "Protestantism" is unknown and has been the subject of much speculation. It came, I think, when he realized that, valuable in many respects as the treatise was, the basic thrust of the *Institutes* of Quintilian misled the soul, and that an *Institutes* (meaning a manual, training course) derived from the Scriptures was required in its place. Goodness is not at the behest of the liberal arts, but waits upon the power of God. Eloquence is not the crowning achievement of a genuinely humanizing education, but may even be at odds with the divine wisdom that alone restores man to humanness. Such conclusions, I suspect, brought about Calvin's "conversion," and set the course of his life.

Calvin's commentary on the passages quoted from I Corinthians indicates how much they troubled him, even after his "conversion." He writes, "Two questions are raised here: 1) Does Paul in this verse (1:17) completely condemn the wisdom of words as something in opposition to Christ? 2) Does he mean that the teaching of the gospel must always be kept distinct from eloquence . . . ?"

Calvin replies: "To the first question I answer that Paul would not be so very unreasonable as to condemn out of hand those arts, which, without any doubt, are splendid gifts of God, gifts which we could call instruments for helping men carry out worthwhile activities. . . . there is no doubt that they have come from the Holy Spirit." Paul is not disparaging eloquence as such, but only its abuse.

Paul, however, does say that wisdom of words voids the cross of Christ, and the second question Calvin has posed is, he says,

> therefore a little more difficult. For Paul says that the cross of Christ is made void, if it is mixed up in any way with the wisdom of words. My answer is that we must pay attention to those to whom Paul was speaking for the ears of the Corinthians were itching with a foolish eagerness for high-sounding words. . . . For the preaching of Christ is bare and simple; therefore it ought not to be obscured by an overlying disguise of words.

On the second passage (I Cor. 2:4) quoted above, Calvin writes, "If the apostle's preaching had been supported by the power of eloquence alone, he could have been overthrown by superior oratory. Further, the truth which relies on brilliance of oratory no one will call genuine. Indeed it can be helped by it, but it ought not to depend on it."

Educated as he was, Calvin never lost his appreciation of the arts of rhetoric and eloquence; he preached sermons of enduring effect and could, when he wished, write powerful and eloquent prose. But St. Paul obliged Calvin to adopt the plain style, characterized by concise and simple language.

The contrast illumined by the comments on Corinthians came into the open when Calvin, having been forced to leave Geneva in 1538, went to Strasbourg. There flourished the famous academy headed by Johann Sturm. "Three men of antiquity were always chosen by Sturm as pre-eminent examples of the eloquent: Aristotle, Cicero, and Hermogenes. . . . In their midst stands Cicero; and Cicero it was whom Sturm, with all those of his generation, appreciated above all, and whose image is his model," so writes Walter Sohm. Sturm insisted, Sohm goes on to say, that eloquence, in the Ciceronian tradition, could rebuild the church. Why? Because, in Sturm's words, "To ideal embellishment, to ideal diction, belongs ideal apprehension. *Res* and *verbum* imply each other." Reality and word are always correlative. This was the conviction of Cicero, of Quintilian, and of the liberal arts tradition after which Sturm had fashioned his academy. Eloquence crowned liberal education *because* expression alone demonstrated impression, and elegant expression proved intimate apprehension. The good man speaking well is not an accidental conjunction— only thus is the attainment of the good by the soul through the arts of education convincingly demonstrated. (In parallel fashion, it may be surmised, Calvin hears another Word saying that faith without works—not faith without education—is dead.)

Calvin appreciated Cicero, but Cicero was never his ideal, neither for himself nor for the products of the Academy of Geneva established by his influence. After his exile, Calvin returned to Geneva with his mind made up, and his *Institutes* developing into a major treatise.

And what, then, has Calvin to teach the active pulpiteer now? First, an overall perspective. The goal of Christianity, for Calvin, is human renovation. In his exchange of letters with Cardinal Sadoleto, written from Strasbourg, Calvin made it clear that concern for the salvation of his own soul is unbecoming the servant of Christ. Salvation is the Lord's business, and He will manage it without hitch. A life lived for the glory of that Lord is the believer's business—and to facilitate his so doing is the work of the church and the aim of the pulpit.

Second, Calvin quite agrees that words are key to influencing the soul. At issue between Geneva and the classical tradition is simply "which words," or better "whose words?"

Third, the good that bears fruit in obedience is not conveyed via the liberal arts, useful as they are to those whose duty it is to proclaim the Word of God. God has ordained that a saving faith, with the life of obedience to which it leads, comes to man through preaching.

Fourth, the preacher performs under twin disciplines: (1) the discipline of his congregation's needs governs his work in the study; and (2) the discipline of strictest obedience to the text governs his proclamation from the pulpit.

Fifth, soteriology has to do with the believer's liberation from the burden of inherited and daily acquired guilt. In Christ, the

Christian is, like Israel, freed from the bondage of Egypt and called to the life of obedience, as taught in the church.

Sixth, the presence of good in the soul is not demonstrable through eloquence, but only by the life of love—as defined by the Scriptures, and summarized in the divine law.

Seventh, the soul, or self, is sculpted into the lineaments of a lost *humanitas* through acts of willed obedience to the proclamation of God's Word. All that man does is done first of all to himself; through choice, that is, not through what comes in but what goes out of the self, is man sculpted into the self he finally becomes—a "sheep" destined for the "joy" of the Father, or a "goat" destined for eternal alienation from his Creator.

Eighth, Calvin's aim, like Quintilian's, is pedagogy. That is why he chooses Quintilian's title for his own classic work. Calvin is fond of speaking of the church as God's school, of the Bible as God's textbook, and of the ministry as God's pedagogues.

With Calvin, the sermon is finally made its own genre in fact. It is enriched in every way out of the classical resources, which Calvin knew intimately, but the homily is freed from the pagan limitations of the rhetorical tradition. Calvin maintains, however, the tradition of oratorical courage dating far back to that time when Demosthenes threw down the gauntlet before the face of Alexander's emissaries. Calvin writes (*Institutes* 4. 8. 9),

Here, then, is the sovereign power with which the pastors of the Church, by whatever name they be called, ought to be endowed. That is that they may dare boldly to do all things by God's Word; may compel all wordly power, glory, wisdom, and exultation to yield to and obey His majesty; supported by His power, may command all from the highest even to the last; may build up Christ's household and cast down Satan's; may feed the sheep and drive away the wolves; may instruct and exhort the teachable; may accuse, rebuke, and subdue the rebellious and stubborn; may bind and loose; finally, if need be, may launch thunderbolts; but do things in God's Word.

The three styles of Cicero have been given Christian baptism. The passion for freedom out of which rhetoric was formed was, by the Calvinists whose pulpits preached according to this prescription, to challenge tyrants in France, the Netherlands, and England—and would set in motion the forces that formed "a more perfect union" on the shores of New England.

Bibliographic Essay

In lieu of disfiguring the text with footnote references, let me suggest some titles that I have found useful in coming to the views discussed above—grouping them roughly in the order of topics discussed.

Linguistics

The names suggested—Rosenstock-Huessy, et al.—are but a tiny fraction of those who have written on the nature of language in this century. There are guides, handbooks, selections.

Eugen Rosenstock-Huessy (who hyphenated his wife's maiden name to his own) lived long enough to see himself the patron of a small but devoted band of disciples who have created an American publishing firm to spread his views. His *Speech and Reality* (Norwich, Vt.: Argo Books, 1970) is a collection of essays expositing Rosenstock's view of language as "the cross of reality," in one of two forms: I/He: :We/Thou, or Inside/Outside: :Past/Future. A longer volume dealing with broader themes, but oriented to the foundational role of the word in history is *Out of Revolution, Autobiography of Western Man*. The reading is not popular, but insightful and stimulating.

Martin Heidegger, the German philosopher whose views so much influenced Rudolf Bultmann, deals with language in his major opus, *Being and Time* (trans. John Macquarrie and Edward Robinson, New York: Harper and Row, 1962), but the density of Heidegger's thought and wording are discouraging. More readable are his *On the Way to Language* (trans. Peter Hertz, New York: Harper and Row, 1971) and his *Poetry, Language, and Thought* (trans. Albert Hofstadter, New York: Harper and Row, 1971).

Franz Rosenzweig, whose promising career was tragically abbreviated by a neural ailment, wrote his major work in the trenches of World War I on bits and scraps of paper; it is *The Star of Redemption* (trans. William Hallo, Boston: Beacon, 1972), a critique of Hegel from the point of view of a Judaic existentialism; language is discussed in this context. Essays and reviews arising out of his collaboration with Martin Buber in translating the Old Testament into German deal more directly with linguistics. Nahum Glatzer has given a highly readable appreciation of the man and his work, *Franz Rosenzweig, His Life and Thought* (New York: Schocken, 1972). An interesting exchange of letters between Rosenzweig (who declined to go over from Judaism into Christianity) and Rosenstock-Huessy (who did) appears in *Judaism Despite Christianity* (New York: Schocken, 1971). "Where," Rosenzweig asks, "should I who never left the Father's house, choose to go?"

Martin Buber popularized his approach to human relations with his distinction between treating the other as a "Thou" and thus enriching yourself, or treating the other as an "It" and thus making yourself a thing. Out of this philosophical perspective Buber developed his own views of the role of language. Among his many books probably *Between Man and Man* deals most explicitly with words (trans. R. Gregor Smith, Boston: Beacon, 1955). Maurice Friedman draws together Buber's views in his *Martin Buber the Life of Dialogue* (New York: Harper and Row, 1960).

Jean Paul Sartre's views are most systematically expounded in his *Being and Nothingness* (trans. Hazel Barnes, New York: Philosophical Library, 1965), but the complexity of this treatise sends one to his fiction for his view of language as "engagement," both with others and the world. His *Existentialism and Humanism* most succinctly exposits his philosophy (trans. Philip Mairet, London: Methuen, 1948).

H. R. Müller-Schwefe surveys the theories of Heidegger, Buber, and Sartre, from the perspective of homiletics, and as prolegomena to his own view of language in his *Die Sprache und das Wort*

(Hamburg: Furche, 1961). The contrast suggested, of course, is that between the speech of man, however perceived, and the Word of God.

Greek Rhetoric

The period under survey here is nowhere better illumined than in Werner Jaeger's three volume *Paideia: The Ideals of Greek Culture* (trans. Gilbert Highet, New York: Oxford, 1939-44). Erudite and yet popular, in it Jaeger brings to life the tensions, aspirations, and teachings and teachers of the flowering of that civilization.

Handbooks to Plato abound. The Platonic dialogues of interest here are his "Gorgias," named after the famous Sophist, whose views Plato rejects; and the "Phaedrus," where he takes a more favorable view of rhetoric. Professor Richard M. Weaver, whose *Ideas Have Consequences* created some stir in its time, has a penetrating analysis of the "Phaedrus" in his *The Ethics of Rhetoric* (Chicago: Regenery, 1953).

Translations of Aristotle's *Rhetoric* appear in various editions: the one I've liked best is by Lane Cooper (New York: Appleton-Century, 1933), perhaps because he intersperses the text with illuminating comments something on the order of William Barclay's handling of biblical terms.

The speeches of Demosthenes have found translators in the last century, but are not common. Without some knowledge of the background and of Demosthenes' long, losing battle to stimulate Athenians' appreciation of their political liberties, the "Orations on the Crown" lose some of their impressiveness. Here Jaeger is helpful, as are introductions to various editions. It is recorded that, after losing the vote of the "judges" on that memorable afternoon, and thus being forced to leave Athens, Aeschines went to Rhodes to teach dramatics (his craft) and rhetoric. He would, it is said, repeat sometimes both his and Demosthenes' speeches, and in response to the enthusiastic applause of his students would say, half musing, "Ah, but if only you could have heard the wild beast himself!" Indeed, if *only* we could!

Roman Rhetoric

Cicero's three essays on the theories that underlay his exceptional oratorial attainments are entitled, "De Oratore," "Orator," and "Brutus, Or Remarks on Eminent Orators." The second is not, though it may so appear, an Englishing of the first. Far more than Demosthenes, Cicero looms over the next fifteen centuries as the ideal combination of polished gentleman, man of action, savant, and one inimitably capable of demonstrating the range of his attainments through rhetorical power. To speak like Cicero, to write like Cicero, to be the politician and lawyer Cicero was were goals that inspired countless youths—and their teachers. It is charged, naturally, that Cicero's defect was the lack of a philosophical view of his own—a charge best left for the reader willing to come as deliberately ingenuous to judge for himself.

Quintilian's *Institutes* are available, as are all the classical texts mentioned, in the Loeb Classical Library. Other editions, and selections, have appeared, but not often. Over a couple of decades as college speech teacher, persuaded that the essence of rhetorical theory is to be found in Aristotle, Cicero, and Quintilian, I suggested without result to various textbook publishers that a compilation be made of selections from these writers for use as introductory speech text. Unfortunately, the pale copies of the classical ideas that constitute the pith of modern speech books sell!

Not quite what I had in view, but a useful substitute is Lester Thonsson's *Selected Readings in Rhetoric and Public Speaking* (New York: Wilson, 1942). The volume excerpts writers from the Greeks to the comparatively modern and provides the reader with very valuable material. Thonsson teamed with A. C. Baird to produce a survey of the history of rhetorical theory, published as *Speech Criticism* (New York: Ronald, 1948), and Lane Cooper does much the same in his *The Art of the Writer* (Ithaca, N.Y.: Cornell, 1952).

Augustine

His *On Christian Doctrine* appears in paperback, and is contained in the volume devoted to his works in the University of Chicago's Great Books of the Western World.

George Kennedy's *Classical Rhetoric, and Its Christian and Secular Tradition from Ancient to Modern Times* (Chapel Hill, N.C.: University Press, 1980) is hardly scintillating, but does provide very useful information on the period covered, and contains a summary of Augustine's essay. It is not always evident, at least to me, that Professor Kennedy's labored summaries catch either the focal point or the enduring usefulness of the writing he has in hand, but the learning is there, though the fire seems lacking.

Calvin

Speculation as to the time and nature of Calvin's "conversion" is assembled by two writers who come to differing conclusions themselves as to what happened.

Jacques Pannier's *Recherches sur l'evolution religieuse de Calvin jusqu'a sa conversion* (Strasbourg: Astria, 1924) leads him to conclude that Calvin's transposition from nominal Catholic to stalwart Protestant occurred like Paul's dramatic change en route to Damascus.

Paul Sprenger's *Das Rätsel um die Bekehrung Calvins*, however, argues that the process was long and undramatic (Neukirchen: Erziehungsverein, 1959). Nothing of great importance is at stake, but Calvin's own reticence about himself has stoked the flames of curiosity.

No writer with whom I am acquainted propounds the theory, which appeals to me, that Calvin's encounter with St. Paul's depreciation of rhetoric obliged him to rethink all the effort he had so far made to fashion of himself a "good man, speaking," and that this confrontation called into question, at the same time, the

Catholicism in which he had been raised at home. The late Ford Lewis Battles, Calvin expert, with whom I occasionally discussed my theory always demurred with, "show me a text!" (Scholars are like that.)

Calvin never repudiated his broad and intensive educational background. In this, as in much else, he differed from Luther whose diatribes against the "whore" Reason are carefully discussed in B. A. Garrish's *Grace and Reason, A Study in the Theology of Luther* (Oxford: Clarendon, 1962).

Walter Sohm's study of the tensions between Calvin and the liberal arts tradition as that tradition was represented by Johann Sturm is entitled *Die Schule Johann Sturms und die Kirche Strassburgs* (Munich: Oldenburg, 1912). The quotation in the text above is from page 35. The issue appears also in slightly different form in the Renaissance humanists' controversy over the priority of rhetoric or philosophy—a clash stemming, of course, from Plato. Jerrold Seigel discussed that conflict in his *Rhetoric and Philosophy in Renaissance Humanism* (Princeton, N.J.: Princeton University Press, 1968). Calvin's own relations with the humanists of his time are detailed by Josef Bohatec in his *Bude und Calvin* (Graz: Bohlaus, 1950). At issue, of course, is the whole nature of man, of virtue, and of the means for humanizing the self.

Francis Hotman's *The Style of John Calvin* draws primarily, and by design, from "The French Polemical Treatises" (New York: Oxford, 1967). But he provides very useful insights into Calvin's attitude toward rhetoric.

Calvin and Calvinism as a revolutionary force is vividly delineated by Michael Walzer in his *Revolution of the Saints* (Cambridge, Mass.: Harvard, 1968), which studies in detail Cromwell's revolt in England, but deals also with the revolutionary dynamic in Calvin. The Calvinist "cleric insisted that political activity was a creative endeavor in which the saints were privileged as well as obliged to participate. The saints are responsible for their world—as medieval men were not—and responsible above all for its continual reformation," Walzer writes. "Luther in his old age," Walzer adds, "was a provincial figure and a political con-

servative. . . . Calvin in his last years was an international figure
and, some would have said, the inexhaustible source of sedition
and rebellion." And the source of that "source" was always the
Calvinist pulpit, the preacher leaning over the open Bible and
expounding it with rhetorical intensity. What this meant for the
pulpits of colonial New England, and for the American Revolution, can be learned from the various works of Perry Miller and
Alan Heimert.

12

Application
John F. Bettler

There is a bakery shop in our town that advertises, "Cakes for Any Occasion." Among the mouth-watering piles of fresh donuts, croissants, turnovers, and tarts, whose ambrosial aromas weaken the resolve of the most dedicated dieter, one will also see an array of decorated cakes. Rainbow colors for birthdays, silver tones for graduations or anniversaries, muted styles for first communions and frosted outlines of Darth Vader, Spider Man, and dozens of others confront the buyer with almost no end of choices and deliver on the promise ". . . for any occasion."

But I have long suspected that the choices lay only on the surface, that below each frosted decoration you would find the same cake. More appropriately the advertising should read: "Cakes Decorated for Any Occasion." Frosting and decorating are not cake baking. They make cakes more appetizing, but they are not essential to cakes.

I'm afraid many preachers have the same approach to sermon application. They think that application is an important—indeed crucial—element in sermon construction and preaching. It is a skill to be developed if a sermon is to be complete, have punch, and prove relevant. So they make a few "here's-what-it-means-to-you" remarks in their conclusions. Or, as the old Puritans, they structure an entire section of their sermon called "uses of the text." Or worse, they reduce application to topical sermon titles, preaching from Proverbs 31 on Mother's Day or Daniel's resolve on New Year's Sunday. But they do not see application as the essence of preaching.

And that is their mistake. For *preaching is application* (or, as Geoffrey Thomas argues a bit later in this volume, biblical preaching is *applicatory preaching*). Application, no matter how skillfully structured or helpfully delivered must never be viewed as an "add-on." It is not a skill to be developed merely as part of a good preaching repertoire. It is not the frosting. It is rather the cake.

Preaching Is Application

Preaching is driving home the Word of the living God to the lives of His people. It is declaring "Thus says the Lord" to people who constantly hear other claims for allegiance and direction. It is, as Samuel Logan has reminded us earlier, bringing the people of God under the authority of God. Preaching is concerned with life. Until the preacher has that vision, sees his task in that light, and structures his sermons by that rule, he is not preaching.

Consider this common definition of application: "After truth has been explained and the facts of that truth are argued, *there remains* the application of that truth. . . . The application then, is *that part* of the sermon which brings the truths of the Word to the listener on a personal basis. It is *the time* when the congregation stops hearing the challenges confronting Moses, Daniel, Luke or Paul and begins to see that these challenges face them as well"[1] (emphasis mine). There are no doubt helpful points in this definition, but note the emphasis. Application is seen as an element that is substantially ("that part") and temporally ("the time") distinct from other aspects of the sermon. Is there really a place for "truth" that does not apply to the listeners? Does "the truth" of God's Word ever stand in abstraction—a brute chunk of fact that is fascinating to study, but removed from the lives of the listeners? Does the preacher *make* God's truth relevant? No! God's truth is relevant; to declare it is to apply it. A preacher would no more look at preaching apart from application than a surgeon would look at cutting apart from healing.

1. Woodrow Michael Kroll, *Prescription for Preaching*, (Grand Rapids: Baker Book House, 1980), p. 176.

John A. Broadus gives a more satisfying definition:

> The application in a sermon is not merely an appendage to the discussion or a subordinate part of it, but *is the main thing to be done.* Spurgeon says, "Where the application begins, there the sermon begins." We are not to speak before the people but *to them* and must earnestly strive to make them take to themselves what we say. Daniel Webster once said and repeated it with emphasis, "When a man preaches to me, I want him to make it a personal matter, a personal matter, a personal matter!"[2] (emphasis mine)

Broadus is simply saying that preaching is application. Preaching *is not* speaking *about* truth *before* the congregation, but rather *speaking truth to the congregation.*

Jay Adams describes this as the difference between a *preaching stance* and a *lecture stance.*

> Preaching that stops short of asking for change that is appropriate to the Holy Spirit's letters to His Church is not preaching at all; at best it is lecturing. The lecturer speaks *about the Bible;* the pastoral preacher speaks *from* the Bible *about* the congregation. He tells them what God wants from them.[3]

The preacher, then, more effectively applies the Word of God by developing the proper attitude toward the task of preaching rather than by learning a few practical skills or helpful hints for better application.

The purpose of this chapter is to develop that attitude by suggesting how the minister might structure his sermons in an applicatory style (or "stance," if you prefer). I would like to emphasize that the entire enterprise, from picking a text to post-sermon discussions, must be understood as *application.*

2. John A. Broadus, *On the Preparation and Delivery of Sermons,* (New York: Harper and Row, 1944), p. 210.

3. Jay E. Adams, *Preaching With Purpose,* (Phillipsburg, N.J.: Presbyterian and Reformed, 1982), p. 43.

The Purpose of Scripture

In Romans 15:4 Paul says,

> For whatever was written in earlier times was written for our instruction, that through perseverance and the encouragement of the Scriptures we might have hope.

Paul refers to the Old Testament Scripture when he says "whatever was written in earlier times." Note that he doesn't say that it was written to be studied as interesting fact; it doesn't stand in isolation ready to be scrutinized and dissected as a thing all to itself. No! It was written for a purpose. What is that purpose? Our instruction. It was written for us. It was written to us to produce in us endurance and encouragement (especially in those times when our brothers in Christ are so hard to get along with; cf. the context of Rom. 14:1–15:6). The Word of God cannot be preached apart from its intended purpose. It is for us. To declare it is to apply it.[4]

Paul also touches on the purposes of Scripture in II Timothy 3:16, 17:

> All Scripture is inspired by God and profitable for teaching, for reproof, for correction, for training in righteousness; that the man of God may be adequate, equipped for every good work.

The fourfold profit of Scripture has been frequently detailed and need not be repeated here. Simply note that Scripture is profitable for life. It shows us what God requires of us, convicts us when we fall short, gets us on the right path again, and disciplines or trains us for righteous living. Through the use of Scripture the man of God (the pastor) is equipped. Equipped for what? The work of ministry. He is ready for any challenge as he ministers to the needs of God's congregation.

4. Cf. other passages that make much the same point: I Cor. 9:8–10; 10:6, 11; Rom. 4:23, 24.

Again we see that the Bible is about life. It is God's manual to show His people how to live. All of its teachings are *for* living. It is application.[5] Scripture grew out of real life situations. When Paul wrote about justification by faith in Galatians, he had in mind real people who were polluting their salvation with attempts at righteousness. The great christological passage in Philippians grew out of a concern about warring women, Euodia and Syntyche, who needed "the mind of Christ" to work out their salvation. Instruction about the second coming was aimed at confused and frightened readers, some of whom had quit their jobs out of ignorance about Christ's return. You see, the Scripture grew out of real life situations. God's Word explains God's redemptive acts among His people. To preach it is to know these real life situations as they exist today in your hearers.

The Example of Scripture

A quick glance at examples of biblical sermons reveals their life-challenging structure. Peter's sermon on the Day of Pentecost (Acts 2:22–42) was designed to produce change in the hearers. He begins with a preacher's stance ("Men of Israel, listen to these words," v. 22), declares Christ to them (". . . a man attested to *you* . . . ," v. 22), addresses his audience throughout (note use of second person in vv. 22, 23, 29, 33, 36), shares how Old Testament Scripture applied to his audience (vv. 25–28; 34–35), and calls them to action (vv. 38, 39). It is also important to note how his audience responded with the question that all good preaching should produce: "What shall we do?" (v. 37).

The pointed application of biblical preaching is also seen in the ministry of John the Baptist (Luke 3:3–14). He preaches repentance (v. 3), addressing his hearers personally ("you brood of vipers . . . bring forth fruits . . ." vv. 7, 8) and gives clear instruction *how* to do it (vv. 10–14). Perhaps the greatest example of how-to preaching is our Lord's ministry, particularly the Sermon

5. Cf. also II Pet. 1:3. In Christ we have been granted "everything pertaining *to life* and godliness."

on the Mount (Matt. 5–7). Note again the use of the second person (5:11, 12, 13, 14, 16, 18, 20, 21; 6:1, 2, 3, 4, 19, 20; 7:1, 2, etc.), the crisp commands ("Beware," 6:1; "Do not," 6:2; "Pray . . . in secret," 6:6; "Do not be anxious . . .," 6:35; etc.), and the marked "how to" emphasis (e.g., "When you pray . . . pray *this* way . . . ," 6:6, 9ff.). We will say more about the importance of concrete application later; but for now note that Christ's preaching not only called for life change, but clearly showed *how* it should come about.

Preaching as application affects every aspect of sermon construction and delivery. When one chooses a preaching portion, he will be sensitive to the existential situation out of which that passage arose and how it relates to his hearers today. As he studies he will keep real people in mind and imagine their response to the main ideas of the text. His language will be simple and concrete, not abstract. His points will be introduced with sentences not titles. His illustrations will grow out of his personal life and out of the lives of his people (maintaining confidentiality, of course).

It is impossible to comment on all of these aspects of preaching. My focus will be on the mechanics of sermon construction and outlining. I believe if the preacher can master a few basic strategies, his entire preaching structure will be practical and pointed. And out of that structure more personal and concrete application will emerge.

How to Put a "How to" Sermon Together

Here is an outline of the steps I follow when constructing a sermon. I will sketch it first and then flesh it out with more detail given to those areas directly impinging on application.

Initial Steps

1. Define the preaching portion
2. Ask, Why did the Holy Spirit put this text here?

3. Write a personalized proposition: a declarative sentence using the second person pronoun
4. Ask a single question of your proposition: Why? How? When? What? Where?
5. Answer the question (answers emerging from the text form the main points of your outline)

Intermediate Steps

1. Study lexical aids, commentaries, original sources, etc. Have I correctly understood the passage?
2. Flesh out sermon with biblical, theological, illustrative, practical content

Final Steps (for me, literal "steps")

1. "Live with" sermon
2. Personalize to my audience

Initial Steps

I do all my initial work in the English Bible, relying on a good translation like the NASB or NIV. There are two reasons for this departure from the seminary dictum, "Always use the original sources." First, I am not fluent in Greek or Hebrew. I know enough to stumble through and to utilize the lexical aids, but not to read fluently and to gain an appreciation for the *flow* of the text. My Greek chops up the text, breaking it into phrases, words, or parts of words that subtly change the meaning. In this initial stage of sermon construction this piecemeal study is not what I want. I must gain an appreciation for the *whole* of the text, reading paragraphs before and after my preaching portion. For most preachers that can only be achieved in a language that is their own.

Second, the initial work of the sermon should be my work, stimulate my thinking, and generate my ideas. This is my sermon; I have to live with it before the congregation does. So, I stay away from the input of others, i.e., lexical aids and commentaries.

There is a crucial place for these later. But not when giving birth to a sermon.[6]

1. Define the preaching portion. This will not be developed fully here. Simply note that a preaching portion is a portion of Scripture that contains a single idea or purpose. A preaching portion could be a single book (e.g., Jude, whose purpose is to motivate his readers to "contend for the faith") even though it may also contain several *sub*-purposes; or a single verse or part of a verse (e.g., Matt. 6:31, "Seek first His kingdom,") even though it is a sub-unit of a broader purpose (e.g., Matt. 6:31 is subordinate to 6:25-34 ["anxiety"], which is part of 6:19-34 ["laying up right treasures"], which is subordinate to 5:1-7:29 ["charter of Christian conduct"]).[7]

A preaching portion cannot be a single word or phrase that does not contain a single thought or purpose. For example, "Jesus wept" is not a preaching portion. The word "so" in John 3:16 is not a preaching portion even though it might make a suitable springboard for a series of sermons on the magnitude of God's love.

2. Ask, Why did the Holy Spirit put this text here?[8] This automatically flows out of choosing the text. What is the Holy Spirit's purpose? Is He correcting error in thinking (e.g., "I would not have you ignorant brethren," I Thess. 4:13ff.)? Is He convincing us of something that we must know or believe (e.g., "But these are written that you might believe . . . ," John 20:31)? Is He

6. I recognize that serious ongoing study of Scripture apart from sermon sources will stimulate sermon ideas. Here I am talking about sermon construction as a thing in itself.

7. For more on selecting a preaching portion see Adams, *Preaching With Purpose*, pp. 21ff. who stresses purpose as the determining factor, and Haddon Robinson, *Biblical Preaching*, (Grand Rapids: Baker Book House, 1980), pp. 53ff. who stresses the single "thought" of a passage. Adams's approach is more in line with the emphasis on preaching as application. Robinson, though helpful, could more easily lead to a lecture stance. A thought or idea can be studied as an end in itself. A purpose is aimed at change, whether in action, thought or belief.

8. Adams and Robinson are again useful. Adams refers to the *telos* or end of a text, Robinson to the "big idea." Again, Adams is more dynamic and Robinson static, but both are helpful.

commanding an action that we must take (e.g., "Earnestly contend for the faith," Jude 3) in the form of particular exigencies?

It is absolutely critical to determine the purpose of a text if I
am not going to pervert it and compromise the integrity of Scripture. The text is not a resource for my ideas. Without knowing
the purpose or intent of a text my sermon becomes the word of
the preacher, not the Word of God! This cannot be overstated.
The authority of preaching is at stake. The purpose must be that
of the Holy Spirit. The goal must be His. The change or response
I desire in my audience must be the change He wants from His
readers. This is, therefore, the most critical point of applicatory
preaching. The application must be that of the text. It must be
aimed at the change the Holy Spirit intended. If I do not know
the purposes of a text, I cannot apply it.

For example, how many "doctrinal" sermons have you heard
on Philippians 2:5-11, the great christological or *kenosis* passage.
The passage is famous not only because it is a rich description of
Christ's humiliation, but also because it is a favorite text of
"teaching" preachers. But how many times have you heard a
preacher talk about this text as an encouragement to unity
through service to one another in the church? The point is, the
purpose of this text is not to inform us of Christ's humiliation
(even though it does that quite nicely), but rather to uphold
Christ as an example of the kind of servant attitude we ought to
have ("let each of you regard one another as more important than
himself . . . ," v. 3) and an encouragement to "work out your own
salvation" (v. 12), probably a reference to *working out of* the
church the disputings (cf. v. 14; 4:2) that had disrupted unity.

How can I apply verses 5-11 if I do not know their purpose? I
can't. Nor can I readily assume I already know their purpose.
Hard work is necessary to examine thoroughly the whole context
of preaching portions.[9] No portion of Scripture dropped into the
Bible in abstraction, complete and unrelated to a live, historical
situation. I must discern that context and then determine its purpose.

9. Adams's suggestion of "telic clues" is especially helpful, *Preaching With
Purpose*, pp. 27ff.

3. *Write a personalized proposition: a declarative sentence using the second person pronoun.* This is an important transitional step in applicatory preaching. A proposition is, simply put, the purpose of the text in sentence form. For example, "The Holy Spirit is informing Christians about the second coming" (I Thess 4:15). Or, "The Holy Spirit is encouraging unity through service" (Phil. 2:1–11). There is nothing new here. Homileticians have been talking about propositions for years.[10] But these are not *personalized* propositions.

I'm suggesting two changes to make ordinary propositions personalized: Make the proposition a sentence, not a title or heading. And make the proposition personal by including a second person pronoun. Both changes will push toward more effective application. Again, for example, "The Holy Spirit wants you to serve one another as Christ served His church" (Phil. 2:1–11). Or, "The Holy Spirit wants you to be informed of Christ's second coming" (I Thess. 4:13). Notice how both automatically involve the audience; both are immediately applicatory. The second coming isn't put "out there" as a subject merely to be studied. Unity isn't a concept for Christians merely to consider. Titles or theme statements lead to such abstractions. But personalized, declarative sentences immediately get the audience caught up in the purpose of the Holy Spirit in that text. Even if I never say another practical thing in the sermon, I have already made application. God is speaking to my listeners in the text. They have been served notice what the Holy Spirit expects of them.[11]

10. Broadus, *Preparation and Delivery of Sermons,* pp. 53ff. remains one of the best treatments of the proposition.

11. It is not within the purview of this chapter to fully develop my concept of the personalized proposition. But I want to offer a few qualifications. The personalized proposition need not always be stated in the introduction of every sermon. I'm here discussing the initial stages of sermon construction, which demand an immediate shaping of the personalized proposition. In the *finished* sermon the proposition may be stated in a number of ways and in a number of places (cf. Matt. 24:32–44 where the personalized proposition is the conclusion of the sermon; cf. John 6:68 where the personalized proposition would best be stated as a question, i.e., "To whom will you go?").

I've noticed that young preachers have a hard time saying "you" to their congregations. We have already seen that preachers in the Bible had no such problem (cf. Acts 2:22, 23, 29, 33, 36). But the problem persists, especially among student preachers and recent seminary graduates. I encourage them to freely interchange "we" or "us" for "you." "We" and "us" are still personal (as opposed to "it" or "them"), and they involve the preacher in the needs of his congregation. They help him avoid preaching "down to" the congregation. But the use of "you" must never be abandoned completely.

4. Ask a single question of your proposition: Why? How? When? What? Where? Here we have the transition from the personalized proposition to the body of the sermon. It is simple and direct. I ask one of the basic five questions: How? What? When? Where? or Why?[12] *I don't ask all of them of a single text*, just one. Which one? The one the text deals with. For example, in I Thessalonians 4:13 the question to ask is What? The Holy Spirit doesn't want us to be ignorant. It follows then to ask what He wants us to know. In Ephesians 5:25-30 the proposition is "Husbands, you must love your wives." The question to ask is How? since Paul is obviously drawing an analogy between Christ's love and a husband's love.

At times a text is rich enough to deal with many questions, at which time a series of sermons might be indicated. But generally an informative text answers What? When? Where?; a persuasive text answers Why?; and a motivation text answers How? This is not a hard and fast rule, but a helpful guide.

5. Answer the question (answers emerging from the text form the main points of your outline). The text provides the answers

12. I must own my indebtedness to Lloyd Perry whose concept of the "key word" stimulated my thinking about transitional questions. I read his book *Variety in Your Preaching*, (Old Tappan, N.J.: Fleming Revell, 1954) almost twenty years ago. Upon rereading it recently I was amazed to discover how differently I have developed the concept from Perry. But the germ of the idea came from him, and I want to acknowledge my indebtedness. A newer book by Perry is his *Biblical Sermon Guide*, (Grand Rapids: Baker Book House, 1970).

to your transition question. When I write them out, I have in front of me my basic outline. Perhaps the best way to illustrate this is to present some examples of the entire initial-step process:

Text: Ephesians 5:25-30

Personalized Proposition: "Husbands, you must love your wives as Christ loved the church."

Transitional Question: How?

Answers: 1. You Must Love Her Sacrificially ("gave up Himself").
2. You Must Love Her Constructively ("removing spots and wrinkles").
3. You Must Love Her Constantly ("as your own flesh").

Text: I Peter 1:3

Personalized Proposition: "God has given you a living hope."

Transitional Question: Why (is this a living, not dead, hope)?

Answers: Your hope is alive because
1. It Flows From the Mercies of God.
2. It Comes Through the Resurrection of Christ From the Dead.
3. You Are Born Into This Hope by the Holy Spirit.

Text: Matthew 6:25-34

Personalized Proposition: God wants you to stop worrying.

Transitional Question: How?

Answers: 1. Recognize Worry as Sin (vv. 25, 31, 34).
2. Remind Yourself of God's Providence (vv. 26-30).
3. Redirect Your Energies Toward Seeking His Kingdom (vv. 33-34).

Text: I Thessalonians 4:13–18

Personalized Proposition: You must be informed about Christ's second coming.

Transitional Question: What (must you know)?

Answers: 1. Christ Will Return (vv. 14, 16).
2. Christ Will Return With Those Who Have Died (vv. 14, 16).
3. Christ Will Return for Those Who Remain (vv. 15, 17).

Please note that I state the main points as full sentences, not titles that stand alone. This not only continues the personalized or preaching stance, but also forces me to restate my proposition or purpose each time I announce a new point. It helps keep everything tightly structured and avoids tangents that distract from the one point of the sermon.

It must also be stated that this is a *working tool* for sermon construction. The finished sermon need not show the tool or structure. Indeed there are some texts (e.g., wisdom literature and narratives) to which this model is very difficult to apply directly (although not impossible). But as a tool for the initial stages of sermon construction it crystallizes my thinking, gives my sermon direction, keeps together a workable structure, and forces me to think in terms of application. With this structure my sermons must apply the text, even apart from the concrete application we will discuss next.

Intermediate Steps

The initial steps of sermon preparation do not take long (perhaps an hour or two) once the preacher has some experience with the demands of preaching twice or three times weekly. He will begin to "think sermonically" or cast studies into a sermonic mold almost automatically.

The intermediate steps will not take much longer (unless of course, you are dealing with an especially difficult text, but that is rare). After I have done my initial work in the English Bible I begin working with the original language, make use of lexical aids, and consult "the experts," i.e., those commentaries I have come to trust. Good commentaries alert me to textual or linguistic problems with a text and point out subtle nuances I may have missed in my initial work with the English. All of this will confirm or cause me to rethink and possibly restructure my initial work.

Now I begin to flesh out my ideas with biblical, theological, illustrative, and practical content. Again, it is not my purpose to develop each of these. Nor will it be possible to comment on the "final stages" of sermon preparation. Application is the concern of this chapter, and I will concentrate on some additional methods of developing practical material in the sermon.

Preaching Is Concrete Application

We have seen that preaching is application. But it must also be noted that preaching is *concrete* application. That is, it not only tells the hearer what to do, but also how to do it. Preaching moves from the general to the particular to the concrete. Like a funnel the focus of the sermon moves downward to a central narrow point. Picture it like this:

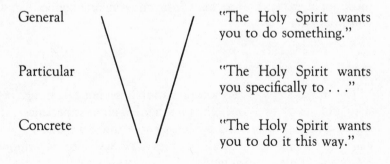

General
"The Holy Spirit wants you to do something."

Particular
"The Holy Spirit wants you specifically to . . ."

Concrete
"The Holy Spirit wants you to do it this way."

Observe how Jesus' preaching moved in this direction in Matthew 6:5–16:

General	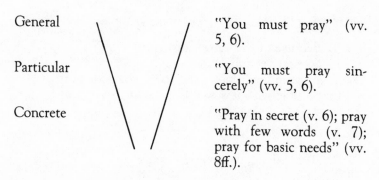	"You must pray" (vv. 5, 6).
Particular		"You must pray sincerely" (vv. 5, 6).
Concrete		"Pray in secret (v. 6); pray with few words (v. 7); pray for basic needs" (vv. 8ff.).

The personalized proposition for this sermon would be, "You must pray sincerely." The transitional question could be "Why?" or "How?"

If "Why?" is my *particular* concern, the sermon structure would look like this:

"You Must Pray Sincerely."

"Why?"

1. Because of the danger of hypocrisy (pleasing men) (v. 5).
2. Because God knows the secrets of your heart (v. 6).

With this structure the concrete or "How to" application could occur under both points, be divided between both points, or be put in the conclusion.

For example:

"You Must Pray Sincerely."

"Why?"

1. Because of the danger of hypocrisy.
   So pray (1) secretly, (2) with few words, (3) for basic needs.
2. Because God knows the secrets of my heart.
   So pray (1) secretly, (2) with few words, (3) for basic needs.

Or,

"You Must Pray Sincerely."

"Why?"

1. Because of the danger of hypocrisy.
   So pray secretly.
2. Because God knows the secrets of your heart.
   So pray with few words; pray for basic needs.

Or,

"You Must Pray Sincerely."

"Why?"

1. Because of the danger of hypocrisy.
2. Because God knows the secrets of your heart.
Conclusion: So pray secretly with few words for basic needs.

Perhaps "How?" is my basic concern. Then the structure is simpler.

"You Must Pray Sincerely."

"How?"

1. By finding a secret place.
2. By using a few words.
3. By sticking to basic needs.

It is obvious that the focus becomes more and more concrete or practical with these structures. Yet we have remained only with what the text provides. What happens when the text doesn't offer such solid suggestions? The preacher must still strive to tell his listeners how to put the text into practice. To be sure, his suggestions will not carry the weight of scriptural authority, but good preaching, modeled in Scripture, demands that they be made.

For example, Peter says that husbands must live with their wives "according to knowledge" (I Pet. 3:7). Husbands must know their wives. The thrust of the text tells *why* they should, but a good preacher will also make suggestions how to do it. He could say, "Why not get a notebook and each day record in it the interesting things you observed about your wife. At the end of a week review it and make some tentative conclusions. Make an appointment with your wife to discuss them." That's "how to" application. The husbands in the audience may use the idea or reject it. But they have at least been stimulated to think about ways of putting the Scripture into practice.[13] Personalized, concrete, "rubber-meets-the-road" application is a difficult skill to master. We want our application to be pointed enough to have punch, but not so pointed that confidentiality is betrayed or personal embarrassment results. But good preachers have mastered the art.[14] You can too. Here are some suggestions that will get you on the way.

Preach in a Pastoral Context

Good preachers know and maintain contact with their people. Good preachers are pastors, counselors, encouragers. They know and work with people, close enough to appreciate their doubts, fears, hurts, and joys. A good preacher must be a people person. Remember, he is not handling ideas or themes (as does a lecturer), but the life-changing Word of God. He must, therefore, know the lives that need changing.

Paul was a preacher. He reminded the Ephesian elders that for over three years he "did not shrink from declaring to you [note personal pronoun] the whole purpose of God" (Acts 20:27). But this was no raised pulpit oratory. Paul was intimately involved with his congregation. He "did not cease to admonish [counsel] each one with tears" (v. 31). His preaching occurred in the context of pastoral ministry. Vitality, immediacy, earnestness are watered and nourished only in the garden of pastoral contact.

Imagine the difference between preaching on the "Blessed Hope" of Christ's return because it occurred in a series on I Thessalonians and preaching it the day after you have conducted

13. For a helpful exercise take each of the following texts and write out three "how-to" ways to put it into practice: Phil. 4:8; I Pet. 3:1–6; Rom. 12:10.

14. Take time to listen to or read the sermons of Jay Adams, Chuck Swindoll, or, in a less evangelical mold, Norman Vincent Peale. These men, among others, have learned to preach concretely.

the funeral of a woman in your congregation and spent several hours afterward comforting her husband of forty-five years. What impact does visiting a man who has been institutionalized for severe anxiety have on a sermon about "the peace that passes understanding?" What difference in character would a sermon on the assurance of faith have if preached as a series on the themes of salvation or after months of struggling with a former elder in your church who had abandoned the faith?

It's the difference between knowing something and living something; between reading a book about swimming and jumping into the water. If you want to preach with power (as Geoffrey Thomas exhorts us all to do), then don't be afraid to get your feet wet!

Of course, such dramatic, life-changing illustrations don't often occur the same week the appropriate sermon is to be preached. That's why a preaching schedule ought to be mapped out months or even a year in advance. Then, as the context of pastoral ministry provides fresh insights or ideas, they can be jotted down and filed with the appropriate sermon. But even if such one-for-one experiences do not occur, an ongoing shepherding contact develops people-sensitivity that will enliven and personalize all preaching.

Although I've been away from the pastorate for ten years, my contact with people is maintained through a regular counseling ministry at the Christian Counseling and Educational Foundation. Counselees are raising issues that force me to the Scripture for answers and direction. But I also find that my study of Scripture, an ongoing discipline removed from any "problem" agenda, triggers pictures of people and their life situations that illustrate or concretize a particular verse or section. You see how it works: *people drive me to Scripture and the Scripture drives me to people.* You can't have one without the other.

Use Personal Illustrations

Nothing perks a congregation's attention or concretizes a text better than a personal illustration (as Jay Adams points out in the chapter following this one). Paul made frequent use of his own experiences to illustrate his points in his letters (cf. II Cor. 12:1–10; Phil. 1:12–26; I Thess. 2:1–12). Hosea's marriage became an illustration of God's loving faithfulness. And Jeremiah's time in a pit and buying a field illustrated God's judgment and blessing upon Israel. Surely, if biblical authors made such frequent use of their own life situations in their messages, we should not hesitate to do the same.

Of course, there are dangers. Personal illustrations can be over-done to the point of robbing a sermon of God's authority (the message is the Lord's, not yours), or can degenerate to a true confessions "can-you-top-this" morbidity (remember you want to share God's victories not just trials), and can easily betray a confidence (I always get someone's permission, including my wife's and children's, before I refer to them in an illustration).

But even with those pitfalls we should use our own experiences as illustrations. Why? Because it forces us to filter the text through life and demonstrates to the audience that the text does apply. After all, if the preacher lives it, so must the listener. There are other benefits too: a personal illustration brings us down to the level of our audience, establishes rapport, maintains interest (everyone loves a good story) and forces us to use personal language. But its chief benefit is that it forces concrete application. We become a living example that the Bible is to be lived.

Two days before I was to preach on Romans 12:9 ("Abhor what is evil . . .") I had an experience with my son in which I lost all patience and berated him for an insignificant mistake. It is precisely that kind of evil occurring among brothers in Christ that Paul says we must abhor. Two days later I told the story to the congregation and concluded: "I hate what I did to my son. Do you hate what you do to one another?" No other application was necessary.

13

Sense Appeal and Storytelling
Jay E. Adams

The preacher was droning on about the Amalekites. And although he was only seven minutes into his sermon, all over the congregation heads began to nod, eyelids drooped, children began to squirm, and teenagers started passing notes. Then an amazing thing happened: suddenly, his audience snapped to attention. Young and old alike strained to hear. What had occurred? What was it that so abruptly transformed this apathetic group of parishioners into an alert, interested body? They came to life when they heard these words: "Let me tell you about an experience that I had during the last war. . . ." The preacher had begun to tell a story!

It hardly matters what age one is; so long as he can understand what is said, he will give rapt attention and almost immediate response to a well-told story. Persons with the most diverse interests and backgrounds will perk up when they hear that they are about to be treated to a story. Why is this? What is this near mystic power that a story possesses? What is the appeal of a story? And what are some of the important implications of the story's attention arousing and holding ability for Christian preaching? These, and others growing out of them, are matters that we shall examine in this chapter.

The answers to the questions in the above paragraph are not hard to find; but the implications inherent in those answers are complex. For instance, it is true that *we learn best what we see, touch, or hear* and that, in discursive language, a story comes closest to the very experience of an event. Moreover, a story, well told, can go beyond the actual, omitting much that is irrelevant or that in real life may distract, while focusing on and emphasizing the major factors in the event. And, a story, by adding just those touches of detail and color that are calculated to inspire, entertain, inform, or stimulate a listener, can do what a reporter's abstract account cannot. In short, a good story is the creation (if fiction) or re-creation (if historical) of an event, or series of events, tailored and told in a way best suited to achieve the purpose for which it is related.

Unlike a historical event, the story may be shaped and manipulated, and through it the audience may be led to see in it whatever the storyteller wishes. Therein, of course, lies both its greatest potential and its greatest danger.

Please do not misunderstand; my use of the word *manipulate* here is entirely neutral. I do not want to imply, or wish for the reader to infer, that the narrator does anything wrong when he molds a story to serve his own ends, so long as he does not thereby misrepresent the truth. Among the advantages that the storyteller shares with the artist are the opportunities that their media offer for simplification, focus, and emphasis. The difference between didactic teaching and a story is like the difference between a photograph and a painting.

The flexibility the storyteller possesses becomes an ethical matter, involving the greatest responsibility. He may not use it to bend or twist the facts either to lead others astray or even to convince them of the truth. Paul plainly denounced all such trickery in the cause of truth (I Cor. 2:4, 5; II Cor. 1:12, 13; I Thess. 2:3, 4).

But it is equally true, when the storyteller has made his audience fully aware that he is about to do so, that he may exaggerate, underplay, take the listener on flights of fancy, etc., in order to make a point. The story is his to do with as he pleases—so long as he does not misrepresent what he is doing, and he uses the story in a way that may be judged moral by the most rigorous use of biblical standards.

Well-told stories also delight because, by them, one may so readily convey suspense, emotion, and surprise. The proper use of pause, inflection, voice, tone, quality, volume, pitch, rate, and bodily action all add to the effectiveness of communication in story form. And, when most effectively used, direct address, dialog, well-chosen vocabulary, engaging style, and the like combine to produce what is perhaps the most powerful mode of human communication that exists. No wonder children and adults alike surface when a preacher moves from mere prose to portrayal.

Storytelling is the life blood of a message; stories can create and hold interest, make a truth clearer than the simple statement of a principle ever could, concretize abstract material, show how to implement biblical commands, and demonstrate how to make truth practical and memorable. No wonder Jesus used so many of them!

The preacher will do well to use them freely too.

But a precautionary explanation is in order at this point. I am not advocating the string-of-pearls method of preparation, according to which the construction of the preacher's message amounts to little more than a number of stories strung along a theme like the pearls of a necklace. In such there is little or no exposition, and hardly any reasoning or grappling with truth. One *focuses* on stories rather than on the biblical passage. As a result, the preacher comes up with a sermon that looks very much like it could have been preached at the Marble Collegiate Church by Norman Vincent Peale.[1] No. We don't need that. Every sincere listener in the congregation should go away from a message knowing

1. What the passage (or group of passages) means; i.e., he should now understand it, even if he didn't before.
2. What the passage means to him; i.e., he should know what the Holy Spirit intended to do to him in the passage.
3. What he must do to obey any commands, appropriate any promises, etc.; i.e., he should know how to convert the passage into life and ministry.
4. That the authority for what the preacher is teaching

1. Peale is a master storyteller and the preacher can learn something about storytelling (not about preaching content) from him.

clearly comes from the Scriptures; i.e., he should be able to see that the preacher got what he is saying from the biblical preaching portion under consideration.

Plainly, if those four elements are necessary for preaching to be biblical (and they are), a sermon may not be only a string of stories—even if they are pearls. Indeed, stories ought to be properly used to help the preacher to accomplish all four objectives; but stories cannot be substituted for even one of those objectives. Within the framework of those four elements, stories have not only a valid, but a valuable use.

There is much, then, to storytelling—much more than can be revealed here. But I shall describe some of the principal factors involved in storytelling, making an attempt to disclose a number of the secrets that for many have remained veiled far too long. But first a word about the title of this chapter.

The original title suggested for this chapter was "Vividness and Illustration." For several reasons I prefer the present title. In the first place, while the word *vividness* has a long history among many homileticians, in my opinion it has played a nefarious part in limiting thinking about the appeal to the senses to one sense alone—the sense of sight. In fact, the possibilities in preaching are much greater. All of the senses—taste, hearing, touch, smell, as well as sight—are fair game for the preacher. I preferred, therefore, to replace the word *vividness* with the two words *sense appeal*.

In the second place, the word *illustration* too shows the very same narrow tendency to confine sense appeal in storytelling to sight (to "illustrate," of course, is to "light up" or "make bright"). Since, through greater use, its etymological coating has worn much thinner than the one in which "vividness" is encased, it might be safe to use it to cover every sort of sense appeal in preaching. But there is already another better word available: *storytelling*. Because it is so much better, I determined to use it instead.

You will have noticed, naturally, that I began the chapter with a short story about storytelling in preaching. I have said quite a bit already about storytelling, but virtually nothing about sense appeal. Because the latter is the broader of the two topics I shall begin with it.

Sense Appeal in Preaching

By sense appeal I refer to the preacher's audio-visual appeal to the five senses.[2] Through sense appeal, the preacher is able to help his audience "see," "feel," or otherwise "experience" what he is talking about in a way that closely approximates the reality about which he is preaching. I say "closely approximates," and I put quotation marks around the words *see, feel,* and *experience,* because while sense appeal stimulates the senses in a way that *approximates* the reality, this arousal of the senses does not always correspond *exactly* to the arousal elicited by the event itself.

But in the successful use of sense appeal there is a reality to what occurs: feelings are stimulated. The imagination (notice how this word also is restricted to the sense of sight—*imagination* is from *image*), or perhaps it is better to use a broader term, the *memory* is activated by the preacher's evocative language so as to arouse the listener's senses and to enable him to "experience" the event about which he speaks.

Sense appeal, then, is concerned not merely with cognitive matters, but especially with those intellectual considerations that affect the emotions; it is essentially *emotional* appeal—an appeal that is successful only when it stirs the members of the congregation emotionally to experience what the preacher is speaking about. Thus to *experience* something is more than to *hear about* it or even to *think about* it. It is an appeal that helps the listener/ viewer to relive or, for the first time, to live through an event. It is the recall of an event, or the recall of aspects of old events stored in the memory creatively reconstructed into a new experience pattern, together with all of the emotions appropriate to the

2. It is important to recognize that, as television has taught us, congregations are not merely *listeners,* but also *viewers.*

event. The difference between merely thinking about something and experiencing it (unless thinking leads to experiencing, as it may and often does) is greater than the difference you see when watching a program on a black-and-white or a color television set. One of the reasons why poor preaching is dull is that the preacher himself fails to experience what he is talking about as he speaks— there is no joy, sense of awe, tingling down his spine, or whatever. When *he* fails to relive the event it is almost axiomatic that his congregation will "experience" that failure. In preaching, it is not enough to talk *about* something; the preacher himself must experience it afresh.

So the major purpose of vividness, or sense appeal, is to add the dimension of reality to truth by helping the listener/viewer to live through or relive (experience) whatever the preacher is teaching.

There are many ways to appeal to the senses in preaching, but we shall consider three:

1. The use of sensuous (not sensual) or evocative language.
2. The appropriate use of sound.
3. The effective use of gesture.

To these may be added storytelling, but I shall reserve a separate section for that discussion.

1. The Use of Evocative Language

Shout "fire!" in a crowded place, and people (who believe you) will think, feel, and act exactly as if the building were on fire, even if it is not. Language, skillfully chosen and used, has power. As the example shows, it has the power to produce the same effects as the actual event. It is clear, also, that context and manner are all important; it is a matter of *shouting,* in a *public place,* in a *convincing manner* that gets the response.

Sometimes, however, the mere use of a word itself will elicit a desired (or undesired) response. Take, for example, Paul's use of the word *Gentiles* in Acts 22:21, 22. There was such hatred for

Gentiles among these Jews, it seems, that they would not accept the idea that God had sent Paul to preach the gospel to the Gentiles. Indeed, when Paul introduced the subject, they would not even allow him to discuss the matter. In that case, the context—the kind of audience to which he spoke, with their racial prejudice—was the critical factor. Like fire in a fireworks factory the word *Gentiles* among them was incendiary. Manner was an unimportant factor, while in the former incident, *how* one informed the public of the fire might have been altogether determinative of their response. Can you picture a crowd believing someone who, in a lackluster manner, casually announces, "Oh, by the way, I should tell you—this place is on fire"? Or how about someone who, as he shouts "fire!" is snickering and giggling? Or suppose there is no problem concerning the manner and the context, but the wording itself creates the difficulty: "I want you to know that this building may be on fire. I don't know this for a fact since I haven't seen any fire or smelled any smoke myself, but it is altogether possible because someone just told me so." That sort of hedging (typical of much preaching) sends a confusing message. So you can readily see that communication—and evocative language as one type of it—is a matter of content, context, and manner. Emotions will be stirred and action elicited only as all three are properly related to the congregation and the preacher.

While keeping these facts in mind, let us consider evocative language a bit more closely. What sort of language is it? It is the language of sense appeal, language aimed at the senses. But, what sort of language is that? How does it differ from other language; what is peculiar to it?

With one group the word *Gentiles* would not be evocative. That is to say, it might be used freely and factually without evoking any emotional response whatsoever. With the Jews mentioned in Acts 22, it was a highly evocative term. It is important, therefore, to recognize the fact that the same word used in one context, with one sort of audience, may be evocative, but when used elsewhere may not be. Learning to choose and use language, then, is not simply a matter of discovering which words are evocative and which are not; it involves other factors (such as context and tone of voice) as well. Indeed, given the proper conditions, it is possible to use almost any word evocatively, and likewise it is possible to reduce or eliminate the evocative effects of any word. Therefore, it is essential for the preacher who wishes to use sense appeal successfully, not only to choose words that properly depict what he wishes to convey, but to become sensitive to how those words relate to times, places, persons, and contexts, etc., and to the manner and tone in which he uses them.

Now, while all of this is true, it is important to note that there is one sort of language that *in itself* especially tends to be evocative: language that by its very nature is *sense-oriented*. Picture words (*green, flashing*), onomatopoetic words (*buzz, bang*), tactile terms (*prickley, soft*), olfactory words (*rancid, fragrance*), and terms that stimulate the taste buds (*sour, briney*) are words of this sort. Often, for full effect, these words must be used in combination with others: "the horror of eating green mashed potatoes," "a sinking feeling at the sight of that flashing red light in the rear-view mirror," "as the saw buzzed through his plaster cast," "his finger was in the car door as it slammed shut with a bang," "a prickley burr stuck to my big toe," "I laid my aching head on a cold, soft pillow," "the dead animal smelled like rancid butter," "the evening air was heavy with the fragrance of rose blossoms," "it was worse than sucking on a sour lemon," "he rubbed briney pickle in the open wound."

As you can see, many feelings (not just those clearly indicated by the terms listed) are evoked by these brief clauses, even without a complete context. Consider also the sentences, "The chalk continually squeaked as he wrote on the chalkboard," and "She slowly rubbed her finger across the skin of the balloon." If you, like many persons, feel a chill run up your back as you listen to the two actions described, chances are that this language *alone* can produce that chill. Read the sentences again; visualize and "hear" what is happening. Am I right? Apart from the act itself, merely imagining it can produce a chill. Of course, authors of erotic novels depend on this power of language to evoke sexual arousal in the reader. The world has learned to appeal to emotions for its sinful purposes; when will the Christian pastor learn to do so in order to present the truth in all its edifying reality and power?

The purpose of using evocative language in preaching is to help the members of a congregation to experience the full reality of the truth and to enter into the event about which the preacher is speaking. The idea is not to change or enlarge on what the preaching portion has to say, but to enable the listener/viewer fully to understand it. Some people can picture, feel, or otherwise experience what a sentence like this means merely by reading it:

> Now when they heard of the resurrection from the dead, some scoffed . . . (Acts 17:32a).

With their "mind's eye," they can "see" the scorn registered on the faces of these Greek philosophers to whom the resurrection was ludicrous, given their view of the body. With their mind's *ear* some people can "hear" the philosophers jeering and laughing among themselves. For most, however, the preacher will have to bring the scene to life for his listeners/viewers in order to draw them into the event. To do so, he will depend largely on evocative language. That is a part of *ministering* the Word.

2. The Appropriate Use of Sound

But language alone will not suffice. In expressing the philosophers' sneers, the preacher might appropriately expel his breath in a hissing sound like that which might have been emitted by the scoffers as they spoke contemptuously of "a resurrected body!" That is to say, the preacher himself will sneer as he speaks the words.

Sound! How important it is as one appeals to the senses. Pitch, rate, timbre (or quality), volume—all of these factors are of significance. Moreover, sounds themselves sometimes count more than words. A preacher is truly free in his preaching when he has reached the point where he can make sounds that cannot be found in the dictionary. There is an illustration that I use about a tin garbage can in which I express the fit of the lid on the can by the word "schunk!" Everyone who has punctured his finger with a needle will respond knowingly to the sound "oooh!" And who doesn't know what "oof!" means when uttered by someone running into an open drawer stomach first? Such sounds and noises, when judiciously used, add immensely to vividness (or sense appeal) in a sermon. Yet, I venture to say that not more than one out of one hundred preachers who may read these lines uses them.

Let me suggest that the next time you listen to an effective communicator—perhaps a television storyteller—listen for nondictionary sounds and noises. You will understand better what I am talking about when you actually *hear* it. The better the preacher, the more freely and easily he uses sound; dull, poor preachers are afraid of sound. One sign of good preaching is a preacher's freedom to make meaningful sounds in the pulpit.

Of course, volume, rate, pitch, and quality are of great importance too. All of these should be governed by content and serve to make content clear. Loud volume when speaking of love makes little sense in most contexts. Reading Matthew 23 without raising one's voice is equally bad. The sound should grow out of and be appropriate to the content at every point. Pitch and rate are automatically controlled by excitement and muscle tension. Quality, or voice timbre—whether melodious, growling, or shrill—also must conform to content. Content-control is the central thing to be kept in mind.

But does one *consciously* "growl" or increase his speaking rate? Rarely. Such things come naturally, without conscious thought, to the seasoned preacher. He *focuses on what he wants to say*, not on *how* he is saying it. But all the while, he allows himself to enter into, relive, and experience the content. Doing so affects the muscle tension, which in turn automatically adjusts pitch, and to some extent quality and rate. His body automatically adjusts to what it experiences. Of course, evocative language, well chosen beforehand during preparation, can help *him* to relive the experience, as well as his congregation.

But he can do more. And the novice *must* do more in order to develop such capacities. At other times, when he is out of the pulpit, he can *practice* choosing and using evocative language. Each day he can prepare to tell the story of something that took place during the day, carefully selecting the best possible evocative language that is appropriate to it. On the way home, he can practice telling it. Then, that evening, he can tell it to a dorm mate, to his wife, or to his family. In such a setting he can feel free to experiment with all sorts of accompanying sounds and gestures. If he does this regularly, for an extended period of time (six months), soon he will discover that what he has been doing consciously on weekdays will have an unconscious effect on his Sunday preaching without any special effort to think about the matter while delivering the sermon.[3] Of course, in sermon preparation, he will work on choosing evocative language too and will be sure that his sermon outlines contain these choices. Soon, he will find it increasingly easier to make such selections. Before long, volume, rate, and pitch will begin to conform more and more to content. They are the product of learning to relive an event.

3. The Effective Use of Gesture

Language and sound are accompanied by gesture (here, I shall use the word to refer to any use of the body in communication, whether overt or covert) when preaching. The body communicates. Smiles or frowns, hand gestures, motion of the body—all are an essential part of sense appeal. When speaking of the "horror of eating green mashed potatoes," a smile would destroy the communication; a wincing grimace of the face would aid it. How can you speak about the "prickley burr" or the mashed "finger in the car door" without appropriate accompanying gestures? Closing the eyes and drawing a long slow nasal breath would be most fitting when speaking about "air heavy with the fragrance of rose blossoms."

Hand gestures (as well as some other sorts of bodily gestures) may be classified in three categories: *emphatic* (e.g., slamming the

3. Tape recordings, studied later, will demonstrate progress.

fist on the pulpit while saying, "We will *not* give in to Satan!"), *indicative* (e.g., pointing while saying ". . . *that* one, over there"), and *descriptive* (e.g., measuring from hand to hand while saying, "It was about *that* long").

Again, practicing gestures is profitable and ought to be done at times other than Sunday morning. Constant practice will pay off quickly. Uncomfortableness and awkwardness in using gestures can be overcome in only one way—the same way that the discomfort of learning how to skate is overcome: by persistence. (For a fuller discussion of this subject, see Gwyn Walters's discussion of "The Body in the Pulpit" in the present volume.)

So, to speak of vividness, or sense appeal in preaching, is to speak of a complex matter. It is not merely a question of painting word-pictures. There are four other senses to which one may appeal, and the means for doing so involve the whole person, including his language (style) and his delivery (use of voice and body). And all of these are controlled by content.

Storytelling

Storytelling, perhaps, has the widest appeal to listeners simply because it makes the greatest use of evocative language. Stories cannot be told without it. The two, therefore, go together.

There are fundamentally two kinds of stories: true and fictional. Of course, many may be a combination of both. These may come in both expanded or condensed forms. The expanded versions, parables, long examples, allegories, and just plain old stories are, properly speaking, stories. Examples and instances, on the other hand, are mini- and miniscule stories: they are shrunken or abbreviated stories.

Stories are constructed in various ways: as analogies, similes, metaphors, extended metaphors (allegories), extended similes (parables), etc. All forms may be used in preaching. The "I ams" of Jesus ("I am the Bread of Life," "Water of Life," "Light of the World," etc.) are little stories. These story-like ways of saying things all triggered off a wealth of meaning to those who knew and appreciated the rich Old Testament background to which they allude. The mini-story, "I am the door," spoken against the background of the entire shepherdly imagery that accompanied it (cf. Ps. 23; John 10), was as much connotative as it was denotative.

So, one principle of storytelling is to be sure that the stories will evoke much from the background of the congregation to which it is told. Agricultural allusions in a rural church (when used accurately) would be more powerful than many narrowly urban references. Of course, a preacher must be sure-footed here; otherwise his choice may backfire. He'd better not speak of the momma, papa, and baby bull to farmers (in some urban congregations a number of persons wouldn't even catch the error)!

And, of course, the opposite principle also holds true: new, unique, and different materials evoke response *when they are carefully described and explained.* The unknown can best be made known by means of the known. Frequently *new* truth can best be communicated in story form.

A third principle of storytelling is to tell about something that is old and familiar in a new and different way. Look at it from a new angle. This is what Jesus did with His "I ams."

A fourth principle is to avoid canned, trite, worn stories. Find your own. Use your own experiences; refer to things around you. When Jesus said, "Consider the lilies of the field . . ." doubtless He gestured with a sweep of the hand toward flowers that were growing all around them. All of creation is God's storybook—read it. Search it until you know all about it. A preacher must develop the capacity to use his senses if he wants to arouse the senses of others. He must become super-alive to the world in which he lives. The God who redeemed us in Christ is also the Creator of the world. Because He is one, there is a correlation between the created world and the new creation in Christ. Everything in creation is in some way analogous to spiritual truth.

How does one go about learning to tell stories? I shall give you two suggestions. First, buy a notebook. As the first order of business every morning when you enter your study, look around you and discover what is there (your initial problem will be to learn how to see, hear, smell, taste, and touch again those things you have learned ordinarily to overlook). Think about that wastebasket containing pages of crumpled, discarded thought—what could it mean? How could it be used to illustrate what truth? Stare at your telephone, that potential link that you have with nearly the entire world. Listen to the scratch of your pen on the paper as you write. Run your finger over the grains in the wood of your desk. Think about the scratch on it and how it got there. Take the cover off a magic marker and smell the ink. . . .

Why, there is enough material in that study alone to keep you in the illustration and storytelling business for several lifetimes! But you must learn to open your senses to it. Because through life we learn to ignore much that exists and much that is happening around us—which we must; otherwise we'd get little accomplished—we go through day after day missing much that could be turned into stories. The ignoring process that we have learned, preachers must learn to reverse. Daily effort will be required to do so.

Each day, in your notebook, write down at least one example, illustration, or some sort of story that you glean from your examination of the study alone. Do that every day for six to eight months. Don't be concerned about whether it is good or bad. Write it down, after prayer, before you do anything else. Soon, you will discover, you will sense more and more—more quickly—and stories will flow. Furthermore, they will get better and better; in time it will become great fun.

The second suggestion is this: take your notebook into the church auditorium, and/or anywhere else that you teach, and (every week) write down at least two more story plots from what your senses tell you is there. That practice will enable you to actually point to, or comment about, something around you in your sermons or talks during the coming weeks ("Do you see that light over there? Well . . . ," etc.).

Now the stories suggested above have to do with *things*. They are good, especially as brief touches (mini-stories) in a sermon. And they are easier to start with. But you will discover that the most effective stories you tell, like Christ's parables, are more extended stories that have to do with persons in action ("A sower went forth to sow . . .") and/or in conversation (note the quotation marks in a modern translation). Dialog is very helpful in enabling the listener to enter into and live the story; it tends to make the events of the story occur at the very moment when it is being told. No wonder Christ used so much dialog.

But how can you develop these stories involving persons in conversation and in action? Basically, in two ways:

1. By making up fictitious stories ("Suppose a farmer had just plowed his field . . .").
2. By keeping your eyes and ears open wherever you are.

When others are relaxing, oblivious of all that is happening, a wise preacher is working. He is *always* looking, listening, searching for such material. If he will only keep awake, jotting down notes immediately so he won't forget, he will collect reams of good material in no time. And most of it will come to him; he won't have to go after it.

So, preacher, after you have worked hard regularly at these activities (daily) for some time, you will notice something interesting beginning to happen: *as you are preaching,* stories of all sorts will pop into your head out of the blue. Some of these will be good; most of those that come early on won't be so good. You will be wise, at first, therefore, not to trust yourself to use them on the spot, *but as soon as the sermon is over,* jot down a note on such story lines and revise them afterward if they show promise. You will find that you may want to use some of them later.

One reason for not using such stories during the sermon is that to tell a story effectively you must think through the *very best way of wording* it. Is there a "punch line"? What should be the *exact* wording of it? What is the best sequence to use in telling it? These and other such questions should be considered.

But, at length, the time will come when, after having done this, even these processes will become largely automatic and, at last, you will be able to use many of these stories *on the spot, as they occur to you.* That is when preaching has become truly free. You will discover yourself writing material into your outline for the next time, things you never thought about until you delivered your sermon. But that stage comes only after much careful, disciplined effort of the sort I have already suggested.

Stories put windows in sermons through which people may see, hear, and smell. But you can never get your congregation to see or hear what you, yourself, have not first tasted and touched. So, above all else, take God's Word seriously enough to come fully alive to its truth and penetrate deeply enough into His creation to discover all the analogies you need. At length your preaching and your congregation will come alive too!

The extended story, as over against the story in mini-form, when complete, consists of five elements:

1. Background or introductory materials.
2. A complication (or problem), which causes . . .
3. Suspense, leading to . . .
4. The climax (or resolution of the problem), ending with . . .
5. A conclusion.

These five elements may be diagrammed in their natural sequence as follows:

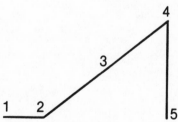

The diagram indicates three things:

1. The natural order of a story.
2. The length of time devoted to each element.
3. The level of interest sustained at each point.

The story's background begins on a normal, acceptable level of expectant interest, rises upon introduction of the problem (complication), and builds as suspense mounts. At the highest level of interest, the resolution (climax) occurs. Then, the interest level drops. That is why the conclusion must be brief (sometimes it is not needed at all; the climax and conclusion come together). Examine Christ's parables in the light of this diagram.

Much more could be said about sense appeal and storytelling, but this brief analysis, plus the practical suggestions introduced, ought to provide a considerable amount of help to those who are willing to earnestly consider and follow them in order to make truth memorable, clear, appealing, moving, applicable, and practical.

PART THREE
THE MANNER

14

Powerful Preaching
Geoffrey Thomas

One of the great perils that face preachers of the Reformed Faith is the problem of a hyper-intellectualism, that is, the constant danger of lapsing into a purely cerebral form of proclamation, which falls exclusively upon the intellect. Men become obsessed with doctrine and end up as brain-oriented preachers. There is consequently a fearful impoverishment in their hearers emotionally, devotionally, and practically. Such pastors are men of books and not men of people; they know the doctrines, but they know nothing of the emotional side of religion. They set little store upon experience or upon constant fellowship and interaction with almighty God. It is one thing to explain the truth of Christianity to men and women; it is another thing to feel the overwhelming power of the sheer loveliness and enthrallment of Jesus Christ and communicate that dynamically to the whole person who listens so that there is a change of such dimensions that he loves Him with all his heart and soul and mind and strength. And this is a New Testament concern: "But I will come to you very soon, if the Lord is willing, and then I will find out not only how these arrogant people are talking, but what power they have. For the kingdom of God is not a matter of talk but of *power*" (I Cor. 4:19–20).[1]

The problem is universal. There is not a denomination or fellowship of pastors that does not designate powerlessness in the pulpit as its greatest weakness, and there is no shortage of homi-

---

1. All citations are to the New International Version unless otherwise stated.

letic literature that suggests to preachers the source of power and a revolution to their ministry. For some the answer is *glossalalia,* but the same powerlessness is evident in Pentecostal pulpits as in non-Pentecostal. For others the answer is intimidatingly austere and almost frighteningly monastic in its tone—agonizing in prayer, fasting, mortification, and self-denial are all absolutized as the only answer to our powerlessness. How it intimidates the young pastor! It is like reading Psalm 23 without the green pastures and still waters, or reading *Pilgrim's Progress* without Interpreter's House and the Shepherds' Fields and Beulah Land, but with only the enemies, the battles, and the conflict. Of course the shadow of the cross falls across everything in our Christian lives including the pulpit. Where is there power in preaching if a man is a stranger to self-denial and cross-bearing? But no man ever became a powerful preacher through mortification alone; neither the Word of God nor our own experience allows us to reach that conclusion.

Where, then, is power for preaching to be found? Certainly not as the rare possession of an elite group of conference speakers or favored ministers. *Every* sermon is to be accompanied by divine power if it is to be a true proclamation of the Word of God. Is it not as sinful to preach the Scriptures powerlessly as it is to misrepresent them by false exegesis? The only way that the New Testament knows of preaching the gospel is with the Holy Ghost sent down from heaven. Whether the matter of our preaching is a doctrine or a word of reproof or practical application, it is to be done powerfully. Whether it is a word of comfort or of sympathy, or a display of the tenderest concern for the weakest evidences of grace, it is all to be done with power. All true preaching, whether evangelistically humbling and awakening or pastorally encouraging and strengthening, is to be suffused with the power of God.

But again, where may such power be found? What is its source? Clearly its only explanation is the life of God in the soul of the preacher. It is born in regeneration by the Holy Ghost. Two hundred and forty years after Gilbert Tennent's famous sermon, the greatest single impediment to the credibility of the Christian faith in the world today is still the unconverted ministry. One need seek no further for the explanation of the powerlessness of so many pulpits than that many men are strangers to salvation through faith in Jesus Christ. John Wesley, Thomas Chalmers, and Abraham Kuyper were all the most weak and pathetic preachers at the beginnings of their ministries for the very reason that they were unconverted men. Powerful preaching is conceived in the new birth and sustained and enriched in communion with our Savior Jesus Christ.

It is, therefore, as both Joel Nederhood and Erroll Hulse pointed out earlier in this volume, the personal relationship of the minister with Jesus Christ that serves as the critical foundation of all he is and does in the Lord's service. This kind of relationship empowers the minister with unction from on high. But beyond this, our gracious God has provided three specific means by which His power undergirds the preacher's proclamation of the Word.

1. The Power of the Word

"The word of God is alive and powerful" (Heb. 4:12). Power in heaven is God: "Ye shall see the Son of Man sitting on the right hand of power" (Matt. 26:64). Power on earth is the gospel: "It is the power of God unto salvation" (Rom. 1:16). The reason for this is that every Scripture is God-breathed (II Tim. 3:16), it is the breath of God; every sentence and every phrase is the sigh of Jehovah. It is all His exhalation because He has supervised its entire process of composition to the jots and tittles. It is not their perfect reliability that gives the Scriptures their unique authority. It is not even their complete truthfulness. The Bible is powerful because it is the Word of God; what it says God says. It is one with that word which said "Let there be" and a cosmos sprang into being, with that breath that breathed into the nostrils of the formed dust of the earth and produced living man. It is one with that word the disciples heard from their seated Lord as He said, "Blessed are the poor in spirit for theirs is the kingdom of heaven" (Matt. 5:3) and went on to preach to them the Sermon on the Mount. The Scriptures are spirit and life (John 6:63).

God has given us this miraculous book, and it is in the center of every pilgrim congregation. What revelatory gifts did at the time of the apostles this perfect gift has done ever since and will continue to do until the parousia. The Word of God is the mark of the church. Surely we are mistaken if we elevate alongside it the sacraments and discipline as two other marks of the church of equal significance. Once the Word of God is no longer believed or preached, where is discipline and what can there be in the sacraments? That is the reason why God's people who have been conquered by that Word will not give up their confession of its inerrant character, because if it is mistaken, it is not the Word of God. There is no need for anyone to lament that apostles and prophets are no longer with us. "But what saith it? The word is nigh thee, even in thy mouth, and in thy heart: that is, the word of faith, which we preach" (Rom. 10:8, KJV). God has taken such care to bring that Word to the church.

This is the confession the church makes concerning the veracity and power of the Bible and it gives rise to a most fundamental question: Why doesn't our preaching reflect the power of that Word? Why are not men feeling the power of that Word? Why is it that people ignore the Word? How can they almost sleep under that Word? Why are congregations so unresponsive to the Word? And if we are honest with ourselves, we must go a step further and confess that we ourselves often do not respond to this Word. We are not moved and changed by it. We are strangers to its power, but why? Surely the Word is not deficient. Jesus Himself testifies to the authority and eternity of the Scriptures (John 10:35). He repeatedly insists that the Scriptures must be fulfilled and are more enduring than the heavens and the earth. Whether men will heed them or be touched by them or not, the Bible remains the Word of God. Whence, then, this absence of the felt power of the Word within the church? A number of questions must be asked.

1. Do We Read the Word?

It is terribly elementary, but it is where we must start. Do we read the Bible? Do we read it more than we read the daily newspaper? Do we read it each day? Do we see it as our duty each day to *search* the Scriptures, to have a set time and pore over them? Do we question them, interrogating and puzzling over their meaning? Do we ransack them? Are we growing in our knowledge of them? Are we making this one of our chief ends in life? Do we read other things for the light they give us on the Bible? In Christian conversation do we talk about the meaning of the Word of God? Are we moved by the Scriptures?

The apostle Paul takes us through all the glories of justification and sanctification and the sovereignty of God in human history and brings it to a prepared climax in Romans 11. He stands back for a moment enthralled as he says, "O the depth of the riches both of the wisdom and the knowledge of God! How unsearchable are his judgments, and his ways past finding out" (Rom. 11:33). He gasps at his own exposition of the truth God has given him. He stands on this peak and he looks down and cries, "O the depth." Have we ever felt like that? If not then our congregations have never felt like that and so have been immeasurably impoverished in their worship. Is it not a duty of the minister to show to people the sheer marvelousness of truth in its Everest-like grandeur? Authentic Christian experience is the influence of doctrinal truth upon our affections (Jonathan Edwards saw this clearly, as Samuel Logan reminds us in his chapter in this volume). But we will not be affected by the Scriptures, we will not tap the power that is in them, unless we read, read, read, and read them yet some more.

I may hold a perfectly sound doctrine of Scripture and know the arguments and proof-texts for its infallibility, but what good is all of that if I am not daily and intimately relating to it? If it is the Word of the Lord then my life is to be spent under its authority. We need search no further for the explanation of the powerlessness of many pulpits, than here: in disobedience to the Savior who said, "Search the Scriptures."

2. Do We Preach the Word?

Paul exhorted Timothy, "Preach the word" (II Tim. 4:2), and that is his exhortation to ministers today. All of Scripture is to be understood by the whole church, and all of Scripture is to be preached to the whole church. That is why God gave it. Are we preaching all of the Bible? Do we go from Genesis to Revelation and back again? The first sermon of the New Testament church was full of Old Testament Scriptures, and it was blessed of God to the conversion of three thousand people. Half of the Bible is historical narrative, but there is no more neglected area of Scripture in our pulpits today. Bible history brings our emotions to the truth, and part of the crippling Stoicism that marks our congregations under our preaching is due to this neglect on our part. There is a great need for series of sermons on the historical narratives of the Old Testament, which could serve as guidelines and models to preachers today. The best model is still John Calvin's sermons.

The exhortation to preach the Word can best be fulfilled by the expository method, that is, preaching systematically through books of the Bible, especially those portions which present the system of redemption. It is the most obvious and natural way of preaching and will impart the greatest knowledge to the hearers, as well as to the minister himself. Texts are found within a certain context, and the connections among the truths are as essential to understanding as the separate propositions themselves. They are not gems to be brought out of a silver casket, brandished to all, and then returned. Verses are not isolated sentences, but are set in narratives or are part of sustained arguments. Preaching through books of the Bible enables us to declare the whole counsel of God and delivers men from imbalance and from riding their own little hobbies. It is also the most interesting method of preaching; it is the rare minister who can make it dull. Only the most superficial kind of Christian is gripped by an Athenian spirit and itches for something new each Sunday, a different voice or the novelty of a verse from a different part of Scripture.

The Word should be preached in its connectedness because that brings the whole counsel of God to bear upon the people and gives to the minister the opportunity to reprove, rebuke, and display every kind of evil without being accused of aiming his preaching at individuals. It also relieves the minister of the hesitation and doubt that otherwise attend the selection of his texts as Sunday grows nearer. Through the course of a year many of the difficulties experienced by members of the congregation will be dealt with and answered. It is enormously important in church planting as the deep satisfaction experienced under this expository ministry of the Word makes people long to know of congregations throughout the entire land hearing such preaching.

3. Do We Proclaim the Word in a Logical and Orderly Way?

Do we do what the Preacher did in the Old Testament? "Yea, he gave good heed, and sought out, and set in order many proverbs" (Eccles. 12:9). The God who made us in His image is a God of order, and we function best when we can comprehend a reasonable and systematic development. Paul set store on five words that were spoken with understanding (I Cor. 14:19). There is an instructive account of a member of the New England congregation of Enfield in July 1741 when Jonathan Edwards preached on Deuteronomy 32:35, "Their foot shall slide in due time." He wrote that Edwards

> . . . began in the clear, careful, demonstrative style of a teacher, solicitous for the result of his effort, and anxious that every step of his argument should be early and fully understood. As he advanced in unfolding the meaning of the text, the most careful tremendous imagery could but inadequately express. His most terrific descriptions of the doom and danger of the impenitent, only enabled them to apprehend more clearly the truths which he had compelled them

to believe. They seemed to be, not the product of the imagi-
nations, but what they really were, a part of the argument.[2]

There is a tremendous power in the reasoned presentation of
truth, and ministers neglect such things as a strong outline and
structure to their peril (see the full discussion of this subject by
Glen Knecht in the present volume). Is not this the manner of
apostolic preaching? Consider how all the *therefore's* of the Epistle
to the Romans hold together the various parts of the letter in
their relationship to one another and give it such movement. Of
course, a sermon is different from an Epistle: it cannot sustain
such a chain of argument. Three or four links are ample, and a
congregation desires to look back after a sermon is over and see
not only that they have passed from "one" to "three" but how
they have made that journey. Too many heads and subheadings
have caused much popular prejudice against logical preaching: it is
too akin to a lecture and is felt to be dry and wearying. The truth
is that the preacher who does not reason has no power. The
ineffective minister is the one who reasons unskillfully and te-
diously. The eloquent preacher argues like Jonathan Edwards,
logically and tersely. He is interesting because he satisfies the deep
longing for order and understanding that is found in the human
mind.

4. Do We Proclaim the Word in a Discriminatory Way?

Discriminatory preaching is that which shows the difference
between the Christian and the unbeliever. Paul tells the Ephesians that the Holy Spirit has a sword in His hand and that
weapon is the Word of God (Eph. 6:17). There is no more salutary and enlightening exercise for the minister than for him to ask
what kind of preaching of the Word of God has the Holy Spirit
used to convict men of sin and bring them to Christ? What characterized the preaching of Martyn Lloyd-Jones, of C. H. Spur-

2. John Gillies, *Historical Collections of Accounts of Revivals*, (Edinburgh: Banner of Truth, 1981), p. ix.

geon, of John Wesley, of George Whitefield, of the Puritans, of the Reformers, of the church fathers, of the apostles, and of the prophets? Why were their ministries so owned of God that many were converted as they heard them? Certainly one thing characterized every one of them: their preaching was immensely searching, reaching the deepest recesses of men's hearts. The Word of God is not a sword in the hands of a circus performer to be thrown up and caught again and again in a dazzling display of virtuosity so that after twenty minutes the performance is over and the crowds go home saying how good a show it was. That sword is more akin to the surgeon's scalpel, and the physicians of the Word must cut deep.

Consider the apostle Peter's preaching on the day of Pentecost. He begins by defending the church against the charge of drunkenness, but swiftly moves on to declare that this event is the fulfilment of prophecy, Joel's day of extraordinary events in heaven and on earth, the day of the Lord and the day of salvation. Did the people of Jerusalem feel they were watching merely another display of oratory? Did they even feel that they had to decide between the charge of drunkenness and Peter's apologia? Not at all! Peter never allowed these people to think they were observers, or members of a jury, or that they were there to pass judgment upon him and his words. Rather he opened their guilt and sin to them as they had never seen it before. They with their wicked hands had crucified and slain the one who had been delivered by the determined counsel and foreknowledge of God. They had murdered God's only begotten Son. They were not passing judgment upon the preacher; he was declaring God's judgment upon them! They had to meet Jehovah, a God to whom right and wrong mattered supremely, and seated at His right hand was the one they had killed! Peter was addressing the most religious people in the whole world, who had travelled to Jerusalem on a pilgrimage to worship this very Lord only to be told that they were inculpated in the death of His only Son. Peter was not brandishing the sword as a performer in some brilliant exhibition of sword play. He was thrusting that sword relentlessly into their hearts, and he would not stop while they rejected the Lord Jesus.

To use terms suggested elsewhere in this volume, Peter was preaching phenomenologically, and the result was that the people were cut to the heart at his words (Acts 2:37).

We are asking why, if the Word of God is life and power, are we seeing such evident weakness in the professing church. And we are suggesting a simple answer—because of a lack of discriminatory ("phenomenological") preaching of that Word, preaching like that of Peter at Pentecost. He spoke directly to the consciences of men. He named their sin, held out the threat of God's punishment, and would not be silent until they began to ask what they had to do. Of course, he spoke lovingly; he loved his hearers. We must love men more than they loved themselves. And yet there was a faithfulness in his witness to them of their real state. Stephen experienced the identical response as he preached a short while later; his hearers were also cut to the heart at what they heard (Acts 7:54). They hated his preaching and they killed him. Our preaching will never approach the power of Peter's at Pentecost unless we too put our heads through the gates of hell and tell the people that they are not ready to die, that they are unprepared for the great judgment, that soon these gates will close upon them in death, and that then there will be no offers of grace, because sinners do not know it.

What do the New Testament Christians ask for so often? What do we need in our lives and ministries? It is boldness, for "the fearful and unbelieving . . . shall have their part in the lake which burneth with fire" (Rev. 21:8). One reason why the gates of hell are not falling before the church is our lack of boldness in preaching. We are not discriminating between Christian and non-Christian; our terminology and application are too general. We are not wielding the sword of the Spirit, but the baton of a conductor.

5. Do We Proclaim the Word in an Applicatory Way?

Applicatory preaching is that which shows the difference between obedience and disobedience in the Christian (a point that John Bettler and Glen Knecht make earlier in this volume). Let me illustrate. When Jesus preached the Sermon on the Mount to His own disciples, He was explaining the true nature of ethics and piety against the whole background of Pharisaic error and hypocrisy. It is often considered that the Pharisees made the law of God more difficult to keep by their casuistry and additional traditions, but in fact these had the reverse effect, and in Matthew 5 Jesus showed the costliness of true obedience by applying to His disciples the full demands of the law of God. Their righteousness must exceed the righteousness of the scribes and Pharisees or there would be no possibility of their entering into the kingdom of heaven (Matt. 5:20). He applied the commandment "Thou shalt not kill" to attitudes and words, as well as to actions: "Whosoever shall say, Thou fool, shall be in danger of hell fire" (Matt. 5:22). He brought the threat of perdition to Christians in order to break the power of remaining sin over them. He applied the seventh commandment in such a way as to warn them that God also hated the lustful imagination and exhorted them to pluck out the right eye rather than go with both eyes to hell. In applicatory preaching, the implications of Christian discipleship are made very plain in order to distinguish between believers who are walking in the spirit and those who in some area of their lives are walking in the flesh. There is no better section of Scripture to learn about applicatory preaching than the three chapters of the Sermon on the Mount.

Let me illustrate this point in another way. It is the duty of the Christian to accept the comfort that the promises of the Word of God offer to everyone who believes: the comfort that the Lord will provide all our needs, that He will work all things together for our good, that He will allow nothing to separate us from His love, and that our faith shall not fail. Whatever has broken our hearts, there is comfort for us in the promises of God. In Matthew 2, there is a description of the women of Bethlehem who had lost their children in the massacre ordered by Herod. We are told that they "refused to be comforted" (Matt. 2:18). The evangelist tells us of that those who refuse to be comforted have no place in the kingdom of God. Of course sorrow in the presence of death is absolutely proper and sanctioned by the example of our

Lord Himself, but there are those who parade their grief for years and declare their total perplexity at God's dealing thus with them, even to justify their unbelief by the action of God: "I can't understand a God who would allow such things to happen." Those people in Bethlehem could have been comforted because the Child, the Messiah, had escaped the sword in order that in the fulness of time He might go to the cross to die for sinners. O mothers of Bethlehem, can't you see how self-centered you are in your sorrow? God's comfort is all mediated to us through His own Son whom He sent to the cross to give us life and peace, however grievous our trials may be. Matthew is saying this to all those who justify their estrangement from God on the basis of their own or others' suffering.

Preaching that lacks application is the bane of the modern Reformed pulpit. How does the Word relate to these people who sit so patiently before us and hear our messages? What should they do as a result? What changes should be affected in thinking, in emotions, and in behavior? The most common criticism that is directed at our worship services is that apart from the hymns we sing, we ask people simply to be spectators. This is what drives them into charismatic meetings, where they are often hoodwinked into believing they have a larger part to play in the worship. The sermon should be the greatest period of participation in the church's assemblies. During a thirty-minute period a Christian should be moved to inward thankfulness and praise, conviction of sin and repentance, determination to love and obey God, new concern for his fellow-believers and his fellow men. The sermon is not for balconeers, but for travellers,[3] for those who are most involved with God; it is the climactic aspect of worship. There is no more common cause of ineffective ministry than a failure in applicatory preaching.

To summarize, there is the power of the Word of God, and yet there is much weak ministry in the churches. The fault for that does not lie with God or with His Word. He has not failed to provide adequate resources for our age. We cannot plead the ad-

3. J.I. Packer, *Knowing God*, (London: Hodder and Stoughton, 1973), p. 5.

vent of TV, or the prevalent philosophy of unbelief, or locked-in false religions, or the hardness of men's hearts and suggest we have meagre provision to deal with these factors. For the Lord would respond, Did not I entrust you with My Word? Is it not living and powerful? Is it not the sword of the Spirit? Every man called by God has been given a Word that is totally adequate for all the possible needs that may arise both in the assembly and in the world. There can come into his life no problem for which there is not an adequate answer in the Scriptures. This is the glory of the church. "Faith cometh by hearing, and hearing by the word of God" (Rom. 10:17). That gift of the Word is accompanied by enormous responsibility: "Every man shall receive his own reward according to his own labour. . . . Every man's work shall be made manifest: for the day shall declare it, because it shall be revealed by fire; and the fire shall try every man's work of what sort it is" (I Cor. 3:8, 13). Then our stewardship of the Bible will be revealed. Did we study it and preach it? Was our preaching logical and orderly? Did we preach with discrimination and application, searching out the hearts of our hearers?

2. The Power of Faith

Today's pulpits have no greater need than to be filled with men of faith who clearly preach the nature of true faith. This is the ethos in which powerful preaching is to be found, and this is the second primary means by which almighty God undergirds our preaching with His power.

1. Men of Faith

John Calvin provides a notable definition of faith: "We shall now have a full definition of faith if we say that it is a firm and sure knowledge of the divine favour toward us, founded on the truth of a free promise in Christ, and revealed to our minds, and sealed in our hearts, by the Holy Spirit" (*Institutes* 3. 2. 7). That understanding, which involves an assured trust that all one's sins are pardoned for the sake of Christ, does not mean that Calvin denied the possibility of true children of God struggling with all kinds of doubts and uncertainties. However, it does mean that he rightly saw a lack of assurance as an abnormal condition for a believer and especially for a minister. It is a contradiction of the biblical pattern of the minister's calling. The experience of the apostles is one of virtually unfailing assurance. A preacher will know the fiery darts of Satan, as will any believer, and he will wrestle with unbelief, but continual uncertainty as to whether he is a true believer debars him from powerful preaching. How can he exhort others when he is uncertain about himself? In the New Testament, assurance is the norm for every preacher. Peter recalls clearly the moment when God begat him again to a living hope (I Pet. 1:3). Paul is sure that the Son of God has loved him personally (Gal. 2:20). John knows that he has passed from death to life (I John 3:14).

Christian biography bears the same witness. George Whitefield records in his journal, "How assuredly have I felt that Christ dwelt in me and I in Him! and how did I daily walk in the comforts of the Holy Ghost and was edified and refreshed in the multitude of peace!" Charles Spurgeon writes in his diary, "Oh the safety of the Christian, as sure, but not as blest, as any saint in heaven! Lord how can I leave Thee? To whom, or whither should I go?" Andrew Bonar records that "for many years (indeed, as many as I can remember), since my first discovery of the way to God by Christ, I have never been allowed to lose my way to the mercyseat for a single day. I have not always had bright sunshine, but I have every day had sunlight, and not darkness, in my soul." He writes similarly nine years later, "The Lord has enabled me to lean upon Christ day by day, for sixty years. He took hold of me that year, and has never once left me in darkness as to my interest in Him all that time."

The church has the right to look to its leaders for strength. If, instead, the pastors themselves are weak, doubting, and uncertain, where is the flock to go? A situation can develop all too easily in which the church exhausts itself trying to assure its preachers and comfort its comforters. It is clear from Acts 6:3-5 that candidates for the ministry should be "full of the Holy Spirit and of faith." Not only believers and not only spiritual but *full.* They should be eminent in their trust in the Lord and with full assurance of faith. That is what gives them power when they speak. David testifies, "I believed and therefore have I spoken" (Ps. 116:10), and Paul testifies to the same experience, "We also believe and therefore speak" (II Cor. 4:13). It was the faith of the Christians of Rome that was so dynamic, it was spoken of throughout the whole world (Rom. 1:8), as was the faith of the Thessalonians (I Thess. 1:8). The same note is characteristic of the Old Testament. Elihu listens respectfully as the older men seek to comfort Job, but finally he can keep silent no longer. "I will answer also my part, I also will shew mine opinion. For I am full of matter, the spirit within me constraineth me. Behold, my belly is as wine which hath no vent; it is ready to burst like new bottles. I will speak, that I may be refreshed: I will open my lips and answer" (Job 32:17-20). He must speak, constrained by his convictions that what he says is the answer to Job's condition. Faith gives boldness and has its own eloquence.

Hebrews 11 is the great section in the Bible on the theme of the power of faith. The author's definition of it is "being sure of what we hope for and certain of what we do not see" (Heb. 11:1), and he illustrates this definition in a number of ways. He tells us it is by this faith that a man may stand in a pulpit and affirm that God created the heavens and the earth. "By faith we understand that the universe was formed at God's command, so that what is seen was not made out of what was visible" (Heb. 11:3). The preacher may affirm that matter did not exist eternally. It did not simply explode into being spontaneously and neither did it emanate as an extension of the essence of God. It owes its origin and continuance to the creativity of almighty God, not to an act of the "Supreme Being" or the "First Cause," but to the word of the God of the Bible, who became incarnate in His Son Jesus Christ, who died on Calvary and rose for our justification. And it was by His word that He made it all. The universe owes its whole origin and dynamic to the mind and utterance of almighty God. This is

Christian proclamation, with all the implications that the doctrine of creation has for ethics, soteriology, and eschatology.

How can a preacher make such claims for His Lord? The author
of Hebrews says that there is only one possible way: "through
faith." No one was there to observe the process. No one heard
God say, "Let there be." It is impossible to run a controlled
experiment to demonstrate this fact. One cannot use one's intellect and reflect upon the universe as it is and use the ontological,
cosmological, and moral arguments for the existence of God to
reach the conclusion that God in Christ made it all by His word.
The only way we know that "without Him was not anything
made that was made" is by faith. We know because God told us.
We have our faith in the Scriptures as the Word of God, and
more fundamentally we have our faith in Jesus Christ who told
us that the whole of the Old Testament record is true. How may
a preacher powerfully declare that Jehovah Jesus spoke the universe into existence? Because it is in Genesis 1, and Jesus Christ
placed His own imprimatur on that great chapter and the whole
book of which it is a part. All our faith in the reliability of the
Old Testament depends upon the credibility of our Savior Jesus
Christ. Of course, it is possible to use observation and the whole
scientific enterprise to show the weaknesses of other theories, but
there is no way whatsoever that we can use scientific processes to
arrive incontrovertibly at the conclusion that the Triune God
spoke the world into existence. There are areas where only faith
can operate, and where the degree of certainty possible is the
certainty of faith.

Faith underlies all our preaching, as it underlies all intellectual
processes. It is not at all that intellectual processes underlie faith.
Life begins in faith; all thinking and speaking and preaching begins in faith. The power of the preacher is the certainty of his
faith, and he must beware of wanting greater conviction than the
confidence of faith.

Faith has the power to make a man go on in the face of great
opposition. It will create in him its own ability to communicate
the greatest truths. So often courses in evangelism are directed at
the methodology of communication. They teach such things as

the opening gambits to conversation, answers to fundamental objections to the faith, and the basic steps of salvation. Useful as such instruction undoubtedly is, it does not strike at the heart of the problem of Christian disobedience to the Great Commission. At the core of the matter is a crisis of faith. We, unlike men of faith, such as Peter and Paul, do not seem really to believe that men are on the broad road to destruction. Thus we are silent and ineffective in our witness, never finding time to evangelize. No course in evangelistic methodology can help us. We need to cry to God, "Lord, I believe, help thou my unbelief." The church has no greater need than preachers with full assurance of faith who continue year after year strengthening the faith of their hearers. Nothing can better serve the cause of true evangelism than that.

There is another statement the author of Hebrews makes that indicates the power of faith. He tells us that it was through faith that men of God have "conquered kingdoms" (Heb. 11:33, NIV). Today men are citizens of enormously influential kingdoms. In this last century there arose leaders whose scepters continue to sway millions of followers. Marx, Darwin, Freud, and Sartre all head vast kingdoms and their subjects are everywhere. They walk the corridors of power in the great capitals of the world. The leading publishing houses are in their pockets. They edit the prestigious newspapers, as well as the popular dailies, and they govern the media. Many universities and colleges are in their service. The most brilliant and cultured leaders of literature, music, and art serve them. The influence of these kingdoms is locked into the whole Western world, and there is no evidence in either Europe or America that their power is coming to an end. What is going to conquer them? The author of Hebrews says that the power that faith imparts to believers can do this. The might of Rome and the glory of Greece were subdued by twelve ignorant and unlearned men. They turned the world upside-down by the power of faith in Christ. What must have seemed to them like impregnable kingdoms, like those facing the church today, collapsed before their confidence in God.

Such power is ours in this hour. Can we not deal with these debilitating doubts that so fearfully weaken our effectiveness as preachers? Let us examine ourselves before God and ask these most basic questions: Am I a true believer in the Lord Jesus Christ? The answer is yes. Has He called me to be a preacher of the gospel? The answer is yes. Has He entrusted me with His own Word? The answer again is yes. Am I preaching that Word logically and with discrimination and application? Again I say yes. Then let me say to myself that what I have is the Word of God, and I am to hold it forth as the Word of life to all the folk of this generation. Let men thus deal with this crippling lack of confidence in the Word of God and in their own calling and preach with boldness as true men of faith.

2. Preaching True Faith

Preachers themselves must know the power of true faith, but they also must be preaching true faith, like Paul "testifying both to the Jews, and also to the Greeks, repentance toward God and faith toward our Lord Jesus Christ" (Acts 20:21). What does it mean to declare to men that they must have faith in the Savior? What are we asking them to do? There is confusion here, especially in Reformed preaching, and a consequent weakness at the very heart of gospel proclamation.

We are not asking the minister to do something after the sermon is over. Many preachers make an appeal to their hearers to have faith in Christ not in and through the proclamation of the Word, but in the time that follows the sermon. They ask for heads to be bowed and all eyes to be closed in order that men should hear persuasive words in as conducive an atmosphere as possible. The appeal often lasts for a long time and is frequently accompanied by a choir or the congregation singing "Just as I Am Without One Plea," while between each stanza the preacher makes one plea after another. Surely such efforts to persuade men to have faith in Christ deny the truth that faith comes by hearing, and hearing by the Word of God (Rom. 10:17). The Word preached has power to convert and save, and nothing more than preaching is required. To ask people to walk to the front or raise a hand is to equate two utterly different actions, an inward spiritual act of a sinner coming to Christ with an outward physical act of a person walking to the front. The confusion is deadly because, whereas the latter physical act is something any man has the ability to do, the inward spiritual act of coming to Christ no man can perform "except the Father which hath sent me draw him" (John 6:44). If coming to Christ were a physical act, then no one would need a special inward operation of the Holy Ghost called "the drawing of the Father." One would simply need the courage to respond to the pleading evangelist who is asking men to get out of their seats and walk to the front, but Jesus said that the action of savingly believing in Him was one that no man could do unless God exercised His divine prerogative and drew that man to His Son.

Neither is believing in Christ the same as believing truths about Him. When Paul testified to men "faith toward our Lord Jesus Christ," he did not present them with three or four simple statements asking men to assent to them. That is not believing upon the Lord Jesus Christ, but rather a limited intellectual activity. The essence of saving faith is not assent to biblical propositions—the devils have such faith. It is as possible to believe in historical facts of the fall of Rome, or the Battle of Hastings, or the War of Independence as it is to believe about the Lord Jesus Christ's life and sayings. No one needs that "drawing of the Father" if we are asking men to assent to basic Bible truths. Any ministry that sees its evangelism in that light should cease to call itself "preaching" and acknowledge itself to be some center for religious study. It is here that Reformed ministry with its confessions, catechisms, and its concept of the "covenant child" is at most danger. Its very discernment and noble emphasis upon the system of truth in the whole counsel of God, and its desire to instruct young people in that system can become a snare. There is an eternal difference between system faith and saving faith. I exercise system faith when, for example, I am far from Aberystwyth and suddenly have an upset stomach. I go to a pharmacist for medicine. He is not the man from whom I usually obtain medication, but I in faith take it from him and drink it. What kind of faith am I exercising? Faith in a system that operates in a country that prevents any Tom, Dick, or Harry from opening a pharmacy and dispensing poisons, drugs, and medicines. The system requires training, qualifications, and licensing; unconsciously I operate in the knowledge and faith of that system. It is the same faith we display when we climb aboard a plane; we don't know the pilot, but we are aware of the system that regulates such responsible enterprises. While faith in Jesus Christ is not believing three or four "laws" about Him, neither is it believing or understanding that whole biblical system that comes to us upon the authority of mother church and is defined so wonderfully, for example in the 107 answers of the Westminster Shorter Catechism. We are not saying to sinners that if they believe truths about Christ, few or many, they will be saved. Devils know that Jesus is "the Son of the most high God" (Mark 5:7), but they are devils yet.

We are not disparaging the need to proclaim the most intelligent belief in the Christ of Scripture. Faith is not a "feeling of dependence" that focuses upon a personal "Jesus." The Scriptures, Jesus said, "are they which testify of me" (John 5:39), and they are the touchstone by which all expressions of faith are to be examined. The Jesus of the Scriptures is true God and true man, two natures in one Person. He is the Son of God equal in power and glory to the Father and the Holy Spirit. He was in a state of humiliation, but now is in a state of glory. He may be found at the right hand of God where He continues to exercise the three offices of Prophet, Priest, and King. That is the only Jesus Christ there is or ever will be, and He is the only Savior. There can be no power in preaching that fails to proclaim *this* Christ and exhorts men to put their trust in Him.

What then is the heart of gospel proclamation? What are we asking men when we preach to them faith in Jesus Christ? It is not the invitation to come to the front; it is not "system faith"; it is not vague, unspecified belief. It is, first, *to show men their need of Jesus Christ.* The preacher's task is to make a person aware of the seriousness of sin. It is not to create false guilt feelings, but it is to show men that the Creator has given laws to those who inhabit His creation, who live and move and have their being in Him, and who must answer to Him for their conduct. There is great power in preaching that addresses the conscience because there is an immediate echo of approval for what is said from within the very being of the hearer. Since men are made in the image of the law-giver, the things of His law are written in their hearts. Therefore men's consciences speak with the preacher to them. It was when Bunyan's Pilgrim felt the weight of the burden he carried that he realized how great was his need of deliverance. The Lord Jesus Christ invited those who labor and are heavy-laden to come to Him for rest (Matt. 11:28), but to others He said, "You would not come to me that you might have life" (John 5:40). Why would they not entrust themselves to Jesus? Because they felt no need of Him, because they were not heavy-laden with their guilt, and thus, when Jesus spoke of the sinner being enslaved in his sins, they protested what freedom they enjoyed. They would not believe in the only one who could make them truly free because they thought they were already possessors of real liberty. No one comes to Christ unless he has been made consciously aware of his need of Him. It is the great task of the preacher to show to men their state as it is before God, to pursue them from every refuge in which they hide, to persuade them that a holy God takes their actions and thoughts so seriously that He knows their every deviation from His will and intends to hold them accountable. This is the bedrock of powerful preaching, that men are in need of Christ because of their sin. Where has there ever been powerful preaching that muted the divine diagnosis and the plight of every man?

Again, proclaiming faith in Christ means *showing sinners how perfectly the Lord meets their needs*. There is little description of the psychology of faith in Scripture, but there is a fulness of teaching concerning the person and work of the Son of God, as though we are being told that faith is conceived and sustained by the constant exposure of the believer to His Lord. Paul's preaching was "in demonstration of the spirit and of power" (I Cor. 2:4) because of his determination not to preach himself, but Jesus Christ the Lord (II Cor. 4:5), and especially "not to know anything among you, save Jesus Christ, and him crucified" (I Cor. 2:2). The power came from that theme, as it still does. The greatest needs men have are pardon for past sins and power for future obedience. All this is found in Jesus Christ: by His death our sins are freely forgiven and through the gift of His Spirit we are empowered to live more holy lives. It is the task of the preacher to turn continually to this theme and show men how perfectly suitable Christ is to meet their every need. Do they need deliverance from the wrath to come? It is to be found in Christ only. Must they have a perfect righteousness? It is found in Jesus alone. And complete and eternal restoration to the divine favor? It is all in Christ. Do men need grace to sanctify their whole nature and make them fit for heaven? It is all in Christ. "He of God is made unto us wisdom, righteousness, sanctification and redemption" (I Cor. 1:30). To have Him is to have all of that. As Edmund Clowney has pointed out earlier in this volume, powerful preaching is Christocentric preaching.

Finally, preaching faith in Jesus Christ means *telling men that they must resign themselves wholly to Him to meet their needs*. The apostles talk about believing *upon* the Lord Jesus Christ and about having faith *into* Him, which expresses entrusting one's whole self, body and soul, for time and eternity, to the person of the Lord Jesus Christ. "Faith in Jesus Christ is a saving grace, whereby we receive and rest upon him alone for salvation, as he is offered to us in the gospel" (Westminster Shorter Catechism, answer 86). Much preaching of faith in Jesus is enfeebled by restricting the focus of the act to the death of Jesus Christ: "Now you must believe that He died for you," men are told. But the apostles said, "Believe upon the Lord Jesus Christ." They made the focus of trust the person of Christ as the one whose death does indeed reconcile God to men, but who is also a Prophet and a King. This great teacher says to all who come to Him for rest, "Learn of Me" (Matt. 11:29) that henceforth His disciples will spend their lives as disciples in His school, finding answers to the greatest questions men can formulate.

What are we to live for? What is the purpose of our existence? Who is God? How may we die in peace? What lies beyond death? What is right, and what is wrong? Who is my neighbor? What is a real church? These questions are all answered by Christ, and for those who come to Him, He can say nothing wrong. We live by all the words that come from His mouth as they are recorded in the Scriptures and preached to us with searching power by His servants. Joseph Alleine, the great Puritan preacher, expressed this concern well:

> The unsound convert takes Christ by halves. He is all for the salvation of Christ, but he is not for sanctification. He is all for the privileges, but does not appropriate the person of Christ. This is an error in the foundation. Whoever loves life, let him beware here. It is an undoing mistake, of which you have often been warned, and yet none is more common. Jesus is a sweet name, but men do not love the Lord Jesus in sincerity. They will not have Him as God offers, "to be a Prince and Saviour" (Acts 5:31). They divide what God has joined, the King and the Priest. They will not accept the salvation of Christ as He intends it; they divide it here. Every man's vote is for salvation from suffering, but they do not desire to be saved from sinning. They would have their lives saved, but still would have their lusts. Indeed, many divide here again; they would be content to have some of their sins destroyed, but they cannot leave the lap of Delilah, or divorce the beloved Herodias. They cannot be cruel to the right eye or right hand. O be infinitely careful here; your soul depends upon it. The sound convert takes a whole Christ, and takes Him for all intents and purposes, without exceptions, without limitations, without reserve. He is willing to have Christ upon any terms; he is willing to have the dominion of Christ as well as deliverance by Christ. He says with Paul, "Lord, what wilt thou have me to do?" Anything, Lord. He sends the blank for Christ to set down His own conditions.[4]

Preaching faith in the Lord Jesus Christ means that the preacher must be able to answer affirmatively all of the following

4. Joseph Alleine, *An Alarm to the Unconverted*, (Edinburgh: Banner of Truth, 1959), p. 25.

questions vis-a-vis his congregation: have they been made conscious of their need through sin and guilt, which only Christ can meet? Have they seen how perfectly the Lord Jesus Christ meets those needs? Have they come to Him in the glory of His person and Word as He is offered to them in the gospel? Powerful preaching will return continually but freshly to these themes, preaching them with tenderness and authority, beseeching and commanding men to believe upon the Son of God. That is the heart-beat of life and power that will throb in every biblical sermon.

3. *The Power of Prayer*

The final means God has provided for empowering His servants is prayer. This is the obvious conclusion to what has already been written concerning the power of the Word and the power of faith, because prayer is simply the articulation of faith in its response to the promises of the Word. As William Gurnal said,

> Furnish thyself with arguments from the promises to enforce thy prayers, and make them prevalent with God. The promises are the ground of faith, and faith, when strengthened, will make thee fervent, and such fervency ever speeds and returns with victory out of the field of prayer. . . . The mightier any is in the Word, the more mighty he will be in prayer.

This rich theme must be dealt with very briefly because it has already been expanded at length by Erroll Hulse earlier in this volume. Someone has rightly said that prayer is the most difficult thing in all the world, and we confess some hesitation in speaking of it as a means of power or a means of anything except ascribing glory to God. Prayer honors God: we declare His sovereignty over all things when we pray. Prayer is an act of worship: God actively seeks men who will worship Him in spirit and in truth. Should not preachers, of all men, honor and worship God? But prayer has also been divinely appointed for our blessing, i.e., as the means by which all the blessings of providence and salvation come to us. Its very privacy teaches us humility; a prayerless preacher is a proud preacher. Prayerlessness is not only a sin, it is a significant denial of our whole theological stance. We are men who affirm that the opening of the heart is the work of God alone (Acts 16:14), and that the opening of the understanding is a divine prerogative (Luke 24:45). So the preacher with the most brilliant gifts of communication and teaching is impotent to plant saving knowledge in a sinner's heart without God's help. If we are not praying, we are saying that we can cope. If we pray, we honor God, confessing that His gifts are to be sought by this means. If we thank Him for the blessings of grace, we are thereby again affirming that all things are of Him.

When ministers are blessed with a spirit of prayer it bodes well for the church and looks as though God intends to give the things they ask for. Such praying is powerful; James says, "The effectual fervent prayer of a righteous man availeth much" (James 5:16). Prayer is vital to the life of the preacher as the biography of every minister indicates. Luther's faithful scribe and companion Veit Dietrich overheard him praying at the Coburg during those anxious days of the Diet at Augsburg in 1530:

> No day passes that he does not give three hours to prayer, and those the fittest for study. Once I happened to hear him. Good God! how great a spirit, how great a faith, was in his very words! With such reverence did he ask, as if he felt that he was speaking with God; with such hope and faith, as with a father and a Friend. "I know," he said, "that Thou art about to destroy the persecutors of Thy children. If Thou dost not, then our danger is Thine too. This business is wholly thine, we come to it under compulsion: Thou, therefore, defend . . ." In almost these words I, standing afar off, heard him praying with a clear voice. And my mind burned within me with a singular emotion when he spoke in so friendly a manner, so weightily, so reverently, to God.[5]

5. Philip Schaff, *History of the Christian Church*, vol. 7, *The German Reformation*, (Grand Rapids: Eerdmans, 1960), p. 463.

The private devotional life of the minister lays the foundation upon which is erected his public prayers upon the Lord's Day and in all his pastoral duties. So often testimony is borne to the power of those prayers as being the very first factor that touched a visitor with the reality of the God whom that minister preached. How often have I heard people say to me that they do not remember anything of the first sermon they heard D. Martyn Lloyd-Jones preach at Westminster Chapel, London, but they were so struck by his praying. None of Professor John Murray's former students at Westminster Theological Seminary, Philadelphia, will ever forget his opening prayers before each lecture in systematic theology, because of their passion, their dreadful awe and their love, all whispered in the most clear but muted tone. Dr. Alexander Whyte speaks of the praying of Robert Candlish in the pulpit of Free St. George's, Edinburgh, a century ago:

> We used to say that his first prayer was enough for the whole of that day. He so "prayed in that prayer." He so came and reasoned together with God in that prayer. Sometimes he would take us to our knees till we had knees in those days like James the Just, as he led us through the whole of Paul's reasoning with God and with man in the Epistle to the Romans. Sometimes he would argue like Job, and would not be put down; and then he would weep like Jeremiah and dance and sing like Isaiah. That great preacher was an Elijah both in his passions and in his prayers. He would put all his passions at one time into an Assembly speech as if he stood before Ahab, and at another time into a great sermon to his incomparably privileged people: but I liked his passions best in his half-hour prayer on a Sabbath morning; he so "prayed in that prayer."[6]

When one turns to Dr. Lloyd-Jones for some advice about praying, one finds a reluctance to make his own habits of prayer a matter of common knowledge. He says, "I confess freely that I

6. Alexander Whyte, *Lord Teach Us to Pray*, (Grand Rapids: Baker Book House, 1922), p. 70.

have often found it difficult to start praying in the morning."[7] Yet there is one important observation that he elevates to a rule:

> Always respond to every impulse to pray. The impulse to pray may come when you are reading or when you are battling with a text. I would make an absolute law of this—always obey such an impulse. Where does it come from? It is the work of the Holy Spirit; it is a part of the meaning of "Work out your own salvation with fear and trembling. For it is God which worketh in you both to will and to do of his good pleasure" (Philippians 2:12–13). This often leads to some of the most remarkable experiences in the life of the minister. So never resist, never postpone it, never push it aside because you are busy. Give yourself to it, yield to it; and you will find not only that you have not been wasting time with respect to the matter with which you are dealing, but that actually it has helped you greatly in that respect. You will experience an ease and a facility in understanding what you were reading, in thinking, in ordering matter for a sermon, in writing, in everything, which is quite astonishing. Such a call to prayer must never be regarded as a distraction; always respond to it immediately, and thank God if it happens to you frequently.[8]

Prayer is just as necessary after preaching—not merely prayer for blessing and fruit, but also prayer for protection against pride so that one's usefulness may not be diminished or hindered. There is nothing more delightful for the preacher than the sense of well-being that follows a sermon characterized by some liberty and power. People have been helped; expressions of thanks have been more profusive than usual, though unnecessary to the feelings of euphoria, for the experience itself is the most stimulating to the minister. As he drives home with his family he is more animated and amusing than usual! All is right in the world: what

7. D. Martyn Lloyd-Jones, *Preaching and Preachers*, (Grand Rapids: Zondervan, 1971), p. 170.
8. Ibid., p. 171.

a wonderful calling is the preacher's! Then we must be on guard lest the great enemy of souls destroy us through pride. Let us then give the glory to the Lord for all that has helped any and keep for ourselves only the imperfect, for that is ours entirely. A sermon that has been the very reverse, wearying to us and to our hearers, one that makes us want to lock ourselves in our studies until all the congregation has left the building, may be more advantageous in teaching us humility. "And lest I should be exalted above measure through the abundance of the revelations, there was given to me a thorn in the flesh. . . . Most gladly therefore will I rather glory in my infirmities, that the power of Christ may rest upon me. Therefore I take pleasure in infirmities, in reproaches, in necessities . . . in distresses for Christ's sake: for when I am weak, then am I strong" (II Cor. 12:7-10). Let us know that for a powerful sermon, more depends upon a spirit of prayer, upon faithfulness in things great and small, upon one's relationship with one's congregation and especially upon humility than depends upon talents and gifts, indispensable though these also are.

Let us make up our minds that for a revival of powerful preaching in the church we must be diligent in the Word, and in the exercise and proclamation of faith, and in prayer. These are the only means of power that the church has, or ever will have.

15

Pastoral Preaching
J. Peter Vosteen

After completing eight years of service in New Jersey, I took up my labors in a new charge. As I stepped into the pulpit for the first time, I was overwhelmed by the realization that I did not know the people to whom I was addressing God's Word. What was I going to say to these people? I could say, "Thus says the Lord," but how could I apply that Word to their lives in a meaningful way? I did not know them. I did not understand their background, their culture, or their particular needs. I could only preach to them in a very general way. "I must visit them," I said to myself. "I must get to know them. I must gain understanding of their wants, desires, dreams, and goals before my preaching can be truly pastoral preaching—worthwhile to them and satisfying to me."

Once again I was reminded of the story told around the potbellied stove in New England and immortalized by Marshall Dodge and Bob Bryan in the "Bert and I" records.

> Rev. Foggs had only one person in church that Sunday, Henry Treat, a farmer of 78. The hymns sounded reedy with only Rev. Foggs, Henry Treat, and Miss Trombly, the organist, singing. The Psalms didn't do so badly since Henry liked to shout the responses right out. Then the Reverend scratched his head and peered over the edge of the pulpit and asked Henry in a whisper if he should go ahead with the sermon with only Henry and Miss Trombly there to hear it. Henry replied that when only one calf appeared at feeding

time, he fed it. Well, Rev. Foggs delivered a spirited sermon lasting two hours. After the service when the Reverend shook Henry's hand at the door, Henry confided that while he would go ahead and feed only one calf, he would not feed it the whole load.

The man of God can be diligent in his task and calling, can preach the Word of the Lord fervently, while at the same time missing the mark because he has not taken into account his audience. Preaching is the proclamation of God's Word. But it is more. It is the proclamation of God's Word to His people. Of course, it remains the Word of God even without the people. If no one listens and no one believes, it is still the authoritative truth of the living God. The prophets of old spoke their word to absent nations (see Isa. 13-21). We do not know the response that was given, but it was a powerfully effective word accomplishing God's design. Nevertheless, under normal circumstances God speaks to living people who are present. The preacher's purpose is to confront these people with God's message for them; to bring them face to face with Jesus Christ; to call them to respond (see the preaching of Peter at Pentecost, Acts 2, and the other sermons recorded in the Book of Acts). This proclamation takes many forms. It is at once exhortation and comfort. It is warning and promise. It is a call to repentance and an assurance that God changes lives. Never may the sermon degenerate into a theological lecture or an ethical treatise, or an emotional appeal. Always it must be God's good news in Jesus Christ. Whether it is the Old Testament or the New Testament that is being preached, it is always Jesus Christ who is before the people. He speaks of judgment and of salvation. He describes the awful agonies of eternal punishment and beckons men to the Father's house, which He has gone to prepare for those who love and serve Him. What a joy it is to preach this magnificent Word which calls men out of a dying hell into a living hope!

But how can we do this? We cannot accomplish it by mounting the pulpit to guess what God might say to people today. Nor can we just read the Scripture and pray that the Holy Spirit will make it clear to the hearers. Nor dare we simply read what John Calvin or John Knox said to his age and parrot that to ours. The uniqueness of the call of God is that He calls new men for each generation. He prepares them in the study of the original languages and cultures of Scripture. He trains them to speak to the people to whom He sends them. He equips them with His Holy Spirit. The moment of truth arrives when the preacher stands before his congregation with the infallible Word in his hand and opens his mouth to speak. The preacher stands between two worlds—the ancient and the modern. He stands between God and his people. He lives with his Bible. He lives with his people. How can he effectively relate to both at the same time and communicate the eternal truths of the one to the other?

1. *The Preacher's Contact With the Word*

Paul had traveled the 100 miles from the gold fields of the Roman colony of Philippi toward the west and the port city of Thessalonica on the Aegean Sea. He had apparently passed by the city of Amphipolis because there was no synagogue there. In Thessalonica Paul found an enclave of Jews. For three successive Sabbaths he entered the synagogue and "reasoned with them from the Scriptures, explaining and proving that the Christ had to suffer and rise from the dead" (Acts 17:2, 3). The result was that some of the Jews and a large number of God-fearing Greeks with a few prominent women were persuaded to join Paul and Silas. What was Paul's personal feeling about his preaching and its results? He tells us in his first letter to the Thessalonians:

> You know, brothers, that our visit to you was not a failure. We had previously suffered and been insulted in Philippi, as you know, but with the help of our God we dared to tell you his gospel in spite of strong opposition. For the appeal we make does not spring from error or impure motives, nor are we trying to trick you. On the contrary, we speak as men approved by God to be entrusted with the gospel. We are not trying to please men, but God, who tests our hearts. You

> know we never used flattery, nor did we put on a mask to
> cover up greed—God is our witness. We were not looking
> for praise from men, not from you or anyone else (I Thess.
> 2:1-6).

For Paul and for us, there must be a conviction that it is God
who speaks in His Word. He is the center of all preaching. It is
His message that is being communicated. The implications of this
for preaching are as follows:

1. The minister must be called of God. We cannot presume to
speak for God. We cannot take upon ourselves the office without
the assurance that it is God who is preparing us all of our life in
all of our ways to do His work. It must be an internal conviction
and an external confirmation by the church. "A prophet who
presumes to speak in my name anything I have not commanded
him to say, or a prophet who speaks in the name of other gods,
must be put to death" (Deut. 18:20). God will not treat lightly
the false prophet. We must have the conviction that we are ap-
proved by God. (Joel Nederhood analyzes in more detail the minister's call earlier in this volume.)

2. The minister in representing God must speak the truth.
God is truth. His Word is truth. Therefore, the person speaking
for God must be most zealous to guard the depository and speak
it well. How sad it is to hear so many men who claim to speak for
God use His Word so lightly. I was appalled at what passed for
the preaching of the Word in one church I recently attended. The
minister read a passage from the Bible and then proceeded to
ignore it while giving us platitudes and human regulations to
govern the way the people lived, all in the name of the living
God. That same Sunday in another congregation the minister
read the Scripture, dealt with the passage, but gave it an interpretation and application that was utterly foreign to what Jesus
Christ had said. If it is Christ's Word that we are proclaiming to
His church, how dare we say what is our thought or our idea.
This is pride in its most strident form.

Consequently, Paul in this passage tells us that he does not
appeal to the people from error or impure motive or trickery. He

assures them that he is not desirous of pleasing them or flattering them. He is not after their money. He wants to serve God alone and to represent Him truly to them. Any preacher who is a preacher indeed must begin with this foundation and remain on it. He must constantly remind himself of his calling because he will be easily tempted to "scratch the itching ears" of his people. When the people are unwilling to hear, instead of widening the scope of his ministry to new people in the community as Christ commanded, he will be tempted to change his message to please those who are now his support base, but who are unwilling to take up their cross daily to follow Jesus Christ. In the interest of popularity and large crowds I have seen many ministers go down the broad way of human psychology and philosophy only to end in destruction. This gives the psyche a temporary feeling of relief, but ultimately starves the soul. The consistent preaching of the gospel of Jesus Christ with a direct application of its message to the hearer is the only food that feeds the soul for eternal life.

If God in His integrity is to be the center of our preaching, then we as His messengers must carry in our persons the integrity of our association with Him. We cannot have impure motives. Paul says, "We never used flattery, nor did we put on a mask to cover up greed. We were not looking for praise from men" (I Thess. 2:5, 6). Jesus condemned the preachers of His day because, as He put it, "they do not practice what they preach" (Matt. 23:3). Often I have seen churches disrupted and their witness destroyed because of the minister. He got involved with the organist. He couldn't handle his personal finances and was indebted to everyone in the congregation. He was lazy and lacked self-discipline so that his work never got done on time. Motivation? What was the motivation of these men? Were they constrained by the love of Christ? Who can look into the heart but God? And what of the men who were always seeking the praise of their congregations? They had to be the best preacher in the city if not the state or the nation. What was their motivation? What of the men who always preach popular topics, saying the words their congregation wants to hear, giving them loads of worship elements that have high entertainment value. What was their moti-

vation? I do not know, only God knows. But this I do know—
that God wants men of integrity who preach and practice the
Word of the living God. It is only as we live out of the Word
ourselves and submit to the power of the Holy Spirit's control
over us that we can avoid the peculiar temptations that befall the
minister.

To accomplish this submission we must be involved in personal group Bible studies with our congregations and receive the
ministration of their gifts. Preachers must do more than give from
the Word; they must also receive, and that on a regular basis. Too
often ministers are only giving out and not taking in. Certainly
we can have fellowship with other ministers and enjoy their exchange of common experiences. However, we must also learn to
have meaningful growth experiences with the people to whom we
minister.

Churches Alive, a parachurch organization with headquarters
in San Bernardino, California, seeks to develop Bible studies in
local churches. It has as part of its policy that ministers should
not lead "Growth Groups." The reason for this lies in the peculiar relationship that most often exists between the minister and
his people. The minister is seen as an authority figure who deserves respect. That is good. However, along with this respect
there often exists the view that the pastor must know everything
about the Bible and have the last word in every discussion. Consequently, in a Bible study where the minister is the leader, the
members of the study often remain silent, deferring their opinions and experiences to him. Instead of participation, the study
becomes a time for the minister to talk and the others to ask
questions or listen. The result is that the minister is on the spot
and the rest of the group goes away unfulfilled. Generally speaking, such groups do not work. As ministers, we have to learn to
participate as any other member in such a study, to teach our
people that their experience with the Scriptures is important too.
As we share in this manner we can grow through interaction and
fellowship with the other members of the congregation sharing
their gifts with us. In this way we buffer ourselves against Satan's
attacks through becoming a vital interacting member of the body

of Christ. We do not lose our positions as ministers of the Word, but we do enhance our positions as members of the church of Jesus Christ.

Furthermore, Jesus taught His disciples not to be called "Benefactors" (Luke 22:25, 26)—those who put others on the dole—but to be servants, those who do for others. As such we teach the Word not only by preaching, but also by putting it into practice in our own lives as we live among God's people. How easy it is to be available to counsel, give advice, and have others hang on our every word. What a massage for our egos! But to go out and put into practice the teaching of Jesus by developing the fruit of the Spirit, by loving our enemies, by walking the second mile, that is much harder. But that is what we must do if our preaching is to be real to our people and have an effect on their lives.

To be an effective preacher, we have seen that it requires our trust in the integrity of God and the development of the integrity of our person. However, it also takes our confidence in the integrity of the Word. Paul calls it a gospel, good news for the people to whom it comes. To be good news it must have an effect on their lives, different from the common perception of life as bad news. We are plagued by our failure and our guilt because of our sin and our inability to conquer that sin. Our God has said that He conquers sin by the life and death of His Son. In the Son there is then truly good news.

For the preacher to communicate that good news he must be absolutely convinced that the Word he preaches to his people makes a difference in their lives. To this end he must believe the promises God has made to him. For example, God said to the prophets through Jeremiah, "But if they had stood in my council, they would have turned God's people from their evil ways and from their evil deeds" (Jer. 23:22). Or the teaching of Jesus when He said, "I tell you the truth, whoever hears my word and believes him who sent me has eternal life and will not be condemned; he has crossed over from death to life" (John 5:24). And Peter's word to God's elect in Asia Minor: "For you have been born again, not of perishable seed, but of imperishable, through the living and enduring word of God" (I Pet. 1:23).

Does God's Word really change lives? That is the question that must be realistically faced by every minister of the Word. Unless we can say a resounding yes, the church of Christ is in deep trouble. Preachers will gradually veer away from the awful truths of God for indirect and less challenging words of men. Gradually the cutting edge will leave the sword, and the sermon will neither penetrate nor judge (Heb. 4:12).

At the same time those who do stay with the Word and preach it in all of its power, who expect God to work through His Word, and who look for results, must be patient. God's work is not done overnight. One man sows the seed, another waters the seed, but God brings the harvest. It has been my experience that we cannot predict the results of preaching God's Word. Some people rejoice in salvation. Some people become angry because God's thoughts are not their thoughts and they will not conform. Some people go to find a different preacher. Some people weep with tears of repentance. The one thing that is certain is that God's Word never returns to Him void. It always accomplishes what God wants it to. And as we embody that Word in our lives and in our speech, we shall exemplify what Paul told the Corinthians: "For we are to God the aroma of Christ among those who are being saved and those who are perishing. To the one we are the smell of death; to the other, the fragrance of life. And who is equal to such a task? Unlike so many, we do not peddle the word of God for profit. On the contrary, in Christ we speak before God with sincerity, like men sent from God" (II Cor. 2:15-17).

2. The Preacher's Contact With His Congregation

How the congregation is to be viewed will determine the relationship of the preacher to his people. In the Old Testament God's covenant people were ruled by God through mediators and, after they demanded to be like the other nations around them, by kings. Consequently the dominant form of the church's structure was that of a nation. Being a nation the relationships were very formal and highly structured. The king had his palace and his throne, which separated him from his people. He had his soldiers and his servants. Coordinate with him were the priests. They too had a very structured relationship with the people. They performed their tasks with great ritual in a temple, which the people could only approach, but not enter. The prophets spoke the Word of God to the people. Indeed this Word brought comfort, consolation, and hope to those who trusted the Lord. However, since the prophet was called to be a messenger from God to return the congregation back to covenant obedience to the law, most of the time the message was that of sin and judgment. Again the people felt the sting of separation from Yahweh, not because of His choice, but because of theirs. Nevertheless, the total impression of the Old Testament congregation was that of distance from God.

But the form of the church in the New Testament age is more that of a household or family. Indeed we are "a chosen people, a royal priesthood, a holy nation" (I Pet. 2:9). In this way Peter related the Old Testament church to the New Testament church on a continuum. But just previous to that he said that the church is "a spiritual house to be a priesthood, offering spiritual sacrifices acceptable to God through Jesus Christ" (I Pet. 2:5). We are then the family of God. "How real is the love the Father has lavished on us, that we should be called children of God! And that is what we are!" (I John 3:1). Jesus is our brother. We are brothers and sisters together in one family. Jesus warns us that we must make this family a priority in our lives even above our natural family to the point where it is necessary to "hate" our father, mother, sister, and brother in order to follow him (Luke 14:26).

This nature of the church as family influences the relationship that the preacher has to it. He is first of all a member of the family. As such he is dealing with the others in the family and not just as the head of the household who controls all things for his purposes. Rather, as a leader in the congregation he is to be a servant and not a master (cf. Luke 22:25, 26). He is to minister God's Word to the family so that the children recognize and give obedience to their one Father who is in heaven. Those who faithfully do this will treat the other members of the family with respect. As Paul instructs Timothy, "Do not rebuke an older man harshly, but exhort him as if he were your father. Treat younger men as brothers, older women as mothers, and younger women as sisters, with absolute purity" (I Tim. 5:1, 2).

At the same time, as a servant it will be necessary for him to cleanse himself from base purposes that originate in the cravings of his sinful nature. Instead, God's servant must "pursue righteousness, faith, love and peace, along with those who call on the Lord out of a pure heart. And the Lord's servant must not quarrel; instead, he must be kind to everyone, able to teach, not resentful. Those who oppose him he must gently instruct, in the hope that God will grant them repentance leading them to a knowledge of the truth, and that they will come to their senses and escape from the trap of the devil, who has taken them captive to do his will" (II Tim. 2:22–26).

Secondly, as the servant-teacher who feeds the family, he must remember that the members of the family are all at different levels of physical development and maturity just as would be the case with any natural family. The course of the natural development of each person will determine his or her interests and needs and comprehension. At the same time the pastor must be sensitive to the spiritual development of each person in his congregation. An individual may be old in years, but still only a babe in Christ. Or he may be only in his twenties, yet be mature in Christ. The instruction of the Scripture is that we must feed the young with milk (I Pet. 2:2) and the mature with solid food (Heb. 5:14). The danger for the pastor lies on two fronts: (1) that he is too intellectual to reach the babes, or (2) that he feeds everyone pabulum, and none grows to maturity. In the region of the church where I minister, the most common complaint is that sermons are like Sunday school lessons: a simple repetition of the Scriptures without depth of understanding or breadth of application. The people claim they return home from Sunday worship services without being edified or challenged.

How can a pastor avoid the Scylla and Charybdis? Only one way. He must be steeped in the Scriptures so that when he opens one passage of the Bible, he relates to the context from which it comes, to the total working of God in the rest of the Scriptures, and to Jesus Christ as the center of all God's redemptive activity (see Edmund Clowney's comments earlier in this volume). Furthermore, there must be a freshness, a vividness, a concreteness, and a contemporaneity in the presentation that keeps the congregation's attention and interest. To reiterate the obvious will not do. To abstract, theorize, or stay in the realm of principle will only bring forth glassy stares and heavy eyelids. The passage being dealt with must be so real to the listener that he can have more than his sense of hearing aroused; he must be able to feel, taste, and see what is happening (as Jay Adams and R.C. Sproul have pointed out). Of course, some passages lend themselves more readily to this than others. When the preacher is talking about Naaman's leprosy and his cleansing in the Jordan, he has all the ingredients for vivid description. However, when he is dealing with Paul's description of justification by faith, it is obviously missing. What does one do then? Well, then the vividness and concreteness must be in illustrative materials, in stories, and in specific application of the scriptural truths to the hearers' lives.

Most especially, every sermon must have a challenging application. A sermon by definition is more than an explanation of scriptural truth. It is also an application of that truth to the lives of the people. When listening to a sermon the congregation expects to have more than their intellect challenged. They expect, and rightly so, that they will receive a message from God that will challenge their lives and their commitment of faith. They expect, as it has been stated to me, that they will receive something that they can carry with them throughout the week ahead. For this to take place, it is absolutely imperative that the minister of God's Word have intimate contact with the people whom he serves. He must know their hopes, their desires, their dreams, their failures, their sins. He must be acquainted with their work and their recreation. The closer he can get to them in all aspects of their lives, the more real will be God's message as applied to their needs. Amos knew the habits of the women of his day when he said, "Hear this word, you cows of Bashan on Mount Samaria, you women who oppress the poor and crush the needy and say to

your husbands, 'Bring us some drinks!' " (Amos 4:1). Jesus likewise had analyzed the ways of the Pharisees when He said to
them, "Woe to you Pharisees, because you give God a tenth of
your mint, rue and all other kinds of garden herbs, but you neglect justice and the love of God (Luke 11:42). Paul understood
the Cretan culture and had read in their literature when he commented, "Even one of their own prophets has said, 'Cretans are
always liars, evil brutes, lazy gluttons.' This testimony is true.
Therefore, rebuke them sharply, so that they will be sound in the
faith . . ." (Titus 1:12, 13). We must do no less.

In making an application it is imperative that the lesson be
drawn directly from the Scripture passage being considered and
not hung on it like a dangling appendage. (Hendrik Krabbendam
warns us of the danger of the moralizing application in his chapter, in the present volume, entitled "Hermeneutics and Preaching.") It is very easy for a preacher to use a biblical text as a
springboard to promote his personal concerns or pet peeves. This
must be avoided at all costs, for should the preacher do this, he
will alienate his people and destroy the power of his preaching.
The Holy Spirit only stirs response to what God says through
man and not what man says on his own.

Assuming then that we are going to make a good scriptural
application, when the congregation is assembled, how exactly is
that application to be made to a greatly diverse group of people
with different interests and different ages? Should the application
be directed just to the adults with no reference to the children?
Should there be a special application to the children? Should we
just use generalities and hope that the message hits someone?

The principle that I have used throughout my ministry is to
use numerous specific applications and weave them into the tapestry of my sermon. Don't save the applications until the end.
Use them throughout the sermon. Some of these applications will
apply directly to the people. Some will apply to them by analogy.
Others will not apply at all, but because they are related to the
culture in which they live they will see the relevance of what you
are saying and will be able to say "Amen."

But what about children's sermons? They have become very popular today. Frankly, I do not like them as they are normally structured, that is, as a separate message designed just for the children. Implicit in this procedure is the idea that this sermon is for the children, but that the regular sermon is for the adults. Worship is a covenantal, family event. The regular sermon is not just for adults, it is for the whole family. Therefore, if I have a large number of children in the congregation and the setting is suitable, I take special time in my regular sermon to address the children. Otherwise I just make passing applications that are directed especially to them. In any case, we must never give the impression to any group, "This sermon is not for you." Every sermon is for everyone.

Earlier in this chapter we stated that we must use directness of speech and simplicity of concept to reach the young and those with limited instruction. This axiom stands. Nevertheless, there is another emphasis that must be made along with this. In earlier generations the masses were passed by and the sermon was directed to the elite of society. But in our society the masses are educated. Therefore, if we direct the entire sermon to those who are the least informed, we leave a large segment of the congregation unchallenged. Those who come to church, by and large, are not biblically illiterate. Although our society as a whole knows more about the newest video games than it does of Moses and Jesus, the people who come to church usually have been instructed in Sunday school or by personal study. Worship must not be simplified to the point where the only message each Sunday is to believe that Jesus died for your sins. The great crying need of the church today is not only to believe on the Lord Jesus Christ, but in believing, to make Him the sovereign ruler of life. The church is crippled by unbelief and disobedience. Therefore, the pulpit must give an ardent call to faithfulness and submission. The only way this can be done is by preaching the whole counsel of God. If we narrow our concept of God and His demands so that we can preach an easy gospel and let the people sit in an easy pew, we ultimately destroy the church.

To illustrate these various principles let me give a sample out-line of Hebrews 12:1–3: "Therefore, since we are surrounded by such a great cloud of witnesses, let us throw off everything that hinders and the sin that so easily entangles, and let us run with perseverance the race marked out for us. Let us fix our eyes on Jesus, the author and perfecter of our faith, who for the joy set before him endured the cross, scorning its shame, and sat down at the right hand of the throne of God. Consider him who endured such opposition from sinful men, so that you will not grow weary and lose heart" (NIV).

Theme: Don't Quit Now

I. Preparations for the Race

   A. Overcoming Inertia

      1. Types of inertia in our lives
      2. Encouragement to the race from the great cloud of witnesses in chapter 11

   B. Stripping Down

      1. Conditioning for the Olympics.
      2. Conditioning for the Christian life
        a. Things that hinder
        b. Sins that beset

II. Running the Race

   A. Getting Out of the Blocks

      1. Running according to the course that God has laid out
      2. Finishing the race you have begun
        a. Need for the Hebrew Christians (Heb. 10:32–34; cf. Heb. 10:19–31; 4:11; 6:11; 10:39)
        b. Need for us—our generation's preoccupation with instant gratification
        c. Involvement of hardship and discipline to complete the race

B. Looking to Jesus
  1. He is ahead of you.
     a. If you look at the crowd, you will be distracted.
     b. If you look at your feet, you will be discouraged.
  2. He has run the race already.
     a. Author and perfecter of faith
     b. He has suffered in the course of His race.
     c. He has triumphed.

Such a structure as this is true to the text and at the same time leads us to God's Word for the direction of our daily lives. It opens up avenues of instruction and encouragement for everyone. Who hasn't felt inertia in his life? Who hasn't felt a lack of interest in life's routine tasks? The menial steps in the house-wife's preparation of meals, the dullness in the accountant's fig-ures, the enigma in the architect's plans. All of this tends to have us avoid the repetitive actions of life for the temporarily exciting. So too in the Christian life, we avoid the daily need of Bible reading, prayer, and fellowship with the Lord for the exhilarating emotional happening. We leave the discipline of our battle against sin for a recreational repast. Each preacher in his own cultural setting can take each need with its biblical solution and encouragement in Jesus Christ and apply it specifically to the people whom he serves when he knows their lives well. Then the Word of God strikes home in a powerful fashion.

Furthermore, this structure enables vivid illustration for the young in its reference to the Olympic games and running the race. This can be related to the present interest in jogging and physical fitness. At the same time, it has a message for the older adults of the congregation in terms of finishing the race and not giving up when the full effects of fatigue set in. It has a word for new Christians as they wrestle against the unnecessary activities of life that hinder the Christian walk, and for older Christians dealing with a besetting sin. It encourages all to look to Jesus to find in His victory over sin our victory as we refuse to give up.

But what further kinds of applications should we be making? Should they be only personal, or should they also challenge the social structure? Should there be words directed to the spheres of education, government, and business, or should these be left out of the pulpit?

The rule has to be that when Scripture makes a direct application of truth to our lives, we make a direct application to the congregation. For example, the Sermon on the Mount says very straightforward things about our personal conduct and attitudes. These words of counsel must be made direct and hard hitting.

Furthermore, the Bible has very definite words to speak about our life together in the church. It tells us how we are to relate to each other as members of one body; it describes the structure of the church; it tells us what kinds of leaders we are to have and how we are to respect them. The Bible describes the elements of worship—the place of the Word, the sacraments, and prayer. It tells us to be a loving, repenting, restoring society with inner discipline.

However, when it comes to specific principles for government, business, and education, the message is not as direct. In the Old Testament the church had a national structure with detailed rules. These rules no longer apply directly to the church today. How they can be applied to civil structure is a very much debated question. The only certain word comes from Paul in Romans 13:1-7 and from Peter in I Peter 2:13-17. But even these words are in a context of personal response to government and are not an exhaustive outline of governmental activity.

Nevertheless, the Bible does have words of instruction for certain areas of cultural life that are related to societal structure. The teaching about marriage, family, employers, and employees is clear and precise (Eph. 5:22-6:9; Col. 3:18-4:1; I Peter 2:18-3:7). Consequently, the preacher can speak out very directly in these areas and draw principal conclusions about other areas where the connection is plain. Beyond that, those who declare the Word of the Lord should be most cautious lest they violate the sacred truth that has been granted to them. Leave the development of principles for Christian social structure to those who have been trained in these areas.

There is still one other area for us to examine. If the New Testament church is seen as the household of God and the children of God, then God alone is her Father. In light of this, Jesus warns us against following the rabbinic custom of calling our teachers and pastors *father* (Matt. 23:9). Nevertheless, Paul refers to himself as father in relationship to the churches. To the Thessalonians he says, "For you know that we dealt with each of you as a father deals with his own children" (I Thess. 2:11). And more directly he says to the Corinthians, "In Christ Jesus I became your father through the gospel" (I Cor. 4:15). Is Paul contradicting Jesus or is he setting an example for us preachers to follow?

Jesus was not concerned about the use of the title per se. Included with the term *father* was also the term *teacher*. "Nor are you to be called teacher" (Matt. 23:10). And yet it is apparent that in the New Testament church, with the full approval of the apostles, the term father continued to be used in the biological households, and the term teacher was used in the church itself (cf. Eph. 4:11 and 6:4). Jesus was concerned with the social standing that accompanied these terms and the hypocrisy embedded in them. Those who are leaders in the church are to be servants for the rest as Jesus Himself came to serve and not to be served. They are not to "lord it over" those entrusted to them, but to be "examples to the flock" (I Pet. 5:3). The church does not exist to exalt its leadership and glory in their abilities, but to join with their leaders in the exaltation of Jesus Christ. When the Corinthian church divided into groups following their various leaders and said that they "followed Paul" or they "followed Apollos" or they "followed Cephas," Paul responded by saying, "What, after all, is Apollos? And what is Paul? Only servants, through whom you came to believe—as the Lord has assigned to each his task" (I Cor. 3:5). No, it is perfectly legitimate for Paul to refer to himself as a father, and thereby to set an example for us to follow. However, we must carefully discern what he means when he uses the term.

First of all, Paul means that he has been used by God to bring others to faith in Jesus Christ. All throughout Asia Minor, Greece, and beyond he has sons not by profligacy, but "in the faith," and children "in Christ Jesus through the gospel" (cf. I Cor. 4:14, 15, 17; I Tim. 1:2; Titus 1:4). Anyone who is going to be a preacher must have a preeminent concern to bring others to a knowledge of Jesus Christ. We can become so preoccupied with the construction of the message and how it will be received by our congregations that we can easily forget the primary reason for preaching. There are, sadly, many preachers whose sermons do not have enough gospel in them to convert a Titmouse. When I was in my first charge, I remember talking with one of the older experienced pastors in the presbytery who had been preaching for many years. He told me that he had recently found out by conversations with his people that they did not know the very basics of the gospel, in particular justification by faith. He was shocked and alarmed that he could have been preaching to them for so long a time and that they could still be so ignorant. He was honest enough to set the blame squarely on his own shoulders and to set about rectifying the situation.

Secondly, by using the term father, Paul is speaking of his intimate concern for those whom he serves. He contrasts his work with that of the tutor or guardian, the *paidagogos* of the Greek home. The *paidagogos* was a slave that had been chosen by the family to direct the education of the child. He was in charge of the entire training including behavior, attire, and deportment. He was principally a disciplinarian who saw to it that the boy toed the mark. If he didn't, then the tutor used corporal punishment to affect a change of ways. The tutor's position was to see to it that the family mores were instilled in the child by way of chastisement. By contrast, Paul deals with the church not by using the rod to chastise, but by coming to them with love and concern. The church has many preachers who will bare their teeth and castigate their congregations from the pulpit for their errant behavior, but not many who will speak to them with the love of Christ as a father desiring that the change comes by way of a new heart. How tempting it is for the minister to take the Word of God and beat his congregation over the head for not attending services, for not giving to the budget, for not reading their Bibles, or for not showing up for the fellowship supper. But what the church really needs is pastors who so love their congregations that they will woo them and urge them by the constraining love of Christ. We need ministers of the Word who go to the heart and seek for total rebirth of the person so that the desire to change behavior starts from within.

To achieve this goal there is one quality of life that Paul emphasizes he had as a parent—gentleness. He says to the Thessalonians, "As apostles of Christ we could have been a burden to you, but we were gentle among you, like a mother caring for her little children." And again in the same passage, "you know that we dealt with each of you as a father deals with his own children, encouraging, comforting and urging you to live lives worthy of God, who calls you into his kingdom and glory" (I Thess. 2:7, 11, 12). Jesus described His behavior among His disciples as "gentle and lowly of heart" (Matt. 11:29).

Surely as the followers of Christ we must have this gentleness in our demeanor. It is necessary for all Christians, but most necessary in the leadership of the church. An elder must not be hot tempered. He must not be violent, but gentle and not quarrelsome. More people are won for Christ with honey than with vinegar. People are lost for the kingdom by arguments. If one argues, he usually wins the battle, but loses the war. When attacked, the soldier of Christ does well to remain silent and by his good behavior win his adversaries for Christ. Peter says, "Always be prepared to give an answer to everyone who asks you to give the reason for the hope that you have. But do this with gentleness and respect . . ." (I Pet. 3:15, 16). The minister who gets upset when things do not go his way, when the church is not growing as he would expect, when he is under fire from some faction in his church, will never achieve his goals. But the man of God who shows his faith under fire and remains calm because his trust is in the Lord to build his church, that man will by his fatherly concern and gentleness win even his enemies to the Lord.

Another biblical image that expresses the concern of the father-preacher is that of the shepherd and his sheep. The shepherd gently leads those who have young (Isa. 40:11). He leads them out into green pastures by day and back into the sheepfold for rest by night. He defends his sheep from the lion and the wolf. He is always there to give them a sense of safety and security. Jesus is the Good Shepherd who genuinely cares for His sheep. He is the one who laid down His life for them. We who minister in His place must also have the heart of Jesus and likewise be willing to lay down our lives for His people.

The need today is as it was in Ezekiel's day. God through Ezekiel complained, "Woe to the shepherds of Israel who only take care of themselves! Should not shepherds take care of the flock? You eat the curds, clothe yourselves with the wool and slaughter the choice animals, but you do not take care of the flock. You have not strengthened the weak or healed the sick or bound up the injured. You have not brought back the strays or searched for the lost. You have ruled them harshly and brutally" (Ezek. 34:2-4).

We must always ask ourselves whether we are interested in our personal advancement in the ministry or the people of God? Are we more interested in the homeless or in our own comfortable housing? Are we more interested in healing the blind or in having people see that we are brilliant? Are we more interested in delivering the lost or in saving our own skin? The power of the pulpit is not in oratory or eloquence. It is in the man who walks with God and uses God's gifts to communicate the love of God in Jesus Christ to his congregation.

Which brings us to the third aspect of the father: he must live an exemplary life before his children. Again Paul says in the context of describing his fatherly concerns, "You are witnesses, and so is God, of how holy, righteous and blameless we were among you who believed" (I Thess. 2:10). To the Corinthians he says, "I urge you to imitate me" (I Cor. 4:16). A father who practices "Do as I say, but not as I do" is in for a disastrous family relationship with his children. The same is true for the pastor-father in the church. The congregation and the community in which we live are watching our lives. Preachers are always in the limelight. Their misdeeds are always magnified. Therefore, we must be on our best behavior, not because of what people might say, but because we are representatives of Jesus Christ and we want to please Him. We don't have to be stereotypes. We don't have to fit the mold of the minister who preceded us. We don't have to lose our individual identity or creativity. However, we must be sensitive to the realization that all people, especially the young, hate hypocrisy. Our lives must be consistent. And when we do make a mistake, we must be open about it. We must confess our sins to our brothers in Christ, asking their forgiveness. We are sinners too. But it must be evident that we are redeemed sinners growing in Jesus Christ. Here, too, we must be elders, "Shepherds of God's flock that is under your care, serving as overseers—not because you must, but because you are willing, as God wants you to be; not greedy for money, but eager to serve; not lording it over those entrusted to you, but being examples to the flock" (I Pet. 5:2, 3).

The preacher then stands in a unique place. He stands before God with the responsibility to be absolutely faithful to His truth and the requirement to proclaim it passionately and persistently. At the same time, he stands before his congregation with the responsibility to address their lives and needs with concern. He must "speak the truth in love" (Eph. 4:15).

How can he ever fulfill both of these demands? How can he be in his study and at the homes of his people? How can he meditate deeply on the Scriptures in solitude while meandering through the throngs of people who call for his aid? We cry out with Moses, "Oh Lord, please send someone else to do it" (Exod. 4:13). I'm not eloquent. I can't talk. The job is too difficult for me.

Yet the Lord uses crooked sticks like Jonah to do His work. He uses thunderbolts like Peter. He uses the under-educated James and the super-educated Paul. He uses the quiet John and the zealous Simon. What He requires of all of us is that we be humble and submit to His will depending on His grace. In the last analysis He expects us to be faithful; faithful to His truth and faithful to His people. "Each one should use whatever gift he has received to serve others, faithfully administering God's grace in its various forms. If anyone speaks, he should do it as one speaking the very words of God. If anyone serves, he should do it with the strength God provides, so that in all things God may be praised through Jesus Christ. To him be the glory and the power for ever and ever. Amen" (I Pet. 4:10, 11).

16

Reading the Word of God Aloud
David A. Dombek

The human voice is a gift of God. He made voices in many colors, intensities, and pitches. Some voices are melodious. Some are crusty. Some have great range and resonance. Some sound frail and thin. But God made them all. Many ministers have not learned how their voices work, or how they can best use them for God's glory and for edifying His people. In this chapter, we will explore briefly the marvel of the human voice. Then we will discuss how the minister should use his voice to read God's Word aloud.

1. The Voice

Did you ever attempt to preach during a downpour on the tin roof of a campground shelter? Did your wife—sitting at the back of the shelter—cup her hand behind her ear to signal to you that she could not hear you? Did you make yourself heard without developing laryngitis?

Did the brand-new sound system in your sanctuary expire at the most important moment of your sermon? Did your shaking voice sound like a squawk amid dunes of silence? Did you strain to make yourself heard? When you finally finished, did your head ache, and were you barely able to talk?

When you understand how God designed your voice to perform, you can meet crises like those related above with greater peace of mind and with less damage to your voice. As you begin

419

to analyze your voice, you might recall the term "voice box" or "vocal cords" first. But do you remember your lungs, throat, tongue, teeth, and sinus cavities, too? Do you think about your diaphragm and your viscera? All these combine to mold your "sound" into articulate speech and melodious song. You cannot use your voice well when you disregard your vocal tools.

The Instrument

"Vocal cords" and "voice box" are misnomers. No Aeolian harp rests atop the windpipe to turn your breath into music. Instead, two folds of muscle form an opening within the larynx. The distance between these folds, narrow or wide, and the tension of the fold muscles, tight or loose, determine the tone quality and the pitch of your voice. When you tighten your throat to yell at your congregation, your voice will only rise in pitch and become shrill in quality. Soon you will be hoarse. Do not press your larynx to perform against its design. God has given you ample vocal power from other parts of your body.

God formed the larynx to block the windpipe—either to prevent unwanted materials (e.g., food) from entering or to prevent air from escaping the lungs. Scientists consider speech a function added to the normal work of the larynx.[1] For proof, they point to rabbits, certain deer, and giraffes—all of which have larynxes yet emit no sound. Since there is no need for these animals to make sounds, scientists reason that the animals did not develop this use of their larynxes.

But speech is more than our adaptation to the needs of our social structure or our manifestation of a superior intellect.[2] We were given larynxes for another reason than the two cited above: The larynx was made to help us to praise the Lord our God. (Besides, who is to say that rabbits do not talk to their Maker? As any farm boy knows, rabbits *do* make sounds!)

1. Virgil A. Anderson, *Training the Speaking Voice* (New York: Oxford University Press, 1961), p. 55f.
2. Ibid., p. 56.

The vocal folds are involuntary muscles. One can do little directly to control them. They react sympathetically with the rest of the body. So, to control the voice, one must control himself. When one can keep his temper or calm his terrors, he will achieve maximum use of the vocal cords and will produce the best tone quality and pitch.

The Power Source

The actual sound of the air whistling through your vocal folds is miniscule. Left to itself, even the most mellifluous voice would be inaudible. But the Lord created the human voice to praise Him. To effect that praise, God gave man a power source, amplifiers, and formulators. Watch a baby cry. It flails its arms wildly. It digs its feet against the cradle's mattress, or it kicks them in the air. Its face reddens with rage. Its eyes squeeze tightly in a horrible grimace. Its mouth trumpets endearing (or offending) screams to serve notice to the immediate world that something is awry. But all these histrionics are side shows to the main event: With its lungs and diaphragm, the infant grabs great chestfuls of air, and then it squanders them on your ears. It comes naturally to the baby.

Such innate vocal prowess comes from the lungs and the abdomen. Once inflated, the lungs naturally contract, forcing out the inhaled air until the pressure within the lungs equals the atmospheric pressure outside them. Inexperienced speakers, enjoined to control their breathing, attempt to force air through the larynx. Soon they become winded, and they find that they are without the necessary power to continue speaking.

To control the release of the air supply, one must employ two sets of muscles, the diaphragm and the viscera. The diaphragm, lauded among voice teachers, rests immediately below the lungs. It forms a platform, which expands when you inhale and contracts (relaxes) when you exhale. "Use your diaphragm!" simply means to control the speed at which you allow your lungs and diaphragm to contract or relax. But the diaphragm exercises no power, no support, for speaking or singing. This power comes from the proper use of the viscera.[3] These muscles in the abdominal area push, piston-like against the diaphragm. Through the diaphragm, the viscera forces the air from the lungs with the power necessary for yelling, singing, or oration. Thus, the speaker controls his exhalation so that he will not lack air when he needs it. And he uses his abdominal muscles to push out the air powerfully. This is how great opera singers can fill a hall with just their voices. They "project" their voices—literally, they push them out to the farthest listener.

The Amplifiers

When the air passes through the larynx, it is set vibrating. Hum. Go ahead, *Hummmmm!* Place your hand over your voice box. Do you feel anything? Probably not. Now repeat your hum and place your fingers upon your nose, your forehead, and your cheeks. You should feel a very slight vibration. Your sinus cavities and facial bones amplify the vibrating air into sound. When you suffer from a cold, you find talking to be unbearable because your head "rings." Those vibrating, resonating cavities throb because they are filled with mucus. To others you sound dull, muted, because those resonating chambers cannot amplify well. The chest cavity itself forms a drum, and it amplifies your voice's sound, especially in its lower ranges. The throat (pharynx) also amplifies your voice.

The Formulators

Now, let us consider how we fashion that vibrating wave of air into speech.

1. *Shaped sounds (vowels).* As a child, you discovered that the sound you made when you blew through your mouth could be changed when you altered the shape of your mouth from narrow

3. For both diaphragm and viscera, see ibid., pp. 28–32.

to wide to narrow ("ooo-eee-ooo"). That is how we make the vowels in our speech. Say the vowels of the alphabet. Notice the shapes and sizes your mouth takes to form the sounds. Vowels are the melody of your language. Repeat the vowels. Now notice the position your tongue takes in your mouth to form each vowel. When the *size* of the opening created by your mouth and tongue changes, the *sound* of the air racing through that opening will also change.

2. *Stamped sounds (consonants).* If vowels are the melody of our language, consonants are the harmony and the percussion to that tune. Originally, consonants were classified in two groups: voiced (musical) and unvoiced. Voiced consonants had a vocal tone in the stop. "M," "n," and "ng" are obvious voiced stops. Other examples of vocal consonants are the following: "v," "z," "j," "dh," and "l." There were four of these consonant types: plosive, fricative, nasal, and glide.

Plosive, as the name implies, denotes an explosion. "P," "b," "t," "d," "k," and "g" are all plosives. Fricatives are formed by two or more parts of the mouth rubbing together. "F," "v" "th," "dh," and "zh" are fricatives. Nasals are musical (voiced) consonants amplified through the nasal areas. "M," "n," and "ng" are nasals. Some consonants are formed by "the gliding of the tongue or the lips or both during the production of the sound."[4] "W," "l," "r," and "j" are glides.

Finally, consonants are classed according to the parts of the mouth that form them. Some consonants are made by the lips ("p," "b," "m," "w"). The lips combine with the teeth to form "f" and "v." The tongue touches the teeth making "th" and "dh." Consonants "t," "d," "n," "l," "s," and "z" are formed when the tongue meets the gums. Touching the roof of the mouth, the tongue makes "sh," "zh," "r," and "j." When one humps his tongue to touch the soft palate at the back of the mouth, he

4. Ibid., p. 269.

forms "k," "g," and "ng." Finally, the "h" sound is formed at the very back of the mouth.[5]

Why should one worry about any of this? Articulation. Slovenly enunciation clouds the congregation's ability to understand what is being said. I do not decry regional accents (some of which are delightfully musical), and I am certainly not criticizing genuine speech defects (e.g., hairlip, lisp, betacism, or mytacism). Articulation goes beyond pronunciation, whatever the accent may be. Articulation seeks to assure that the word, spoken or sung, is understandable.

What can you do to improve your articulation? Use your cassette tape recorder as your critic. Hear how you actually sound to others. Be relentless on yourself. Discover what consonants you cannot enuniciate clearly. Good speech books contain sections of exercises to help you to conquer the practice of slurring your speech.[6]

I regret that we cannot explore this area in greater detail. We are fearfully and wonderfully made. Remember, as ministers, that spoken words are our stock in trade. Are we concerned to make them understandable? Slipshod speech habits belie the speaker. Some people deem it pious to care more for sermon content than about the way it is presented. We should not malign concern to preach the Word faithfully, but we should also care to present the Word of God well, using the tools of speech He has given us.

2. Why Read Interpretatively at All?

One of the most wonderful facets of our duty as proclaimers of the Word of God—whether in family devotions or in the worship of the Lord—is the oral reading of His Word. Through it we proclaim the Word of our Father directly to His people. Yet

5. The technical terms for the above are as follows: *bilabials, labio-dentals, lingua-dentals, lingue-alveolar, lingua-palatal, lingua-velar,* and the *glottis.*
6. Not public-speaking books, but books on speech, like Anderson. Consult your local high school's speech teacher for advice.

many of us, ministers and laymen alike, read God's Word aloud dully.

I trembled when I chose that adverb *dully*. Yet, it was hard for me to find a word that would not question the motives of dedicated servants of God. *Dully* describes the quality of the oral reading of the Word of God and not the minister's or layman's personal devotion toward God's Word.

The Bible's writers were men of flesh and blood. Their message, the gospel, brings one to seraphic joy (Ps. 119; Luke 2:14), or it drives him to demonic terror (James 2:19). The gospel's cutting edge rescues, or it slays. Yet, by the way this awe-inspiring, God-given document is read aloud, a stranger to that Word of grace would never discern that the gospel of Christ should mean anything worthwhile to those who read it or to himself.

Dramatic reading of the Scriptures has been criticized for subjecting the Scriptures to a foreign interpretation: "Let the Scriptures speak for themselves," say the critics. "We don't need some actor telling us how *he* thinks the words were said." Consider, however, what this argument overlooks. There is no such thing as a neutral, nondramatic reading of Scripture. Bland, phlegmatic reading of God's Word connotes one's indifference to the text. Such an analysis may be wrong, to be sure, but the bland reader is giving his family or congregation two subliminal impressions: first, that he considers his sermon to be more important than the way he reads the text (he has spent much more time on his sermon), and second, that God's Word must await the preacher's weekly interpretation to be meaningful to his listeners. Do not forget that the reading of your Scripture text has already begun your sermon—the exegesis of that text. It is imperative, therefore, that your reading coincide with the exegesis. The exegesis, in turn, should help one to read the text correctly. The one is indispensable to the other.

The question of the interpretative reading of Scriptures is not Should I read the Bible interpretatively? Rather, it is Does my oral reading of the Bible paint a perspicuous, enthralling picture of the text? The point is that *any* reading of Scripture is an oral interpretation of Scripture, and we must be fully self-conscious as to the interpretation we are offering when we read.

To offer an appropriate oral interpretation of any scriptural passage, one must first *personally* confront that passage. To do this involves first of all an immersion in the "grammatical-historical" context of the passage. For example, imagine yourself telling, or prophesying, or singing the text to the world of Isaiah or of Paul. Use the research that has been done into the background of the text to provide an understanding of the people who originally heard that text.

The oral reader represents the author of the text to the hearers. He seeks to re-create the text for the hearers from the viewpoint of its author. In Philippians 3:17–21, Paul displays his "mercurial" emotions. In seeking to exegete the serious charges that Paul levels at his opponents, one must not muffle Paul's personal sadness. At the end of this text Paul took the Philippians to the throne room of Christ. The reader must sense and communicate Paul's joy. When one reads dramatically, it surely is not necessary to weep as he reads ". . . and now say again, even with tears" (NIV). But we cannot ignore such personal revelations. We must read Paul's anguish for us as much as we read his joy, which immediately follows it.

When you read dramatically, be prepared to be surprised by what the text will tell you. In Philippians 3 again, Paul listed a number of sins that drove him to tears. Among them, he linked gluttony with idolatry, and he called gluttons traitors to Christ's cross! Is gluttony that bad? Would you read the passage with the shock in which Paul wrote it? Scripture abounds with similar surprises, which we dull by bland reading. Dramatic reading of Scripture will reveal to you, and to your people, in a fresh and vivid way, the demand to repent and the joy of believing God.

3. The Art of Reading Aloud

Oral, or dramatic, reading does not mean stentorian, emotional delivery. Some ministers read and preach that way, but dramatic reading does not require it. Histrionic bombast has serious drawbacks for the oral reader and the preacher. Have you ever heard a preacher whirl toward a clamorous climax only to exhaust his energy before he reached it? He was demanding too much from his voice. Too much emotion is bad and may be even worse than not enough of it. Theatrics is not what I mean by dramatic reading or speaking.

Dramatic reading paints pictures for the ear that the author has painted for the eye. When one reads aloud, he uses a number of pitches and hues to color the text. He can stress one word, or several, above the rest of the sentence. He can vary the pace at which he reads the sentence. He can change the tone quality with which he reads—a scratchy voice for an old man. He can alter the pitch of his voice—a male reader might raise his voice when he reads a woman's words. And he can vary the rhythm, or beat, at which he reads. These various forms of emphasis are sharpened by the reader's use of silence. The conscious employment of pauses can add a great deal of color to a reading.

Before we begin our discussion, we must remember an old actor's adage: "There's no good way to read a line; but there are many wrong ones." This sage meant that there is no systematizing that actors can follow to guarantee them a flawless interpretation. Actors change the reading of their lines frequently as they look for a better interpretation. I mention this not to disquiet, but to comfort. Being able to interpret correctly one text in several different ways gives a vivid freshness to oral reading.

1. Emphasis on Certain Words

Let us begin by discussing the various ways a reader emphasizes the words he reads. Sentences of action revolve around their verbs. Say "Bill hit the ball." Emphasize each word by turns. The meaning you desire will determine where the stress is put:

a. *Bill* hit the ball. (Not John or Harry)

b. Bill *hit* the ball. (That is what he did. He did not pitch it or catch it.)

c. Bill, *hit* the ball! (A command)

d. Bill hit *the* ball. (That particular ball, an unusual stress.)

e. Bill hit the *ball.* (Not the dog or the barn.)

A number of elements combine to help us understand the relation of Bill to his battered ball. For a statement of simple fact, one would slightly emphasize the main verb (b). "Hit" is an action verb, and it tells what happened in the sentence. One should stress the action verb, unless there is a good reason to emphasize another word—and there are such reasons. Indiscriminate emphasis of words can make the reader "seasick" from going up and down. He can put himself to sleep—to say nothing about his listeners. (One obvious exception to this rule is "said" in "he said" preceding or following most quotations. Here, one should emphasize the quotation with its main verb.)

Linking verbs (*to be, seem, appear, become, feel, taste, look,* etc.) equate the subject and its compliment. Say Psalm 23:1a, "The Lord is my shepherd. . . ." Emphasize each word by turns.

a. *The* Lord is my shepherd. (That particular Lord. An unusual emphasis!)

b. The *Lord* is my shepherd. (As opposed to someone else's being my shepherd.)

c. The Lord *is* my shepherd. (Right now! Stresses the reality of the relationship.)

d. The Lord is *my* shepherd. (Who's?)

e. The Lord is my *shepherd.* (The nature of that relation.)

For the plain statement, the last example is the correct reading. In Psalm 23 David described his relation to God as a sheep's to his shepherd. Many of the verbs in the psalm are simple, strong, action verbs. Though you may not wish to read the psalm stressing all its action verbs, practice it that way once or twice to capture the psalm's vigor.

The preceding examples also illustrate how oral reading depends on how one understands the text (i.e., exegesis). When a text is read blandly, the reader gives the erroneous impression that the author of the text has an indifferent attitude toward what he wrote. After discovering what the writer is saying, the reader must read the writing in a way that pushes the *writer's* concerns to the fore.

Oral readers often trip over pronouns and prepositions. In Psalm 23:1a, we noted that emphasizing "my" connoted a possessiveness on the author's part, or "my" set up a contrast between the author's shepherd and an implied shepherd for the reader of the psalm. Neither of these was the point of the statement. When pronouns are used as adjectives, they rarely require emphasis. As subjects, especially of linking verbs, pronouns may be stressed, with sufficient reason: "I" [and no other] am the light of the world . . . (John 8:12). But we should resist the temptation to stress the pronouns in the remainder of that verse: "*Whoever* follows *me* will never walk in darkness, but will have the light of life" (NIV). Rather, it would be read, "Whoever *follows* me will *never* walk in darkness, but will have the *light* of life."

Isaiah 53 is frustrating for the oral reader. Isaiah wrote verbs of graphic and compelling force: *stricken, smitten, afflicted, pierced, crushed,* and *cut off.* But Isaiah strongly contrasts the Messiah and His people: "he"/"we," "him"/"us," "his"/"our." This pronoun contrast begs for emphasis. One cannot emphasize both the verb and the pronoun:

> But *he* was *pierced* for *our* transgressions,
>   *he* was *crushed* for *our* iniquities . . . (NIV)

If one does not emphasize the helping verb "was," his reading sounds like a roller coaster—up and down. How can the reader avoid this ludicrous result?

Read Isaiah 53:1–10 emphasizing all the action verbs. Make the words preceding those strong verbs lead up to the action of the verb, to climax in it. Read the words following the verb to descend from the main verb. Now reread the passage stressing the pronouns. Can you feel the change in the passage's thrust when you change the emphasis of the sentence's words? Both sets of nuances are correct, though different. Emphasizing the verbs un-derlines the heinousness of the abuse done to Christ. It stresses His agony. Emphasizing the pronouns confronts you and your listeners with the astounding revelation that *He* should undertake and suffer such a humiliation for *us*. Both outlooks are valid. Both deserve the attention and the understanding of you and your listeners. How can you read this passage so that both the aspects are patent at once? You cheat!—you bend the rules.

Because Isaiah wrote in parallels, he made our dilemma some-what easier. Try,

> But he was *pierced* for our transgressions,
> *he* was crushed for *our* iniquities . . .

In the first phrase, stress the strong verb. In the second, stress the pronouns (or, vice versa). The "he" need not be stressed much since it is obvious that "he" is the subject of the section of this prophecy.

When reading a rhythmic passage that the congregation already knows, like Isaiah 53, one may remind himself to read the passage dramatically by typing a manuscript and marking the stresses, pauses, and the melody line (the ups and downs) for his voice. Then he should practice it assiduously. Thus, he may free himself from traditional reading patterns and may start a wonderful and thoroughly edifying experience for himself and his congregation.

Besides emphasizing pronouns incorrectly, oral readers should beware of stressing prepositions or their objects. Prepositional phrases act as adjectives and adverbs. They direct your attention to something else in the sentence, a noun or a verb; or they make a transition to a new thought or introduce one:

> *In the beginning,* (or, *In* the beginning)
> God created the heavens and the earth.
> (Gen. 1:1, KJV)

It is difficult to resist the temptation to emphasize the opening phrase of the Bible, simply because it is the first word from God. But Moses' point was not "when"—that is obvious, the begin-ning—God created the world. Rather, Moses stressed the one who was at work, and what He did, and what was the result of God's work:

1. *God* created the heavens and the earth.
2. God *created* the heavens and the earth.
3. God created the *heavens* and the *earth*.

The reader may use his discretion here. He might read the verse each way, depending on which of Moses' points he wished to stress: the Creator, His action, or the product of His action. But he should certainly read it with gusto, pealing the words like a set of bell changes, calling his listeners to worship God as he reads to them. Investing emphasis in prepositional phrases leaves the interpreter "broke" when he comes to the point of the verse. Like an eager runner, he has spent his energies in the early part of the race. He can do nothing but fade on "God created," which was Moses' whole point in Genesis 1.

Prepositions rarely point to themselves and thus rarely require emphasis. However, prepositions without objects and used as adverbs may be stressed with, even more than, the verbs they modify—e.g., "get *up*" (command), "come *to*" (regain consciousness), "pick *out*," "follow *on*" (ensue), etc. The reader should experiment with different emphases, different degrees of stress, until he achieves a natural reading. As a rule, prepositions and their objects should not be emphasized.

In this section we have discussed simple emphasis by the stressing of particular words. Emphasis is much more complex than that. I have warned against falling into certain emphasis "traps": pronouns and prepositions. The field is open for the reader to discover many subtle combinations of stresses with which he can accent the oral picture his listeners will hear.

One of the best emphases is silence. If the congregation or family follows the reading of Scripture in their own Bibles, the reader should wait until everyone has found the text before he begins to read them. I am not thinking only of the frustrated listener who is forced to forage for the text while it is being read to him. I am thinking also of the reader. A pause of several seconds, after rummaging has ceased, quiets the congregation or the

family and brings their minds to concentrate on what is about to
be read to them.

Silence, known as "dramatic pause," is also very effective *within*
a reading. Like other accents, silence upsets the familiar rhythm
of the reader and jars the listener's mind to hear what is being
read to him. John 13:30:

> As soon as Judas had *taken* the bread,/he
>   went out.///And it/was//night.
> (One slash mark indicates a slight pause,
>   two a longer one, etc.)

Pause between these two sentences. Read the second sentence
more slowly than you read the first one, and read it with the toll
of doom. A noticeable pause alerts your listeners to Judas's imminent disaster.

Dramatic pauses establish the author's meaning: "The shepherds found Mary and Joseph, and the baby lying in the manger"
(feeding trough). Why are they all lying in the manger? One's
exegesis will determine the answer of this question, but I would
suggest reading the passage as follows:

> They . . . found Mary and Joseph,//and the baby,
>   who was lying in the manger.
> (No stop is necessary for the comma after "baby."

Dramatic pauses can also help to communicate the author's
astonishment to the listener.

> You *foolish* Galatians!//Who has *bewitched* you?//
> Before your/very/*eyes* Jesus Christ was clearly
>   portrayed as//*crucified* . . .
>   (Gal 3:1, NIV)

Here, and in the following verses, Paul's rhetorical questions,
which naturally call for pauses, could chop to pieces the reading.
The pace and the length of the pauses should be varied. The
reader should himself imagine and then communicate Paul's an-
guished and unbelieving astonishment.

Read verse 2 slowly, pointing your finger at those "dear idiots of Galatia" (Phillips). Increase your speed through verses 3 and 4. But do not stifle Paul's sarcasm. Actually ask the questions Paul has asked, for today they are real dangers, not philosophical abstractions. Read verse 5 slowly. Allow Paul's crucial question to soak into your "Galatians." Do not ramble through such passages indifferently.

John 18:38 (NIV) shows us another use of silence.

"What//is//truth?" Pilate asked.///
And with this/he went out again . . .

The slashes give the listeners time to realize that Pilate's concern is artificial and sardonic, sneering. Later, terrified by the Jews' allegation that Jesus Christ claimed to be "Son of God," superstitious Pilate begged Jesus,

"Where *do* you come from?" . . .
///but Jesus gave him no answer (or,
but Jesus gave/him/*no*/answer).
(John 19:9, NIV)

The pause in the second citation underlines Jesus' silence as the judgment of Pilate's earlier, cynical attitude toward the truth (i.e., toward Christ, John 14:6). So, pauses, long and short, are effective aids to stress words and ideas.

2. Variety of Pace, Quality and Pitch, and Rhythm

Insipid oral reading of Scripture comes from a tedious uniformity of speed, tone, pitch, and rhythm. Again, I make no judgment of the minister's personal piety. He may not lack devotion, but he may need training that will develop his "ear," his ability to listen to himself read while he reads.

Today, cassette recorders abound in the land. If you have one of these, tape yourself doing a reading. At first, you will experience "otic-shock syndrome": "Do I *really* sound like that?" Most of us disapprove of the recorder's representation of our voices. We hear our voice and its resonance from inside our bodies. The tape recorder cannot portray that perspective of our tonal quality. But we had better accustom ourselves to the notion that, like it or not, the tape recorder's representation of our voices *is* the way we sound to other people. We can improve our tone quality by using proper speaking techniques, but our voices will always sound better to us than the voice that speaks to us from the recorder.

After you have listened to your recorded reading, ask yourself some questions: Did your mind wander as you listened to yourself read? (If your own mind wandered, what about the minds of your listeners?) Do you need to vary your tone, pace, and rhythm more? Do not be easy on yourself. Do not rationalize a mediocre job. How can you vary your reading? How can you enliven it and make it interesting?

We have already discussed one form of variation—the stressing of particular words. One can also vary his pitch and rhythm when he stresses a word. Already he is on the right road. Let us discuss other things that can be done.

Variation of pace. This is a day of speed. We are continually inundated with printed material, which demands our "immediate attention." Doctors, lawyers, and theologians have an impossible task keeping up with the scholarly information multiplying in the chosen areas of their own disciplines. So, they use speed-reading. Then they transfer optic speed to oral reading. That is sad. But I am not concerned with speedy reading (or with slow reading, either). Rather, I wish to discuss the pace at which one reads. This pace should vary. We noted this above when we discussed silence as a form of emphasis.

Consider the familiar example: "Our Father, who art in heaven, hallowed be thy name." "Who art in heaven" is an appositive, parenthetical phrase; hence, it is set off by commas (on punctuation, see below). When we say parenthetical phrases, we lower the pitch of our voices and we say the phrase a bit faster. Thus, we connect the main subject and the main verb of the sentence: "Our Father, . . . hallowed be thy name." Grammatically, "who art in heaven" is not a part of the main sentence. Dramatically, it should be read thus: "Our Father (who art in heaven), *hallowed* be thy name."

The Apostle's Creed is a string of parenthetical phrases. It should be read (or recited) more slowly, thoughtfully. Emphasize the verbs and use pauses judiciously. Granted, congregational recitation (choral reading) is difficult to control, but it can be taught. One Sunday morning adult class will give a good start. The congregation will love such training. Recitation need not be vain repetition. Choral reading may be practiced with one's family to hone its beauty.

When the minister leads in a recitation of the Apostle's Creed, he should not charge through ". . . suffered under Pontius Pilate, was crucified, dead, and buried. He descended into hell. The third day he rose again from. . . ." He should try this instead:

. . .*suffered* under Pontius Pilate,/
was *crucified,*///*dead,*//and *buried.*///
He *descended* into hell.///The third day
he *rose* (again) from. . . .

The pauses help to emphasize more easily the verbs. The adverb *again* is parenthetical and interrupts the flow of the sentence "he rose . . . from the dead." We should teach our families and congregations to recite these formulae meaningfully. Can choral reading be worse than the monotone with which we now recite these creedal professions?

Sometimes one *may* emphasize parenthetical phrases. This should be done when the writer is prodding his reader or when he is being sarcastic with him. To emphasize the parenthetical phrase above the main sentence, one might read it in a higher or lower pitch than the main sentence and, in addition, read the phrase more slowly than the rest of the sentence.

One example of this is Philemon 19:

I, Paul, am writing this with my own hand, I will pay it back—not to mention that you owe me your very self. . . .

First of all, the main statements should be identified: "I am writing this. . . . I will pay it back. . . ." Everything else is secondary to these thoughts. Three phrases—an appositive, a prepositional phrase, and a parenthetical one—are grammatically not in the main sentence. But depending on how these phrases are emphasized, they can add enormous weight to the meaning of the sentence.

Whole stories require changes of pace. When we read the arrest of Jesus, we should begin slowly. We should build the tension as the disciples wait, awkwardly, for someone to move. Peter draws his sword, and the reading quickens. Jesus yells at Peter, "Put your sword back into its sheath." The pace reaches a fever pitch. Then the tempo should be slowed as we read of Peter, forlorn and desperate, following his accused Lord. The oral reader is the reporter. He is Matthew, Mark, Luke, or John. This is true, no matter how their accounts are read. Varying the pace at which they are read will draw the reader himself into the text, and his listeners with him.

Variation of tone quality and pitch. I have used "tone quality" to mean the sound of the voice. Here, the cassette recorder will help greatly. With implacable sternness, it will teach how the voice sounds at any pitch or quality. If the preacher will use the tape recorder relentlessly, he will become able to hear himself when he reads in the pulpit. He should continue to criticize his own reading and to experiment with new vocal nuances and shades of color and emphasis. Then he will become a "sight reader"—like a musician who sight reads his music.

One may vary the tone quality of his voice also by changing his voice to represent a character who is painted in the story. For the witch of Endor, one might make his voice high and shrill. For Goliath, perhaps a deep voice—sneering and proud. "Oh, I can't do that," someone might say. But if the voice is used properly, as we have discussed above, practically anything can be done. One may change his emotions when the psalmist does, as if he were the psalmist before the congregation or family. Whether one characterizes (acts) in his oral reading or not, he must use good tone quality to transmit the author's meaning.

The pitch of your voice arrived when you did, and it grew from the shrill little squeal to your present baritone. Pitch depends on the length, thickness, and elasticisty of the vocal folds. Thick, long folds produce a low pitch. Narrow, thin, and tense folds issue a high pitch. One's normal vocal pitch is the range of notes he uses when he talks. Most of us use very little of our vocal range. The best stage actors have a speaking range of two octaves, and the singing range may be greater. If you are to improve as an oral reader, you must constantly develop the whole range of your voice. Good speech books have exercises for widening your range.

Variation of rhythm. We have already touched upon this, but I want to stress the importance of our not letting ourselves stumble into a misuse of reading rhythm. Chanting is great, but not when God's Word is being read to His people. When we read the psalms or when we recite a portion of Scripture we have memorized, we should read it so that its sense, and not its rhythm, stands out. Most of us read John 3:16, "For God so loved the world," as "ta-TA-ta-TA-ta-TA." Such rhythm blurs the message of the verse. Why not read it, "For God so *loved* the world that he *gave* his only begotten Son. . . ." This breaks the rhythmic recitation and manifests the heart of the verse's message. Further we must be careful in our treatment of scriptural lists. They are not to be rattled off mindlessly.

The fruit of the Spirit (Gal. 5:22, 23) should be read thoughtfully, with various emphases and rhythms. Each one of the fruit has its own music and flavor. They are not identical words.

Punctuation. One cause for poor, rhythmic reading is inattention to punctuation. The end of a psalm's line does not always mean that the reader should drop his voice. The vocal stop could come in the middle of the next line. Yet, the poetic portions of Scripture are often read according to the way the printer has set them on the page. Modern translations have helped this problem somewhat. But stay awake!

One familiar example is the way we pray the following:

". . . Thy will be done/
On earth as it is in heaven."

The prepositional phrase that modifies the verb "done" should not be separated from that verb in this prayer. When we pause after "done," we vivisect a very important thought. We should read it,

> ". . . Thy will be done on earth,/
> as it is in heaven."

Punctuation marks are the traffic signs for oral readers. They are stop signs or yield signs. The stop signs include the period, the question mark, the exclamation point, and, generally, the semicolon. These punctuation marks should give few problems. But the "yield signs" of punctuation can frustrate the reader. Commas, parentheses, colons, and dashes require various sorts of pause and stress. The comma may join independent clauses, as well as tack dependent clauses to the main clause. Then the comma acts as a bridge between the main clauses. When we read clauses joined by a comma, we must not drop our voices as far as when we read a period. The comma joins the independent clauses together, so our voices must show that the clauses are attached.

Unlike the semicolon, which separates main clauses, the colon introduces the main clause to an appositive, or to a series of appositives that follow it. A colon can also introduce its main clause to another main clause that will explain or amplify the first clause. The type of pause your voice makes depends on what sort of stop is necessary. Commas, parentheses, and dashes set off parenthetical phrases that need different degrees of dramatic emphasis. It is difficult, if not impossible, to distinguish vocally between a set of commas and a set of parentheses. Both denote the subordination of their enclosed phrases.

Dashes mark parenthetical expressions—even sentences. But they emphasize that what they enclose is important, or that it is emotionally charged. Dashes represent abrupt breaks in the flow of the writer's thought.

In Philemon 8–10 Paul writes,

> Therefore, although in Christ I could be bold and order you
> to do what you ought to do, yet I appeal to you on the basis

of love. I then, as Paul—an old man and now a prisoner of Jesus Christ—I appeal to you for my son Onesimus, who became my son while I was in chains . . . (NIV).

In this situation, the reader must first find the main sentence. He must eliminate the introductory clause, prepositional phrases, and parenthetical expressions. The result will be the following: ". . . I appeal . . . I appeal . . ." That is it. The other clauses amplify Paul's appeal: (1) Paul reminds Philemon, and not too subtly, of Paul's authority in Christ. (2) Paul softens this reminder of his authority by founding his request not on that authority, but on love—(3) love for an old, imprisoned man, (4) to whom Onesimus was bound by the most intimate chains in the universe—the father-son relation in Christ. (In the Roman Empire, Philemon had the right to have Onesimus executed. This grim reality underlay Paul's solicitude.)

How do these four clauses modify "I appeal"?

(1) . . . although in Christ I could be bold and order you to do what you ought to do . . .

Paul says, "I'm appealing to you instead of ordering you." Thus, the clause could be read as a warning to Philemon. Or one could read it as a choice that Paul has thoroughly rejected. But then the question arises, "Why did Paul even mention it?" A good reading will have a little of each element in it. (There is no need to stress "bold." The rest of the clause stresses it.)

(2) . . . on the basis of love . . .

Paul defines the motive for his appeal as Philemon's love for Paul! Paul's problem was to convince Philemon that Paul himself could actually love a useless slave who had turned thief and fugitive. Paul must convince Philemon that to harm Onesimus was to harm Paul himself. So, one should read "I appeal to you on the basis of love . . ." levelly, stressing "appeal" and "love." But Paul should be allowed to reveal the sincerity and the depth of that

love in the rest of his letter. The line must not be read too dramatically.

(3) . . . as Paul—an old man and now a prisoner of Jesus
Christ . . .

Paul reminds Philemon (a) of Paul's authority and now (b) of
his circumstances—an old man and imprisoned. Phrases 1 and 3
are parenthetical. Although they are important to the thrust of
Paul's appeal, one must not let them overwhelm the main verb of
appeal.

(4) . . . (I appeal to you for my *son///*Onesimus) who became my son while I was in chains . . .

The bomb! The last time Philemon had seen Onesimus, an
indolent, good-for-nothing (whose name meant "useful"), he
would never have expected to receive by him a letter from Paul,
Philemon's own friend and spiritual father. Paul? Moreover, Philemon reads that (a) as an old man Paul has become a father (b)
while he is locked away. (c) And the child's name?—why, Onesimus! Philemon reads on that (d) Onesimus is now Paul's beloved
(v. 12) and that (e) Onesimus gave the same sort of care to Paul
that Philemon would have given him had Philemon been with
Paul (v. 13)! Imagine Philemon's shock (and joy?) at this revelation of God's wonderful grace. Verses 8-10 should be read like
this. Thus we see how crucial it is to understand both the author
and the receiver of the letter. We must seek to understand what
Philemon's reaction to Paul's letter could have been when he first
saw the Epistle, and we must read it accordingly.

Yield sign punctuation marks serve to catch our attention, to
alert us that something is about to happen. But we must also
remember to read the interludes—set off by commas, parentheses,
and dashes—in such a way that they do not drown the message of
the main sentence, but rather adorn it. "But," one might ask,
"how can I see whether the end of a line has a stop sign or a yield
sign, or, indeed, any punctuation at all? When I get there, it's too

late." We obviously must read ahead of what our voice is speaking. This is not as difficult as it sounds, but it can be confusing. We must practice looking ahead of what we read, and we must prepare to read it. At the same time, we must not break concentration on what we are reading. This is like sight reading music before it is played. Soon it becomes natural.

4. Conclusion

The Bible is always being told by someone. It is one long conversation—story or lesson—punctuated with prayer and praise. Since we cannot but read it dramatically, an important question arises, "How dramatically should I read the Bible?" I have an old record of Charles Laughton reading four stories from the Bible. This great actor immersed himself completely in these narratives. As the serpent beguiled Eve, Laughton lisped with a sinister hiss. (He ignored the simple fact that the serpent did not become what we associate with the ominous snake until after God had judged it.)

It is not necessary to snarl, hiss, or wail to read God's Word dramatically. You may find that sort of reading to be repugnant. What is required is that you "tell me the story of Jesus." I do not mean that you should preach to me about Jesus. I mean that you must tell me Jesus' story as He has had it revealed, from the beginning to the end, in His Word. After you have told me that story convincingly with all the verve, joy, and pathos necessary to make it ring true, then you may comment on it.

In this essay I have made no attempt to give you a complete account of the voice or of how to use it to read God's Word orally. But I trust that I have whetted the appetite to begin to explore the joys of reading God's Word aloud well.

Here's how to start:

1. Consult a voice teacher. Tell him or her that you have no aspirations for the Met, but that you are a minister who wishes to learn to use his voice properly. After you pick him up from the floor, drop a few words like "diaphragm," "tone quality," "vis-

442	*Reading the Word of God Aloud*

cera," "projection," etc. to revive him. He can help you over several months, to develop the conscious use of your diaphragm, viscera, and larynx and resonators to project your voice.

2. Check your local library for recordings of oral readers. There are many recorded albums. Imitate (do not impersonate) a good reading into your cassette. Compare it with the record. Become conscious of rhythm, accents, and the pace of the reading. Try to reproduce these yourself. Be relentless on yourself. (P.S. When you do a good job, admit it, if only to yourself.) The point is not to see if you can sound like someone else. Rather you are trying to open your mind to the possibilities around you.

I recommend that you stay away from recordings of Scripture reading. Many Bible readers suffer from trying to make the Bible sound "sacred." They read in soft, solemn tones that suggest shafts of sunlight through the cedars of Lebanon. However, much of Scripture is rough-hewn, even shocking. Dramatic reading should not smother this shock. Perhaps part of the problem is that few of these oral readers have the intimate knowledge of Scripture and its backgrounds that seminary gives to its students.

3. Get a good book on the human voice, complete with exercises for your growth and development (see the bibliography, below).

4. Listen! Develop a good ear. We have discussed this in relation to yourself. But now listen to other people—common people. Listen to the music of their voices. As you grow in your ability to hear others, you will be a better oral reader.

5. Finally, read aloud. Read your private devotions aloud. Let God surprise you there. Read large portions of Scripture—whole books if possible. It is possible to read twelve chapters aloud in half an hour. When you work on sermons, read aloud the larger context of your passage. Develop your sense of the flow of the narrative or the argument within your passage. This will be helpful when you narrow your work to a verse. But read it aloud. If you have young children, turn off the television and read stories to them. When they adjust to the change—after a few sessions of total war, they will be a most appreciative audience. Read to your wife. Trap her in the kitchen and read to her while she washes the

dishes. Enjoy yourself even as you discipline yourself to read dramatically.

The minister in a church I once attended had one New Year's sermon. Without comment, he read Matthew 5–7, the Sermon on the Mount. Hearing that whole sermon, as the yardstick for our conduct during the coming year, humiliated and edified all of us. That might not be a bad assignment for you to work on. The performance takes about twenty-five minutes.

God's Word is quite capable of convicting sinners without your or my explanation of it. When we read it as a contract from our Maker, we aid the Spirit, removing the fig bushes in which men try to hide to escape their approaching Lord. It is an awesome task—the public reading of God's holy Word—but it is a responsibility we cannot dodge.

Let us teach our children and our people to reverence the Word of God not only because of what they know about it, but also because of how they hear the holy drama of the history of redemption dramatically read weekly to them.

Selected Bibliography

Care of the Voice

Anderson, Virgil A. *Training the Speaking Voice*, 2nd ed. New York: Oxford University Press, 1961. This is the best book on the subject short of a speech therapist's manual. Anderson's detailed discussions may seem abstruse, but he is well worth wading through till the end is reached.

Brodnite, Friedrich S. *Keep Your Voice Healthy: A Guide to the Intelligent Use and Care of the Speaking and Singing Voice*. New York: Harper Brothers, 1972. Good and not as complex as Anderson.

Seuss, Theodore (Dr.). *Fox in Socks*. New York: Beginner Books (A Division of Random House, Inc.), 1965. One might wonder at seeing this piece of nonsense among a roster of scholarly tomes, but there is a method to my madness. *Fox in Socks* is an articulator's nightmare. It is prefaced with the warning, "Take it slowly. This book is dangerous!" The book closes, assuming the reader has made it that far, with, "Now is your tongue numb?" Between these warnings are a number of numbers for the tongue. Not everyone will have trouble with the same pages, but everyone will have trouble somewhere in this book. *Fox in Socks* is available at any children's book section, but *beware!*

Oral Interpretation

Lantz, J. Edward. *Reading the Bible Aloud.* New York: MacMillan, 1959.

Lee, Charlotte I. *Oral Interpretation,* 2nd ed. Boston: Houghton Mifflin, 1959. Northwestern University has been famous for the oral readers it has produced—Charlton Heston, for example. Charlotte Lee teaches oral interpretation at Northwestern. In this book, she devotes attention to the different forms of literature—prose, poetry, and drama. She stresses the need for analysis of organization, structure, and style. Your ability in exegesis should help you here. A third edition has been published in which the examples for reading and analysis have been changed, but the text is virtually the same.

————. *Oral Reading of the Scriptures.* Boston: Houghton Mifflin, 1974. Here Miss Lee analyses Scripture with the same tools she uses to take apart literature in general. Some of this is valuable, but it can be overdone. In my own opinion Miss Lee is too restrained in her coaching.

Sessions, Virgil D., and Holland, Jack B. *Your Role in Oral Interpretation.* Boston: Holbrook, 1968.

17

The Body in the Pulpit
Gwyn Walters

At first sight the chapter title "The Body in the Pulpit" might bring to mind a corpse lying pathetically in the pulpit, much to the dismay of an onlooking congregation, and much in need of a miraculous revival. We *do* sometimes hear of preachers who *literally* die in the pulpit, but that is not our subject in this chapter. More often we hear of those whose lifeless manner in the pulpit reflects the need for the revived use of their bodies in preaching. An urgent (and devout) call must go out, "Is there a doctor in the house?" to bolster their vital signs, assuming (in faith) that the need is for a doctor, not a mortician.

This chapter will seek to supply a homiletic doctor's prescription for bodily vitality in the pulpit.

Biblico-theological Considerations

Preoccupation with the physical body of the preacher might be regarded as suspect by those among us who lay greater, if not exclusive, stress upon the biblico-theological content of preaching and upon dependence on the Holy Spirit as the power behind preaching. Wisdom then prescribes the mention of some biblico-theological basis for such preoccupation.

Scripture is frugal in its description of the use of the body in the proclamation of the Word of God. Ezra, flanked by six men on his right and seven men on his left, stood on a high wooden platform (pulpit) built for the occasion—for visibility and audibility—and ceremoniously opened the book of the Law in view of the audience below, which likewise was standing (Neh. 8:4, 5). Our Lord sat on a mountainside and on the prow of a boat (Matt. 5; Luke 5). Peter stood with the eleven for his Pentecost sermon (Acts 2). Paul stood up and motioned with his hand, a gesture common to orators, sometimes to command silence or attention (Acts 13:16; cf. 12:17; 19:33; 21:40; 26). This could be a vigorous shaking of the hand up and down as when shaking fruit from trees. In Acts 14:9 the crippled man listened to Paul as he was speaking. Paul looked directly at him, saw that he had faith to be healed, and called out, "Stand up on your feet."

In Acts 14:14 when the apostles, mistaken for Zeus and Hermes, heard that the crowd wanted to offer sacrifices to them, they tore their clothes and rushed into the crowd, shouting, "Men, why are you doing this? We too are only men, humans like you. We are bringing you good news. . . ."

The symbolic action of clothes tearing reminds one of similar bodily actions in the Old Testament. Isaiah walked naked (i.e. without his outer robe) and barefoot to convey his message (Isa. 20:2). Jeremiah wore a yoke (Jer. 27:2). Ezekiel not only lay first on his left side and then on his right for many days, but used visual aids of clay models and baked bread (Ezek. 4). In the New Testament Agabus bound himself with a girdle (Acts 21:11).

These instances, however, though interesting, are peripheral to the more basic considerations of the use of the body in preaching.

Preaching involves one use, albeit a most important use, of a Christian's body. It is thus related to the use of the body in Christian living. This, in turn, is inescapably linked with the incarnation of our Lord.

God was pleased to embody, to flesh out, His Word in the incarnate Son, using a human body with bones and limbs, muscles and skin to express His thought. When the church is described as Christ's body, it is not unspiritual to think of His expressing Himself through the human bodies of those who compose the body. Individual bodies are included in the redemptive incarnation of Christ; they are bought with a price and are to be used to glorify God (I Cor. 6:20). They can be the habitation of

God (I Cor. 6:19), presented as living sacrifices, holy and pleasing to God (Rom. 12:1) in spiritual worship, their members becoming instruments (weapons) of righteousness (Rom. 6:13).

Just as we are not to be Docetic in our view of our Lord's humanity, denying His actual coming in the flesh and regarding His humanity as an accommodating illusion, so we are not to minimize the role of our bodies in Christian living. We are likewise to avoid Manichaean tendencies to denigrate the body as a fit vehicle for spiritual expression. Not least, in the activity of preaching we need to maximize the use of the body for God.

The Preacher's Appearance

The preacher's own feelings about his physical appearance affect him as he assumes the platform or the pulpit. His own feelings are affected by what he conceives to be the congregation's reaction to his appearance. His appearance may indeed be conditioned or modified by the congregations' expectations and preferences.

The self-image and self-confidence of preachers will vary (unless the grace and Spirit of God intervene) in terms of how they feel bodily. They are helped if they feel they can convey that they are disciplining their body through diet, exercise, and rest and look and feel healthy with radiant color and the absence of pain, weakness, and fatigue. A clear conscience regarding gluttony, overindulgence, lethargy, and laziness as they affect physical appearance also helps.

Lest we conclude that such factors as these are indispensable, we must hasten to remember that God has been pleased to use and equip preachers who have functioned while emaciated, undernourished, and suffering from many grievous ailments. Calvin is a case in point of a preacher who was rarely without pain. Bodily weakness is often the best vehicle for spiritual strength. Normally, however, physical health and strength and the absence of deformities in preachers allows them to concentrate more on what is being said with voice and actions.

Healthfully self-respecting preachers attend to sanitary and toiletry needs, allowing due time for doing so prior to public appearance. Feeling dirty, unwashed, and unkept is inhibiting to most preachers. If preachers choose to be clean shaven they should be such and try to avoid "5 o'clock shadow" at 11:00 a.m. Mustaches and beards should be distinguished from overgrown undergrowth. Hygienic, suitably styled hair also contributes to a preacher's composure. A receding hairline, however, should not impede a preacher.

Some of the aforementioned factors are givens—such as height and hair, handsome or plain features—and preachers have to learn to live with them. It is worth remembering that through the grace of God, it was a dwarf who was described as "Athanasius contra mundum." Diminutive, disfigured Athanasius did not allow his handicaps to inhibit his preaching any more than did Whitefield allow a squint to deter his.

Dress, however, is not as much a given, though fashion and social context may dictate to some extent. Preachers help themselves when they dress appropriately to the occasion so that they feel comfortable physically, socially, and ecclesiastically rather than like the "man without a wedding garment."

The more time and thought preachers devote to how they look in public before they get to the public place, the freer they will be to do what they are called to do when they are there. While they ever remember that God looks at the heart and not the outward appearance, they also realistically recognize that their human hearers, weaker or stronger brothers and sisters, see the outward appearance and are affected by it. Though there is more to "adorning the gospel" than bodily appearance, they seek a clear conscience in regard to unnecessarily offending their spiritual siblings.

A congregation is as much a "visience" as an audience and is affected as much (if not more) by what it sees as by what it hears—especially in today's television-shaped culture. Several factors may accentuate a preacher's bodily presence or detract from it. Adequate and rightly directed lighting is important so that preacher and congregation are visible to each other, unnecessary shadows being eliminated and a gaunt visage avoided. The preacher should not be silhouetted against a window nor placed between two windows whose light may dazzle the congregation. Neither preacher nor congregation is helped if the pulpit platform and the front wall are too "busy" with objects, pieces of furniture, inscriptions, or pictures. A plain background allows the congregation to see the preacher more clearly. An auditorium without intercepting pillars also facilitates unimpeded view of the preacher as does one with a sufficiently high pulpit or a sloping or terraced floor fanning outward and upward from the pulpit.

What then, in preachers' natural appearance, affects the congregation? Much depends on the composition and sociological context of the congregation and the cultural influences upon it. Where tall people predominate in the pew (as, e.g., in many Dutch churches) a Zaccheus in the pulpit-tree is noticeably small; where small people occupy the pews (as, e.g., in Taiwan) even "five-foot six" preachers are gargantuan. The smaller may lack credibility in the eyes of the bigger; the bigger may be overpowering in the eyes of the smaller. In either case certain compensatory accommodations may need to be made in style of delivery or in position relative to the pulpit height. Height is an unalterable given, but it can be managed.

Weight and shape, however, are alterable. Preachers in the isle of Tonga might flaunt their corpulence whereas they might find it to inhibit their preaching in a culture more enamored of the slim and sleek. In the latter they might lack credibility were they to preach on discipline and self-control or stewardship or kindred topics. They would do well to lose weight. Of preachers' character and conduct it has been said, "What you are speaks so loudly that I can't hear what you say." Sometimes sheer weight can carry too much weight and be a block to communication.

Other blocks to communication may be caused by the preacher's apparel. In a word, he may either overdress or underdress. Where the details involved are truly *adiaphora* and not regulated by biblical principle, the preacher simply must take his guidance from the expectations and practices of his congregation. An economically depressed congregation is as likely to be distracted by an obviously expensive pin-striped suit as a wealthy congregation is distracted by a ragged jacket and slacks that are three sizes too small. Argue as we might that these things should not matter to God's people, the fact is that they do, and the sensitive preacher considers them carefully before he enters the pulpit. His purpose is to communicate the Word of God, and he must do all that he biblically can to be sure that his physical appearance never becomes a barrier or stumblingblock for those to whom he is preaching.

But with all of these details to consider (in addition to the extraordinarily difficult task of preparing the sermon itself), the preacher-to-be may fall into despair, and may cry, "Who is sufficient for these things?" As in all things, "our sufficiency is of God." Our appearance, be it average or distinguished, bland or magnetic, plain or handsome and beautiful, can be immaterial when the Holy Spirit lays hold of us and places His unction upon us. When the Spirit rests anointingly upon a preacher seated behind or standing in the pulpit, He can override both negative and positive elements in the preacher's appearance. Even though we must give full and sensitive attention to our appearance in the pulpit, we can be confident that it is ultimately His Word that the Spirit honors and blesses. As we preach that Word, we may, like Moses, not even know that our faces shine or that "with unveiled faces they reflect the Lord's glory, being transformed into his likeness with ever-increasing glory, which comes from the Lord, who is the Spirit" (II Cor. 3:18).

The Effect of a Preacher's Action in the Pulpit

Evan Roberts, God's instrument in the revival that swept Wales in 1904-5, had moved around from place to place during that year of energetic enterprise. At its end, however, he suffered from exhaustion and, instead of preaching or addressing the congregation, would sit immobile on the platform "more a spectacle than a prophet." Many were surprised and saddened by his silence; but in some senses his silence spoke volumes. His very silence was communicating, for we are never not communicating. His nonverbal language was eloquent, for good or ill.

Many preachers, far from being exhausted by service in the faith, are more spectacles than prophets, the body-language of their appearance speaking loudly whether or not they open their mouths. We now, however, must consider, beyond appearance, the action of the preacher in the pulpit. Such action may be undesigned or deliberate and calculated or almost choreographed or healthfully spontaneous. It may or may not be accompanied by vocalized words. "Action! Action! and Action," said Demosthenes, are the three cardinal virtues of effective public speaking.

Since the gospel is intrinsically alive and life-giving, inwardly moving and changing and impelling toward outward action in a host of ways, it is incongruous for its proclaimers to be neither inwardly moved nor outwardly active and expressive. An earlier chapter by Geoffrey Thomas has dealt with "passionate preaching," and Jay Adams has pointed out the necessity for the preacher himself to experience what he preaches. Passionate experiential preaching is hardly conceivable without the body participating as cause and/or effect. Inward passion and body expression are closely interrelated. Inner feelings may not only cause bodily changes, but also be caused or helped along by them. It is surely unlikely for a gospel that is the dynamism (*dunamis*) of God to leave the body-channel of the one who experiences this dynamism untouched by it. What is more naturally to be expected is that the dynamic meaning experienced will be dynamically expressed in and through the preacher's body, so that hearers/viewers may experience the same dynamic meaning.

Among the dynamic aspects of the gospel that are amenable to bodily expression are the more negative facets of conviction of sin, separation, alienation, hostility, guilt, and judgment; and the more positive facets of repentance and conversion: justification, reconciliation, forgiveness, regeneration, adoption; as well as new creation, new life; new allegiance, following, obedience; the sanctifying energies of the Holy Spirit; the call to evangelism, mission, social action; the challenge to service, sacrifice, suffering; the exhortation to unity and cooperation; and the inspiration of an active hope till Christ's return.

The inward feelings associated with these facets are varied. They include gratitude, indignation, indebtedness, awe, reverence, zeal, excitement, intensity, urgency, love, joy, tenderness, compassion, and optimism. None of these could be adequately experienced and conveyed without involving the body's "bones, muscles, nerves, and blood cells."

We need now to ask more particularly how bodily action in the pulpit affects the congregation.

"Let us remain seated while we sing meditatively 'Stand up, stand up for Jesus.' " Any congregation has a right to resent such an incongruous injunction from the pulpit. The preacher has cheated them out of an action that would be not only logical, but conducive to the spirited singing of the hymn. Preachers have foolish ways of cheating themselves out of many actions that could enhance and facilitate their public performance. Right or wrong bodily actions affect how preachers communicate the truth of Scripture and must therefore be carefully considered in preparation for preaching.

A simple two-stage exercise convinces student preachers of the way body position and actions affect both our and our congregation's feelings. Without having the resulting emotional effect described in advance they are directed to stand pigeon-toed, to clasp their hands tightly in a controlled fashion, to pull both shoulders forward, to bend the torso forward from the waist, press the chin on the chest toward the right shoulder and look up to the left. They spontaneously describe their feelings without any prompting in such terms as *twisted, distorted, contorted, crooked, disfigured, malformed, grotesque, awkward, unbalanced, ugly, squeezed, pressurized, afraid, hunted, haunted.* After about two minutes in this position they are told to stand on their toes, feet pointing forward, their bodies erect, flinging their arms upward and widely apart with fingers open, their faces upward, their eyes and mouth wide open. Unhesitatingly they express themselves in such terms as *released, free, open, exposed, light, happy, praising.*

Preachers need to remember from this how their bodily actions can help them be confirmed in their sense of call to preach and their authority in preaching. If they allow their inward sense of the august urgency of preaching, its privilege, responsibility, delight, and joy to inform their bodily action, the latter in turn will affect their feelings, and a cyclic continuum will be established.

As one begins to preach, the sense of awesome privilege should affect one's body performance. A healthy admixture of humility and confidence should exude. Whatever bodily posture or movement confirms or conforms to these should be adopted.

Beyond the very fact that preaching affects and is affected by the preacher's body, the content of preaching is related to the preacher's body. The prevailing mood of the occasion and the sermon text or topic will, ideally, have been experienced bodily throughout the earlier part of the service. If holiness, righteousness, sin, and judgment are prominent realities in the service, facial expression, posture, and gestures will have been, and will continue to be, appropriate accompaniments helping our inner realization of them. They will be more restrained, deliberate, and solemn than when the more lightsome, exhilarating aspects of the gospel are in focus. A tall friend of the author's (a university long-jump champion) used to leap up pulpit steps four at a time. This was not so unbecoming when the opening hymn contained "and leap, ye lame for joy" and the sermon was upbeat, but it was a trifle incongruous when the service mood was more sombre. In the latter case he would not have been helping himself.

When we come to the moment of proclaiming the truth, body resiliency, malleability, and adaptability are very advantageous. The faith we hold is so variegated that it makes total demands on our total selves, including especially our bodies. The truth is vibrant, alive, not static, impassive, immobile. It is moving, progressing, climactic. It is freeing, not freezing. How odd if, when speaking of the liberty that is in Christ, we ourselves are in locked bodies with locked muscles in arms and face, virtually paralyzed. Should we not be feeling the truth and be inwardly liberated in such a way as to free us up for bodily expression of it? At the same time a sense of hypocrisy because of the disparity between the truth we say we believe and what we are actually experiencing can be dissipated to some extent from the body inward. Freer movement of our bodies, especially spacious gestures can help us experience the liberty of which we speak. This is not psycho-somatic autosuggestion, but one of the means the Holy Spirit is pleased to use with us who are His temples and instruments.

When our bodies have helped us internalize the meaning of the truth and have established an inner mood, ethos, and ambience appropriate to the text, we are more able to externalize and extend it to the congregation. Our bodies being liberated, we want to give ourselves heartily and wholeheartedly to them. Having known how our bodily actions have helped us actualize meaning for ourselves, we shall more spontaneously use them to express to others the gamut of truth-feeling that is within. We shall find natural vent and expressions of excitement, urgency, intensity, awe, zeal, reverence, love, joy, tenderness, compassion, indignation, abhorrence, strength, animation, aliveness, and more.

Without choreographing ourselves with stilted movements we shall punctuate our speech with properly timed emphatic gestures and help ourselves portray the truth that we "see" and "sense" with descriptive gestures. The bodily actions that flow naturally from our inner realization of the truth that we proclaim do not automatically guarantee articulate communication, but they move us well in its direction. The congregation as it decodes our actions may have different formulae and perspectives to which we may need to learn to accommodate.

The congregation does not need to wait for a preacher to open his mouth and utter words before they are "spoken" to by him. Much in-depth study is now being undertaken in "nonverbal communication," which refers to "all communication except that which is coded in words."[1] "Body language" is being "spoken" all the time preachers are in public view on platform or in pulpit. It is often unconscious, but very revealing, sometimes betraying. It

1. T.W. Chadwick, A Study to Determine What a Pastor Is Communicating Nonverbally From the Pulpit. D.Min. Thesis, The Eastern Baptist Theological Seminary, 1976.

goes on apart from words and often accompanies speech. We need to consider it before we deal with the more deliberate use of "speaking with the body" and its effects on a congregation.

Much audience ("visience") research indicates that nonverbal language is more potent than verbal language. Most communication of feeling from the pulpit is on the nonverbal level. Credibility and trust are possible for the hearer/viewer only when there is congruity between the verbal and the nonverbal messages. Where they are incongruous, the nonverbals prevail. Hans Van Der Geest claims that "body language is more persuasive than words; it speaks directly to the spectator's subconscious, and thus has a deeper effect than the intellectual word."[2]

We might often wish that our nonverbals said less, but we cannot keep them quiet. Spiegel and Machotka, dealing with "the fact that men use gestures, postures, costumes, facial expressions, and styles of movement to reveal their thoughts, feelings, intentions or personalities,"[3] give examples of body communication in the Bible: "A naughty person, a wicked man, walketh with a froward mouth: he winketh with his eyes, he speaketh with his feet, he teacheth with his fingers" (Prov. 6:12, 13).

Aware then of the power of nonverbals we need to be alert to and avoid those idiosyncracies, mannerisms, offensive actions, repetitive movements, and gestures that are counterproductive and undermine what we are going to say or are actually vocalizing.

A nervous shuffling of hymn book, Bible, bulletin, and sundry notes or manuscript hardly comports with a message of strength, confidence, and peace any more than does a mechanical thumping of the lectern (as in the case of an ex-miner who became a preacher and who forgot to leave his pick-axe when he came from coalpit to pulpit). It doesn't help to have legs akimbo like a depressed Eiffel Tower or to wobble on one's feet or to turn one ankle or both ankles outward or to wrap a leg around the lectern

2. Hans Van Der Geest, *Presence in the Pulpit* (Atlanta: John Knox Press, 1981), p. 42.

3. J.P. Spiegel and P. Machotka, *Messages of the Body* (New York: MacMillan, 1974), p. 3.

stand. Better avoided is a swaying to and fro or back and forth as though on ship deck in turbulence. This nautical movement is nauseating to some viewers. Involuntary shrugging of shoulders, the twitching of a jacket edge, the removing and replacing of a handkerchief, the holding of both coat lapels, the repeated adjusting of a tie, coat, robe, or hood or of glasses that are forever forsaking their high position on the nose—all these should be corrected. Finally, the preacher must withstand the temptation to stroke the nose, the ear, the lips, the chin, the mustache, the beard. An old Scottish preacher intermittently would say, "Notice this brethren," drawing attention to some point, but inadvertently he would accompany it with a stroking of his beard!

While congregations may be humored or harmed by the all-too-eloquent body language we have instanced, they would not, if they could, eradicate all body language, certainly not the deliberate body language of a competent preacher.

Congregations vary in their desires for physical, visible action in the pulpit. Some liturgically conservative, conventional, traditional ones prefer the preacher to err on the side of being staid, proper, impassive, motionless. They equate these characteristics with being more rational, sober, and balanced and less threatening, embarrassing, and demanding. They feel less nervous and self-conscious. They are afraid of and resent the more dramatic, theatrical, demonstrative, emotional, interferingly personal style. The latter they associate with Bible-thumpers, soapbox orators, saw-dust trail evangelists, and charismatics. They tend to identify pulpiteers with puppeteers and are chary of being manipulated by heartstring pullers who deftly move their hands and other parts of their bodies. Even these reserved congregations, however, do not really wish to obliterate action. When it is done "decently and in order" they desire it and benefit from it.

Most congregations, it would seem, according to audience research, favor liveliness, action, and expressiveness in the preacher because they are thereby helped to understand and celebrate the truth. As Chadwick suggests, they come with a desire for security, trust, dependability, and a sense of love expressed visibly by the preacher; there is likewise their hope for the future, for deliverance, and for release to be catered to, and furthermore their need to have their faith clarified and their understanding quickened. They want these conveyed through the preacher's personal presence. All congregations at times need a variety of body language: sometimes relatively restrained action and sometimes more vigorous action. If a congregation is called to an active response by an immobile preacher, they cannot be blamed if they "respond" in kind. They may well feel that such preachers are not responding to their own sermon since there is no visible indication of any response. It is as though they are hypo-stimulated, unaffected by the truth of the Word within and the turmoil of the world without.

In experimenting with his own congregation Chadwick preached six sermons, the fourth of which was presented in an uncharacteristically stiff, immobile style of manuscript reading. One of his congregational appraisers wrote afterward, "I feel the need for your arms and hands to grasp the lectern! It's not your usual presentation of a sermon. Especially this topic requires physical motions that let me know you care. You're manipulating yourself. You're not reading naturally! . . . arm clasp—practice what you preach. Talk about concern—I feel that you've left us."[4]

Chadwick found that as the nonverbals of a speaker decrease, the "nonverbals" of the audience increase: they talk, turn in their seats, look around, shuffle bulletins, look through their papers, some even going back and forth to the rest rooms! He provided some scales for testing nonverbal cues and asked observers to appraise the preaching by deciding, between pairs of opposites, which were most evident: for example, controlling or controlled, happy or unhappy, despairing or hopeful, important or unimportant, aggravating or soothing, interested or bored, dominant or submissive. One might easily forecast how the stiff fourth sermon would rate using these categories.

It is ironic that the inhibition of the spontaneous expression of feeling in bodily action tends to increase with higher education. It is lamentable when preachers' growth in erudition and in exper-

4. Chadwick, *Study.*

tise in important aspects of their ministry results in a restricting rather than a releasing of their body language. They need to be helped to avoid such a danger by knowing how to engage in valuable body actions.

As the preaching moment begins, a congregation is helped when the preacher stands straight, with shoulders level, parallel to the lectern, head upright, chin neither too high nor too low, feet firm and slightly apart, with one somewhat more forward than the other for balance and mobility. The lectern, at waist level, allows access to Scripture and notes (if needed) and gives freedom for arm movement in due course. At this stage the hands can be in a neutral position just behind the lectern, the back of one hand almost resting in the palm of the other. When called upon, the arms will be ready for movement.

Within the sermon itself the most powerful instruments of the preacher's body for impact upon a congregation are his eyes. The members of the congregation must see the preacher looking at them throughout the sermon. They say, "Look at us when you're talking to us." Maximal eye contact is ideal. There may be brief exceptions to this direct eye contact, but the main contact with the congregation will be eye to eye. We must let our audience know that we value their presence and wish to meet them interactively as they contribute to the preaching event—not only as units, blocks, or sections, but as individuals into whose eyes we look.

"The hearer asks for a preacher who sees a vision and concentrates on the hearer while he is seeing the vision. If the hearer sees the preacher seeing and senses him sensing, the hearer will also see and sense."[5] How can this "visual" rapport be brought about? If a congregation asks this of the preacher, how can he give himself to them? How can he be there personally involved and involve them personally?

Some might suggest that impromptu preaching would attain this in that the address being unpremeditated, its substance and form and expression would be left to the moment of delivery.

5. P. Harms, *Power From the Pulpit* (St. Louis: Concordia), p. 31.

This would mean that the preacher would have to depend on his gift of recall of unassorted material in his mind, his general knowledge of Scripture and of life, his gift of speech, and the Holy Spirit. This supposedly would guarantee an immediacy between him and the audience, an on-the-spot co-working on the sermon with no notes or manuscript to interfere with eye contact.

Such an approach would horrify most preachers, not only or so much because it would be so threatening, so risky of breakdown midstream in preaching or of drawing a blank, but rather because of the danger of arrogant independence from Scripture and consequently misrepresentation of God's Word. This is too great a sacrifice for eye contact. In any case such preachers might need to be looking too much at word after word, or phrase after phrase of the Scripture passage chosen as text and be so preoccupied with what they were going to say next that authentic person-to-person eye contact would not materialize.

Some would swing the pendulum to the other extreme and meticulously prepare a full manuscript to which they adhere sacrosanctly in the pulpit as though it were the inviolate oracle of God signed, sealed, and delivered in their study four days previously and to be opened and read verbatim at sermon time. Some have achieved considerable expertise both in oral/aural writing of their sermons and in "over-the-top," unobtrusive reading of the manuscript with vivacity and dramatic expression, meanwhile attaining a good degree of eye contact. Some go the next step and memorize the entire manuscript so that, at least ostensibly, they can look at the congregation throughout. Some half-memorize and half-read their script or memorize and use notes to trigger their memory. Again there seems to be eye contact through these methods.

Various researchers indicate, however, that there is something lacking in each of these cases. There is more to "eye contact" than is here achieved—and more to preaching. Many, some might say most, preachers who use these methods would fall under Calvin's judgment when he wrote to Protector Somerset: "Monseigneur, it appears to me that there is very little preaching of a lively kind in the kingdom, but that the greater part deliver it by way of reading from a written discourse."[6]

Calvin favored extemporaneous preaching, preparing substance meticulously but leaving the actual verbal expression of the message for the time of delivery. He would agree with the Bern Preacher Act of 1667 that required an extemporaneous sermon: "They must not read the same in front of the congregation from notes or paper, which is a mockery to have to watch and takes away all fruit and grace from the preacher in the eyes of the listeners."[7] Many agree with Van Der Geest that "the personal style, the direct address indispensable for the awakening of trust, is in general seriously impaired by reading from notes . . . the sermon does not *emerge*; it comes from yesterday. The preacher misses the 'act of restructuring during the moment of speaking.' . . . The sense of words is grasped more clearly and quickly while listening to a speaker than while reading a book because the tone, pace, mimicry, indeed the whole appearance of the speaking is itself a language not found in reading."[8]

While complete freedom from notes and manuscript might be interpreted as "show-off" on the part of the preacher who seems like the boy riding a bicycle saying "Look Ma—no hands," it is more often appreciated by the congregation as signifying that the preacher has internalized the message, that it comes from the heart and is more involved with them than with what is written, that there's more direct dependence on the Holy Spirit at the moment of delivery. The congregation is more likely to react immediately to the sermon and to remember it more vividly. The preacher is not competing against the congregation, but eliciting the cooperation of the congregation and is enhanced in their eyes in regard to integrity, earnestness, and credibility—*sine qua non* for preaching the truth.

One of the most lamentable casualties of notes or manuscript

6. C.E. Edwards, ed., *Devotions and Prayers of John Calvin* (Grand Rapids: Baker Book House, 1976), p. 6.

7. Quoted by Van Der Geest, *Presence*, p. 47.

8. Ibid., p. 48.

dependence, alongside minimal eye contact, is body language—
involuntary and deliberate—especially free, fluid, authentic ges-
turing. "Students of gesture have estimated that there are at least
seven hundred thousand different symbolic physical manifestations (gestures) that are capable of conveying fairly precise meanings."[9] Too few of these are used by most preachers; fewer still by
those tied to reading. In the latter case the too safe presence of
the words affects the preacher's energy level and diminishes the
preacher's power and liberty. Some, when reading, cannot gesture
at all, but hold both hands on the lectern or clasped behind or in
front of the body or hanging limply to the side. When used,
gestures tend to be stylized, restricted, stilted, forced, angular.
When wide or high gestures are used they may inappropriately
accompany a downward look, e.g., speaking of heaven, pointing
up but looking down at the manuscript. When the message is
internalized the gestures can come from within as a natural spontaneous flow preceding or accompanying speech rather than as
something added externally and mechanically. R.C. Sproul discusses in even greater detail the value of preaching without a
manuscript in "The Whole Man" in this volume.

We are to be immersed totally in sermon and congregation
together and this demands kinesic behavior on both parts, especially the preacher's. But this should not be frantic, frenetic determination to get into sermons for a kind of therapeutic release
from tensions, pathological exhibitionism, nervous gesticulation,
but rather a concern to have the audience feel and respond to the
action and meaning of God's Word. "Purposeful body movement
in conjunction with what the sermon is doing at a given moment
also gains and holds attention and thereby creates a climate for
meaning."[10] The hearer will find himself experiencing the same
muscular response and "similar feelings inspired by them. In this
way, the audience shares . . . [the preacher's] emotion rather than
observing it."[11]

9. Oliver, Zelko, and Holtzman, *Communicative Speaking and Listening* (New
York: Holt, Rinehart, and Winston, Inc., 1965), p. 180.
10. Quoted by Harms, Power, p. 35.
11. Ibid.

Effective gestures come from the "heart"—the "center," the mid-upper torso just below the sternum or breast bone. When the center follows the direction of a gesture—the body turning and the body weight distributed in that direction—the gesture gains strength. Otherwise it lacks strength because the body is at variance with the arms and hands. "In preaching, if your center leans in the direction of your listeners, it suggests assertiveness on your part, a measure of commitment to what you are saying, and it makes your listeners the focus of your attention and concern."[12]

There are mainly two kinds of arm or hand or finger gestures: the emphatic and the descriptive (though they sometimes merge). The emphatic reinforce and impress the truth to be conveyed. They include the raised forearm with the forefinger pointing up or a clenched fist held up or brought down on the pulpit.

The descriptive gestures are more conceptive and directive and are akin to a music conductor's usages. In referring to God in His holiness and love, the right arm could be swept upward. In referring to man in his sin the left arm could be swept downward. Other descriptive gestures would be moving both arms up and down, widely extending both arms with a welcoming motif, and so on.

These are hesitantly suggested because some preachers admit to being unable to think of appropriate gestures. While ideally the felt meaning of the truth preached should spontaneously constrain the apt gesture, these "conventions" may trigger in time the more naturally outgoing ones. Some may even practice before a mirror or be video taped. Even the mightily gifted nineteenth century preacher John Elias used to "rehearse before a mirror practising holding his index finger straight when he pointed because he believed that a bent finger suggested weakness. He was intent on mastering his craft not (surely) to be an effective actor, but to be a disciplined preacher, wholly obedient to the demands of his message."[13]

12. C.L. Bartow, *The Preaching Moment* (Nashville: Abingdon Publishing Company, 1980), pp. 95–96.
13. R. Tudur Jones, *John Elias* (Bridgend, Wales: Pregethur and Phendefig, 1975), p. 20.

More especially, whatever use we may make of the body in the pulpit—its appearance, posture, facial expression, eye contact, gestures, expressive movement, mime, acting—our concern must be not with any of them as such or with ourselves and our rating with the people, but rather with the message of the Word we bring and with the people for whose sake God puts us as a "body in the pulpit."

Our concern must be that of Calvin when he wrote to Somerset:

> Now this preaching ought not to be lifeless, but lively, to teach, to exhort, to reprove, as St. Paul says in speaking to Timothy (2 Tim. 4:2). So indeed, that if an unbeliever enter, he may be so effectually arrested and convinced as to give glory to God, as Paul says in another passage (1 Cor. 14). You are also aware, Monseigneur, how he speaks of the lively power and energy with which they ought to speak, who would approve themselves as good and faithful ministers of God, who must not make a parade of rhetoric, only to gain esteem for themselves, but that the Spirit of God ought to sound forth by their voice, so as to work with mighty energy.[14]

14. Edwards, *Devotions*, p. 6.